TEXAS

FODOR'S TRAVEL GUIDES

are compiled, researched, and edited by an international team of travel writers, field correspondents, and editors. The series, which now almost covers the globe, was founded by Eugene Fodor in 1936.

OFFICES

New York & London

Fodor's Texas:
Editor: Andrew E. Beresky
Editorial Contributors: Carol Barrington, Richard Erickson, Edna Gundersen, Frances Kay Harris, Eleanor Mortensen, Judy Williamson
Illustrations: Ted Burwell
Maps and Plans: Pictograph, Burmar

FODOR'S®

TEXAS

1986

Fodor's Travel Guides
New York & London

ISBN 0-679-01281-8 (Traveltex edition)
ISBN 0-340-38433-6 (Hodder & Stoughton edition)

The following Fodor's Guides are current; most are also available in a British edition published by Hodder & Stoughton.

Country and Area Guides

Australia, New Zealand & The South Pacific
Austria
Bahamas
Belgium & Luxembourg
Bermuda
Brazil
Canada
Canada's Maritime Provinces
Caribbean
Central America
Eastern Europe
Egypt
Europe
France
Germany
Great Britain
Greece
Holland
India, Nepal & Sri Lanka
Ireland
Israel
Italy
Japan
Jordan & The Holy Land
Kenya
Korea
Mexico
North Africa
People's Republic of China
Portugal
Scandanavia
Scotland
South America
Southeast Asia
Soviet Union
Spain
Switzerland
Turkey
Yugoslavia

City Guides

Amsterdam
Beijing, Guangzhou, Shanghai
Boston
Chicago
Dallas–Fort Worth
Greater Miami & The Gold Coast
Hong Kong
Houston
Lisbon
London
Los Angeles
Madrid
Mexico City & Acapulco
Munich
New Orleans
New York City
Paris
Philadelphia
Rome
San Diego
San Francisco
Stockholm, Copenhagen, Oslo, Helsinki & Reykjavik
Sydney
Tokyo
Toronto
Vienna
Washington, D.C.

U.S.A. Guides

Alaska
Arizona
California
Cape Cod
Colorado
Far West
Florida
Hawaii
New England
New Mexico
Pacific North Coast
South
Texas
U.S.A.

Budget Travel

American Cities (30)
Britain
Canada
Caribbean
Europe
France
Germany
Hawaii
Italy
Japan
London
Mexico
Spain

Fun Guides

Acapulco
Bahamas
London
Montreal
Puerto Rico
San Francisco
St. Martin/Sint Maarten
Waikiki

MANUFACTURED IN THE UNITED STATES OF AMERICA
10 9 8 7 6 5 4 3 2 1

CONTENTS

EXPLORING TEXAS

FOREWORD

Texas is a big state, and 1986 is a big year for Texas. This year, the entire state will be celebrating its sesquicentennial, the 150th anniversary of its independence from Mexico. One of the prime statewide events is a wagon train, which will cover 3,000 miles within the state, taking a circuitious route from Sulphur Springs and ending in Fort Worth in July. The journey will take six months to complete, and anyone with a wagon and mule or horse can join the train along the route.

Some 3,500 events—statewide as well as on a local city or community level—are planned for the year-long celebration. For information on what events are being held where and when, contact the Texas 1986 Sesquicentennial Commission, Box 1986, Austin, TX 78767; 512–475–1986. Or, you can contact the Chamber of Commerce, offices listed in the *Tourist Information* section of each chapter in this guide for local happenings.

Because of its size, it is only natural that Texas is a state with staggering contrasts— ultra-urban sophistication versus moonlike landscapes, tropical beaches versus deserts, French restaurants versus rustic dance halls, crowds versus solitude, and much more. Our task in *Fodor's Texas* is to choose and concentrate on segments of the state most likely to be of interest to the traveler. This means that *Fodor's Texas* doesn't include such vast regions as central Texas around San Angelo, or even cities such as Waco or Texarkana. Though these places may hold some interest for visitors, we have had to make hard decisions about them in view of the limited space in the book.

For those cities and areas with more interest to the traveler that we do cover, our Texas travel writers and journalists—each a resident of Texas—have put together information on the widest possible **range** of activities and, within that range, present you with **selections** of events and places that will be safe, worthwhile, and of good value. The descriptions we provide are just enough to enable you to make your own informed choices from among our selections.

All selections and comments in *Fodor's Texas* are based on the editors' and contributors' personal experiences. We feel that our first responsibility is to inform and protect you, the reader. Errors are bound to creep into any travel guide, however. We go to press in the fall of the year, and much change can and will occur in Texas even while we are on press and certainly also during the succeeding twelve months or so when this edition is on sale. We cannot, therefore, be responsible for the sudden closing of a restaurant, a change in a museum's days or hours, a shift of hotel ownership (for the worse), and so forth. We sincerely welcome letters from our

(Continued on page **x**)

Santa Fe
Albuquerque
Amarillo
40
Palo Duro Canyon
27
Childress
25
Lubbock
83
385
84
Lamesa
Carlsbad
62
20
NEW MEXICO
Midland
El Paso
62
Monahans
Odessa
87
Juarez
Pecos
San Angelo
Rio Grande
Van Horn
10
277
Fort Davis
Alpine
Pecos R.
Marfa
90
67
385
Langtry
Presidio
Amistad Reservoir
Del Rio
Santa Elena Canyon
BIG BEND NATIONAL PARK
Eagle Pass
Piedra Negras
MEXICO

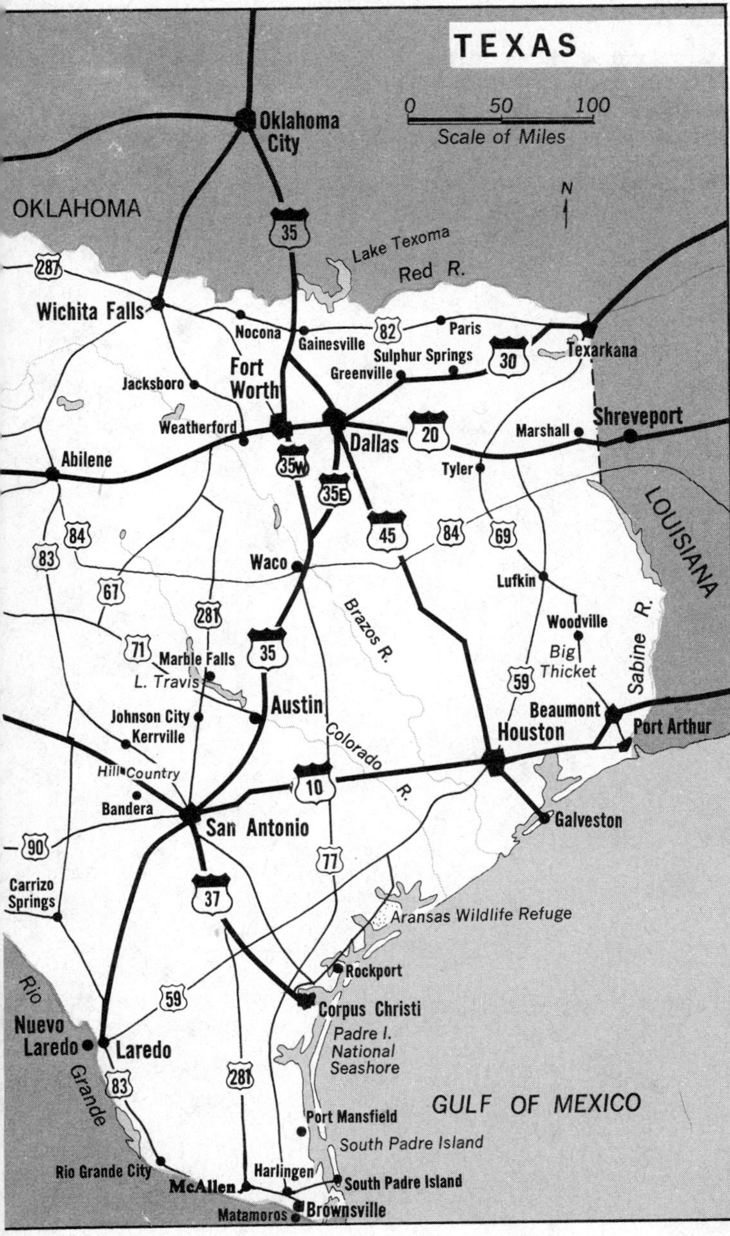
TEXAS
0 50 100
Scale of Miles
N
OKLAHOMA
Oklahoma City
Lake Texoma
Red R.
Wichita Falls
Nocona
Gainesville
Paris
Sulphur Springs
Greenville
Texarkana
Jacksboro
Fort Worth
Weatherford
Dallas
Marshall
Shreveport
Abilene
Tyler
LOUISIANA
Waco
Lufkin
Brazos R.
Woodville
Big Thicket
Sabine R.
Marble Falls
L. Travis
Austin
Beaumont
Port Arthur
Johnson City
Kerrville
Houston
Colorado R.
Hill Country
Bandera
San Antonio
Galveston
Carrizo Springs
Aransas Wildlife Refuge
Rockport
Corpus Christi
Rio Grande
Nuevo Laredo
Laredo
Padre I. National Seashore
GULF OF MEXICO
Port Mansfield
South Padre Island
Rio Grande City
Harlingen
McAllen
South Padre Island
Matamoros
Brownsville
287
35
82
30
20
35W
35E
84
45
84
69
83
67
281
71
35
59
10
90
77
37
59
281
83

readers on these changes, or from those whose opinions differ from ours, and we are ready to revise our entries for next year's edition when the facts warrant it.

Send your letters to the editors at **Fodor's Travel Guides, 2 Park Avenue, New York, NY 10016.** Continental or British Commonwealth readers may prefer to write to Fodor's Travel Guides, 9-10 Market Place, London W1N 7AG, England.

FACTS AT YOUR FINGERTIPS

FACTS AND FIGURES. Texas, the "Lone Star State"—a sobriquet derived from the state flag—is known for bigness. In a state with an area of more than 2,675,300 square miles, it's easy to understand where the preoccupation with size comes from: Texas is larger than the whole country of France. You will appreciate the long distances when you drive across the state. It is 821 miles (1,321 kilometers) from Texarkana in the northeast to El Paso in the west and 872 miles (1,403 kilometers) from Dalhart in the far north to Brownsville at the southernmost tip. And to get you where you are going, there are more than 70,000 miles of highway in Texas.

But land area is not the only measure of Texas bigness. The state's population topped fourteen million in 1980, making Texas number three in the nation. Texas' population is currently growing faster than that of any other state, owing largely to immigration from the Midwest and East Coast states. Today, it is not uncommon to hear a Boston brogue or a Pennsylvania dialect on the streets of Austin or Houston, alongside the celebrated Texas twang. Fifteen Texas cities have more than 100,000 inhabitants, and Houston, with almost two million people, is the fifth largest city in the United States. Texas' seven largest cities—Houston, Dallas, San Antonio, El Paso, Fort Worth, Austin, and Corpus Christi—all have detailed chapters in this guide.

Because nineteenth-century Anglo settlement of Texas generally moved from east to west, the most fundamental geographical regions in the state are considered to be East and West Texas. Thick pine forests, flat, lush coastal plains, and grassy, rolling hills are most typical of East Texas; dry, wild regions and the forbidding, empty prairies dominate West Texas. But such a geographic division of the state is imprecise and can pose problems for the uninitiated. In East Texas, the term *West Texas* includes the Panhandle, the northernmost extension of Texas, which resembles the handle of a skillet, whereas in the Panhandle, *West Texas* means the area of desert and mountains west and southwest of Odessa.

For the people of the Panhandle, the top of Texas is simply the Panhandle, a vast land of high plains, endless fields of wheat and cotton, and kaleidoscopic starry vistas at night. Likewise, the term *East Texas* should not include the Central Texas Hill Country, the rather mountainous and water-rich region bounded by Del Rio, San Antonio, Austin, Temple, and San Angelo. *North Texas* indicates the region around and north of the Dallas–Fort Worth metropolitan area. South Texas comprises San Antonio and anything south of there to the Mexican border. Thus, Dallas is in North Texas; Houston, in East Texas; Austin, the capital, in Central Texas; and the port of Corpus Christi, in South Texas. Of course, any native Texan will be glad to argue with you over this breakdown of geographical regions. Go ahead; disputing is a favorite pastime in the state.

Texas is truly a land of contrasts. Mountains more than eight thousand feet dominate the skyline in West Texas, whereas on the plains of the Panhandle's golden spread, you are sometimes lucky to spot a prairie dog mound high enough to break the uniform flatness. In East Texas are some of the thickest, marshiest forests in the nation, but the flat brush country south of San Antonio is almost devoid of high trees—though frequently almost as impenetrable as East Texas forests.

The state possesses great cultural and ethnic diversity too. In addition to the Anglo-Saxon, Hispanic, and black populations, there are long-standing communities of Poles, Czechs, Germans, Lebanese, and other more recent arrivals such as Vietnamese, Cambodians, and Haitians. Each November the Scottish clans of Texas gather in Salado for music and games. The Alabama-Coushatta Indian reservation and village near Livingston draws numerous visitors yearly. In addition, the Cajun-French influence of Louisiana extends across the border into Texas near Orange and Port Arthur.

PLANNING YOUR TRIP. Making reservations for travel and lodging can be tedious, so if you would rather not bother, use a travel agent. The services of a travel agent seldom cost a penny; the agent gets his fee from the hotel or carrier you use. Agents are helpful if you desire a package tour, in which case your pretrip planning would be minimal. If you prefer standardized hotel and motel accommodations, remember that most of the large hostelry chains publish free directories of their members' locations and special qualities.

Auto clubs are a good idea. They are helpful for itineraries, brochures, and emergency services on the road. The American Automobile Association (AAA) is a respected choice. If you live in the United States or Canada, check your local telephone directory for the nearest AAA office; if you are visiting from abroad, call AAA in the first U.S. city you arrive in. If you make your own trip itinerary, be sure the map you use is up to date. For Texas, get the Official Highway Travel Map and other information on places to visit from the state tourist agency.

Make arrangements to board the pets, discontinue newspaper deliveries, and ask a neighbor to keep an eye on your home and pick up the mail. Look into trip insurance (including baggage insurance) and be sure your other policies are up to date. Major credit cards (especially Visa, MasterCard, and American Express) are accepted throughout Texas, so plan on using "plastic" for lodging, gasoline, tickets, and major meals. Consider the safety of carrying at least half of your cash in traveler's checks, and be sure to have on hand sufficient identification (including a photo ID) to avoid undue waiting when cashing them.

TOURIST INFORMATION. The Texas highway department operates 10 tourist bureaus across the state on major highways, plus another bureau in the state capitol in Austin and one in the Judge Roy Bean Visitor Center in Langtry. The bureaus are open daily from 8:00 A.M. to 5:00 P.M. and offer the car traveler valuable brochures on Texas points of interest and copies of the

Official Highway Travel Map. Their travel counselors can chart your route, give you comprehensive information about your destination, and suggest things to see and do along the way. Stop by the bureaus or write the State Department of Highways and Public Transportation, Travel and Information Division, P.O. Box 5064, Austin 78763; (512) 475-2877. Write for their book, *Texas! Live the Legend,* which includes detailed information on most Texas cities and towns—as well as lakes, state and federal parks, hunting and fishing, wildlife, and flowers—and will be invaluable to anyone touring the state outside the big cities. (Recently the Texas Tourist Development Agency published *Point/Counter Point,* a more generalized presentation of the state; this publication can be had free by writing to Point Counter Point, Texas Tourist Development Agency, Dept. FG 3, Box 12008, Austin, TX 78711; (512) 475–4326.)

The tourist bureaus are located in:

Amarillo	on I–40 (from Oklahoma and New Mexico)
Anthony	on I–10 (from New Mexico)
Denison	on U.S. 75 & 69 (from Oklahoma)
Gainesville	on U.S. 77 & I–35 (from Oklahoma)
Laredo	on I–35 (from Mexico)
Orange	on I–10 (from Louisiana)
Texarkana	on I–30 (from Arkansas)
Harlingen	on U.S. 77 & 83 (from Mexico)
Waskom	on I–20 (from Louisiana)
Wichita Falls	on U.S. 277, 281, & 287 (from Oklahoma)

Note: For Texas Sesquicentennial events, contact the *Texas Sesquicentennial Commission,* Box 1986, Austin, TX 78767; phone 512–475–1986; or your destination's chamber of commerce. (See *Tourist Information* section in each chapter.)

TIPS FOR BRITISH VISITORS. Passports. You will need a valid passport and a U.S. Visa (which can be put only in a passport of the 10-year kind). The visa will be good for multiple entries for the life of the passport. You can obtain the visa either through your travel agent, or directly from the *United States Embassy,* Visa and Immigration Department, 5 Upper Grosvenor St., London W1 (tel. 01-499 3443).

No vaccinations are required for entry into the U.S.

Customs. If you are 21 or over, you can take into the U.S.—200 cigarettes, 50 cigars or 3 lbs. of tobacco; 1 U.S. quart of alcohol; duty-free gifts to a value of $100. Be careful not to try to take in meat or meat products, seeds, plants, fruits, etc. And avoid narcotics like the plague.

Insurance. We heartily recommend that you insure yourself to cover health and motoring mishaps, with *Europ Assistance,* 252 High St., Croydon CRO 1NF (tel. 01-680 1234). Their excellent service is all the more valuable when you consider the possible costs of health care in the U.S.

Air Fares. We suggest that you explore the current scene for budget flight possibilities, including the much ballyhooed *People Express* and *Virgin Atlantic*

Airways. People Express in particular are worth considering as they have connecting flights from the arrival airport in New Jersey directly to Houston for much less expense than the regular commercial fares. Be warned, however, that these cut-rate flights are fiendishly hard to come by, so be sure to book well in advance. Check, also, on APEX and other money-saving fares, as quite frankly business travelers who needn't watch the price of their tickets are the only ones to fly full price these days!

WHEN TO GO. Because of long summers and moderate winters in much of the state, the month of your visit really depends on when you *can* go. Outdoor activities that flourish during the spring and long summer include boating, sailing, cycling, golf, tennis, swimming—the list is almost endless. Of course, Texas is not famous for its winter sports— unless you consider hunting, fishing, and January golfing and picnicking as part of a winter-sports regimen. If weather is the determining factor for your trip, however, be advised that from the first of July to mid-September, the weather is *hot* across the whole state and that December through February can be quite cold in the northern half of Texas. If we consider the entire state and all the climatic zones, the best months for touring it are probably April to mid-July and October. But whatever time of year you visit, you are sure to find the sun, and definitely the fun, during your stay.

CLIMATE. Texas could be called the land of the six-month summer, May through October. In fact, the summers might be even longer were it not for the occasional early and late cold snaps that roll down from the Great Plains states in the north. Springtime is March and April, and autumn hurries by in November and early December. Mid-December to the end of February is usually all there is of winter, but even that season is temperate in the southeastern part of the state.

Texas has a continental climate, with the corresponding seasonal extremes in temperature, but the relatively low latitude and the adjacent Gulf of Mexico tend to moderate extremes over much of the state. Draw an imaginary line from Laredo, on the Mexican border, to Waco and then to Marshall, near the Louisiana line: The area southeast of the line has warm to hot, humid summer days and nights, fair springs and falls, and very moderate winters (plenty of sunny January days for golfing and picnicking).

Now draw another line from Del Rio, again on the Mexican border, to Wichita Falls, near the Oklahoma border: The area between the two lines is higher, dryer, hotter in summer and colder in winter. Seasonal extremes are greater, as is the daily temperature range. Indeed, among Texans, Wichita Falls is known as both the hottest and the coldest place in the state.

Draw your last line from Del Rio to the corner of New Mexico that borders Texas near Odessa. The area due north of Del Rio all the way to the Panhandle high plains is high in elevation, is semiarid, and has hot days and cool nights in summer and cold, sometimes snowy winters. West of the third line lies Far

West Texas, part of the mountainous Chihuahua Desert that extends up from Mexico. The higher elevations may have snow in winter, but the valleys and plains are arid all year long and very hot in summer.

PACKING. The easiest way to accomplish this task is to make a list for each member of the family, then check off each item as you pack it. Remember to keep accessible items you will need for having fun. Pack the film and cameras, the suntan lotion and insect repellent, toilet articles, writing supplies, swimwear, hiking shoes, sun hats, radios, maps, your guidebook, and your vacation reading material in a backpack, a kit bag, or a large purse where you can get at items quickly and easily. If you wear glasses or contact lenses, do not forget to carry spares. If you fly, be careful with your film. No matter what airport security guards may say to the contrary, the X-ray machines at the boarding gate frequently destroy photographic film.

Make sure everyone has the appropriate footwear for walking. Sturdy leather shoes or boots for the countryside and tennis or jogging shoes for urban asphalt are good choices. You might consider putting all the rain gear in one place. If a downpour strikes, you won't have to hunt everywhere for protection.

Do not take too many clothes. Nothing is more tiresome on a vacation trip than lugging around lots of heavy luggage or trying to find room in an overstuffed car trunk for things purchased on the road.

For most of the year and for most people, the heat, not the cold, will be more of a factor in planning what to wear. From March to October, you will generally encounter warm to hot, dry days and cool nights in West Texas and the Panhandle, whereas in Central Texas and East Texas the tendency is toward warm to hot days and warm, humid nights. But watch out—Hill Country nights can get nippy, even in June.

Women will want to stick to one or two basic colors in order to limit the number of accessories. Skirts and blouses, pantsuits and sundresses, and shorts are necessary items. For dressy evenings in Dallas and Houston, take along your basic cocktail or evening wear. Don't forget that Houston nights are pretty warm most of the year. In winter, take sweaters and a lightweight coat, preferably one that is wind and water repellent.

Men will need ties and jackets for some big-city restaurants and clubs, but casual dress is the rule in most places. For sightseeing in the cities in summer, jeans or khaki slacks, shorts, sandals, and T-shirts are fine.

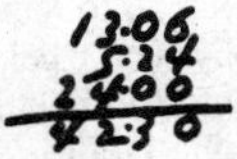

WHAT WILL IT COST? Of course, this is *the* crucial question for most of us. Gasoline and other transportation expenses are somewhat determined by your style of traveling, but they are far more subject to your destination's distance from home and the vagaries of transportation costs. Lodging and food costs, however, depend more on you, your way of doing things, and your tastes. Two people can tour comfortably in Texas for about $130 a day (not counting gasoline or other transport costs), as you can see in the table below.

Typical Daily Expenses for Two People

Room at moderate hotel or motel, including tax	$58
Breakfast at restaurant, including tip	10
Lunch at inexpensive diner, including tip	12
Drinks, dinner with beer or wine, and tip at moderate restaurant	25
Miscellaneous admissions, tour fees, movie tickets, small purchases	25
	$130

Such is a typical cost breakdown for a very comfortable trip: spacious room with TV (but no room service) and not much stinting on meals and incidental drinks and purchases. But in each of these categories you can cut cost corners and free up money for those fun miscellaneous expenses and shopping. Take lodging, for instance. There are several budget motel chains that furnish the same amenities as their more famous competitors but who do so with much less panache. The *Motel 6* chain is one frequently found in Texas. A simple, clean room for two costs under $25 a night, including tax. What do you give up? Well, there is no color TV; maybe there is only a shower instead of a shower-bath; you have to pay a quarter for ice; there is no restaurant attached. All in all, though, you definitely get your money's worth. Two more lodging suggestions are to look for reduced rates in urban hotels on the weekends, when visiting businessmen depart, and to search out motels on the old highway thoroughfares.

As for meals, why not try picnicking once a day and switching to pastries and coffee for breakfast? A portable ice cooler packed with drinks, some sandwich supplies, and a good Thermos can really dent those lunch bills. And a leisurely luncheon in a city or roadside park can be more relaxing than sitting in a busy restaurant. Just make sure to keep your picnic kit accessible in the trunk.

HINTS TO THE MOTORIST. Because of the fine highways, a wide variety of landscape, and limited rail and bus routes, traveling by motor car is definitely the best way to see Texas.

Although sometimes you may doubt it, Texas observes the national 55-mph (89-kph) speed limit (except, of course, where otherwise indicated). A large anti-55-mph lobby exists in the state, because there are such long distances between the cities. Remember, it is almost 1,000 km. from Houston to Amarillo and more than 1,200 from Houston to El Paso. But the lobby won't help you if you exceed the limit and are stopped by a Texas Department of Public Safety officer. Keep to 55 mph unless lower speeds are posted. Traffic fatalities have decreased since the nationwide speed limit was instituted.

Lower speed limits are enforced in communities. Watch for signs saying "Speed Zone Ahead" and be prepared to decelerate. Keep alert when driving on weekdays during the school year (August-June); school zones are usually marked with flashing yellow lights and permit only very low speeds. And if you find yourself behind a loading or unloading schoolbus, don't pass or overtake it—it's against the law. Of course, you will encounter few speed zones and schoolbuses on interstate highways and urban expressways.

Before leaving home, have your regular mechanic thoroughly check your car. It might be wise to join an auto club that renders emergency and repair services on the road, or to investigate your auto insurance to see if you are covered for towing and emergency charges. While you are doing that, make sure your insurance policy is in force and take proof of that fact with you.

If you need repairs en route, look for a garage displaying the National Institute for Automotive Service Excellence (NIASE) seal. You may need to check the Yellow Pages of the local telephone directory for auto-parts stores that are open 24 hours a day; quite a few cities have them. But if it is Sunday, you're far from a metropolitan area, and you need that fuel pump or special fan belt for your disabled car, your chances for fast service are slim. To avoid such a scenario, carry some emergency parts and tools in the trunk of your car, along with the jack, the spare tire, and your jumper cables.

Locating gasoline is rarely a problem. If gas stops are few and far-between on a U.S. or a Texas state highway, road signs will indicate the distance to the next service station.

Texas maintains a splendid system of interstate, U.S., and state highways, with an aggregate length of more than 70,000 miles. You will find that your pleasure and knowledge of the land will be increased if you drive some of the many farm-to-market and ranch roads that crisscross major routes. Most of these secondary roads are comparable to regular two-lane, shouldered highways in other states. So if you have the time, be adventurous. Take a few of these not-so-well-traveled roads. For a detailed map of all Texas highways and roads, pick up the Official Highway Travel Map from one of the Texas tourist bureaus. "F.M." means "Farm-to-Market Road," and "R.M." means "Ranch-to-Market Road."

DRIVING HAZARDS

Desert driving in West Texas is not to be considered a problem. As long as your radiator is serviceable and your tire pressure is correct, you should not have trouble. Nor does mountain driving pose any threats. The only steep grades in the state-highway system are found in the Guadalupe Mountains and the Big Bend country, but the highways there are excellent and were constructed for the average vehicle.

Texas does have its share of driving hazards, however. A serious one is game and livestock on the road, especially at night. On secondary roads and highways, be prepared to stop to avoid deer, cattle, sheep, and other animals that may suddenly cross in front of you. The main danger comes from deer, as evidenced by the recurrent deer-crossing signs that mark highway sections where frequent collisions have occurred. Other hazards are primarily weather related. Make sure your radio works and use it when you encounter threatening weather. Find a local station or, if you have a weather radio, tune it to 162.4 MHz or 162.55 MHz for continuous weather broadcasts.

One special hazard in Central and West Texas: flash flooding. During and just after heavy rainfall, a narrow, dry gully or creek can become a raging torrent of brown water in minutes. The porous limestone aquifers cannot retain the water from sudden large amounts of precipitation. The runoff can convert a normally dry *arroyo,* or streambed, into a flood channel, and the resulting wall of water is often strong enough to wash a car or truck off the road and into the current at low crossings. If water covers the road at a low crossing, do not try to reach the other side. Find an alternate route.

TRAILERS

Towed vehicles or trailers more than 55 ft. (16.8 m.) long or 8 ft. (2.44 m.) wide require special permits in Texas. The permits are good for single trips not exceeding 10 days. The $5 fee is payable only by cashier's check or money order, and you must supply the license number, make, model, and weight of the trailer, plus the license and engine numbers of the towing vehicle. The permits are available from any State Department of Highways and Public Transportation district office and from the Texas tourist bureaus (see *Tourist Information,* above).

WHAT TO DO WITH THE PETS. Will you take your pet dog or cat on the trip? More and more motels accept them now. Check before you register. If this is your first voyage with your pet, accustom the animal to car travel before you leave. Don't let a dog ride with its head out the window; wind, sand, dirt, and gravel might damage its eyes permanently. Just crack the glass enough for his nose. See that the pet exercises regularly. Highway comfort stations and rest stops are excellent places to halt for a spell and unwind, and many have the bonus of being scenic. Don't forget your pet's water and food dish. And never, never leave a dog or cat in the car on a hot day, even with the window cracked open. The blazing Texas sun can heat the inside of a car to more than 115 F. (46 C.) in a matter of minutes.

HOTELS AND MOTELS. *General tips.* Always make advance reservations whenever possible. Otherwise, you are sure to waste time and energy at least once in your trip looking for accommodations that, in the end, may not suit your needs. If you don't have reservations for the night, start looking for a hotel or motel early, say four o'clock. Remember that special sporting or cultural events of which you are unaware may cause all the vacant rooms in a city to disappear on a certain day—the day you might arrive in town without a reservation. During the football season (Sept.–Jan.), floods of weekenders descend on places like Austin, Houston, Dallas–Ft. Worth, Waco, and Lubbock. And San Antonio hosts so many special events that hotels book up fast there, too.

When you make advance reservations, advise the hotel or motel operator when you expect to arrive. Most hostels will not keep reservations after 6:00 P.M., so if you want to be absolutely sure to have a room when you arrive late, give the number of one of your credit cards over the phone to pay for the lodging in advance. Many chain or associated motels and hotels will make reservations with their affiliates at your next destination.

Whether to choose a hotel or a motel for your lodging is a difficult decision, since the amenities in each category are so similar. But in general, you will find that hotels offer a bit more personalized service to their guests. Also (in general) hotels run a bit more expensive than motels of comparable quality. Many hotels have one-day laundry and dry-cleaning service, whereas motels are more prone to offer a coin-operated laundromat, if anything. Room service is rare in motels but almost always available in hotels. Seldom, if ever, do you have to pay for parking at a motel; in hotels, there is usually a charge for use of the hotel garage, in addition to the tip you give the parking attendant. You won't find porters and bellmen in motels (unless you are in a resort area), but, on the other hand, you will probably be able to park quite near your room. Television, bedside telephones, and in-room toilets, baths, and showers are standard fare for motels and hotels in all price categories. Many have swimming pools, even in downtown areas. As for motels and motor inns in the urban areas, you will find that they offer about the same conveniences as the older, sometimes more elegant hotels, the only exception being more personalized service in hotels.

Hotel and motel chains. In addition to the hundreds of fine independent motels and hotels in Texas, many lodging establishments belong to national or regional chains. Two advantages to staying in chain motels are the ease of making future reservations and the great degree of standardization among the affiliates. You know almost exactly what kind of room you will have tomorrow night by looking at the one you have tonight. The main hotel chains in Texas are *Hilton Inns, Hyatt, Marriott,* and *Sheraton.* The major motel chains are *Best Western, Holiday Inn, Howard Johnson's, La Quinta, Quality Inns, Ramada Inns, Days Inns,* and *TraveLodge.* In all the hotel and motel chains mentioned above, you can expect at the least to find rooms with full baths, color TV sets, telephones, desks, carpeting, and usually double or queen-sized beds. Budget motel chains also exist in Texas, and they offer almost the same amenities (right down to the swimming pool) but at a substantial savings. Two economical chains worth mentioning are *Rodeway Inns* and *Motel 6.*

Categories. Hotels and motels in all the Fodor's guidebooks to the U.S.A. are divided into five categories, arranged primarily by price but also taking into consideration the degree of comfort, the amount of service, and the atmosphere that will surround you in the establishment of your choice. The dollar ranges for each category are clearly stated before the listing of establishments for each city. Remember that prices and ratings are subject to change on rather short notice. We should also point out that many fine hotels and motels had to be omitted for lack of space.

Super Deluxe. A category reserved for only a few hotels that render deluxe accommodation in a special atmosphere of glamour, good taste, and dignity. The hotel will probably be a meeting place for local high society. The tops in everything, including price.

Deluxe. The minimum facilities must include bath and shower in all rooms, suites available, a well-appointed restaurant and bar, room service, color TV and telephone in room, air conditioning and heat, and ample personalized service including laundry service if it is a hotel. In a deluxe motel or motor inn, fewer services may be available by employees and more by automatic machines.

Expensive. All rooms must have bath or shower, TV and telephone, attractive furnishings, and heat and air conditioning, and there must be a restaurant within or next door to the establishment. Motels in this category may have laundromats, which should be in a convenient location.

Moderate. Each room will have a bath or shower and (unless in a resort area) TV and a telephone; a restaurant or coffee shop should be nearby. Functional lodging, perhaps not in the best location.

Inexpensive. Almost always the rooms will have a bath or a shower, but occasionally such facilities might be down the hall. TV and telephone may be included, optional, or unavailable. Clean, functional rooms are the minimum. In *Motel 6* and *Rodeway* there is always a pool. Motels in this price range are usually good bargains; in hotels you might want to look over the room before you take it.

Other lodging tips: Bed-and-breakfast establishments are becoming more prevalent in Texas, especially in the Hill Country and along the Gulf coast. Country inns rely for their business on weekenders from the cities who want to get away from everything. They are usually in areas of scenic beauty about 50 to 125 mi. from major metropolitan areas. For the out-of-state tourist who also appreciates rustic, rural inns, the best solution is to seek information from a chamber of commerce, a tourist association, or even a courthouse in the small villages and towns that appeal to you.

Another solution to the comfort-in-the-wild problem is to get reservations in a state-park cabin. The state-park cabins sleep four to a dozen people, and the rates start as low as $12 a night. Kitchen and utensils, linens, and towels are provided. Since the cabins are such a bargain, many use them. Reservations and a deposit are absolutely necessary, perhaps months in advance. For more information on the state parks, including the address and telephone number, see the *State Parks* section below.

DUDE RANCHES. Theoretically, a dude ranch is very similar to a resort, whereas a guest ranch is a working ranch that takes in guests as a sideline. Both types are to be found in Texas, especially in the Hill Country. Bandera is the most widely known community in Texas for dude ranches. The town lies about 45 mi. northwest of San Antonio on Texas Hwy. 16 in some of the most scenic splendors of the rolling country. Kerrville, 26 mi. to the north, is also known for ranch resorts, as is the small community of Hunt, about 14 mi. farther west. For more information on dude ranches, check with the Bandera and Kerrville chambers of commerce: Bandera County Chamber of Commerce, P.O. Box 171, Bandera, TX 78003; (512) 796-4312. Kerrville Chamber of Commerce, P.O. Box 790, Kerrville, TX 78028; (512) 896-1155.

Woodcreek Resort in Wimberley, west of Austin and north of San Marcos, provides horseback riding, barbecue, rodeo, and golf, swimming, tennis, and other sports, all in a tranquil setting of huge cypress trees on the Blanco River. The lodge has a restaurant, a bar, and frequent entertainment. Write to Woodcreek Resort, 1 Woodcreek Drive, Wimberley, TX 78676; (512) 847-2221.

DINING OUT. Except for a few fancy establishments in the major cities, evening meals are the only ones for which you should occasionally worry about reservations. To make matters complicated, more and more restaurants refuse to accept reservations, preferring instead to have you sit in their bar or lounge drinking expensive liquor until a table is ready. In Austin, for instance, there are only about a half dozen good restaurants where you can reserve a table. On a busy night (Friday, Saturday, Sunday) you should call up before leaving your hotel and ask how long a wait there will be before getting a table. Seven o'clock is usually when the largest crowd arrives.

Texas is a state for casual dress. Few are the restaurants where a man would be turned away for want of a tie. "No shoes, no shirt, no service" is a much more common warning to customers than "Gentlemen need jackets." Women should encounter even fewer problems as long as they don't wear shorts or jeans to a swanky restaurant in Dallas or Houston. If you are traveling with children, you may want to call ahead to a restaurant to see whether it offers a children's menu. Lower-priced plates for kids are rapidly disappearing.

Restaurant Categories. Restaurants in the main cities of Texas are classified in this volume according to type of cuisine served and the price for a typical meal (without extras). In less-populated areas, the restaurants are classified only according to price: deluxe, expensive, moderate, inexpensive. Limitations of space make it impossible to list every establishment. Instead, you will find what we consider to be the best selections in each category. As a rule, prices in metropolitan areas are higher than those in rural regions. Although the various restaurant categories are the same throughout the Fodor's series of guides, the prices in each category may differ from region to region. You will see the dollar ranges for each category clearly stated before the listings of the restaurants. Menus are volatile; prices might go up after press time. In all our categories, the price range *does not* include cocktails, wines, cover charges, tips, or extravagant house specialties.

Deluxe. This category will concern only the major cities or their surrounding areas. The category denotes an outstanding restaurant with a lavish or particularly attractive atmosphere. These restaurants are indeed difficult to get out of for less than $15–$20 per person, even if you skip dessert and alcohol and order the cheapest thing on the menu. Deluxe restaurants should have a superb wine list and a good bar (where local law permits), excellent service, and delectable food.

Expensive. In addition to the expected dishes, an expensive restaurant will offer one or two house specialties, a good wine list, cocktails, air conditioning, good service, and a good atmosphere for dining in comfort.

Moderate. Cocktails or beer available, air-conditioned, better-than-average service, and a reputation for wholesome food.

Inexpensive. Good food at bargain prices. Frequently there are house specialties, too. Availability of beer, wine, and drinks may vary. Air conditioning, tables (or tables and counter), good service.

Restaurant chains: There are several chain eateries in Texas, some of which operate nationwide. *Denny's, Pizza Hut, Red Lobster,* and *Bonanza Steak Houses* are but four in Texas offering reliable menus at budget prices.

TIPPING. Giving tips expresses your appreciation for service well received. You should reward courteous, efficient service fairly. Likewise, when you receive poor or surly service, you should express polite dissatisfaction by reducing or withholding your tip. In many service establishments, especially restaurants, waiters and waitresses are paid far below the prevailing minimum wage. Much of their income depends on the tips they receive. This system is intended to induce good service. But we, as customers, must remember that courteous and efficient service is all that should be required for an employee to receive the standard gratuity. A waiter can render extra-special attention to your desires only if that attention is not at the expense of other customers. When you get such special attention, it merits extra compensation.

The standard tip for restaurant, bar, and cocktail-lounge service is 15% on the amount of the bill *before* taxes. Do not include the tax when figuring your tip. Good service, however, might be more easily rewarded by simply dividing the pretax amount by six and then rounding off to the nearest quarter. This calculation provides a tip of about 16.7% and is often quicker to determine than figuring exactly 15% when you're in a hurry or if you're not an arithmetic whiz. Similarly, if service was not quite up to par, dividing the pretax amount of the bill by 8 or 9 will render 12.5% or 11.1%. You can be assured that the difference will be noted by the employee. In many Texas establishments, a service charge (usually 15%) is included in the bill for parties of six or more. When it is, an extra 5% tip is necessary only if you made many special requests or if you genuinely appreciated the waiter's attention. When you drink something at a bar or at the counter in a restaurant, leave at least 10% (25¢ minimum). There is no tipping in fast-food restaurants, self-service eateries, and outdoor concession stands.

A hotel bellman gets 50¢ per suitcase, unless you load him down with a lot of extras. If you do, give that extra $1 or $2. Doormen and parking attendants usually receive $1 for parking or fetching a car. For short stays in hotels and motels it is not necessary to tip the maid unless you throw a party in your room or make a mess. If you stay longer than two nights, leave the maid about $1 a day, on the last day of your stay. Room service gets about 15% of the bill before tax (but be sure to check the bill first for any included service charge). Tip barbers and hairdressers 10%, minimum $1. The person who washes your hair gets 50¢ (unless it's the barber or hairdresser who does it). Manicurists get 10% of their bill, and so should shoeshiners.

Tip 15% on taxi fares. If the driver helps you with your luggage, give 25¢ per item for loading and unloading and 50¢ per item if he helps you carry them any distance. On the train, give 15% to dining-car waiters and $1 a night to the sleeping-car attendant. Remember, there is never any tipping on a plane. Tip airport porters and redcaps the same as hotel bellmen for carrying your luggage.

SENIOR-CITIZEN AND STUDENT DISCOUNTS. Since there is no uniformity in age-related discounts, the only thing to do is to ask each time you purchase an admission. Some attractions in Texas—especially museums, cultural spectacles, and movie houses—offer discounted admissions to senior citizens (generally 65 and older) and to bona-fide students. Some proof of age and affiliation will be required. Usually, places offering student discounts will be more strict—they may require a high school or college ID or possibly an international student travel card. Most cinemas now require the student to provide proof of age and then to purchase a special student pass in order to get student admission at that theater. Few, if any, discounts remain for air, rail, or bus tickets. One place to look for special senior-citizen rates and privileges, though, is the state and national parks.

DRINKING LAWS. The minimum age in Texas for consumption and possession of alcoholic beverages is 21. Other liquor laws vary from county to county. Out of 254 Texas counties, 69 are wholly dry—that is, no alcoholic beverages are sold. In 14 counties, only beer or beer and wine are marketed. In 171 counties, which include all the major cities, the status is wet, at least in part.

Bottled distilled liquor must be purchased in state-licensed package stores, which may be open from 10:00 A.M. to 9:00 P.M. except on Sundays and certain holidays. Beer and wine can be bought in liquor stores, supermarkets, and convenience stores between 7:00 A.M. and midnight, except on Sundays, when beer and wine sales begin at noon.

BUSINESS HOURS, HOLIDAYS, AND LOCAL TIME. Except for El Paso and the last 100 miles of Far West Texas, the state is on Central Standard Time from the last Sunday in October to the last Sunday in April. (CST is the same as Chicago: one hour earlier than New York and the East Coast, six hours earlier than GMT.) El Paso is on Mountain Standard Time, one hour earlier. As in the rest of the United States, on the last Sunday in April the clocks are advanced one hour to establish Daylight Savings Time. On the last Sunday in October, they are turned back an hour.

Texas banking hours are generally from 9:00 A.M. to 2:00 P.M., but you can usually find "mini-lobbies" and drive-in windows in major banks that are open before and after the main-lobby schedule. Most large banks operate their drive-in facilities on Saturday, too. Remote self-service stations are now being used by banks; these require bank or credit cards and are accessible 24 hours a day seven days a week in most shopping centers and some grocery stores. Currency-exchange services are found only in the larger banks in the main cities, so be sure to change foreign monies in sufficient amounts or carry your funds in U.S.-dollar traveler's checks.

Shops and boutiques usually open at 8:30 or 9:00 A.M.; department stores and shopping malls, at 10:00. Many malls, and some stores, stay open until 9:00 P.M. Otherwise, the closing hour is generally 5:30. Most professional offices, businesses, and government bureaus open at 8:00 A.M. and close at 5:00 P.M..

The banks, most businesses, and some restaurants are closed on the following holidays: New Year's Day; Presidents Day, mid-February; Easter; Memorial Day, end of May; Independence Day, July 4; Labor Day, early September; Thanksgiving Day, late November; and Christmas, December 25. The banks and some other establishments are also closed on Columbus Day in mid-October and Veterans Day in early November. Texas state holidays are also celebrated, but they usually affect only state-government offices. Texas Independence Day, a big hoo-ha, is March 2nd.

POSTAGE. Don't forget that U.S. domestic airmail rates apply to Canada and Mexico, too. The current airmail rate is 22¢ for letters of 1 oz. (28 g.) or less and 14¢ for postcards. International airmail rates for Europe, Africa, Asia, Australia, New Zealand, and most of South America are 44¢ per ½ oz. (14 g.) up to 2 oz. The international airmail postcard rate is 33¢. Airmail rates for the Caribbean, Central America, and parts of South America are less than regular international rates: 39¢. International aerogrammes cost 36¢—but do not enclose anything in them.

WATER SPORTS. Don't by any means succumb to the old, Hollywood-fostered stereotype of Texas as being an arid wasteland. With 624 mi. of coastline and more than 6,000 square mi. of inland freshwater lakes and streams, water sports flourish in the state through the long summer and the mostly moderate winter.

Along the Gulf coast, you will find sailing, boating, and yachting; deep-sea, pier, and surf fishing; and swimming, water skiing, and surfing. The principal beaches and resorts for water enthusiasts are Galveston Island, Port Aransas–Corpus Christi, and Port Isabel–South Padre Island (see the individual listings in this guide). But if you desire isolation along with your beach activities, as do many campers and anglers, be sure to investigate the smaller coastal communities, such as Brazosport, Freeport, Port O'Connor–Indianola, Rockport-Fulton, and Port Mansfield. In all the resorts, and in the smaller towns above, you will find more than adequate facilities for lodging, camping, meals, and supplies.

Inland, there is a real treat in store for water-sports buffs: the lakes of Texas. It would take several long vacations to see them all and a whole book just to list them. Most lakes and impoundments provide plenty of recreational amenities for water skiing, swimming, fishing, etc., and many are large enough and deep enough for sailing and scuba diving. Get detailed information on each one from this guide or from a Texas tourist bureau (see *Tourist Information,* above), but for now, here are a few exceptional water playgrounds.

Running northwest from Austin for about 80 mi. along the Colorado River are six beautiful impoundments called the *Highland Lakes:* Lake Austin, Lake Travis, Marble Falls Lake, Lake Lyndon Baines Johnson, Inks Lake, and Lake Buchanan. Created and maintained by the Lower Colorado River Authority (LCRA), the lakes offer myriad water sports, including sailing, windsurfing, and water skiing, plus campsites, motels, and several renowned golf and tennis resorts (especially on Lake Travis). For maps and detailed information, write the LCRA headquarters, 3700 Lake Austin Boulevard, Box 220, Austin, TX 78767, or the Highland Lakes Tourist Association, 901 W. Riverside, Austin, TX 78704. *Amistad* (Friendship) *Dam,* on the Rio Grande near Del Rio, is a joint project of the United States and Mexico that impounds 67,000 acres of water extending 74 mi. upstream. Buoys on the lake mark the international boundary. Two marinas are currently in use, and more are planned. Sailing and, especially, fishing are excellent here. But beware strong winds when you're in a small craft; the lake can get very choppy.

Caddo Lake, near Marshall and the quaint southern-colonial town of Jefferson, is 38,000 acres of calm water draped with Spanish moss hanging from lofty cypress trees. Although quite shallow as Texas lakes go, Caddo is replete with water-sport possibilities and is superb for bass fishing. Forty miles of marked "boat trails" help you wind your way through this jungle-like paradise. *Canyon Lake,* between Austin and San Antonio, is a crystal-clear gem set in the evergreen-shrouded Hill Country. One of the most popular corps-of-engineers impoundments, Canyon Lake provides a full regimen of water sports, fishing, and excellent parks for camping. Below the dam, canoeing, kayaking, and innertubing the tumbling rapids of the Guadalupe River draw thousands of tourists and weekenders from March to October every year. The first six or seven mi. of river below the dam are also a haven for anglers who want to try their luck against wily trout and smallmouth bass. This stretch of water is great for stream fly fishing.

Lake Meredith, near Borger in the Texas Panhandle, features 22,000 acres of water for boating, fishing, and sailing amid the stark beauty of the Canadian River Valley. Parks are available for camping. There are several boat ramps for launching and one marina. An interesting and charming natural-history museum of the area is in nearby Fritch. Fishermen here go after walleye, crappie, bass, and catfish.

Toledo Bend Reservoir, along the border of Texas and Louisiana, is an enormous impoundment more than 65 mi. long and covering 187,000 acres in the Sabine National Forest. The vast waters permit boating and sailing of all kinds, and there are beaches, swimming, fishing, and other water sports. The fishing here is especially famous.

More than 125 other lakes with sporting facilities are scattered throughout the state for your enjoyment. For most Texas destinations, a water-sport recreation area should be nearby.

OTHER SPORTS. Participant Sports. If you enjoy knocking little white balls around beautiful countryside, don't leave your *golf* clubs behind when you visit Texas. There are municipal courses and golf clubs galore all across the state: courses with forest-lined fairways and deep water hazards in East Texas; with rolling hills and tight doglegs in the Hill Country; and with wide-open, long, straight five-pars in the Panhandle. In Far West Marfa, you can play on a mile-high municipal course while sail planes soar on thermal currents far overhead. Many Texan golfers choose an area of the state and play every course in it for their vacation relaxation. The Hill Country, the Rio Grande Valley, and the region around Austin are good for such intensive encounters with your handicap. True championship courses are found in Fort Worth, San Antonio, Houston, Austin, The Woodlands, Horseshoe Bay on Lake LBJ, Lakeway (a Jack Nicklaus course on Lake Travis), and Dallas.

Texans are into *tennis* in a big way. Several pros have come from Texas, and several still live there. Championship municipal courts and clubs abound in the cities, but for casual exercise you can find free courts in almost any public park. Some state parks also have courts.

Racquet ball is becoming popular, and more and more private courts in fitness centers are being built. Supreme Courts is a widespread chain. Squash courts are more difficult to find. Check for courts at institutions of higher education. You might be permitted to play for a fee.

Runners should definitely bring their togs and shoes. Texas can boast of many scenic and manicured hike and bike trails. Austin has more than once been called the best city for runners in the United States by specialist running publications. In Austin, try the Town Lake Hike and Bike Trail, 10 km. of beautiful packed sand-gravel that circumnavigates the city's most charming park.

Of course, *horseback riding* is popular in the most cowboy of all states. Western-style riding prevails. Palo Duro Canyon (see *State Parks,* below) is a good place for riding, especially for the novice. English riding, show riding, and steeplechase are found only in or near the largest cities, and without an invitation you may be limited to being an onlooker.

Bicycling is gaining ground every year in Texas, especially in Austin, where more and more students and commuters have given up four wheels for two. The fine secondary roads in the Hill Country and the coastal piedmont offer a wide range of cycling conditions and are perfect for touring.

Hiking and *backpacking* havens are found primarily in state and national parks (see below). Lost Maples State Park, Guadalupe Mountains National Park, Big Bend National Park, Garner State Park (and surrounding area), Padre Island National Seashore, and the national forests in East Texas are the best recreation areas for these sports.

Spectator Sports. One word that just about sums up this category is *football.* From August to the end of January, the football fever runs amok in the state. During your trip you can measure just how passionate and serious a disease this is by counting the bumper stickers praising the Dallas Cowboys, the Houston Oilers, or any of the hundreds of university and high school teams. College football season runs concurrent with the professional schedule. Most of the Southwest Conference football teams are based in Texas. For some real Texan excitement around a real American experience, take in a game in one of the enormous stadiums bedecked with Astroturf and bright lights. It is unforgettable.

Baseball follows football today as the most popular spectator sport, but it is still the most all-American one. Professional games are held in Dallas and Houston. Good college encounters can be found during the spring in several Texas cities.

Rodeos are held regularly in both large and small communities all over the state. Check local newspapers and magazines for times and locations. If you are visiting Dallas, you can take in a rodeo in nearby Mesquite on any Friday or Saturday from April to September. Year-round rodeos are held at 8:00 P.M. Saturdays at the Roundup Rodeo in Simonton (west of Houston) and KowBell Rodeo in Mansfield (south of Dallas-Fort Worth).

HUNTING. Texas is a mecca for hunters, with the white-tailed deer leading the list of game animals. White-tails are more densely distributed in the Central Texas Hill Country than in any other place in the nation. Mule deer and pronghorn antelope are hunted in West Texas and the Panhandle. Game birds include a great variety of migratory waterfowl that winter in the state, plus quail, dove, pheasant, prairie chicken, wild turkey, and woodcock. Also, several privately owned exotic-game ranches offer year-round hunting for imported antelope, sheep, and deer. The principal difficulty for hunters is finding a place to pursue the sport. No large areas of public land are open to hunting, so special arrangements must be made with landowners. The daily, weekly, or annual hunting-lease system is popular. For information, get a recent copy of a newspaper from the area you wish to hunt in and check the classified advertisements under "Hunting Leases."

A nonresident general hunting license (good for all species of game) costs $100.75 per year; a nonresident small-game license, $37.75 (no hunting for turkey or deer with this permit). Licenses (and necessary stamps) are available at most sporting-goods stores. For more information, get the free *Guide to Texas Hunting and Sport Fishing Regulations* from the Texas Parks and Wildlife

Department, 4200 Smith School Road, Austin, TX 78744. Or call toll free 1 (800) 792–1112 (in Texas).

FISHING. Angling is a year-round sport and pastime in the Lone Star State. With more than 6,000 sq. mi. of inland waters, plus the tidal bays and 624 mi. of shoreline on the Gulf of Mexico, Texans are blessed with plenty of places where they can wet a hook. Native freshwater game fish include largemouth (the natives say "black") bass, spotted bass, crappie, bluegill bream and other sunfish ("perch" in Texas), white bass, catfish, and the rare Guadalupe bass in the Hill Country streams. In recent years, the Texas Department of Parks and Wildlife has succeeded in several stocking experiments, so you can now fish for Florida bass, smallmouth bass, walleye, northern pike, hybrid striped bass, freshwater flounder, and even rainbow and brown trout in some of the lakes and streams across the state.

Along the Gulf Coast there are more than 250 species of saltwater fish waiting for your bait or lure; they include speckled trout, king and Spanish mackerel, wahoo, redfish, sailfish, red snapper, marlin, and flounder. You can angle from boats, by wading the flats, or from piers and jetties. A five-day nonresident fishing license good anywhere in the state costs $7.00 for fresh or saltwater angling. Licenses are available at most sporting-goods stores. For more information, call or write the Parks and Wildlife Department (address and telephone number listed under *Hunting* above).

STATE PARKS. There are some 90 Texas state parks, historic sites, and recreational areas. Entrance to most parks is $2.00 per vehicle for day use, or you can purchase an economical annual entry permit for $15 that is, good at all parks for unlimited visits. Reservations are advisable for camping, RV hookups, and the rustic but comfortably furnished cabins available in some parks. You can buy the annual entry permit and make reservations at any park entrance gate during business hours, or you can write or phone the Texas Department of Parks and Wildlife, 4200 Smith School Road, Austin, TX 78744; (800) 792–1112 (in Texas).

Fifty-four parks provide facilities for camping (fee), and primitive camping is permissible in others. Forty-nine parks have water and electricity hookups for a moderate charge; 23 of those also have sewage hookups. Fishing is allowed in the parks, subject to state licensing, but no hunting of any kind is permitted. The parks and historic sites preserve Texas' heritage amid scenic natural phenomena. There are well-maintained nature trails, historic markers, and, sometimes, guided tours. Below are a few highlights.

Davis Mountains State Park, 6 mi. west of Fort Davis, near the Fort Davis National Historic Site, has almost 2,000 acres of rugged mountain hiking and a multilevel hotel called Indian Lodge, modeled after a pueblo. Camping and trailer facilities are also available, as is an interpretive center.

Lost Maples State Park, near Kerrville, north of San Antonio, features a large stand of splendid bigtooth maples in a rugged series of box canyons. In November the trees put on a dazzling display of colors unparalleled in the mesquite- and cedar-dominated Hill Country. Deer and other mammals are numerous. Fishing is available, as are primitive campsites and RV hookups and paved nature trails.

McKinney Falls State Park, on the southeast outskirts of Austin, at the confluence of Onion and Williamson Creeks, has long quiet pools, nature trails, campsites, showers, restrooms, and hookups for camping in comfort. A convenient and inexpensive place to stay while visiting the state capital and the surrounding area.

Mustang Island State Park, 14 mi. south of Port Aransas, near Corpus Christi, is a beachfront recreational area with all the conveniences, plus surfing, swimming, fishing, birdwatching, and more.

Palo Duro Canyon State Park, 12 mi. east of Canyon, in the Texas Panhandle, is the state's largest park, at the bottom of 1,000-ft. cliffs of iridescent sandstone. Once the wintering grounds for Charles Goodnight's gigantic herds and the site of a major Indian battle in 1874, today the canyon offers modern camping facilities and an open-air drama, *Texas,* to visitors in summer.

San Jacinto Battleground State Historic Park, 22 mi. east of downtown Houston, marks the site where Texas won its independence from Mexico in 1836. The limestone and concrete monument rises 570 ft. above the coastal flatlands. The Battleship *Texas* is moored here, too. The behemoth ship was constructed before World War I and served as Eisenhower's flagship during the Normandy invasion on D-Day in 1944. Both are open daily.

Texas State Railroad, operating between Rusk and Palestine, is a train ride complete with an antique steam engine that the Texas Parks and Wildlife Department operates through a 24-mi.-long state park—the thinnest state park in the nation. Trains run weekends from March through May and in October, and daily (except Tuesday) fron June to Labor Day. Fun for the whole family.

TEXAS TRAVEL TRAILS. Several years ago, the Texas Department of Highways and Public Transportation devised a novel approach to giving the motor-car tourist a taste of the vastness of Texas. The department established 10 Texas Travel Trails in different regions to aid visitors and natives who like to see the sights and sense the history of the state as they travel.

The trails consist of 10 great loops, mostly on secondary highways away from the beaten path. The loops vary in length from 500 to 800 mi. Since the trails are circular, the motorist can start anywhere and proceed in either direction for as long as he or she likes. A narrative, detailed map exists for each trail. You can use these maps in conjunction with the Official Highway Travel Map. Travel Trail markers in blue and white have been placed along each route: Rectangular signs with the name and symbol of the particular trail identify and confirm your route from time to time, and round signs with white arrows guide you at intersections where the trail changes highways or at points of possible confusio

Although the highways the Travel Trails use are often Texas state highways and farm-to-market and ranch roads, all the routes are well paved and enjoyable to drive on.

The Travel Trail maps and the Official Highway Travel Map are available free from any Texas tourist bureau or by writing the Texas Department of Highways (see *Tourist Information,* above). Be sure to ask specifically for the Travel Trails maps. For some reason, the trails are not as publicized as they once were, even though the maps and information are still obtainable.

The **Texas Forest Trail** "begins" at Tyler, famous for its roses, and takes you on a long, wooded loop through the East Texas piney woods, where lumber, oil, hunting, and fishing are important activities. In addition to the treescapes, some of the most interesting sites along the trail are Jefferson, the town that defied Jay Gould's railroad empire, and hosted Oscar Wilde; Kilgore, home of "the world's richest acre," an intensely drilled oil pool; San Augustine, with historic homes that have seen the likes of Davy Crockett and Sam Houston walk across their floors; and Woodville, a town that is a bird sanctuary and the site of a dogwood festival in the spring (late March or early April).

The **Texas Forts Trail** "starts" in Abilene, moves down to San Angelo and Mason, turns north up to Mineral Wells and Throckmorton, and returns to Abilene. The region holds a series of ruined forts that once stood between the land-hungry frontier settlers and the resentful Indians. Eight forts lie on the trail. Some are no more than heaps of rubble, but others, including Forts Griffin, Belknap, Concho, Richardson, and McKavett, have substantial remains, with reconstruction still going on.

The **Texas Hill Country Trail** is a scenic delight. The trail itinerary takes you through the Edwards Plateau and Llano Estacado geologic regions north of San Antonio and west of Austin. Numerous campgrounds, resorts, and dude ranches are scattered about in this water-rich area, where deer, sheep, and goats are abundant. This is predominantly a German-settled area. It was also the home of LBJ.

The **Texas Tropical Trail** wanders down from Corpus Christi, the second largest port in Texas, along the coast to the Rio Grande Valley. Old Mexico is always nearby, historical markers are frequent, and delicious citrus fruits and vegetables are plentiful.

The **Texas Pecos Trail** ushers you through the forbidding land of cactus and Judge Roy Bean. West of the Pecos, once a formidable barrier to frontier settlers and Indians alike, lies a harsh land that was known for its harsher law at the turn of the century. Today, the Trans-Pecos produces cattle and oil, but looking out your car windows, you may often think you are back in the Wild West. The trail is 734 mi. long.

The **Texas Mountain Trail** guides the motorist through a high, arid region studded with 90 peaks more than a mile in elevation. There are two national parks, one national monument, and the calm border towns of Presidio, Texas, and Ojinaga, Mexico. In Alpine, you can take in a rodeo at Sul Ross University, and in Marfa, after dark, you can try your hand at figuring out what the eerie Marfa lights really are. No one else seems to know. Visit the University of Texas

McDonald Observatory and peer at the heavens through an 87-in. telescope. The historic town of El Paso is also on the Mountain Trail.

The **Texas Plains Trail** is the way to see the Panhandle and the Staked Plains of Coronado fame. Kit Carson was frequently here in the 1870s as a scout for the Indian wars. You will drive across fertile flat plains and then plunge suddenly into deep canyons. Oil, natural gas, wheat, cotton, and cattle provide the basis for the economy. Most of this region of Texas was not settled until the mid-1880s. This is real cowboy land.

The **Texas Brazos Trail** and the **Independence Trail** are both pilgrimages to Texas history that wind through the coastal piedmont, where Texas won its independence from Mexico. Both trails are convenient to Houston, San Antonio, and Austin. The **Texas Lakes Trail** tours the many lakes of the Dallas–Fort Worth region. All three are excellent one- or two-day round trips from Texas' major cities.

NATIONAL PARKS. Actually, there are only three national parks in Texas, but since there are national monuments, forests, a seashore, and several wildlife refuges in the state, we will treat them all together.

Despite limited or primitive facilities in many national parks, more and more visitors are heading for them each year to escape from the fast pace of urban life. The boom in backpacking, primitive camping, and general outdoorsmanship has led to an increase in park use. The parks are relatively undeveloped, however, because their purpose is to preserve the natural order of things from man's litter-prone and automobile-manic behavior. If you use the parks, be conscientious and leave the environment just as you found it, as pristine as possible.

Alibates National Monument, north of Amarillo and about 6 mi. south of Fritch, is a flint quarry that was in use from 10,000 B.C. until possibly the 1800s. The monument is still under development and archaeologists continue to scour the site. Two ranger-guided tours per day are available from Memorial Day (late May) to Labor Day (early September). Collecting specimens is prohibited.

Big Bend National Park, along the Rio Grande in West Texas, encompasses more than 708,000 acres of mountains, plains, deep canyons, and desert where 2,000 species of plants and animals exist. More than 350 bird species have been spotted in the park. But one flying creature birders have not seen recently is the Big Bend pterodactyl, the largest flying creature ever known (50-ft. wingspread). Today, only his fossil remains. Spectacular scenery meets the visitor at every turn in the park. Hundreds of miles of trails are at your disposal for hiking: easy walks to strenuous climbs. There is a Visitor Center (open 8:00 A.M. to 7:00 P.M. in summer; 8:00 A.M. to 5:00 P.M. in winter), a post office, three campgrounds, two trailer parks, four store-gas stations. In the Chisos Mountains Basin, a few rooms and cottages are available, but reservations are strongly advised all year long. Write the Chisos Mountains Lodge, Basin Rural Station, Big Bend National Park, TX 79834. Several ways of approaching the park are available, but be sure to drive the panoramic Camino del Rio (FM 170) either coming to or leaving Big Bend. The winding road is definitely worth a trip, even if you have to go out of your way.

Big Thicket National Preserve, just north of Kountze in East Texas, is a labyrinthine forest set in swamps, where the visitor can hike and boat for miles in a Texas jungle. The visitor station is on FM 420. The *Big Thicket Museum,* in nearby Saratoga, is open Tuesday through Sunday.

The *Fort Davis National Historic Site,* in Fort Davis in Far West Texas, has been called the most outstanding example of a Southwestern frontier fort still in existence. Between 1854 and 1891, the fort was the center of military operations against the surrounding Indian tribes. A museum, some reconstructed barracks, and a reenactment of an 1875 military retreat all await the traveler. Fort Davis is a necessary stop on the itinerary of any Wild West history buff.

The *Guadalupe Mountains National Park,* 64 mi. north of Van Horn on the New Mexico border, is a naturalist's delight. Deer and elk graze in the high alpine meadows amid the stark beauty of the rocky peaks. The hiking trails are ideally suited for the experienced backpacker, especially in the interior of the park, but a few easy paths and one day-use area are available. Primitive camping is available only in the highlands, and you must carry your own water. There is one small RV-and-tent campground near Pine Springs. All overnight visitors must check in and out of the Frijole Information Station near Pine Springs on U.S. 62/180.

Lyndon Baines Johnson National Historical Park, Stonewall and Johnson City, about 70 mi. due north of San Antonio, provides guided-tour buses and horse-drawn wagons to show the visitor the birthplace, boyhood home, school, ranch, and grave of the only U.S. president to come from Texas. It operates in connection with LBJ State Park. Ranch tours start in the State Park. The Hill Country scenery, especially in the spring when the fruit trees are in bloom, warrants a stopover by itself. Two state parks in the area afford camping and fishing; the park at Stonewall even has a swimming pool and tennis courts. Great destination for a weekend in the Hill Country.

Padre Island National Seashore, southeast of Corpus Christi on Park Road 22, is on one of the longest (113 miles) islands in the nation. The park preserves the fragile natural barrier island of shifting sand dunes as an isolated, subtropical paradise for the beachcomber. Swimming beaches and a long, almost deserted beach for primitive camping. At the information station you can get maps and use the snack bar, rent equipment, or receive first aid. Showers are available, too. No collecting of artifacts allowed, and no metal detectors in the park. Fine place for bird watching.

There are six national wildlife refuges in Texas open to the professional and amateur naturalist. Each has its own rules, hours, and purpose. Some allow camping and fishing; others do not. Entrance to most is permitted during daylight hours only. The best months for viewing wildlife are usually October through March.

Aransas National Wildlife Refuge, southeast of Tivoli, is the most famous, because it is the principal wintering ground for the nearly extinct whooping crane. But there are sometimes as many as 300 other species of birds in the park.

A network of roads, hiking trails, and observation towers allow the visitor to watch and photograph the fauna. Best time here: November through March. There is an interpretive center where literature and slides are available, and picnicking is allowed. Open daily.

Other national wildlife refuges include: *Anahuac,* northeast of Galveston, for geese and ducks; *Santa Ana,* the southernmost refuge, near Reynosa, on the Mexican border, for native plants and Central-American birds; *Hagerman,* on Lake Texoma near Denison, for migratory fowl on the Great Central Flyway; *Laguna Atascosa,* east of Harlingen, for waterfowl from October to December; *Muleshoe,* south of Muleshoe, in the Panhandle, for prairie dogs, waterfowl, and especially sandhill cranes.

Four national forests are found in the piney woods of East Texas. Primitive camping is allowed in all areas of the forests except where posted. Be advised that there are no electric, water, or sewer hookups for recreational vehicles at any primitive camping area. Hunting and fishing are regulated by the Texas Department of Parks and Wildlife. Deposit of fees for overnight camping or day use of developed swimming beaches is required.

Each forest has several recreation areas for camping, etc., but we will list only the one area in each forest that provides the maximum number of facilities. Caney Creek, in *Angelina National Forest,* on Lake Sam Rayburn, about 14 mi. southeast of Zavalla via Texas Hwy. 63 and FM 2743, offers camping, swimming, boating, shelters, concessions, restrooms, fresh water, and hiking trails. Ratcliff Lake, in *Davy Crockett National Forest,* on Texas Hwy. 7, 20 mi. east of Crockett, has the same facilities as Caney Creek. Red Hills Lake, in the *Sabine National Forest,* about 3 mi. north of Milam via Texas Hwy. 87, lacks only a concession stand. And Double Lake, in the *Sam Houston National Forest,* about 4 mi. south of Coldspring via Texas Hwy. 150 and FM 2025, has full facilities.

For more information on national parks contact a Texas tourist bureau (see *Tourist Information,* above).

CAMPING AND RV FACILITIES. Camping facilities are widespread in Texas, and more are springing up each year. National parks, state parks, municipal parks, as well as private firms and individuals, provide campgrounds for tents and hookups for recreational vehicles.

Of 90 state parks and monuments across Texas, 49 have at a minimum electricity and water hookups, restrooms, and cooking facilities, and some of those also have sewage hookups and showers, swimming pools, and tennis courts. Hookups cost an additional fee of about $5 to $7 a day. Reservations for camping spots in state parks are strongly recommended, especially during the summer. For more information, see *State Parks,* above.

Municipal parks in the larger towns and cities also provide limited camping and RV facilities. If you are unsure whether a municipal campground is situated in a city, call the local chamber of commerce tourist bureau or refer to the municipal listings in the blue or Yellow Pages of the phone book.

Private campgrounds and RV parks are often small and here-now-gone-tomorrow enterprises. That is not to say that they offer fewer or poorer services, just that they are more difficult to locate. Look for private campgrounds near the state parks and recreation areas, since their private counterparts will be trying to capitalize on the excess of visitors to the parks. One chain campground that is an exception to this is *Kampgrounds of America* (KOA), a series of well-maintained RV and camping parks near recreation areas and cities. For more information, write KOA, Inc., P.O. Box 30558, Billings, MT 59114, or check the local phone book for a nearby listing. KOA grounds often have grocery stores, telephones, and swimming pools.

For information on camping in U.S. national forests see the *National Parks* section, above. Fees here are usually small, but the amenities are limited too.

Roughing it. Primitive camping—frequently no water and, of course, no car—really should be part of any excursion into one of the wildernesses of the national and state parks. The primitive camper can find plenty of places to pitch his tent around the many Texas lakes and in the national forests. Cities, however, usually frown on or ban camping in municipal parks, except in occasional designated camping areas.

For more camping information, you may want to contact a Texas tourist bureau (see *Tourist Information,* above) to get a copy of the *Texas Public Campgrounds Guide.*

THEME PARKS. *Alamo Village,* about 32 miles east of Del Rio, near Brackettville, is a Wild West recreation center. The replica of the Alamo here was the movie set for John Wayne's 1960 film, *The Alamo.* A frontier village, a stagecoach, and lots of country-and-western music. Open May through September; horse races on Labor Day (early September).

Aquarena Springs, in San Marcos near Austin on I-35, features glass-bottomed boats, a submarine theater, an aerial tramway, and a Hill Country nature trail with the ruins of an early Spanish mission and a functioning water-powered mill. Open year-round.

Astroworld, adjacent to the Astrodome in Houston, has more than 100 rides, shows, and amusements for the whole family. A real fantasyland, it is open weekends in April and May; daily, except Monday, from June 1 to Labor Day; and weekends from Labor Day to December 1.

Hanna Barbera Land. North of Houston on I–45. Open daily Memorial Day to Labor Day; weekends in spring and fall. Information: (713) 350–0914.

International Wildlife Park, between Dallas and Fort Worth, off I-30, is a drive-through game preserve of African animals brought to Texas for protection and breeding. Its entertainment "village" offers a petting zoo and rides. Open daily late April to late September, weekends spring and fall.

Sea-Arama Marine World, on Seawall Boulevard in Galveston, puts on shows with trained dolphins and sea lions and lets visitors see up close the food and game fish native to the Texas Gulf coast, as well as more exotic species. Open daily at 10:00 A.M. year-round, continuous shows until dusk.

Six Flags over Texas, between Dallas and Fort Worth, off I-30, is 200 acres of blended history and fantasy, set against the half dozen sovereign flags that have flown over the state. (See *The History of Texas,* below.) The admission ticket lets you enter 100 rides, shows, and exhibits. Food, souvenirs, and a gaming arcade are available. Open weekends in March, April, and September through November; daily from mid-May to Labor Day.

This is a selection; for other theme parks, see the individual chapters in the "Exploring Texas" section.

GOING INTO MEXICO. Entrance Requirements. U.S. citizens who plan on visiting the border areas (defined as anything within 75 miles south of the border) for a length of time less than 72 hours are not required to present any form of entrance permit.

Entrance requirements for persons other than U.S. citizens are more stringent, however. A green tourist card is necessary, as well as an American Multiple Entry Visa and passport. Visitors should check with the Mexican consulate for further information on the necessary permits. Tourist cards and Multiple Entry Visas are available at no charge through the Mexican Consulate in any major Texas border town of entry, as well as from various travel agents.

Tourists may not be stopped crossing into Mexico, but upon re-entering the States, be prepared to show all of the above listed forms. Canadian citizens are exempt from these requirements.

HINTS TO HANDICAPPED TRAVELERS. All federal and state and most city office buildings; the state universities, colleges, and parks; and most municipal street departments have instituted, or are in the process of instituting, special privileges and facilities for the handicapped. More and more curbs, especially in downtown areas, have antislip ramps for wheelchairs. Reserved parking spaces are often seen. And public bathrooms and toilets have special stalls. Most businesses have been following suit.

Many hotel and motel chains, including *Holiday Inn, Hyatt, Ramada,* and *Sheraton,* have made efforts to provide special rooms for the handicapped in most of their establishments. Be sure to ask the hotel or motel if they have special accommodations when you call to make reservations.

Many state parks have paved, level nature trails that easily accommodate handicapped visitors. Call the individual park before your visit, to find out for sure. For travel tips for the handicapped, write the following organizations: Consumer Information Center, Pueblo, CO 81109; Society for the Advancement of Travel for the Handicapped, 26 Court St., Brooklyn, NY 11242.

Access to the National Parks is a handbook that describes facilities for the handicapped at all national parks. It costs $3.50 and is obtainable from the U.S. Government Printing Office, Washington, D.C. 20402. For a free copy of *Access Amtrak,* a train guide for the handicapped, write Amtrak, National Railroad and Passenger Corporation, 400 N. Capitol St., N.W., Washington, D.C. 20001.

INTRODUCTION TO TEXAS

by
MOLLY IVINS

Molly Ivins is an East Texan who has been in the newspaper business for twenty years, including a stint as a correspondent for The New York Times. *For six years she was editor for the* Texas Observer, *and she is currently a columnist for the* Dallas Times-Herald.

Texans are actually just like everyone else in this country, only more so. That's why John Bainbridge called his book about us *The Super-Americans.* Everything that is good and, I regret to report, most of what is bad in America exists in Texas in an exaggerated form. I don't know why the state has this slightly larger-than-life quality. I suspect it has something to do with a lack of self-consciousness; for some reason, Texans almost never worry about making fools of themselves.

Let me confess right away that I love Texas passionately; but I regard that as a harmless perversion, and I discuss it only with consenting adults. I cannot promise you will see "my" Texas as you wander through this exuberant, uproarious nation-state. But I urge travelers to approach it the way a good Texan approaches an adventure. You may learn much here about history, different cultures, and racism; you will see glorious natural beauty and architectural wonders; and for all I know, you may suffer self-improvement as a result. But if I were you, I'd come to Texas just for the fun of it. Let 'er rip. EEE-YAH!

Texas—I believe it has been noted elsewhere—is a big state, and in it are any number of symptoms of civilization: symphony orchestras, theater companies, museums, universities, poets, scholars, and fern bars. But I think what makes Texas Texas is more in the EEE-YAH! vein. Texas is a wonderful, funny, and astonishing place, but it helps if you are not afflicted with excessively refined sensibilities. Texas can be real tacky.

The state is considerably more complicated than its Hollywood stereotype. Geographically and economically, it can be divided into five separate and distinct regions. It is also a mosaic of cultures; the pieces of the mosaic overlap from one region to the next, and the darker ones always wind up on the bottom. The cultures of Texas are black, Hispanic, southern, standard suburban, and kicker (short for shitkicker). The kickers are dominant.

Kickers used to be mostly country people, but the combination of migration to the cities and the spread of the drugstore-cowboy culture has erased that distinction. Nowadays, kickers are more likely to be refinery workers, insurance salesmen, or secretaries than real cowboys. And a lot of the kickers one sees in Texas grew up in Michigan.

There used to be a great animosity in Texas between the freaks and the kickers. Fifteen years ago, if a longhair wandered into a kicker bar by mistake, he was apt to have his carcass stomped. All that has been radically changed by the most revered artist in Texas, Willie Nelson, the great singer and composer of progressive country music. Willie is a longhair his own self, and those two cultures somehow got married around his music: The kickers took to letting their hair grow and the longhairs turned in their sandals for boots, and now it's kind of hard to tell one from the other.

The redneck tribes of Texas are identified by certain distinctive totems; your pick-em-up truck with guns slung across the back window racks is a solid clue. Drivin' down the highway real fast, throwin' beer cans out the window while your country music plays real loud on the radio is also a giveaway. Necks are noted for gettin' drunk on Saturday nights, usually makin' it to church Sunday mornin', and tellin' Rastus-

and-Liza jokes. Most everybody in the whole state loves football, country music, and beer.

Texans are not particularly civilized people; they shoot, knife, and stomp one another to death with some frequency, and they fight in bars all the time. They're slightly obnoxious to be around when they're having fun. They laugh real loud, hoorah a lot, bang their beer bottles on the table, and just do carry on. They do not shout when they get mad, and they tend to get very quiet just before they become violent. That's when you should leave the bar. Texans are a great deal like Aussies—they cuss a lot, drink enormous quantities of beer, and don't put up with much . . . uh . . . guff.

By way of compensation, we are a notably friendly lot. There is, of course, no way to prove this, but it is my own observation that the level of civility in common daily encounters is considerably higher in Texas than elsewhere in America. When folks speak to you in a public place, they don't usually want your body, your money, or your time. As a rule, they're just being friendly. There's a lot of "ma'am-ing" and "suh-ing" that goes on. "Hidy" is the universal conversation opener, whether you've just been stopped for speeding by the Highway Patrol or you're approached by a lady of the night.

We Texans are a sadly chauvinistic lot, with a highly developed sense of state identity. When wandering around the continent most of us call "Yurip," Texans will, if asked where they are from, generally reply, "Texas," rather than, "The United States." Some of this chauvinism stems from our history. We were an independent nation before joining the United States—and sometimes act as though we still are. Some of it comes from the vagaries our school system; we study as much Texas history as we do American history. If visitors will kindly bear in mind that provincialism is a universal characteristic, our bragging will be easier to take.

Texas is mostly too hot. I recommend spring (which comes early) and fall (which starts late) as the best times to travel the state. In winter, anywhere south of Austin is apt to be fine, but if you come in the summer, well, it's just hot, that's all. No matter what time of year you come, there'll be some kind of civic whoopee and fandangle going on—the Cuero Turkey Trot, the Luling Watermelon Thump, or the Houston Fat Stock Show. Just about every city and town in Texas has its own annual hoorah. In Pharr, they celebrate onions, and in Athens, it's black-eyed peas. And there are rodeos and county fairs year-round. The friendly folks at the Texas Tourist Development Agency can provide you with a list of all these municipal kickups.

"To a Texan, a car is like wings to a seagull," Ronnie Dugger once wrote. "Our places are far apart and we must dip into them driving." There are a few good train trips in the state, and if you are interested only in cities, you can do it by plane, but this is a place best traveled by car. The great slabs of freeways will get you from one city to another in jig time, but the better way, I think, is to wander the primary highways, the better to see the landscapes and visit the towns.

Texas music includes mariachis, blues, country, and soul. Texas has produced two significant variations on country music. The first was country swing, a cross between country and the big-band sound, invented by the late Bob Wills. The second innovation was progressive country, a country style more sophisticated in both music and lyrics than Nashville country music. All over Texas, music is best enjoyed in your basic honkytonk. Every town has a few of 'em, down-home nightclubs. The dress is boots, jeans, and cowboy hats. Texans like to dance—either the two-step or a kind of country-music jitterbug. You can pick up the steps to the Cotton-eyed Joe, where folks dance four or eight to a line with their arms slung across each other's shoulders, in any honkytonk.

Some of the best-known honkytonks are Billy Bob's Texas in Fort Worth, Gilley's in the Houston suburb of Pasadena, the Cotton Club in Lubbock, and Rio Palm Isles in Longview. Tejanos (Texas Chicanos) are producing an amazing amount of good new music these days in styles called Tex-Mex, *norteño, ranchero,* and *conjunto.* The best-known Tejano band is Little Joe, Johnny y La Familia. They play constantly in halls across Texas, and should you run across them, don't miss the performance. Leadbelly (the late Huddie Ledbetter) and Lightnin' Hopkins were the greatest of the black blues artists. In most big Texas cities you can find good black blues or R & B clubs.

Perhaps the prettiest part of the state is the Hill Country of Central Texas. The Balcones Fault marks the line where the plains crumple up into the hills and the start of limestone country with its springs, rivers, and lakes. San Antonio remains the Hispanic capital of Texas and is crammed with history and fine attractions like the lovely riverwalk Paseo del Rio. I'm afraid it's impossible for me to debunk the Alamo: We may have lost, but we put up one hell of a good fight there, really an all-timer, like Thermopylae or Carthage. Besides which, we got so mad about losing that we went and stomped the Mexicans at the Battle of San Jacinto while yelling, "Remember the Alamo!" and we have been bragging about it ever since.

Austin, the state capital, is a mellow place noted for its innovative country music. It's the home of the university and the legislature, the finest free entertainment in Texas. The Lege meets for the first four months of odd-numbered years and during unpredictable special sessions after that. It beats the zoo or the circus, so catch it if it's in town. Austin's Sixth Street has become the Bourbon Street of Texas, and there's good live music all over town.

El Paso and its sister city of Ciudad Juárez have a flavor all their own. Both cities are markedly Mexican in feel, and the best restaurants serve real Mexican food, not Tex-Mex. Juárez nightlife ranges from chi-chi clubs to funky bars.

The two great cities of Texas are Houston and Dallas, both of which have almost as many detractors as avid fans. Houston has been described as "Los Angeles with the climate of Calcutta," and indeed the weather is so thoroughly miserable (hot and humid except for a few days a year when it's cold and humid) that before air conditioning took over, foreign diplomats used to get hardship pay for being posted there. Visitors will find that Houston has a compensating vitality and optimism about it that like to bowl you over. The sheer, raw energy of the place is astounding; it runneth over in all directions, sprawling across the Gulf coastal plain with complete abandon. No city planner has ever touched Houston; the nation's fourth largest city just grows like Topsy.

Dallas is considered Texas' "Eastern" city, by reputation a formal, proper, dressy place, self-consciously "cultural." It's a clean, well-lighted city, and compared to Houston it's almost fussy in its orderliness. A businessman's town, Dallas was built on the paper industries of insurance and banking. Its downtown is deader'n a doornail at night, but there's a cheerful night life in the Oak Lawn area and along Greenville Avenue. Neiman-Marcus remains one of the great class acts in the world of retail merchandising, and the lively apparel business in Dallas probably accounts for the city's "dressiness."

Fort Worth is the "cowtown" across the Trinity River that Dallas likes to look down on. It has a spunky, unpretentious charm of its own, and its old stockyard area is worth a visit.

THE HISTORY OF TEXAS

by
CONNIE SHERLEY

Connie Sherley has lived within a thirty-five-mile radius of Austin her entire life. Before becoming a freelance travel writer—she is a member of the Society of American Travel Writers—Mrs. Sherley was travel editor of the Fentress Group Newspapers in Texas.

When Columbus discovered America, Texas was inhabited by several Indian tribes on a permanent basis, and some others as they felt the need to roam. The Caddoes were primarily farmers who got along with one another and stayed put. Hunting was good in the dense forests of North and East Texas where they lived, worked the land, and kept to themselves.

The Lipan Apaches covered the territory from San Antonio up into West Texas in a nomadic manner, leaving the coast to small tribes of less-tranquil Indians, the most notorious of whom were the Karankawas. After the first guidebook to Texas, Cabeza de Vaca's *Relación,* pointed out that the Karankawas were cannibalistic in addition to being mean *hombres,* knowledge of their presence discouraged casual landings along the Gulf of Mexico.

The first notice of Texas by Europeans came in 1519, when Alonso Álvarez de Pineda mapped the Gulf coast from Florida to Vera Cruz, Mexico. He did no exploring; that came nine years later, when remnants of an ill-fated Spanish expedition washed up on the coast near Galveston. Led by Cabeza de Vaca, three survivors finally escaped from the Karankawas and made their way across Texas and down to Mexico City in 1536.

Cabeza de Vaca faded from New World history, but the seeds of greed he had sown with the tales of golden cities took root. The most famous search for the Seven Cities of Cibola was made by Francisco Vásquez de Coronado, who marched into Texas with three hundred well-armed conquistadores in 1540 and spent two years in the plains region, wandering as far as the Grand Canyon of the Colorado. The expedition failed to find cities of gold, but they left behind a boon to the Indians by releasing horses, which were to make the nomadic Indians more mobile.

The First Flag

The Spanish flag, first of six to fly over the state, was now firmly planted in Texas soil, but the new rulers made no attempt to colonize until the French fleur-de-lis flag was brought to the area in 1685 by Robert Cavelier Sieur de La Salle, an explorer with a splendid name but little sense of direction or luck. He and his men were looking for the mouth of the Mississippi but ended up at Lavaca Bay instead. He established Fort Saint Louis and began a search for silver and gold but then was killed by one of his own men. Disease and Indian raids eventually wiped out the fort, eliminating the French flag.

Actually, it took nearly two years for news of the French invasion to reach Mexico City and be relayed to Spain, where the absentee rulers decided that time had come for positive action. The first step was to give the territory a name. In 1689 Damian Massanet reported meeting Indians who proclaimed themselve *thecas,* or friends. There was debate about whether the word was *tejas, tayshas, texias* or *texas,* but the latter finally was accepted. In 1691 Texas-Coahuila was declared a dominion of Spain. Missions were established to Christianize the Indians, which was no small task, considering their nomadic nature. Initial attempts were made in East Texas, where the Caddos' stay-at-home ways created a better climate for conversion. The missionaries had some success, but it was the introduction of pigs, horses and cattle, farm implements, and European know-how, rather than religion, that laid a foundation for a culture destined to attract settlers.

A milestone in Texas history was the establishment of San Antonio de Valero mission and San Antonio de Alamo presidio, a garrison supplying military support, in 1718, as an outpost for the Mexican viceroy. Four more missions, San José, Concepción, San Juan Capistrano, and Espada, followed on the banks of the San Antonio River.

Canary Islanders became the first of many outside ethnic groups to settle in Texas, when fifteen families were brought over in 1731 and given land at San Antonio. During the 1750s towns were formed on the Rio Grande, and in 1779 Nacogdoches was permanently established. Spanish paranoia about possible United States designs on the territory was fanned by the 1803 Louisiana Purchase and the Aaron Burr conspiracy, but problems were growing in Mexico. After Father Hidalgo led an unsuccessful revolt there in 1810 and 1811, Spain virtually ignored Texas.

The Old Three Hundred

Just before the Spanish period ended with Mexican independence in 1821, Moses Austin came to San Antonio from Missouri and applied for a colonization permit. The request was approved, but Austin died before he could make the next move. His son, Stephen F. Austin, a New Orleans attorney, took up the quest, obtaining permission to settle three hundred families. The Texas pilgrims, now called the Old Three Hundred, arrived by wagon train. Within a decade the original families had been joined by seven hundred more, and the colony at San Felipe had a population of five thousand.

Continuation of the empresario system begun by the Spanish encouraged colonization through land agents who received large grants for themselves and cheap land for settlers who accompanied them. Between 1821 and 1836 the population of Texas jumped from seven thousand to nearly fifty thousand as empresarios from both the United States and Mexico took advantage of the rulings.

Among the new arrivals was a Virginian named Sam Houston, who had grown up in Tennessee among the Indians and had developed an understanding of their ways that led to his distinguished service as a scout during the Indian wars. He subsequently became a lawyer, served in congress, and was governor of Tennessee when his bride, the daughter of one of the state's most influential and wealthy men, left him after their honeymoon. The scandal caused Houston to resign the governorship and head down the Texas Road to the Oklahoma Territory, where he stayed among his old boyhood friends, the Cherokees. Three years later, President Andrew Jackson asked Houston to go to Texas on a mission. Leaving his Indian wife, Tiana Rogers, behind, Houston went to San Antonio and later decided to settle in Nacogdoches.

Distance, language, and other cultural differences were rapidly corroding relations between Mexico and the Texas colonists. The Mexicans couldn't understand the Anglos' regard for law in the abstract or their dissatisfaction with a new constitution that failed to provide trial by jury and the right to bail. Neither could the Mexicans comprehend why the predominantly Protestant settlers were upset about a "paper law" requiring them to become Catholic. Sensing that the situation was getting out of control, the Mexican government decided in 1830 to cut off further settlement and imports from the United States.

In an attempt to work out some of the problems, Stephen F. Austin went to Mexico City and was promptly put in prison there. The experience convinced him that independence was the only answer.

The Alamo

Skirmishes between the colonists—now called Texians—and Mexican soldiers soon erupted into battles. On Oct. 2, 1835, Gonzales became the Lexington of Texas, but the Mexican president, Santa Anna, didn't become especially concerned about the rebels until they captured San Antonio on December 9, 1835. The defeat made Santa Anna angry enough to take command of the army and begin a march to San Antonio. By the time he arrived, the Texas force there had dwindled to fewer than two hundred men.

The Texians' commanders, Lieutenant Colonel William Barrett Travis and Colonel James Bowie, ordered their men into the walled chapel called the Alamo, hoping reinforcements would arrive before their situation became hopeless. Bowie was seriously ill with typhoid-pneumonia and had to be taken in on his cot. The seige began on February 24, the day after Santa Anna arrived with the first wave of his troops. The Mexican commander's daily demand for surrender was answered each time with a cannon shot.

Travis's appeals for help brought 32 men from Gonzales, who made their way through Mexican lines and entered the Alamo on March 1. Their arrival raised the Texians' ranks to 187 men. Three days later the remainder of Santa Anna's troops marched into San Antonio, which was now surrounded by 5,000 men.

On March 6, 1836, Santa Anna hoisted the red flag of no quarter on the San Fernando church tower. Just before dawn, with bugles sounding the *Deguello* ("Death to the Defenders"), columns of Mexican soldiers attacked all four walls. Twice they were driven back, but the third attack on the north wall was successful. Travis died at his cannon, and Davy Crockett and his Tennessee Boys fell in hand-to-hand fighting in front of the doors into the chapel. Bowie emptied his pistols and utilized his famous Bowie knife before he was killed. The thirteen-day siege ended in a few hours. The Texas force had no survivors. Santa Anna ordered the defenders' bodies burned.

During the siege the constitutional convention was in session at Washington-on-the-Brazos. Former members of the United States Congress, constitutional-convention representatives from Alabama and Missouri, fifteen attorneys, and six doctors were among the forty-four men who signed the Texas Declaration of Independence on March 2, 1836. David G. Burnet was named provisional governor, and Sam Houston continued as commander in chief of the army.

Military disasters continued for the Texians. Three weeks after the fall of the Alamo, Santa Anna ordered the massacre of more than three hundred prisoners at Goliad, fanning to a roar the rebels' fire of rage and indignation.

Sam Houston took his time regrouping the Texian forces as Santa Anna marched south to a point on Buffalo Bayou near the present site of Houston. The ragtag Texas army stalking the Mexicans had no uniforms and little artillery. On April 21, surrounded by 1,600 men, Santa Anna felt confident enough to take his usual siesta. After the camp had settled down for naps, 783 Texians came charging across the terrain shouting, "Remember the Alamo!" and "Remember Goliad!"

The Battle of San Jacinto was over in eighteen minutes. The Mexicans counted 630 dead, 280 wounded, and 730 taken prisoner, including Santa Anna, who remained a captive for six months. Nine Texians were killed or mortally wounded and thirty others sustained less-serious wounds. A rifle ball shattered Houston's ankle.

The Republic of Texas

The Treaty of Velasco, signed May 14, 1836, sent Santa Anna back to Mexico City, where he promptly denounced the new republic, but the United States, France, Great Britain, Holland, France, and some German states recognized the country, providing Texas with powerful diplomatic friends who discouraged full-scale invasion by Mexico. Sam Houston was elected president and Mirabeau B. Lamar vice-president. The people also voted in favor of annexation by the United States, but the Missouri Compromise of 1820 precluded Texas' becoming a state, since most Texas landowners had slaves. In 1838 the annexation proposal was withdrawn and the government settled into the job of organizing the republic. The distinctive red, white, and blue flag with the lone five-pointed star was officially adopted.

The republic period was a collection of financial and strategic disasters. Ships of the Texas navy were repossessed when repair bills couldn't be paid. Mexico refused to recognize Texas' independence, which led the republic into skirmishes and foolhardy expeditions into Mexico and New Mexico that cost both lives and money.

The capital was moved from Washington-on-the-Brazos to Columbia to Houston. Finally Austin was selected as the permanent capital site during Lamar's presidency, much to Houston's displeasure. Austin citizens suspected that after his reelection, Houston might try to move the capital back to his namesake city, so they put a protective watch on the state archives.

During one of the periodic Mexican invasions, Houston did, indeed, send two Texas Rangers to move the archives to Washington-on-the-Brazos for "safekeeping." A woman caught the rangers loading the archives and sounded the alarm by firing a six-pound cannon kept loaded for the purpose. The rangers and the archives took off in a wagon, but the citizen recruits, dragging the cannon, caught them as they camped overnight and gave the rangers a choice of fighting or surrendering the archives. They selected surrender, ending the Archives War and returning the government records to Austin.

The only commodity the republic had was land. At this time the Texas Republic's boundary followed the Rio Grande to its source through New Mexico into what is today southern Colorado, where it took a stovepipe cut into Wyoming and included portions of Kansas and Oklahoma. The General Land Office was established to handle this huge public domain. The empresario system was continued, further spurring settlement, which in turn stirred up the Indians.

The prospect of cheap land in a climate of personal choice and freedom attracted settlers from the southern United States, where slavery was increasingly becoming a heated issue. Several hundred Germans, including noblemen who hoped to make a profit as empresarios, formed the Verein zum Schutze Deutscher Einwanderer, which sponsored 7,380 German colonists from 1844 to 1846, when the Verein went bankrupt. A second group, Irish settlers, arrived in 1848, and Czechoslovakian families, eager to escape the wars that regularly overran their homeland, began to immigrate in large numbers. Poles, Swedes, Danes, and Wends arrived in Galveston and pushed inland, bringing their religions, skills, and cultures to a new setting. In all, twenty-six ethnic groups formed the nucleus of early Texas settlement.

Statehood

Eventually, it was Great Britain's interest in Texas that led to statehood. The British had no intention of adding the republic to their empire, but they felt that an independent Texas would be a deterrent to the United States' western expansion, since Texas' far-flung borders would create a barrier. Trade with Texas offered Britain commercial advantages, as well as an opportunity to muddy American economic and social affairs.

After the United States senate again rejected annexation in 1844, the question became an issue in the presidential campaign. When James Polk, who favored annexation, defeated Henry Clay, President John Tyler carried out the electorate's wishes by pushing Texas statehood through congress as one of his last acts of office.

With prodding from Great Britain, Mexico offered to recognize Texas' independence if statehood was refused, but sentiment in Texas was for annexation. Sentiment aside, the Texas public debt had risen to nearly eight million dollars, and the support of United States revenues was welcome. An annexation ordinance was adopted in Texas July 4, 1845. The following October the people approved a state constitution in which Texas reserved ownership of its public lands and retained the right to divide into five separate states—a plan that has been proposed at least sixteen times but never approved. The United States congress accepted the Texas constitution December 29, 1845, making Texas the twenty-eighth state in the union.

The Lone Star flag was lowered from the capitol in Austin February 19, 1846, and the Stars and Stripes became the fifth flag to fly over Texas. Texians became Texans when they became Americans, for a reason shrouded by history but probably having something to do with logical spelling.

Almost immediately Mexico launched an attack, and the United States retaliated. The Mexican War ended February 2, 1848, with the Treaty of Hidalgo.

Then Texas got into a boundary dispute with the United States, after which the Compromise of 1850 brought Texas ten million dollars in exchange for claims to land on either side of the Rio Grande. The windfall allowed the state to pay its debts and set two million dollars aside for a permanent school fund that, in 1854, led to a statewide network of free public schools.

Sam Houston returned to the political arena, serving as a United States senator for two terms before successfully running for Texas governor in 1859. Because of the vast distances within the state, and to get goods to distant markets, Texas was eager to have railroads. An offer of five sections of land (3,200 acres) for each mile of track was made to the companies. When there were no takers, the land grant was raised to sixteen sections. The plan eventually gave the railroads more than thirty-two million acres, mostly in West Texas, where it was subsequently sold to settlers for $1.50 an acre.

Hostile Indians and lack of water slowed West Texas development, but one of those problems was eliminated in 1854 by the first American windmill. The railroads brought the invention to Texas, primarily to supply water for steam engines, but its use quickly spread, making the vast dry areas of the Panhandle and West Texas inhabitable.

Texas in the Confederacy

Before the economic benefits that would result from railroads and the windmill could be felt, the issue of secession, in the dispute over slavery, became paramount. Houston, now governor, opposed secession, but the people were predominantly southerners. As states' righters, they opposed a strong federal government even if they weren't pro-slavery. Texas seceded from the Union January 28, 1861, and the Confederate flag replaced the Stars and Stripes to become the sixth flag. When Houston refused to take an oath of allegiance to the Confederacy, the Secession Convention removed him from office.

The Texas coast was blockaded during the Civil War, and the state's prime port, Galveston, was captured by the United States and then recaptured by the Confederates. For the most part there was little fighting on Texas soil; however, the war's last land battle took place deep in the Rio Grande Valley near Brownsville, an area so remote that a Confederate force captured eight hundred federal soldiers May 13, 1865, only to have their startled prisoners tell them that Lee had surrendered at Appomattox more than a month earlier.

Reconstruction was a bitter period. The predominantly rural population was busy trying to revitalize farms and ranches neglected during the war. Cattle provided the only bright economic note. The hardy longhorn had multiplied at a tremendous rate on the open range. The problem was getting them to markets hundreds of miles away. Fortunately, the longhorn is a fine traveler. Herds of twenty-five hundred to three thousand were moved north along the famous cattle trails—Chisholm, Western-Dodge, and Shawnee—to slaughter pens as far away as the Canadian border.

Cattle raising was a hard life that created cattle kingdoms and spawned the cowboy, who learned professional rudiments from the *vaqueros* and also borrowed the Mexican cowboy's trappings: leather chaps, bandannas, spurs, the lariat, boots, and a broadbrimmed hat capable of warding off the weather, be it rain or the fierce Texas sun.

Range Wars and Railroads

It was 1879 before barbed wire was sold in quantity, but John "Bet a Million" Gates soon became its leading salesman and set up manufacturing companies to meet demand. Enclosing the open ranges set off feuds between cattlemen and ranchers, and the feuds led to fence cutting. In 1884 a special session of the legislature was called to deal with the problem. As a result, fence cutting and malicious pasture burning became felony crimes in Texas. The fenced range brought a new era in cattle breeding, which had gotten off to a fancy start in 1848 when two cows and a bull from Queen Victoria's Durham herd were imported to a North Texas ranch.

The railroads were developing quickly. Dallas was served by one line, but word got out that the new Texas and Pacific Railroad had selected a site twenty miles away as the point where the new line and the existing railroad would intersect, creating an important cross site that would challenge Dallas in importance. When the legislature passed the Texas and Pacific charter, the charter contained a provision written in at the last minute by a Dallas legislator stipulating that the cross site must be "no more than a mile from Browder Springs." The bill became law before the legislators from the rest of the state discovered that Browder Springs was in effect part of Dallas, the source of Dallas' water supply, about a mile from the site of Neely's first cabin—the beginning of Dallas. The strategic rail position caused a growth flurry that raised Dallas' population from twelve hundred to seven thousand in a few months. The town quickly became a leading distribution point for the Southwest, attracting ambitious merchants and businessmen with a penchant for establishing banks and insurance companies.

After the capitol burned in 1881, plans began for a new building on the grounds in Austin, although the state had no money. To finance the project, three million acres of Texas Panhandle land were offered in exchange for a building contract. An Illinois syndicate took up the offer and turned the land into the famous XIT Ranch.

The late nineteenth century was a period of slow development for Texas' agricultural economy, but important changes were taking place in other ways. Fifty miles inland, upstart Houston had dredged Buffalo Bayou into a channel capable of handling oceangoing ships. Houston's port status, combined with its excellent rail facilities, gained added importance in 1900 when Texas' more important port, Galveston, was hit by the worst natural disaster in American history—a hurricane that killed more than six thousand people and virtually closed Galveston.

Black Gold

Oil had been something of a nuisance in Texas for years. People dug for badly needed water, only to have the well ruined by seeping oil. The first producing well, drilled in 1866, was abandoned because there was no market for the product. In 1896, with a market for oil slowly developing, the Corsicana oil field led to the building of the state's first refinery.

Texas' big-time entry into the oil age came January 10, 1901, when Spindletop blew in near Beaumont. During the wild period that followed, hundreds of oil companies were formed. Some survived. The barbed-wire king, "Bet a Million" Gates, started the Texas Company, which would become Texaco. Gulf and Humble also began with Spindletop leases. Black gold would upstage cotton, wheat, and cattle in the state's economic picture.

The flat land around Houston was perfect for pipelines, and the ship channel made an ideal refinery site. Best of all, Houston bankers were willing to take chances on exploration financing. The new port city was a natural headquarters for the fledgling oil industry.

In Dallas on September 10, 1907, oil money got a new market when Neiman-Marcus opened for business. Political destiny entered the world with the birth of Lyndon Baines Johnson, August 28, 1908.

More rich oil fields were discovered throughout East and West Texas. (In 1923 the University of Texas became one of the richest schools in the country when Santa Rita Number 1 came in on land set aside for the university during republic days.)

The state's mild winters and dry climate made it a military headquarters during World War I. The forerunner of the Army Air Force was founded at Fort Sam Houston in San Antonio in 1910 and expanded to Kelly Field during World War I. Originally all pilot training took place outside the Alamo City at Randolph Air Field, the "West Point of the Air."

Texas became the first state to elect a woman governor in 1924, when Miriam "Ma" Ferguson ran for the office because a prior impeachment made her husband ineligible. She lost a bid for a second term but made a successful comeback six years later and served two more years.

Water had always been one of the state's biggest problems. There was either too little or too much. Heavy rains set the rivers on rampages that caused loss of property and life. Droughts wiped out farms and ranches. In the late 1930s, construction began on a series of dams that would tame the rivers and provide new sources of irrigation and power, as well as a mammoth watery patchwork of recreational lakes.

World War II and After

When the United States moved into the defense period that preceded World War II, Texas' low tax rate, excellent climate, and good labor market brought an influx of industry. Government aircraft plants were built in the Dallas–Fort Worth area, and additional army, air force, and naval training bases were opened in Texas.

Lyndon Johnson was elected to the United States Senate in 1947 by a margin of eighty-seven votes that earned him the nickname "Landslide Lyndon." Within four years he was the senate majority whip, and, with Sam Rayburn of Texas serving as Speaker of the House, Texas had unprecedented influence in Washington. By 1950 Texas businessmen were wooing large companies and industries to relocate in the state, and the industrial migration was in full swing. For the first time in the state's history, the census showed more Texans living in cities than in rural areas.

By now irrigation had become the greatest thing for Texas farmers and ranchers since the windmill. Sophisticated networks of manmade rainfall turned the high plains into one of the nation's prime wheat-, grain-, and cotton-growing areas. The oil industry evolved to the petrochemical industry centered on the Gulf coast.

Since the Aerospace Medical Center and the Air Force's Air Training Command headquarters were in Texas, it seemed logical that the Manned Space Center (MSC) should be built on a thousand acres of former swampland outside Houston donated to the government by Rice University. Naturally, there were those who felt Vice-President Johnson's role as chairman of the National Aeronautics and Space Council had as much to do with the decision as the free land, but be that as it may, the MSC put Texas up front in the space age.

Nov. 22, 1963, John F. Kennedy was assassinated in Dallas and Lyndon Johnson became president of the United States.

By the 1970s Texas was the world's most air-conditioned area, and its citizens were noted for dashing from air-conditioned homes to air-conditioned cars to air-conditioned offices and shopping malls. Surrounded as they were by oil and its byproducts, the world petroleum crisis took on an ironic aspect for Texans waiting in gas-station lines.

The increase in oil prices turned the Texas weather into a valuable natural resource and made the state the most attractive notch in the much-publicized Sun Belt. Space-age industries followed the lead of electronics companies that had relocated in Texas during the 1950s and '60s. Population boomed, particularly in the Houston, Dallas, and San Antonio areas, putting the three among the eleven largest United States cities in the 1980 census.

TEXAS FOOD AND DRINK

by
CONNIE SHERLEY

Texans are born knowing the difference between chile, chili, and chile con carne. This intuitive hereditary touch complements the asbestos palates with which we also are said to come into this world.

Consider that chile is to chili is to chile con carne, a formula outsiders find more difficult to comprehend than the theory of relativity, which is precisely what it is; but instead of being relative to the universe, this matter is relative to Tex-Mex, the state's own cuisine. Without chiles there would be no chili, and without chili there would be no Tex-Mex.

Chiles are peppers that grow in a variety of sizes packed with a wide range of sizzle. Chili is the traditional "bowl of red," produced by slowly cooking chopped beef, chiles, and the chef's own blend of spices, which always includes cumin, a special ingredient brought to Texas in 1731 by Canary Islanders who settled in San Antonio. True Texas chili is never cooked with beans. The subject is undebatable.

Since *chile con carne* translates to "peppers with meat," chili con carne (if such a thing existed) would be a meat dish with meat, a redundancy on a par with "Rio Grande River"—which, incidentally, is where it all began when Mexican chiles were brought north and combined with slow cooking to make tough, stringy beef from the hardy Texas longhorn palatable.

Like most things Texan, the origination of chili is steeped in legend made more colorful with each passing decade. Many historians—and the state abounds with experts on the subject—claim that chili was created in the San Antonio jail during Texas Republic days when an imaginative cook chopped up meat of questionable vintage before simmering it with chiles and anything else he thought might mask the taint. The dish got better with each reheating, and prisoners supposedly developed such a passion for the pungent mixture that they refused freedom when their sentences were completed.

The story is certainly plausible, for the addiction has been handed down as part of the Lone Star heritage. When the first norther puts a nip of fall in the air, twentieth-century Texans are overcome by a craving that can be sated only by a steaming bowl of chili and a stack of crisp saltine crackers, which are lovingly crumbled into the bowl of red. (Dipping saltines into the dish is a *faux pas* of the highest magnitude.)

West Texans attribute the origination of chili to chuck-wagon cooks called upon to satisfy the palates of cowboys who snacked on pequins, small wild chiles considered the most potent of peppers.

If time hadn't wiped out, or at least blurred, the tracks of truth on the subject, credit probably would go to a combination of sources that merged in San Antonio, where *lavanderas* began a moonlighting operation to augment their incomes as laundresses and developed the first fast-food operation, ladling chili from wash pots set up around the plazas. Nineteenth-century writers vividly describe the chili queens' stands ringing the squares and the mouthwatering, spicy scents that drew customers into the area.

The era ended in 1937, when modern health ordinances forced the chili queens out of business. By then their menus had been expanded to include tortillas and tamales served on long portable tables made of sawhorses and boards. The outdoor enterprises were the forerunners of Tex-Mex restaurants.

Tex-Mex

During the chili-queen period, almost every Texas town was fortunate enough to have a man of Mexican heritage who mounted a big tin can filled with steaming tamales packaged in corn shucks on a pushcart and set up shop along Main Street. As financial pressures of the Depression began to ease, tamale salesmen sensed their clientele's desire for expanded services, as well as an opportunity to get in out of the fickle Texas weather, and opened restaurants in their homes. The three-generation businesses utilized Grandmother's talents in the kitchen, Mama's and Papa's supervision in the dining room, and the children's energy taking care of the tables.

As word of mouth spread, additional rooms furnished with second-hand tables and chrome chairs were opened. The less atmosphere a place had, it seemed, the better the food was. South-of-the-border recipes were adapted to north-of-the-border tastes, but chili gravy, which is chili with a minimum of meat, was the cohesive ingredient. The menu was based on the regular plate: an enchilada, rice, refried beans, and a tamale, which evolved to the special plate with the optional addition of either a taco or *chile con queso.*

For the uninitiated, an enchilada might best be described as a Mexican crepe. It begins with a tortilla made of masa, a special corn flour, combined with exactly the right amount of water. The dough is patted out to a flat pancake and baked on a grill. Some cooks heat the tortilla in chili gravy; others douse it in hot lard before rolling the softened tortilla around grated longhorn or Monterey Jack cheese and chopped onion. The rolls are covered with more chili gravy, sprinkled with additional grated cheese and onion, and heated until the cheese melts and the sauce bubbles.

The first Tex-Mex restaurants heated and served the food on the same heavy brown pottery plates. The feast was always presented with the admonition, "Hot plate—very hot plate."

After World War II the taco took on added dimension and crumbling power when an Austin restaurant, El Matamoros, began serving a tortilla that erupted with thin bubbles when deep fried. The crisp, puffy product exploded into tiny pieces if touched by a fork, a misfortune that befell only outsiders bent on adhering to Emily Post's rules. Texans know that tacos, like fried chicken, were meant to be eaten by hand.

The innovation made Austin the state's acknowledged Tex-Mex cuisine capital. Around the state, restaurants advertised, "We serve Austin-style Tex-Mex," which meant that a puffy tortilla would be wrapped round the seasoned ground meat garnished with chopped tomato and lettuce if you ordered a taco, and the same base would be used for *chile con queso,* a blending of at least two cheeses and chiles. The two dishes, combined with a serving of guacamole, make up the popular salad plate, guaranteed not to offend the most timid taste buds.

The original regular plate has evolved to include a variety of combinations through the years, as Tex-Mex has gradually embraced new dishes. Guacamole was a natural addition inhibited only by the availability of the avocado. The basic ingredient is mashed to a lumpy consistency, perked up with seasonings, and combined with finely chopped tomato.

Chile rellenos slipped into Texas from New Mexico, and were allowed to stay because the bland chiles, stuffed with a variety of fillings before being batter fried, are such a delicious addition. The same goes for fajitas, skirt steaks the Mexicans turn into a delicacy by marinating them and quick grilling them over charcoal. The meat slices are served in flour tortillas, refined cousins of the masa variety. Carne asada is similar, but the chunks of beef are usually garnished with pico de gallo, a sauce of tomatoes, chiles, onion, chopped avocado, and cilantro leaves.

Which brings us to sauces. The quality of the *salsa picante* can make or break a restaurant. The basic condiment is freshly made of chiles, tomatoes, onion, garlic, and cilantro, finely chopped. It is a dip for tostados, the quartered, crisply fried tortillas served in baskets, and provides added zip when Texans want more fire in a dish. It should be capable of clearing the sinuses when the dosage is doubled. Beware of seeds in salsa. They carry capsaicin, the chiles' punch.

Of the seemingly endless array of new dishes on Tex-Mex menus, only the nacho was conceived north of the border. June 1, 1971, was a date that changed the Texas restaurant scene. Among other things, the arrival of liquor by the drink through a change in state law created a need for an appetizer on Tex-Mex menus. Who can sip margaritas without nibbling? Tortillas were quartered, fried to a crisp, topped with refried beans and cheese, popped into the oven until the cheese melted, and then crowned with a sliver of jalapeño (hal-uh-*pain*-nyuh). The nacho is the supreme Tex-Mex hors d'oeuvre.

The Margarita

The margarita was on the south bank of the Rio Grande, just waiting for Texas to shake off its archaic liquor laws. One part each of pure lime juice (connoisseurs use only the Mexican variety) and triple sec or Cointreau, and two parts tequila are either given a good tumbling with crushed ice in a cocktail shaker and strained or served on the rocks after being blended sans ice. The glass rim is doused with lime juice and dipped in coarse salt, so the margarita can be sipped through the coating. Definitely not for those on a low-sodium diet.

Just as Tex-Mex is blasphemed through fast-food sour-cream "tacos" garnished with ripe olives, the margarita has been desecrated with a frozen version of the drink that amounts to a tequila-touched snowcone piled into fancy glasses. Powders and bottled "reconstituted" lime juice, touted as substitutes for fresh lime juice, have found their way into bars, but just as sure as chiles make chili, there is no shortcut to a fine margarita.

On the changing Tex-Mex scene, two things remain constant. The first is the last: the dessert course. Forget the pastry cart and other devious offerings meant only to appeal to the sweet tooth, pad the tab, pour on calories, and/or make you forget how lousy the entree was. Tex-Mex needs only a pecan praline or lime or pineapple sherbet.

The Lone Star praline bears no resemblence to European confections of the same name. Texas pralines are made by cooking sugar and cream or buttermilk to a golden brown. The syrup is beaten until creamy, laced with pecans, and dropped by spoonfuls to harden into patties. Pralines stretched with coconut merit the same disdain as frozen margaritas.

Texans are about equally divided between pralines and sherbet as the perfect ending to the meal; however, the sherbet isn't meant to be a palate-clearing sorbet. The idea is moot because of Tex-Mex's natural lingering qualities.

Tex-Mex Champagne: Beer

Beer, the other constant on the Tex-Mex scene, has been legal in Texas since the repeal of Prohibition, so there has never been any problem concerning what to drink with a Tex-Mex meal. Wine does nothing for the cuisine, but cold beer, served in an icy mug, complements each bite. Beer drinkers are loyal to Lone Star, Pearl, and Shiner, the last of which remains the principal product of the South Texas town (population 2,213) bearing the same name.

Where else but in Texas will you find a beer garden on the National Register of Historic Places? Scholz Garten, on the fringe of the University of Texas in Austin, has been pouring suds since 1866. Customers order by the pitcher or in the Lone Star trademark, the long-neck bottle. German immigrants endowed the state with a beer culture that continued without interruption through Prohibition, with homebrew produced in cellars and smokehouses.

Texas Barbecue

Beer also lends itself nicely to barbecue, the second most renowned eating habit in the state. The predecessor of modern bar-b-q began in ranch pits where whole steers were cooked over wood coals. Texas barbecue got international attention, or notoriety, when Lyndon Johnson had the barbecue master Walter Jetton cater gatherings in Washington and at the Texas White House.

The statewide popularity of barbecue goes back to the time when Saturday was set aside for weekly shopping. Farmers brought their families to town and spent the day gathering supplies. The rural folk were skeptical of what few restaurants existed, and boardinghouses were always crowded already. To feed the crowds, meat-market owners built pits in back of their shops and started slow cooking brisket, ribs, and rings of sausage, known as hot links. The patient process began on Friday night. By Saturday morning the air floated with the delicious smoky aroma, whetting the appetites of townspeople, who quickly joined the Saturday barbecue tradition. Meats, sold by the pound, were eaten picnic-style off heavy, rosy-pink butcher paper.

The best barbecue is found in unpretentious small-town establishments with interiors permeated by the essence of smoked meats. Anyone who thinks all barbecue is dry and tough should drop by Joe Cotton's in Robstown, Louie Mueller's in Taylor, or the Kruez Market in Lockhart.

Add cole slaw, potato salad, sliced onions, dill pickles, jalapeño peppers, sliced white bread, iced tea, and kegs of Lone Star, Pearl, or Shiner beer to barbecue, and you have an occasion that has won votes for many politicians and marked holidays, weddings, anniversaries, and birthdays in Texas for several generations.

Other Texas Favorites

Oh, yes, "ahst" tea, another Lone Star phenomenon. Failure to specify hot tea when ordering in Texas will get you a tall glass of iced tea, regardless of the time of day. Texans drink vast amounts of iced tea morning, noon, and night. Nothing takes the sting out of a hot summer day like a big, thirst-quenching glass of orange pekoe over ice.

The native soft drink is Dr. Pepper, prepared from a formula worked out by a Waco druggist who wanted something different to bring customers to his soda fountain. For years Dr. Pepper, like Fritos, was marketed only within the state. Traveling Texans who carried private stocks of the soft drink and the crunchy snack based on corn tortillas are credited with creating a demand for the products all over the world.

One of the joys of driving through Texas is the opportunity it provides for sampling local specialties: homemade breads from the bakeries at Fredericksburg; wursts from the meat markets of New Braunfels; and kolaches, the fruit- or cheese-filled Czechoslovakian pastries from West. Be alert for festivals and fairs where local cooks strive to excel by producing ethnic dishes seldom seen other places.

Texas home cooking was heavily influenced by Southerners who brought along a love for fried chicken, hot biscuits, and rich sweet desserts when they migrated to Texas. Because corn was more plentiful than wheat, cornbread became the staff of life. Today nutritionists have declared beans and cornbread, the pioneers' staple, to be one of the best-balanced, most protein-rich dishes.

In a spirit of making do, cooks substituted peaches for apples and pecans for walnuts in recipes. And somewhere along the line beef was given the batter treatment, and the infamous Texas chicken-fried steak came into being. This entrée is the mainstay on menus of small-town cafés and city restaurants catering to rural expatriates. Non-Texans have been known to describe chicken-fried steaks and the mandatory cream gravy that accompanies them to a shoe sole coated with batter, fried, and slathered with well-peppered Elmer's glue. Texans excuse the comparison as ignorance of the better things in life. They remember that it has taken the rest of the country a long time to get tuned in to the culinary joys of fried okra and good-luck-producing quantities of black-eyed peas eaten on New Year's Day—joys long recognized in Texas.

The need to disguise Texas beef evaporated years ago. Some of the most flavorful and tender steaks available are served at restaurants like Cattlemen's in Fort Worth and the Night Hawk in Austin. There's no charge for the 72-ounce sirloin at the Big Texan in Amarillo, provided you clean your plate within an hour. Yes, it's even possible to get a steak cooked rare, a bit of progress few Texans would have bet on a decade ago.

You must be wondering if a visit to Texas is going to limit you to provincial eating. Remember the statement that June 1, 1971, changed the Texas restaurant scene? The new liquor laws did more than end brown bagging and legalize margaritas. As wines began to flow freely in the state, the need arose for foods beyond Tex-Mex, barbecue, and steaks, all of which lend themselves best just to beer and iced tea.

Young Texans who had developed a liking for foreign cuisines while traveling abroad opened trendy cafés to showcase their newly acquired cooking abilities. The opportunity for a profit margin from the sale of cocktails and wines encouraged excellent chefs who'd been imported to the state by hotels to leave the corporate kitchens and start their own restaurants.

New arrivals from the Far East, lured by wide-open spaces in the Sun Belt and the Lone Star mystique, have introduced Indian, Szechuan, Thai, and Vietnamese dishes that sound foreign but taste familiar because of that common denominator, the chile. Their family-owned and -operated restaurants are reminiscent of the first Tex-Mex places that made eating out so much fun.

Chefs specializing in nouvelle cuisine and Continental cooking are making the most of the excellent fresh shrimp, crab, red snapper, and flounder brought in from the Gulf of Mexico. In the past five years, some of the country's finest restaurants have emerged in Texas cities. The reputation of several Dallas haute cuisine establishments is so widespread that reservations were booked two years in advance by delegates to the 1984 Republican convention.

Texans have always believed the best is none too good, which is why they point with pride to places like Jefferson, the East Texas hamlet with a firm hold on the past. Few meals served anywhere compare to the tradition and excellence of the plantation breakfast at Jefferson's Excelsior House: grits, cured ham, scrambled eggs, and the lightest biscuits and orange muffins you'll ever put into your mouth.

There have been many changes since the late Helen Corbitt introduced a new level of eating excellence in the Zodiac Room at Neiman-Marcus, but one thing remains constant: The sure way to start a debate is to walk up to a group of Texans and ask directions to the best Tex-Mex restaurant in town. Eight people will come up with at least five different answers—and they'll all be right.

EXPLORING TEXAS

HOUSTON

by
CAROL BISBEE BARRINGTON

Carol Bisbee Barrington, an award-winning travel writer and photographer, lives in Houston and specializes in magazine and newspaper feature articles on Texas. She is the author of a book, Day Trips from Houston, *and is a member of the Society of American Travel Writers. John Ashby Wilburn, who produced part of the Practical Information section, is the Editor of* VIVA, *and has been the Managing Editor for* Houston City *magazine.*

Given Houston's national media billing as "The Golden Buckle on the Sun Belt," visitors come to this young city with high expectations and strong misconceptions. In short, the city they experience is not usually the utopia they expect.

First of all, is this Texas? The mind's eye often equates the Lone Star State with sagebrush, and many visitors are amazed by the vast acres of forest, water, and green pastureland surrounding Houston. The second blow is the weather—subtropical, changeable, and often uncomfortable. From its founding as a real-estate development in 1836 until the mid-1950s, Houston was actually considered an unhealthy place to live. It is no coincidence that the city's first spurt of significant growth came with the advent of affordable commercial and residential air conditioning.

Clean and almost starkly modern with scant respect for restrictions, also-rans, and yesterday, Houston may well be the last hangout in continental America for the rugged individualist, a lodestone to the entrepreneur eager to seek his fortune amid the canyons of commerce. Unhampered by zoning, planning, or strong unions, Houston in the last decade has grown seven days a week wherever the developers' dollars have beckoned, covering thousands of acres with cement and buildings that weren't there the month before.

As vital as Houston is, it doesn't always work. Those same elements which have nurtured its enormous growth have created "jumble city." Islands of magnificent architecture often look out on slums or are built to the very edge of sidewalks, forever forcing traffic through four-lane funnels. Many ordinary municipal services such as adequate police protection, cheap and reliable public transportation, and decent roads are in very short supply. Human planning in terms of new parks, green belts, historic preservation, and the like have been very far down the list of civic priorities.

As Houston begins to strangle on its own unbridled growth, things are changing. A new businesslike attitude in City Hall promises improvement and some responsible planning for the future, but for now, there's some tarnish on that golden buckle. Visitors should come prepared to deal with the city on its own terms.

You'll need two basics: a car to get around and plenty of money or "plastic" to enjoy the city's swinging lifestyle. Houston's heyday as one of the least expensive entertainment cities in America is long gone, victim of inflation and the proliferation of corporate expense accounts.

And it helps to understand the natives. Less conservative than Dallasites and far less relaxed than San Antonians, Houstonians seem to live in their cars, always en route somewhere. And they come in several major guises, ranging from the corporate businessperson (often a transplant from California or New York) to the redneck. The latter is a Texian term for local boy whose daddy probably farmed some and raised cattle on the land that today sprouts subdivisions and shopping centers. He is easily identifiable by his cowboy boots and well-washed jeans, a name like Bubba or Jim Bob tooled into the back of his belt, and the guns on the rack in his pickup.

Enjoy both types. The first keeps contemporary Houston prosperous, and the second gives it character.

And "folks talk funny here," as a visiting friend once commented. Yankee or Michigan dialects aside, the local patois is a unique blend of black, Chicano, and lazy-South accents and can be difficult to understand. Just ask folks to slow down until you get your ears in tune.

On the Banks of Buffalo Bayou

"The town of Houston is located at a point on the river which must ever command the trade of the largest and richest portion of Texas." So did those first promos put out in the eastern press by the Allen Brothers sell the sizzle of their new real-estate speculation in August, 1836. That river the ad refers to was muddy, narrow, and barely navigable Buffalo Bayou, and the town was nonexistent—just half a league (four thousand acres) of coastal prairie the Allen Brothers bought for a thousand dollars down and four thousand dollars more whenever.

Their timing was as good as their promotion. Sam Houston's forces had just defeated Santa Anna and his vastly superior Mexican army near this dubious hunk of real estate, and suddenly the fledgling Republic of Texas was ripe for settlement and commercial exploitation. Naming the new town-to-be after the hero of the revolution was a genius of a higher sort, and when the seat of government moved to Houston from West Columbia in 1837, the settlement began to earn its promotional label: "The City of the Future."

Things haven't changed much in the nearly century and a half since. Houston today remains a real-estate developer's dream of opportunity, still growing through entrepreneurial capitalism. Those short, square downtown blocks laid out by the Allen Brothers now sport massive skyscrapers, one of the most contemporary civic panoramas in America. Downtown Houston has become an architectural showcase.

Still bounded on the north by the natural bend of Buffalo Bayou but otherwise encircled by freeways, the downtown district is slowly becoming a "people place" in spite of itself. New parks and plazas, plus fun things like plays, programs, art shows, etc., are beginning to curb the 4:30 P.M. exodus to the suburbs, and weekend festivals often lure folks back into town. Do be aware, however, that few people actually *live* downtown and that after dark this core of the city is usually a ghost town, a dangerous place to wander. Nor is it possible to see it all by foot at one time. Best make a windshield tour first and then either explore on foot or take one of the walking tours conducted by the

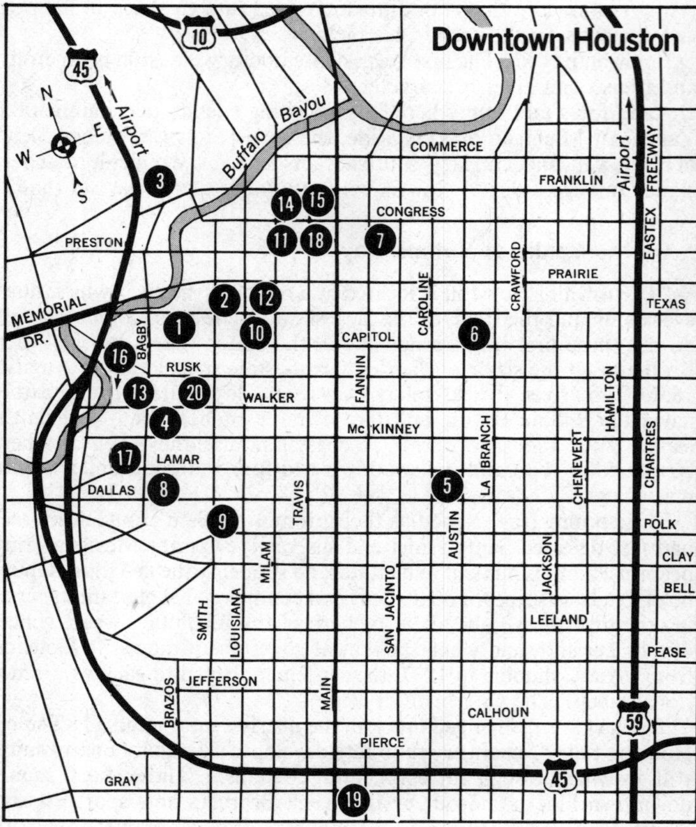

Points of Interest

1) Albert Thomas Convention and Exhibit Center
2) Alley Theater
3) Amtrak Station
4) City Hall
5) Four Seasons Hotel
6) Greyhound Terminal
7) Harris County Courthouse Square
8) Hotel Meridien
9) Hyatt-Regency Hotel
10) Jesse H. Jones Hall for the Performing Arts
11) Kennedy Bakery (La Carafe)
12) Lancaster Hotel
13) Music Hall
14) Old Cotton Exchange
15) Pillot Building
16) Sam Houston Coliseum
17) Sam Houston Park
18) Sweeny-Coombs-Fredericks Building
19) Trailways Bus Terminal
20) Tranquillity Park

Greater Houston Preservation Alliance on the third Wednesday (12 noon) of each month (223–8367).

Plans to develop Buffalo Bayou into a residential-recreation corridor park have not yet moved forward. For now, both the bayou and Allen's Landing are unremarkable and, aside from their history, have little to offer of tourist interest. The area bounded by Commerce, Fannin, Texas, and Louisiana Streets was the heart of old Houston, but only a handful of the original buildings remain. Best of the lot are the Old Cotton Exchange (1884), 202 Travis; the old Kennedy Bakery (1860s), now La Carafe, 813 Congress, thought to be the oldest commercial building still on its original site; the Pillot Building (1860), 1016 Congress, the last of many iron-fronted buildings in the city; and the Sweeny-Coombs-Fredericks Building (1889), 301 Main, a marvelous Victorian recently restored by Harris County.

If you're in this district at lunchtime, stop for some Cajun cuisine at the Cloisters, an inexpensive cafeteria-style lunchroom operated by the Altar Guild of Christ Church at the northeast corner of Fannin and Texas. Built in 1893, this is the oldest church in the city and the second oldest in the state. Just ask at the church office for a tour and a glimpse of its famed Tiffany window. Incidentally, that Cajun food comes from Treebeard's, four blocks away on Travis in Old Market Square.

For a look at today's Houston, park your car in the Civic Center garage (directional signs on Smith, Bagby, Rusk, and Walker) and begin at Tranquillity Park. A Bicentennial project commemorating the Apollo space flights, this futuristic oasis is an ideal vantage point from which to survey the monoliths of downtown. Among those within walking distance west of Main Street are Pennzoil Place (1976), twin towers separated by a twelve-foot space and still one of the most distinctive buildings in town; the Texas Commerce Tower (1982), at seventy-five stories the world's tallest composite tube tower, with Miró's *Personage and Birds* for comic relief in its front plaza; One Shell Plaza (1971), at one time the tallest reinforced-concrete building west of the Mississippi; and Allied Bank Plaza (1983), fifty stories of reflective glass a wag once described as a Dunhill lighter. From the air this last building curves like a fat dollar sign, appropriate since its estimated value is approximately $160 million.

Many of these buildings overlook tiny Sam Houston Park, where the Harris County Heritage Society gives guided tours of five historic buildings (see the *Tours* section below).

Tranquillity Park is the threshold of Civic Center, home to the Albert Thomas Convention and Visitor's Center, the Alley Theatre, and the Jesse H. Jones Hall for the Performing Arts. The underground garage serves these and other facilities. Walk around the blocks bounded by Louisiana and Texas streets—you may catch the Houston Sym-

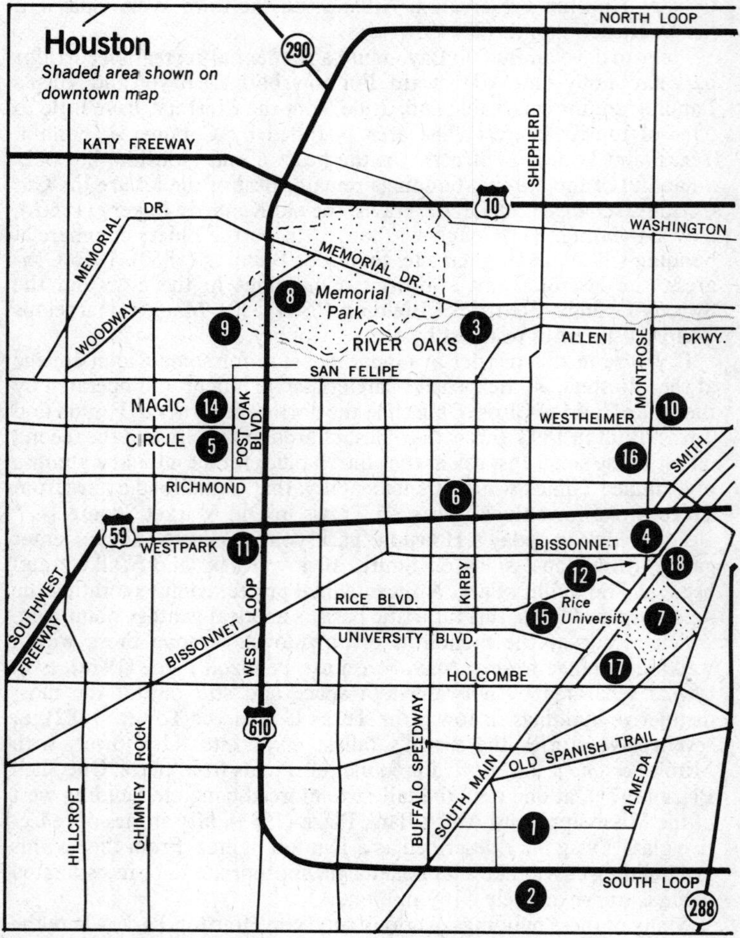

Points of Interest

1) Astrodome
2) Astroworld
3) Bayou Bend Branch, Museum of Fine Arts
4) Contemporary Arts Museum
5) Galleria
6) Greenway Plaza
7) Hermann Park, including the Museum of Medical Science, Museum of Natural Science, Hermann Park Zoo, and Hermann Park Garden Center

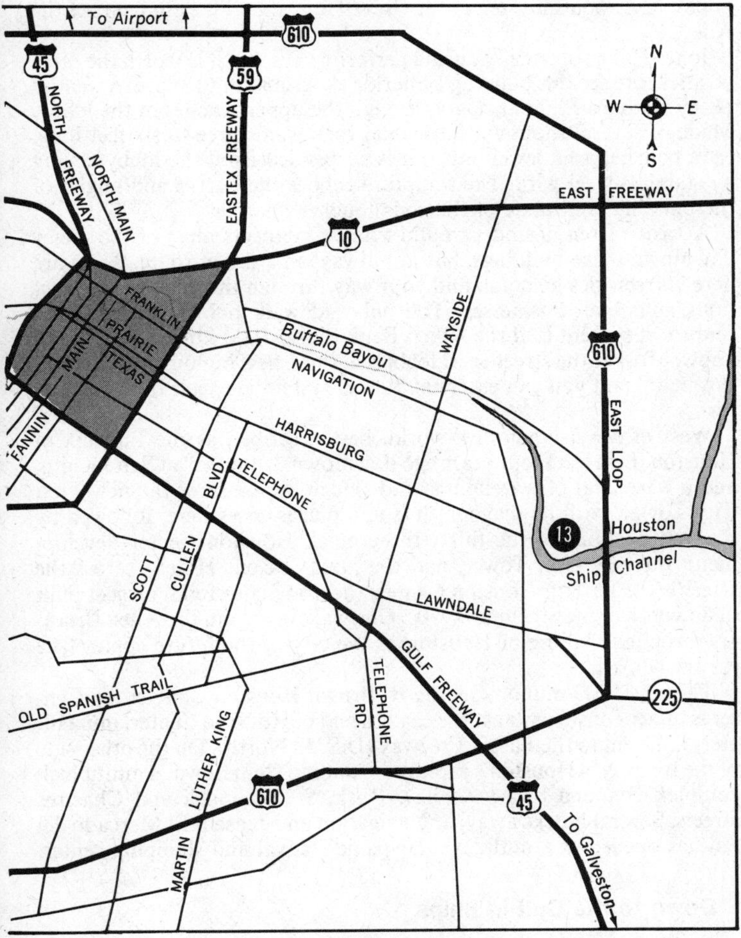

8) Houston Arboretum and Nature Center
9) Inn on the Park Hotel
10) Montrose Neighborhood
11) Mountain Park
12) Museum of Fine Arts
13) Port of Houston
14) Post Oak Shopping Sector
15) Rice University Institute for the Arts
16) Rothko Chapel
17) Texas Medical Center
18) Warwick Hotel

phony in a noontime concert in Oscar Holcombe Plaza in front of the Alley.

Jones Hall is open only during performances, but it is worth the price of a ticket to see this building's interior. A fascinating sculpture, *Gemini II,* by Richard Lippold, soars through the upper reaches of the lobby. Made of several thousand hexagonal rods from three to six feet long, each polished to a jewel finish, it is suspended from the lobby ceiling by stainless-steel wire. The sculpture echoes the curves and angles of the building, and none of the rods touches another.

A vast warren of underground tunnels connects most of the major downtown office buildings, but not always in a direct route. "You are here" directories help you find your way through the maze of intersections and retail businesses. The only sidewalk public access to the tunnels at present is at the Allied Bank Plaza, 1000 Louisiana. Nice to know: Most of the street-level lobbies of these new buildings are "walk-through," and you can enter the tunnel system via their down escalators.

West of Main is another world, best described as the Phoenix of Houston. Less than four years ago downtown "stopped" at San Jacinto, and a wasteland of warehouses and shlock began. Now the new First City Tower, with its diagonal line and plazas, rises here, followed by the first beauties of the thirty-three block Houston Center development, the new Gulf Tower, and the Four Seasons Hotel. Across the street is the Park in Houston Center, the first major retail project built in downtown since the mid-1950s. One walk here, and the Allen Brothers' prophetic billing of Houston as the city of the future comes true for the tourist.

The new $200-million George R. Brown Houston Convention Center is under construction at the eastern end of Houston Center, immediately adjacent to the Eastex Freeway (U.S. 59 North). On the other side of the freeway is Houston's rapidly expanding Chinatown, a multiblock complex bounded by McKinney, Rusk, St. Emanuel, and Chartres streets. Several blocks away, at Navigation and Jensen, El Mercado del Sol has opened as a multilevel Hispanic festival and shopping center.

Down to the Gulf in Ships

Even though Houston lies fifty miles inland from the Gulf of Mexico, it is the nation's third-largest port, owing to a forty-foot-deep ship channel dug through shallow Galveston Bay and up Buffalo Bayou in 1915. You can watch the action in the busy turning basin from the free observation deck on the top of Wharf 9. Just go through Gate 8 from Clinton Drive, east of downtown and accessible from the 610 loop. A boat tour of the port must be reserved in advance (see the *Tours* section below). Crews from the ships as well as Houstonians love two w holes nearby: Shanghai Red's, 8501 Cypress, for its free happ ering shrimp Monday through Friday, and the Athens Bar and Grill, ur Clinton, for its Greek music and dancing.

Next stop east of town is the San Jacinto Battleground State Histor Park (see the *Historic Sites* section below), after which you can ride the free Lynchburg Ferry back and forth across one neck of the bay. The San Jacinto Inn between the park and the ferry is another Houston tradition, an all-you-can-eat, family-style place featuring fresh oysters or shrimp, depending on the season. En route back to Houston, swing by Gilley's, 4500 Spencer Highway. Long before it was the setting for the movie *Urban Cowboy,* Gilley's was one of the top country-and-western hangouts in this part of Texas.

South of Downtown

The Texas Medical Center, three miles due south of downtown via Fannin and Main streets, is a city unto itself. More than twenty major health facilities are crowded onto 180 acres, among them the M. D. Anderson Hospital and Tumor Institute, famed for its cancer treatments, and the Texas Heart Institute (see the *Tours* section below). Just getting to the Med Center from downtown is one of the quiet pleasures of the city. From the Mecom Fountain at the Warwick Hotel to University Boulevard, South Main is lined with marvelous old oaks as it goes past Hermann Park.

South Main and the 610 loop south are the main arteries to Astrodomain—Astroworld, Astrohall, and the Astrodome. Tours of the latter are interesting, but it's much better to see the place in action. Check with the box office, 799-9555, to see who's playing what. When it opened in 1965, the Astrodome was called the eighth wonder of the world, for as the first domed stadium larger than a football field, it was the prototype of things to come.

Houston's southern section extends twenty-five miles south from downtown via the Gulf Freeway (I–45) to the Nassau Bay/Clear Lake area and includes the Johnson Space Center. Weekends are nice here—there's usually a speedboat or sailboat race on Clear Lake, and the return trip can include a venture into the wilderness of Armand Bayou (see the *Parks* section).

Houston's Other Business Centers

Like satellite cities, Greenway Plaza and the Galleria sprout among the trees west of downtown. Begun in 1967, the 127-acre Greenway Plaza encompasses ten office towers, apartments, a Stouffer's hotel, and

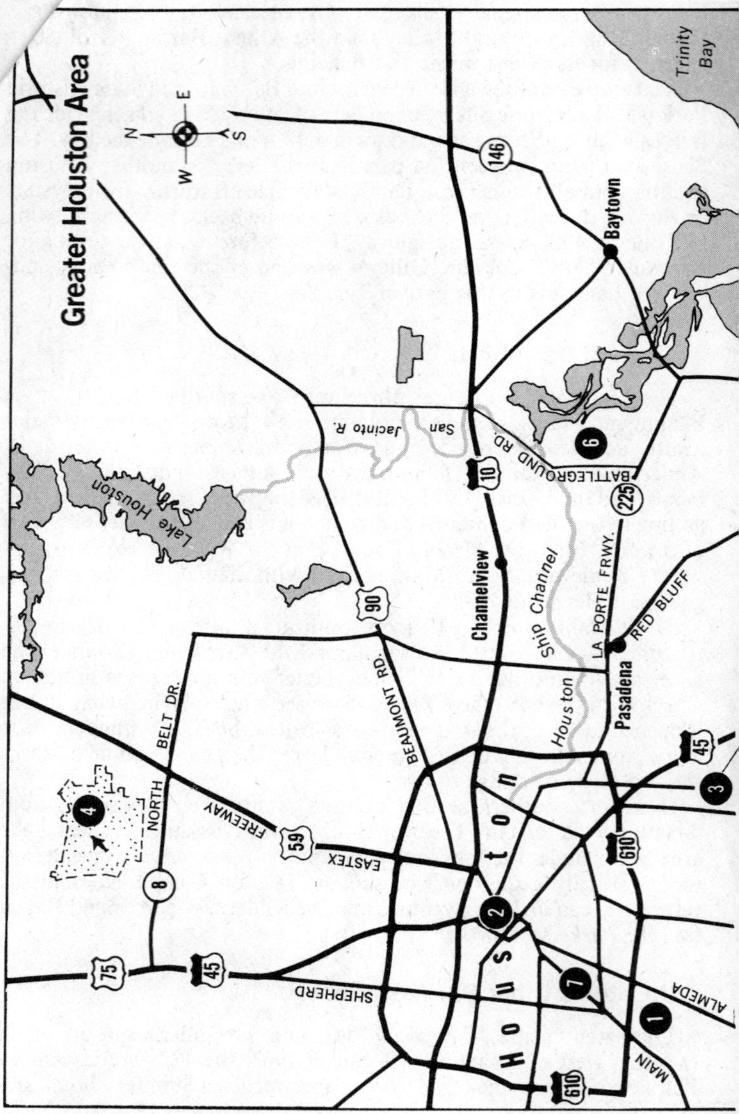
Greater Houston Area
N
E
S
W
Trinity Bay
146
Baytown
San Jacinto R.
Lake Houston
6
BATTLEGROUND RD.
10
225
Channelview
Ship Channel
LA PORTE FRWY.
RED BLUFF
90
Pasadena
Houston
BEAUMONT RD.
NORTH BELT DR.
4
FREEWAY
59
EASTEX
45
3
610
8
2
H o u s t o n
75
45
SHEPHERD
7
1
ALMEDA
MAIN
610

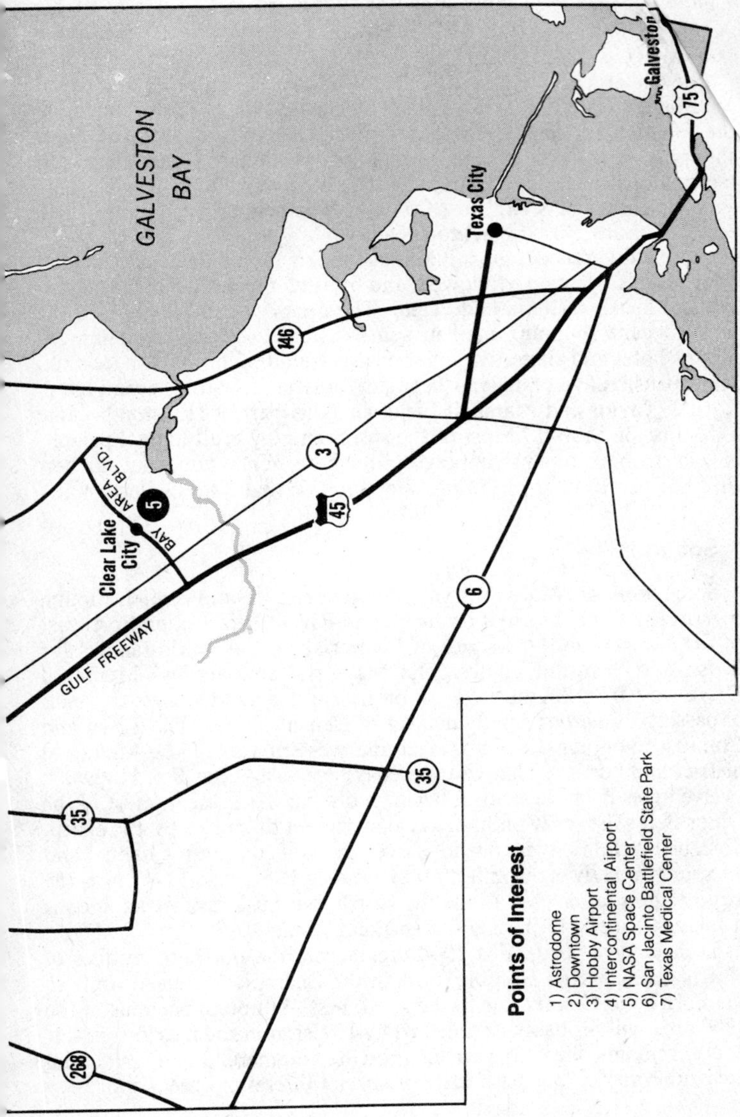
GALVESTON
BAY
Texas City
Galveston
75
146
3
45
5
Clear Lake
City
BAY AREA BLVD.
GULF FREEWAY
6
35
35
268
Points of Interest
1) Astrodome
2) Downtown
3) Hobby Airport
4) Intercontinental Airport
5) NASA Space Center
6) San Jacinto Battlefield State Park
7) Texas Medical Center

an excellent multi-sport and entertainment facility, the Summit. You can't miss the place—just look for high-rises and a cluster of big American flags near the Buffalo Speedway exit from the Southwest Freeway (U.S. 59 South).

The Galleria is both a specific place and an area, the latter also called the Magic Circle. These few golden blocks just west of the 610 loop in the Westheimer–San Felipe–South Post Oak locale sport the finest shopping in the city as well as high-rise headquarters for numerous international businesses. Amazing that little more than twenty years ago, the corner of South Post Oak and Westheimer was an open field edged by a little-used blacktop road.

What a difference some millions can make! First came Sakowitz and then Joske's. Neiman's followed, and by 1965 the design of the adjoining and lavish Galleria had begun. The doors opened in 1971 on the most elegant shopping mall in southwestern America, containing a luxury hotel and three tiers of shops surrounding an indoor ice rink. An expansion five years later brought Galleria II, with a second hotel, Lord & Taylor and Marshall Field, and this part of Houston became a destination in itself. Most of the stores employ multilingual personnel, so strong is the international traffic here. When you want the best this city has to offer in dining, shopping, or nightlife, Galleria is it.

Suburbia

Some other areas of Houston crop up in conversations often enough to warrant some information here. The River Oaks section northeast of the Galleria and just south of Memorial Park is world-famous for lavish and beautiful homes. The Memorial area follows Memorial Drive west from Memorial Park on its curving ramble west to Texas 6, passing numerous small enclaves of elegant homes. The Town and Country Shopping Center is near the western end of the Memorial district and borders what will someday be a vast Outer Belt Highway, twelve miles from the central business district. At present, most of the Outer Belt exists only on highway-department dream maps, the exceptions being the Beltway 8 bridge over the Houston Ship Channel and an approximately eight-mile stretch between U.S. 59 and I–45 near the airport. This latter road forms the North Belt business district and, as it merges with I–45, passes Greenspoint Mall.

Even farther north, FM 1960 arcs across the northern reaches of Harris County from Humble through the Champions area en route to the Fort Bend County line in the southwest. Although portions of the 1960 area will probably be annexed by Houston in the near future, for now it remains one of the fastest-growing commercial and residential areas in America but with little of special interest to the visitor.

PRACTICAL INFORMATION FOR HOUSTON

HOW TO GET THERE. By car. As I–10 crosses Texas from the Louisiana border on the east to the New Mexico border on the west, it passes through the heart of Houston. U.S. 59 runs northeast to southwest, and I–45 northwest to southeast.

The approximate driving times to Houston from other cities, in hours, are: New Orleans 7; Dallas 5; Galveston 1; Corpus Christi 4; South Padre Island 7½; Austin 3½; and San Antonio 4.

By train. *Amtrak* passenger service connects Houston three times a week with New Orleans, Los Angeles, and San Antonio. The station is at 902 Washington Ave., at the intersection of Bagby; 224-1577. Reservations also can be made at 1 (800) 874-2775.

By air. Confirm in advance which of the city's two airports you will be using. Some airlines have flights into both.

W. P. Hobby Airport is 9 mi. southeast of downtown via I–45 and Broadway Blvd.; 643–4597. A new garage adjacent to the terminal has relieved serious parking congestion.

Houston Intercontinental Airport is 15 mi. north of downtown, accessible from either I–45 or U.S. 59 via North Belt.

In all, Houston is served by 9 commuter, 14 domestic, and 11 international airlines, including American, Continental, Delta, Eastern, Frontier, Ozark, Pan Am, Piedmont, Republic, Muse, Southwest, TWA, USAir, United, Western, Aeromexico, Air Canada, Air France, British Caledonian, Cayman Airlines, KLM, South African Airways, TACA, Tan Sahsh, and Viasa. Many of these carriers offer excellent nonstop overseas flights.

By bus. Houston is served by *Greyhound Bus Lines,* 1410 Texas (222-1161 or 800-292-7030 toll free), and *Trailways Bus System, Inc.,* 2121 Main (759-6500).

TELEPHONES. The area code for Houston and most of the surrounding area is 713. You do not need to dial the area code if it is the same as the one from which you are dialing. However, some of the 713 area numbers outside Houston require that you dial a "1" first, then the seven digit calling number. A new area code, 409, now covers some outlying areas, such as Beaumont, Galveston, Sealy, and the Liberty-Dayton sectors. If your call requires a "1" or the new area code, an apologetic voice will tell you so in electronic pear-shaped tones after you have dialed. For local information within the 713 calling area, dial 1411. For directory information outside the 713 area, dial the area code, then 555-1212. If you need operator assistance, dial "0" (zero). Pay-telephone calls are 25¢.

HOTELS AND MOTELS. Few cities can match Houston when it comes to accommodations. The economic vitality of the past decade has brought a hotel-motel boom of surprising proportions, and yet room costs are generally somewhat below what you would find in many other major American cities. The challenge is finding the right place to stay in terms of location and budget. Fortunately, there are fine choices all over town, particularly in the *Super Deluxe* and *Deluxe* categories.

Some hotels, such as those in the Galleria, are destinations in themselves. Others are convenient to downtown, the Texas Medical Center, or a specific business district. We've noted general areas along with addresses so you can select a hotel near where you will be spending most of your time. We've also noted those which offer complimentary transportation to the in-town airline terminals, Medical Center, or shopping, and there is a special category for accommodations worth checking for long-term stays in the Medical Center. With careful selections you may be able to get along without a rental car after all.

Also, Houston is a businessman's city, and even the swankiest hotels have low occupancy rates on weekends. Most of the rates noted are slashed from 30 to 60% on special one- or two-night weekend packages, with some nice extras like champagne or breakfast tossed in for good measure. If you'll be in town over a Friday or Saturday night, ask about these special packages when you reserve. Many hotels and motels also offer family plans, free cribs, and free accommodations for children sharing the parents' room.

Hotel rates are based on double occupancy, European Plan (no meals). Categories, determined by price, are: *Super Deluxe,* $150 and up; *Deluxe,* $100 to $150; *Expensive,* $75 to $100; *Moderate,* $50 to $75; *Inexpensive,* $50 and under.

Most of America's major hotel and motel chains have properties scattered around Houston; space precludes listing every one. If you have a favorite "brand," call its toll-free number and ask about Houston accommodations. Again, select on the basis of location, not cost. Houston is a tough city to move around in.

And sometimes it's a tough city to rent a pillow in. Hotel space is extremely tight in Houston during the annual Offshore Technology Conference the first week of May and the Houston Livestock Show and Rodeo the last week of February and the first week of March. During these periods or when three or more conventions are in town, the Greater Houston Convention and Visitors Council (see the *Tourist Information* section below) keeps computer track of available hotel space and will be happy to advise you. Try first on your own, however, and stress to the hotel that you are *not* in town for a convention.

Super Deluxe

Four Seasons Hotel, Houston Center. 1300 Lamar (77010); 650-1300. Occupying one full block in the new 33-block Houston Center redevelopment area downtown, this is without a doubt the finest hotel in a fine hotel town. New yet ageless, spacious yet intimate, Four Seasons seems like the home you always knew you would create if only you had money. The lobby and rooms have wade-through carpeting, the three-story staircase would serve a queen's entrance, and even the elevator is a refined elegance in its own alcove. Amenities include video games in the indoor recreation area, but it's hard to imagine children in this environment. Then again, it may be the rare civilizing influence that makes a difference—bring on the rascals. The fourth floor is a small resort in the city's concrete heart, centered on a year-round heated swimming pool, sun deck, and large whirlpool. Garden rooms overlook this area. The remaining 391 guest rooms are pages from *House Beautiful*—custom-made furniture, fine linens, fresh flowers, bay windows. Guest robes and French-milled soap are included, along with complimentary downtown transportation, overnight shoeshines, in-house movies, concierge and turn-down service, etc. The concern for the guest is incredible—the maid even turns the shower head to the wall on her twice-daily calls. Guests have courtesy privileges at the adjacent Houston Center Athletic Club at a nominal charge, and there are several excellent restaurants on the premises.

Inn on The Park. 4 Riverway (Woodway, just west of the 610 loop) (77056); 871-8181. When a hotel spends $12,000 a month to fly fresh flowers in from Amsterdam, you know quality counts. Beautifully situated in its own park complete with lake and swans, this Four Seasons operation is lovely and hard to leave. Among the surprises: underwater stereo music in the dual swimming pools and some of the more innovative nouvelle cuisine in town in its restaurants. The public rooms are appointed with fine furniture and lavish bouquets, and the 383 guest rooms have the quality linens, marble baths, and the other extras common to Four Seasons operations. Amenities include a fully equipped health club with whirlpool and sauna; jogging trails; concierge service; and courtesy limo transportation to the nearby Post Oak Airline Terminal and Magic Circle–Galleria shopping. The only thorn on this rose of hotels is the limited and inconvenient self-parking. For the nonce, play the role to the hilt and indulge in the valet parking.

The Lincoln Hotel Post Oak. 2001 Post Oak Blvd. (in the Galleria area) (77056); 961–9300. Designed by I. M. Pei and completed in late 1982 at a cost of more than $70 million, this new property is making a high-stakes bid to become one of the world's great hotels. The location can't hurt—just off the 610 loop in the heart of the Magic Circle—and the amenities follow suit. There are multilingual 24-hour concierge service, a soaring atrium lobby humanized with thick rugs and antiques, a garden deck with pool and sauna, and complimentary transportation within the neighborhood. The 455 rooms come with either contemporary or traditional furnishings; just state your preference when you reserve. Security is assured with Uniqey, which reprograms the room door lock with each new occupant.

The Remington on Post Oak Park. 1919 Briar Oaks Lane (inside the 610 loop near the Galleria) (77027); 840–7600, (800) 392–4659 inside Texas, (800) 231–9802 outside Texas. This 12-story hotel developed by the Rosewood Corporation and the Caroline Hunt Trust Estate of Dallas is on a private three-acre site inside the loop and facing Memorial Park. Access to the walled entrance is from San Felipe. This hotel was designed for the upper limits of the carriage trade: The service personnel are dressed by Ralph Lauren, the 248 rooms were developed at a cost of $200,000 each, and the suites run to such niceties as 7-ft. marble whirlpool baths, baby grand pianos, and formal dining rooms for eight. Service is all-important here—the staff will know your name and park your car, the maid will turn down your bed, and the businessman's center will provide dictation and secretarial services via telephone to your room.

The Warwick. 5701 Main (77251); 526–1991 or (800) 231–5701. Refurbished by Texas oilman John W. Mecom and family in the 1960s, this sumptuous 310-room hotel reigns like a dowager queen in the Hermann Park–Rice University–Medical Center area south of town. Aubusson tapestries, Baccarat chandeliers, and an outstanding collection of European antiques and art fill the public rooms, with service to match. The upper-floor guest rooms offer some of the best views in town, and the Sunday brunch is a Houston tradition. Med-center transportation via complimentary limo.

Wyndham at Travis Centre. 6900 Fannin (in the Rice University/Med Center are) (77030); 524–6633.

Deluxe

Guest Quarters–Galleria West. 5353 Westheimer (Galleria) (77056); 961-9000 or (800) 424–2900. All luxury suites here, one- and two-bedroom, plus dining areas, fully equipped kitchens, and 24-hour room service. There is also a fine restaurant, a swimming pool, and guest memberships with free transportation at the Houston City Club's all-sports facility. The complimentary transportation covers a 5-mile radius of the Galleria location. Transportation to the Med Center can be arranged.

Hotel Inter-Continental Houston. 5150 Westheimer (Galleria) (77056); 961-1500; (800) 392-5477 in Texas; (800) 231–6058 elsewhere in U.S. This sleek hotel is the Inter-Continental chain's debut into the highly competitive Houston luxury-hotel market—so expect the best. On the western edge of the Magic Circle area at the intersection of Westheimer and Sage, this three-building contemporary has 518 rooms in two high-rise towers; a heated indoor-outdoor pool; full-scale health club with sauna, massage, whirlpool, and exercise rooms; lighted tennis court; and three racquetball courts. The guest rooms will have oversized beds, in-house movies, and bathroom telephones and television. Parking for more than 500 cars is available.

The Houstonian Hotel and Conference Center. 111 N. Post Oak Lane (Galleria) (77024); 680-2626, (800) 392-0784 inside Texas, (800) 231-2759 outside Texas. Nestled in an 22-acre pocket of forest near the 610 loop west and Galleria, this in-city resort also is a health-and-fitness facility that includes a preventive-medicine center and a women's health-and-beauty spa called the Phoenix. The 247 rooms are quiet and well-appointed, and guests are welcome to use the indoor and outdoor running tracks, the Olympic-size swimming pool (usually set up for lap swimming), and assorted courts for tennis, racquetball, volleyball, handball, etc. Complete three-hour physicals ($495) can be arranged to evaluate your personal health and to prescribe an intensive exercise-and-nutrition program. If all that sounds too rugged or scientific, you can loll by the inn's second pool, walk through the woods, or just generally recover from the world. On the fringe of one of Houston's major business districts, this is one of the more unusual hotel-resort facilities in the country.

Hyatt-Regency Houston. 1200 Louisiana St. (downtown) (77002); 654-1234, (800) 228-9000. The tomorrow hotel in the tomorrow city when it was opened in 1972, the Hyatt still holds its own in the downtown area, as much for its eateries and central location as for its outstanding design and accommodations. The 350-foot-high atrium lobby with its zipping glass elevators makes you feel like a movable piece inside a Mondrian painting. The 1,000 guest rooms have oversized beds and are well-appointed. The 29th floor is the Regency Club, terribly exclusive, with full concierge service and discreet privacy. The sixth floor has 18 lanai rooms with private patios adjacent to the swimming-pool terrace. More than $250,000 worth of original art is scattered here and there, and a full-time horiculturist tends the flora. A semi-sidewalk café, Whistler's Walk, is an affordable oasis in downtown.

Hotel Meridien. 400 Dallas (downtown) (77002); 759-0202. The premier property for Air France in America, this sleek 360-room hotel is part of Allen Center, yet it overlooks Houston's past in Sam Houston Park. A touch of France shows where you least expect it. After your genteel check-in seated at a small reception desk, the concierge takes over your cares. The rooms are very attractive, the staff uniforms are French couturier, and Le Restaurant de France is *tres magnifique,* arguably the best French restaurant in a high-dining town.

The Lancaster. 701 Texas Ave. (downtown) (77002); 228-9500, (800) 231-0336. An $18-million-dollar facelift has turned the old Auditorium Hotel into the elegant Lancaster. The location, directly across from both the Alley Theatre and Jones Hall, is ideal for culture hounds or downtown-bound businessmen. The amenities class it with the elegant small hotels of Europe. The 93 guest rooms have fine furniture, marble baths, fresh flowers, and original art, and the services include a multilingual staff, full-time concierge, in-house valet, etc. Although thick terry towels and complimentary bathrobes are no surprise, this may be the only hotel in town to provide umbrellas, bath scales, and four telephones in every room.

Stouffer's Greenway Plaza Hotel. 6 Greenway Plaza East (77046); 629-1200, (800) HOTELS–1. Sparkling from a $5.5 million renovation, this high-rise hotel in Greenway Plaza has 389 sound-proof rooms with walk-in closets, dressing rooms, turn-down service, complimentary shoe shines, plus coffee and the morning paper that come with your wake-up call. There's an outdoor pool and whirlpool, plus a health club on the premises. Guests can also use a nearby indoor tennis-jogging-racquetball facility, and there's free transportation to the Galleria, Med Center, and nearby airline terminal.

The Westin Galleria. 5060 W. Alabama (Galleria) (77056); 960-8100 or (800) 228-3000. One of two Westin hotels that anchor wings of the Galleria, this 495-room hotel is tops in amenities and service. A new in-your-room-dining feature literally brings formal restaurant service upstairs, and some of the bedrooms convert to living rooms, courtesy of beds that fold into the walls. There is also a concierge in the lobby plus complimentary shuttle service to the Post Oak Air Terminal.

The Westin Oaks. 5011 Westheimer (Galleria) (77056); 623-4300, (800) 228-3000. This handsome hotel serves the corporate traveler and tourist, whereas groups and convention business tend to stay at the Westin Galleria, down the mall. In addition to direct access to the shops, skating rink, and major department stores of the Galleria, the Oaks is glowing with a $1.7 million refurbishing that created four executive floors for VIPs, with more to come. Most of the frills, such as concierge, pool, and complimentary transportation within the Galleria area, are standard here. The newly reopened Galleria Roof atop the hotel is splendid, a Houston favorite for its view and romantic mood.

Expensive

Adam's Mark. 2900 Briarpark at Westheimer (far west Houston) (77042); 978-7400 or (800) 231-5858. One of the best hotels in the city's western hinterlands, this contemporary house borrows architecturally from the Hyatts, with its 10-story atrium lobby, glass elevators, cushy cocktail-lounge area, etc. Big pluses: an indoor-outdoor swimming pool, fine furnishings in the 604 rooms, and an in-house health club. Guests have privileges at the nearby Westside Tennis Club, and there's shopping in the huge Carillon Shopping Village flanking the hotel.

The Doubletree Hotel. 15747 Drummet Blvd. (North Belt-Intercontinental area) (77032); 442-8000, (800) 528-0444. Considered by a national rating service one of the three top airport hotels in the country, this 315-room hotel sits on 10 wooded acres and has courtesy transportation to Intercontinental Airport, 5 min. away. Rooms are of residential quality, soundproof, and they have good security. A swimming pool with whirlpool-spa sits in a shady courtyard, and there's golf at the nearby World Houston course.

Holiday Inn–Crowne Plaza. 14703 Park Row (east of the TX 6/I-10 interchange) (77079); 558–5580. This second entry in the luxury sweepstakes is ideal for those needing a far west Houston/Park 10 locale.

Holiday Inn–Crowne Plaza Galleria. 2222 West Loop South (Galleria) (77027); 961-7272. This $60-million, 501-room hotel has won awards for its contemporary decor. Guests find a relatively inexpensive but luxurious comfort here, including one private floor that includes a concierge, happy hour, continental breakfast, honor bar, and personal secretary in the room rate. All guests can enjoy the free self-parking; sauna, whirlpool, and indoor swimming pool; and the complimentary limo service within the Galleria area.

L'Hotel Sofitel. 425 North Beltway, at Imperial Valley Dr. (North Belt–Intercontinental area) (77060); 445-9000 or (800) 231-4612. The emphasis on quality food and wine in its three restaurants, plus a take-out bakery, shows the French touch at this fine 337-room hotel. Even the check-out comes with a complimentary loaf of French bread. The rooms are well furnished and have a small sitting area, and there are a concierge, turn-down service, indoor pool and sauna, and new fitness club with exercise equipment as well as complimentary transportation to the airport.

Hyatt Regency West Houston. 13210 Katy Freeway (Eldridge exit; far west Houston) (77079); 558-1234, (800) 228-9000. This elegant newcomer has six five-story buildings connected by a large garden atrium, part of the Woodcreek development that includes Conoco and Shell facilities. A lake wanders through the hotel and grounds. There's an outdoor heated swimming pool, whirlpool, health club, two tennis courts, and two restaurants. Maps show running trails nearby, plus there's complementary transport to nearby shopping centers and golf course. Free self-parking and scheduled airport-hotel transportation ($10).

Sheraton Crown Hotel. 15700 Drummet Blvd. (North Belt–Intercontinental area) (77032); 442-5100 or (800) 325-3535. There's a resort atmosphere here, thanks to the indoor and outdoor swimming pools, game room, health spa, whirlpool, and lively bars and restaurants (two of each). The 439 rooms are comfortable and well done, and there's complementary transportation to the airport, Greenspoint Mall, and nearby golf and tennis.

Westchase Hilton and Towers. 9999 Westheimer (far west Houston) (77042); 974-1000. Primarily a corporate hotel serving the southwestern and far western business districts. The 308 rooms are large and well-furnished, with complimentary in-room movies. The two top floors have VIP concierge service, complete with the *Wall Street Journal* at your door, and Continental breakfast. Also here: pool, hot tub, and guest membership at the nearby Westside Tennis Club. Also helicopter service via Airlink Airways (see the *How to Get Around* section below). Reserve through your local Hilton hotel.

The Woodlands Inn and Conference Center. 2301 N. Millbend Dr., the Woodlands (north of Houston in southern Montgomery County) (77380); 367-1100 or (collect) 363-2000. Surrounded by three superb golf courses in the woods 27 mi. north of Houston via I–45, this 268-room lodge and resort is in a world of its own. In addition to challenging golf, the facilities include extensive men's and women's health clubs, a beauty spa, ice skating, tennis, bicycle rentals, swimming, jogging trails, and one of the nicest swimming pools in the greater Houston area. Ideal when you want to mix pleasure with business in the far north reaches of Harris County. Intercont. airport van ($12).

Embassy Suites. 9090 Southwest Freeway, Gessner exit (far southwest Houston–Baybrook area) (77074); 995-0123 or (800) EMBASSY. Ideal for families, all 243 rooms are one-bedroom suites with two oversized beds, sitting rooms, and fully equipped galley kitchens. All face into an inner atrium courtyard. Complimentary cocktails in the late afternoon and breakfast in the morning are served in the Mexican-style patio and are included in the room price, as is use of the indoor pool, sauna, and whirlpool.

The Hobby Airport Hilton. 8181 Airport Blvd. (Southeast Houston, within sight of Hobby Airport) (77061); 645-3000. Southwestern flavor two blocks east of Hobby Airport. A new nine-story tower, plus a three-story cabaña section around the pool. Of the 310 rooms, 30 have separate sitting areas and nine have in-room hot tub–whirlpools. Courtesy transportation to the airport and nearby shopping.

Houston Airport Hilton Inn. 500 North Belt East (77060); 931-0101. Convenient and comfortable, with an indoor-outdoor swimming pool, sauna, and new health club as well as courtesy transportation to Intercontinental Airport.

Sheraton Houston Place Hotel. 6800 Main (Medical Center area) (77030); 528-7744. Bright and fresh, this 280-room hotel is popular with overnight corporate travelers as well as short- or long-term visitors to the nearby Med Center. More than 200 multiroom suites have fully equipped kitchens and king-sized beds. The complimentary shuttle makes stops at a supermarket as well as the Med Center, Hobby Airport, and the South Main Terminal for Intercontinental Airport flights. Plenty of free parking, plus a cheerful staff and quality housekeeping.

Note: The following **Marriott** hotels can be reserved by calling (800) 228-9290.

Marriott at the Astrodome. 2100 S. Braeswood at Greenbriar (77030); 797-9000. Motel-style rooms in a garden setting south of downtown and the Medical Center, near the Astrodome and Astroworld.

Marriott Brookhollow. 3000 North Loop West (T. C. Jester exit) (77092); 688-0100. Adjacent to the Brookhollow business park and across from Northwest Mall in northwest Houston, this 10-story contemporary hotel has "double doubles," oversized beds, or parlor rooms (where the bed folds into a cabinet). There is also a swimming pool and sauna, plus complimentary transportation to the Galleria, Northwest Mall, and the Post Oak Airline Terminal.

Marriott Hotel–by the Galleria. 1750 West Loop South (San Felipe exit) (77027); 960-0111. This contemporary high-rise is a good value for Magic Circle hotels. Comfortable rooms with cable television in each, movies, plus indoor pool, outdoor sundeck, sauna, game room, and free parking in the attached garage. Free shuttle to Post Oak Airport Terminal and Galleria shopping.

Marriott Hotel at Houston Intercontinental Airport. 18700 Kennedy Blvd. (77032); 443-2310. Tucked between terminals B and C, this was formerly the Host International. Now freshened up, the rooms are comfortable and soundproof, and the roof-top restaurant shows off just how much of Houston's land remains undeveloped. Swimming pool, plus intra-airport transportation by tunnel train.

Marriott at the Medical Center. 6580 Fannin (77030); 796–0080. Newly opened, this 398-room hotel has complimentary van service within the health complex, indoor pool and whirlpool, and access to the fitness center at the Institute of Preventive Medicine next door.

Marriott Northbelt. 255 North Belt East (Greenspoint–Intercontinental Airport area) (77060); 875–4000. In the heart of the North Belt business district, this new high-rise has comfortable rooms, indoor-outdoor swimthrough pool with sundeck, whirlpool spa, sauna, and exercise room for working off those stresses. A free shuttle serves the airport and nearby Greenspoint Mall.

Nassau Bay Hilton. 3000 NASA Road One (Nassau Bay/Clear Lake area) (77058); 333–9300. Sparkling new, this 14-story contemporary hotel is very convenient to the Johnson Space Center and has its own marina on Clear Lake. Boat rentals are next door, and there's a swimming pool on the premises. The 244 rooms all have oversized beds and views of the lake, and the top-floor rooms come with concierge, Continental breakfast, and other niceties.

The Residence Inn Astrodome. 7710 S. Main (77030); 660-7993, (800) 331-3131. Ideal for long-term corporate or medical stays, both studio and two-level "penthouse" suites have fully equipped kitchens, some fireplaces. A pool, spas, laundry, and sports court are on-site, plus there's a comp shuttle within a three-mile radius.

The Shamrock Hilton. South Main at Holcombe Blvd. (Medical Center–Astrodome area) (77030); 668–9211. It's said when this grande dame of Houston hotels opened on the empty prairie five miles south of downtown in 1949, all Hollywood was deserted—the stars were here for the gala party. That prairie now is filled with the vast Medical Center complex, and the Shamrock, built by colorful entrepreneur oil man Glenn McCarthy at a cost in excess of $21 million, continues to hold its own amid the newcomers. The public rooms remain among the most striking in town, and the swimming pool is the largest and longest hotel pool in the world. The 785 rooms may not be quite as classy, but they are spacious, comfortable, and quiet. In addition to the South Main Airport Terminal across the street, there's complimentary transportation to the Med Center and helicopter service to Intercontinental Airport (see the *How to Get Around* section, below).

Moderate

Allen Park Inn. 2121 Allen Parkway (77019); 521-9321, (800) 392-1499 (in Texas), (800) 231-6310 (outside Texas). Comfortable rooms in the near-downtown area, plus a sauna-whirlpool and exercise room.

Astro Village–Holiday Inn. 8500 Kirby (near the Astro complex) (77054); 799–1050. No surprises, in the south part of town.

Astro Village Hotel Complex. 2350 South Loop West (610 South and Kirby) (77054); 748-3221, (800) 231-2360 (outside Texas). The man who brought the world the Astrodome also created this hotel, complete with the most extravagant and expensive suite in the world stretched across the top floor. This Celestial Suite goes for $3,000 a night and has 13 rooms, ranging from the circus and Tarzan rooms to an opulent master bedroom. The standard guest rooms in this hotel-motel are comfortable but unremarkable; the nicest are around the pool and garden. Great south-of-town location within sight and a long walk of the Astrodome and Astroworld.

Brookhollow Hilton. 2404 North Loop West (T. C. Jester exit) (77092); 688-7711. Comfortable accommodations and an excellent seafood restaurant, The Anchorage, near the northwest corner of the 610 loop.

Harvest House Hotel. 7901 Southwest Freeway (Gessner exit from U.S. 59 South) (77074); 777-2389. Near the Sharpstown area.

Hilton Inn West. 12401 Katy Freeway (I–10 West) (77079); 496-9090. A good choice if you need housing in the Dairy-Ashford area of far west Houston.

Holiday Inn–Downtown. 801 Calhoun (77002); 659-2222. Lots of freebies here: covered parking, in-room movies, and transportation to the Med Center, to the Galleria, and throughout downtown based on availability. When the sun shines between the skyscrapers, you can get a tan around the outdoor pool.

Holiday Inn–Memorial Plaza. 2100 Memorial Dr. (midway between downtown and River Oaks) (77007); 869-8261. Overlooks the Allen Parkway Recreation Area near downtown. A courtesy van serves the Downtown Airport Terminal.

Quality Inn–Intercontinental Airport. 6115 Will Clayton Parkway. (77205); 446-9131, or (800) 228-5151. In the woods east of the airport and midway to Humble and U.S. 59. Comfortable rooms, some with steam baths and whirlpools. Courtesy satellite television, tennis, biking, and transportation to the airport.

Ramada Inn–Northwest Crossing. 12801 Northwest Freeway (U.S. 290 northwest of 610 loop) (77040); 462-9977, or (800) 2–RAMADA. Excellent accommodations in the city's newest business area. Some rooms have private spas and whirlpools.

Ramada Hotel—Southwest/Sharpstown. 6855 Southwest Freeway (Bellaire Blvd. exit) (77074); 771-0641 or the 800 number above. Comfortable and convenient to the southwest part of Houston.

Sheraton Houston Hotel. 777 Polk Ave. (downtown) (77002); 651-9041, (800) 325-3535. Acceptable accommodations across from the Downtown Airport Terminal.

Sheraton Kings Inn. 1301 NASA Blvd. (Nassau Bay–Clear Lake area) (77058); 488–0220 or the 800 number above. Central to the area and to the Johnson Space Center.

Sheraton Town & Country. 910 West Belt (77024); 467-6411. Well located at West Belt and the Katy Freeway (I–10) on the corner of an expanding shopping center with Neiman-Marcus, Marshall Field, and more than 100 other stores. The top-floor suites are nice, and 32 other rooms open on to the outdoor swimming pool. Helicopter service to Intercontinental Airport is nearby, or bus shuttle to both airports is available for $10.

Viscount Hotel. 2828 Southwest Freeway (Kirby Dr. exit) (77098); 526-4571 or (800) 255-3050. Pleasant accommodations, all with oversized beds. Convenient to Greenway Plaza, Bellaire, and the Rice University area.

Inexpensive

The Grant. 8200 S. Main (77025); 668-8000. Clean and comfortable with extra-long beds, this small motel is close to the Astrodome and on the bus route to the Med Center. Swimming pool and playground.

Hobby Regency Motor Hotel. 6161 Gulf Freeway (Griggs exit from I–45 South) (77023); 928–2871 or (800) 892–8100. Comfortable accommodations near Gulfgate.

La Quinta Motor Inns. Eleven locations around Houston. Call 800-531-5900 for specifics.

Southern Manor 1001 NASA Road One (77598); 332-4581. Just east of the I–45 interchange and convenient to the Johnson Space Center–Nassau Bay area.

The Bed and Breakfast Society of Houston. 921 Heights Blvd. (77008); 468–6220.

The following offer suites with kitchens, maid service, and other amenities in the Galleria area:

Galleria Gardens Executive Lodging. 2450-2500 McCue (77056); 622-4400.

Galleria Oaks Corporate Inn. 5151 Richmond (77056); 629-7120.

Galleria Place Executive Inn. 4723 West Alabama (77027); 621-2797.

Oakwood Garden Apartments. 2424 S. Voss, Suite A101 (77057); 783-4651.

In addition to many lodgings already listed, the following are convenient to the Texas Medical Center. Though not luxury or expensive properties, they offer long-term rates and/or family plans, and free transportation within that district.

The Chief Motel. 9000 S. Main (77025); 666-4151.

Holiday Inn–Medical Center. 6701 S. Main (77030); 797-1110.

Medical Center Visitor's Lodge. 1025 Swanson (77030); 790-1617. A 12-unit apartment hotel with kitchens, just off Fannin.

Surrey House Motor Hotel. 8330 S. Main (77025); 667-9261. Two swimming pools, plus kitchenettes, coin laundry, and a playground.

Tides II Motor Inn. 6700 S. Main (P.O. Box 25006, 77005); 522–2811. Motel-style rooms and a pool in a palm-tree setting. Daily buffet in the adjacent restaurant, plus airport pickup by advance arrangement.

The Rodeway Inn Towers. 2130 W. Holcombe (77030); 666-1461. Restaurant, coin laundry, pool, and parking garage on premises; no kitchens.

Special note: **The Ronald McDonald House,** 1550 La Concha, provides a residential setting for families of children under 19 years of age being treated at the Medical Center for cancer or other life-threatening diseases. In addition to a community kitchen, laundry, and recreation facilities, there are 21 bedrooms, each of which will sleep four comfortably and six maximum. The rate is $15 per room per night. All applications must be submitted to the social worker at the hospital where the patient is registered.

HOW TO GET AROUND. Unless you know the city well, you will need a good map and a lot of patience, and it helps if you understand the local names for some of the major freeways. When someone talks about the Katy or the Katy Freeway, they mean I–10 west of town (it parallels the Katy Railroad tracks, hence the name). I–10 east of downtown is called the East Freeway. Don't confuse that with the Eastex Freeway, which is U.S. 59 North. U.S. 59 South (from downtown) is called the Southwest Freeway. North of downtown, I–45 is called the North or Dallas Freeway, and south of town it is called the Gulf Freeway. A portion of U.S. 290 West is known as the Northwest Freeway. Few if any of those names appear on the official highway signs, so you'll have to make some mental translations when getting verbal directions.

The confusion multiplies into an Abbott and Costello "Who's on First?" joke when it comes to I–610, better known as the 610 loop, which circles the city. Be prepared to hear "North Loop East," "South Loop West," etc. The first direction refers to the road in relationship to downtown Houston; for example, the north loop is I–610 north of town. The second direction is generally a post-office address used for mailing purposes and has no value to someone trying to find a specific place. Always ask which exit you should use and which direction you should then travel on the frontage road.

From the airport. The *Trailways Bus System* provides shuttle service between Intercontinental and four in-town passenger terminals ($6 one way). A similar limousine service shuttles passengers to and from Hobby ($4–5 one way). Call Trailways at 759–6500 for schedules from any of its Houston terminals: Downtown Terminal (at the Hyatt Regency on Polk St.); South Main Terminal, 7011 S. Main (across from the Shamrock Hotel); Post Oak Terminal 5000 Richmond (just outside the 610 loop); and the Greenway Plaza Terminal, 3769 Southwest Freeway (south frontage road between the Wesleyan and Edloe exits). A taxi ride to downtown would be about $20 from Intercontinental Airport, $24 to the Galleria area.

Executive Airlink provides transportation between Intercontinental and five Houston locations several times a day in three air-conditioned Bell 206L2 helicopters. For schedule and fares, call 230-1254. *Airlink Airways* operates three air-conditioned Bell Jet Ranger helicopters between Intercontinental and five locations; 975-8989.

By Bus. The *Metropolitan Transit Authority* (Metro) operates a citywide bus system at a modest fare of 55¢, slightly more if you ride a special express route. Although comfort and efficiency are improving, the buses do not serve all the places you'll want to go. You'll need a car if you intend to explore beyond your lodgings. The one exception to the generally poor bus service is the Downtown Shoppers Special that runs on Main between Franklin and Pierce Sts. These buses are marked with signs or red flags and require an exact fare of 10¢. For more bus information, stop at 403 Louisiana in the Hogg Building downtown or call 635–4000.

By car. Unfortunately, Houston's growth has not been accompanied by an equal expansion of the highway system, either in areas served or in car capacity. You can count on stop-and-go traffic from 7:00 to 8:30 A.M. and 3:30 to 6:00 P.M. weekdays, whether inbound to or outbound from downtown. Visitors should be aware that both the Katy Freeway (I–10 west of downtown) and the North Freeway (I–45 north of downtown) have controlled transitways in the center median that can be used only by authorized van pools and buses. Construction delays should be expected. These restricted lanes are clearly posted and closed to general traffic.

Nor do the surface roads offer much relief. Both Houston and surrounding Harris County have developed area by area, without much attention to a comprehensive overall road system or construction for anticipated growth. There are very few limited-access surface roads connecting the various parts of town, and roads engineered to handle local traffic two generations ago are now being pressed into service as major arterials. Streets stop and then start up again miles away, and such niceties as freeway-access signs on the surface streets are rare. Allow twice the amount of time a trip should take based on its actual mileage.

Once on the road, it's every driver for himself, particularly on the freeways. Newcomers often feel that Houston is still the raw hell-bent-for-leather West but that the cowboys have traded in their ponies for pickup trucks. Unfortunately, courtesy on the road is rare, and defensive driving is highly recommended.

On-street parking is limited, and illegally parked cars are towed away and impounded until fines and storage charges are paid. It's best to use one of the many public garages. Rates are generally reasonable, and the covered parking helps handle Houston's weather.

Rental cars. Most of the major car-rental companies are well represented, both at various hotels and service locations in town and at or near the airports. Rates and conditions of rental vary widely. Do some preliminary investigating via the toll-free reservation numbers listed in your local telephone directory, or see a travel agent. Above all, *do not arrive in town without a rental-car reservation* or you may be stranded without wheels.

By taxi. Four taxi companies operate in and around the city. Although they are permitted to cruise and can be hailed from the street, most are lined up outside the major hotels and at the airports. Rates are uniform: $2.10 for the first mile, $.875 cents for every mile thereafter. A ride into town from the airport is approximately $20.00. Cabs can also be called: Liberty Cab Co., 695–6700; Sky Jack Cab Co., 523–6080; United Cab Co., 654–4040; and Yellow Cab, 236–1111.

By limousine. More than a dozen rental services provide classy chauffeured transport. A list is available from the Greater Houston Convention and Visitors Council. (See the *Tourist Information* section, below).

By helicopter. Because of Houston's choking traffic, this is becoming an increasingly popular means of getting around. *Armadillo Airways* flies every hour, Sunday–Friday, between 7:00 A.M. and 7:00 P.M., linking Intercontinental Airport, Westchase Hilton, Galleria, Shamrock Hilton, and Sugar Grove; 975-8989. *Executive Airlink* flies Monday–Friday, 6:15 A.M. to 8:05 P.M., and Sunday from 1:00 to 7:00 P.M. between Intercontinental, Park 10, Marriott Astrodome, Town & Country, Galleria, and Greenway Plaza; 230-1254.

TOURIST INFORMATION. The *Greater Houston Convention and Visitors Council* (GHCVC) publishes free maps and an excellent series of multilingual brochures on local attractions, accommodations, downtown walking tours, shopping, restaurants and entertainment, and general public information. They also prepare a monthly *Day and Night* calendar with detailed information on all sports, theatrical events, and special events going on in the city and surrounding area.

Most of the brochures are available at the information kiosks in the three airport terminals, and the *Day and Night* folder is widely distributed by restaurants, hotels, and businesses throughout the city. All are available by advance mail from the Greater Houston Convention and Visitors Council, 3300 S. Main, Houston, TX 77002. There is also a drive-up information booth with a multilingual staff at that location. Open Monday through Friday, 8:30 A.M. to 5:00 P.M.; Saturday, 9:00 A.M. to 3:00 P.M.; 523–5050, (800) 392–7722 (in Texas), (800) 231–7799 (outside Texas).

The *Gateway Receptionists* in red-and-blue uniforms give out information and directions at both airports, including the customs and immigration areas. The information kiosks are staffed from 7:00 A.M. to 11:00 P.M., seven days a week, and the international-arrivals area has personnel on duty from 9:00 A.M. to 11:30 P.M. daily.

Another source of help is *Traveler's Aid,* a United Way agency with volunteers at all three airports and at the main headquarters at 2601 Main, Suite A. Almost any travel emergency or problem is their specialty. If the airport staff is unavailable, call 668–0911 for emergency help 24 hours a day, seven days a week.

The *USO* provides local recreation facilities, programs, and services for active-duty members of the armed forces; 443–2451.

Harbinger Limited provides visiting executives with business services and Houston trip coordination/consultation. Information: P.O. Box 6753 (77265); 847-7688.

Emergencies have a way of cropping up, even during vacations. Here are a few numbers you may need: Poison Control Center, 654–1701; Emergency Dental Service (after 5 P.M.), 790–9690; Dental Center, 975-9336, 222-2517, and 623-4540; and Galleria Clinic, 961–4050. The following emergency rooms are equipped to handle medical or surgical emergencies around the clock seven days a week: St. Joseph's Hospital, 1919 La Branch (downtown), 757–1000, ext. 1495; Twelve Oaks Hospital, 4200 Portsmouth (off U.S. 59 South), 623–2500. Four others are within the Medical Center complex: Ben Taub General Hospital, 1502 Ben Taub Loop, 791–7300; Hermann Hospital, 1203 Ross Sterling, 797–4060; St. Luke's Episcopal, 6720 Bertner, 791–2011; and Texas Children's Hospital, 6621 Fannin, 791–2222. The universal emergency number, 911, will not be in service in Houston until 1986.

During your stay the following numbers may be handy: weather, 529–4444; road conditions throughout Texas, 869–4571; road conditions in Houston, 222–3131; time, 844–7171.

Banks are generally open Monday through Friday from 7:30 A.M. to 5:30 P.M. International currency can be exchanged at the Texas Foreign Exchange Co., 1130 Travis, Monday through Friday, 8:30 A.M. to 6 P.M., and they'll quote the current rate of exchange by telephone; 654–0999. Terminals A, B, and C at Intercontinental Airport have foreign-exchange kiosks, at least one of which is open daily from 7:00 A.M. to 11:00 P.M.; 443–0070. However, they may limit the amount of the transaction because of limited monies on hand.

Houston is one of the few cities in America with high-quality resident companies in opera, symphony, and ballet, as well as professional teams in the major sports. On any given evening, something is going on somewhere in town, from soccer to little theater, from symphony to rodeo. Game and performance information is published monthly by the GHCVC, *Houston City* magazine and the *Texas Monthly,* and daily by the *Houston Post* and the *Houston Chronicle. Arts for Everyone, Inc.,* publishes a free performing-arts calendar every two months, You can either request it by mail: 1950 W. Gray, # 19 (77019) or call them when you are in town to find out what is playing and whom to contact for tickets; 522–3744.

There are several ticket sources. *Ticketron,* 526-7220, gives telephone information, and tickets can be bought by credit card through *Teletron;* 526-1709 (9:00 A.M. to 8:30 P.M., Monday through Friday; 11 A.M. to 8:30 P.M. Saturday). *Houston Ticket Center* is in Jones Hall, 615 Louisiana; 227-ARTS (9:30 A.M. to 5:30 P.M., Monday through Friday; noon to 5:00 P.M., Saturday). Ticketron sells in all *Joske's* stores; at the *Downtown Ticket Center,* 1100 Milam (222-7469); and through 17 *Ticketmaster* outlets around town (799-9555). A new *SHOWTIX* booth sells advance tickets as well as half-price day-of-performance tickets in Tranquility Square downtown (522–9292).

Tickets for performances of small theater or university groups can be ordered by calling them directly (see the *Music* and *Stage* sections, below).

SEASONAL EVENTS. January. The *International Boat, Sport, and Travel Show* draws crowds to the Astrohall, and feline lovers head for the *Houston Charity Cat Show* at the Albert Thomas Convention and Exhibit Center downtown. This vast facility fills again at the end of the month with a major antique show and sale sponsored by the *Houston Antique Dealers Association* (HADA), one of the best shows of its kind in America.

February. The roar of *motorcycle races* fills up the Astrodome as competitors rev up for short track and steeplechase competitions. Two weeks later the Astrodome-Astrohall complex is the site of the city's biggest annual shindig, the *Houston Livestock Show and Rodeo.* This kicks off "Go Texan" celebrations all over town. Traffic stops as trailriders come in from outlying areas, camp in Memorial Park, and then parade through downtown. Everyone wears western duds during the 14 days of rodeo and livestock competition, and major national entertainers are part of every evening's show.

March brings a blaze of floral color across the city, the most beautiful of which can be viewed on the annual *Azalea Trail* through the River Oaks–Tanglewood residential area. The grounds of *Bayou Bend* (see the *Museums* section, below) are always part of this two-weekend show. By mid-month the *Houston Festival* has begun, a series of successive weekend celebrations and performances in downtown parks and plazas that ends with a grand finale *Tardi Mardi Gras* bash in Sam Houston Park downtown. This month also brings the first of the *wildflowers* along the roadsides, and by early April the bluebonnets and Indian paintbrush literally cover the hills of the counties west and northwest of Houston.

Early **April** recharges the street fun with the *Westheimer Arts Festival,* and the *Reeking Regatta* navigates Buffalo Bayou from San Felipe St. to Allen's Landing downtown.

On **May** 5, *Cinco de Mayo* celebrations show off the city's strong Mexican-American spirit, and in midmonth the *Old Market Square Arts and Crafts Show* brings fresh weekend life to the city's oldest district.

Warm **June** evenings herald the first of a summer series of ballet, music, and play performances in Miller Outdoor Theatre in Hermann Park. One of these, the *Juneteenth Blues Festival,* is a major party for the city's black community, a musical celebration of the delivery of the Emancipation Proclamation in Texas.

July brings an *Old Fashioned Fourth Celebration* to Sam Houston Park, followed by fireworks there and at various other spots around town.

The Astroworld series of *dog shows* in Astrohall at the end of the month ushers in the infamous "dog days" of **August,** and the following weekend pooches are usually replaced by pistols as the *Houston Gun Collectors* move in with their special exhibition. Meanwhile, back in Hermann Park, the best of the Bard struts the stage of Miller Theatre during the annual *Shakespeare Festival.*

September brings national and jazz musicians to the *Annual Houston Jazz Festival* in Miller Theatre. This is also *British Festival* month, and there is a special arts-and-crafts show complete with bagpipes in Old Market Square.

A *Greek Festival* and *German Oktoberfest* get equal billing in **October,** along with two special day trips out of town. The *Texas Prison Rodeo* at Huntsville is a go-for-broke show unequaled in America, and the *Renaissance Festival* in the woods north of Magnolia re-creates the sounds, sights, food, and fun of the sixteenth century.

If you can't leave town, you'll find the Albert Thomas Exhibit Hall brimming with the elegance of the *Theta Charity Antique Show* and the 100 to 1000 blocks of Westheimer closed to traffic for another swinging *arts festival.*

Early **November** brings *Houston Camper Show* to the Albert Thomas, and then things quiet down until Foley's Annual *Thanksgiving Day Parade* through the heart of downtown. The following Sunday *Santa* arrives at Sharpstown, along with 17 tons of real snow.

The wonderful old homes in Sam Houston Park glow with *candlelight tours* in early **December,** and the world's largest *office party,* free and open to the public, swings at the Galleria a few days before Christmas. The **Bluebonnet Bowl,** a clash of collegiate football teams in the Astrodome, closes out the year on December 31.

TOURS. Several firms offer commercial tours of the city, NASA, and Galveston—a good way to get your bearings and some historical insight. Among them are: *Adven-Tours,* 522–6390, which uses town cars or vans to tour Houston and NASA ($30) and Galveston and NASA ($65, including lunch), and will design a tour to fit your special interests.

Angel's Travel & Tour, 988–0648, offers a variety of tours for Japanese and Chinese tourists only.

Grayline Tours of Houston, 691–1220, has three tours, multilingual guides, and free pick-up upon request at major hotels. Choices include a 2½-hour tour of the city's highlights ($12, plus $1.50 for admission to the Astrodome); a 5-hour tour of NASA ($15); and, Mondays and Thursdays, a 7½-hour tour of Galveston ($25 including admissions). For groups of 20 or more, there are charters to Gilley's, the San Jacinto Battleground and Port of Houston, and a working cattle ranch in Hungerford, west of Houston.

Japan Tours & Travel, 850-0199, shows off the Houston area with guides fluent in Japanese, Korean, and Chinese.

The NASA-Galveston Tour Agency, 521-0329, which is not affiliated with either the space center or the city, uses either a 15-passenger van or a seven-passenger limo on a three-hour morning tour of the city ($25) and an evening tour that includes a complementary drink at the Hyatt Regency downtown. Other destinations include the San Jacinto Battleground, San Antonio, and Austin.

Four limousine services offer private guided tours on a per-hour basis, usually with a 3-hour minimum: Limousines of Houston, Inc., 699-1444; Limousine Service International, 524-8468; and Royal Limousines, Inc. 928–5544.

There also are some special local tours:

Sam Houston Park has guided tours of four old homes, a church, and an 1824 log cabin, all within the shadow of contemporary skyscrapers and I–45 downtown. Open Monday through Saturday, 10:00 A.M. to 4:00 P.M. (last tour at 3:00 P.M.); Sunday, 1:00 to 5:00 P.M. Adult admission is $2; children 12 to 17, 50¢; children under 12, 35¢; 223–8367.

The Astrodome, the first indoor stadium in America, has tours that include a multimedia presentation at 11:00 A.M. and 1:00 and 3:00 P.M., daily unless there is a game ($2.75 per person, kids under 7 free), 799-9544.

The Lyndon B. Johnson Space Center, better known as NASA is 20 mi. south of Houston via I–45. Tours are self-guided, beginning at Rocket Park alongside the parking lot and continuing through museum buildings. Sign up for Mission Control Center briefing at the Information desk, Bldg. Two; 483–4321.

The Port of Houston has a 90-minute narrated tour aboard the M-V *Sam Houston* that is well worth the three-month wait for reservations. If you just drop in, you can view port activity from the observation platform on Kirby Drive, open daily, 9:00 A.M. to 5:00 P.M. Boat tours are at 10:00 A.M. and 2:30 P.M., Tuesday, Wednesday, Friday, and Saturday; 2:30 P.M., Sunday. For information and reservations, write the Port of Houston at P.O. Box 2562 (77001) or call 225–4044.

Free van tours of the *Texas Medical Center,* including a 35-min. orientation film, are given Monday through Friday at 10:00 A.M. and 1:00 P.M. Reservations should be made at least two days in advance; 790–1136.

Five universities in Houston welcome visitors. For guided tours, contact *Houston Baptist University,* 774–7661; *Rice University* (Admissions Office), 527–8101; *Texas Southern University,* 527–7760; *University of Houston* (Admissions Office), 749–2321; and the *University of Saint Thomas* (Public Relations), 522–7911, ext. 292, 243.

Out of Town. A number of regional businesses and industries welcome visitors with a sincere interest in that specific field. For information, contact the GHCVC (see the *Tourist Information* section, above).

The city also is surrounded by varied agriculture, and free tours can be arranged through rice and soybean farms, dairy farms, and cattle ranches. For information and reservations, contact the Texas Agricultural Extension Service, 406 Caroline, Rm. 203 (77002); 221–5020.

The 500-acre *J.D. Hudgins Ranch* specializes in Brahman cattle and welcomes visitors with advance reservations, 55 miles west of Houston. A Hudgins bull was the 1984 Houston Livestock Show International Grand Champion. P.O. Box 145, Hungerford 77448; (409) 532–1352.

PARKS. Hermann Park's 545 acres are southwest of downtown via Main and Fannin Sts. Surrounded by class—an 18-hole public golf course on the east, the Medical Center on the south, Rice University on the west, and the Warwick Hotel and Mecom Fountain on the north—this is the city's in-town playground. Scattered around the fringes of the park you'll find the *Museum of Natural Science* and the adjacent *Burke Baker Planetarium;* the *Houston Zoological Gardens;* the *Hermann Park Garden Center* with its special plantings of roses and camellias, and a fragrance garden for the blind; the *Miller Outdoor Theatre;* and the *Houston Belt and Terminal Railway Co.* kiddie train that chugs along a 2-mi. track through the park and woods.

For simple relaxing there are numerous picnic sites and shelters, children's playgrounds, and grassy fields shaded by huge oaks here. A large cast-bronze statue of Sam Houston stands at the northwest corner of the park—Sam's hand points toward San Jacinto, where his Texian army won the republic's independence from Mexico in 1836—and a newly refurbished reflecting pool and landscaping fronting the zoo.

For the blessing of **Memorial Park** west of downtown, thanks go to Will Hogg. In addition to the Midas touch, he must have had second sight. One of the movers and shakers of Houston in the early 1900s, Will Hogg developed the city's most elegant residential area, River Oaks, in 1924. Then, perhaps foreseeing the unplanned, unzoned, mercilessly concrete development that is today's Houston, he donated 1,000 acres of virgin woodland to the city with the stipulation that if it was ever used for anything but park purposes, it would revert to the Hogg estate. An additional 500 acres was later purchased, and today Memorial Park not only commemorates those who lost their lives in the First World War, but it also adds quality to life in Houston.

In addition to a challenging public golf course, Memorial Park includes a tennis center, jogging-hiking-biking-exercise trails, polo grounds, an archery range, picnic areas, and the wilderness along Buffalo Bayou that is the *Houston Arboretum and Nature Center.*

Sam Houston Park, bounded by Bagby, McKinney, and Dallas Sts. downtown, preserves a handful of the city's historical structures in a small, rolling green. The only building on its original site is the *Kellum-Noble House* (1847), the oldest brick house in the city. The *Nichols-Rice-Cherry House* (1850) was once the home of William Marsh Rice, founder of Rice Institute (which later became Rice University), and next to it is *St. John's Church* (1891), with its original altar, pulpit and cypress pews. The simple lines of the *San Felipe Cottage* are typical of thousands of homes around the Lone Star State about 1875, and its neighbor the lovely *Pillot House* (1868) has what is believed to be the first indoor kitchen in Houston. The area's pioneer origins are preserved in the *Old Place,* built around 1824 and moved here from the west bank of Clear Creek. It is the oldest structure still in existence in Harris County.

Entrance to the park is open and free, but tickets for guided tours and access to the buildings are available in the *Yesteryear Shop* in the Long Row, which fronts on Bagby. The *Tea Room* serves great soup/salad/sandwich lunches Monday through Friday, 11:00 A.M. to 1:30 P.M., plus you can buy a sandwich from the back patio door for a picnic in the park. Few things in Houston are as pleasant as picnicking in this small park. For more information, call the Harris County Heritage Society at 223–8367.

Two blocks north on Bagby, **Tranquility Park** tops an underground parking garage with a Bicentennial tribute to the Apollo flights. An intricate walk-through fountain with waterfalls and reflecting pools forms the heart of the park, and assorted grassy knolls represent the earth, lunar mounds, and other celestial bodies. Bronze plaques at the entrances tell the Apollo story in 15 languages, and a replica of Neil Armstrong's footprint on the moon is a good search-and-find project for children. The best time to visit is late afternoon, when the angle of the sun can turn the fountain into a shower of golden light.

While you're in the neighborhood, jog across Walker to **Martha Hermann Square,** which surrounds the reflecting pool in front of Houston City Hall. If you can't find a hotel room, not to worry. You can legally sleep here undisturbed by the law (no guarantees about other problems). That was a stipulation of George Hermann when he gave this pocket park to the city in honor of his mother some years ago.

A long green corridor of grass, trails, and playgrounds called the **Allen Parkway Recreation Area** borders Buffalo Bayou and Allen Parkway immediately west of downtown. Access is from Allen Parkway or Memorial Drive, but don't go alone any time or linger after dark.

For a look at Houston as it was before the Allen Brothers began their real-estate promotion, journey south of town via I–45 and then east on Bay Area Blvd. to the **Armand Bayou Nature Center.** This park and wilderness center preserves plant and animal life in its natural habitat. In addition to free explorations of the esturary by pontoon boat, you can follow nature trails or explore by canoe. For information, call 474–2551. For boat ride reservations, call the Bay Area County Park System, 326–6539.

ZOO. Alas, there is only one, officially known as the **Houston Zoological Gardens but generally just called the Hermann Park Zoo.** One of the few major zoos in the country that is free, it includes among its many pleasures an excellent children's petting zoo, an unusual nocturnal-animals exhibit, a walk-through aviary, and the new Kipp Aquarium. If you have children in tow, bring some bread or crackers to feed the ducks in the pond outside the zoo, and save some time to ride the train (75¢). Both the zoo and the train are open daily, year-round, but the hours change with the season.

During the summer they are 9:30 A.M. to 8:00 P.M. Parking is free. Information: 523–5888.

GARDENS. The 155-acre **Houston Arboretum and Nature Center** is on the western edge of Memorial Park, a towering buffer of native East Texas trees within a toot of traffic on the 610 loop. Yet when you walk the more than 5 mi. of trails, civilization seems very far away. Guided tours are given on Sunday afternoons whenever a small group forms, and self-guiding maps are available daily in the headquarters building. Buffalo Bayou is au naturel here, so the mosquitos can be fierce—come prepared. Free and open daily, year-round. Information: 681–8433. From the west loop (610) take the Woodway exit and turn east toward downtown.

More than 200 species of plants native to Texas thrive at a vest-pocket arboretum and natural-science museum in the Spring Branch area, the **R. A. Vines Environmental Science Center,** 8856 Westview; 465–9628. Another 17 acres bordering Rummel Creek in the Memorial area forms the **Edith Moore Sanctuary,** operated by the Houston Audubon Society. There's good access from the northwest corner of the parking lot of Memorial Drive Methodist Church, 12955 Memorial Dr., or from the sanctuary entrance at 440 Wilchester. Information: 932–1392 or 228–0037.

The gardens of **Bayou Bend** are beautiful and open to the public any time of the year (see the *Museums* section, below). In the spring, this is one of the most comprehensive showcases in the South for azaleas. Rose and camellia growers will find much of interest in the test gardens of the **Houston Garden Center,** 1500 Hermann Dr. in Hermann Park; 529–5371.

Several commercial nurseries offer interesting looks at Houston's tropical flora. *Aerial Gardens,* 6205 Skyline in the Hillcroft-Richmond area off U.S. 59 South, specializes in bromeliads and orchids and is one of the few places in town that sells bonsai. For directions, call 783–2182. *Condon Gardens,* 1214 Augusta inside the west loop (I–610), specializes in specimen plants laid out in garden fashion, a delight just to visit. Information: 782–3992. Two other noteworthy gardens lie some distances from town: *Lilypons Water Gardens,* just south of I–10 on FM 1489 in Brookshire (36 mi. west of downtown Houston), specializes in water lilies, lotus plants, etc., including the fauna to make your water garden come alive. Best of all, you pick and they mail, even the goldfish: 934–8525. An hour's drive north of Houston via I–45 or U.S. 59 and assorted country roads, the *Hilltop Herb Farm* occupies a fragrant corner of the Sam Houston National Forest west of Cleveland. The local gurus on herbs, their use, and their culture, owners Madeline Hill and Gwen Barclay also give tours and serve some fantastic meals by advance arrangement. For information, write Box 1734, Cleveland, TX 77327; 592–5859.

CHILDREN'S ACTIVITIES. Astroworld and **Waterworld** top the lists. Adjacent to the south loop (I–610) east of Kirby Drive and across from the Astrodome, both are part of the Six Flags chain. Astroworld has more than 80 rides and several stage shows for the $13.50 admission price. Waiting areas are covered and air conditioned. Open daily Memorial Day through Labor Day, weekends in spring and fall. Waterworld is 15 acres of wet family fun. Open daily May 18 through August 16, weekends only in May and September. ($8.95; $6.95 after 5:00 P.M.) Information: 799–1234.

Appleseed Park, 800 Rosine (one block off Allen Parkway, west of Waugh Dr.), is a physical fitness center designed specifically for kids 2–12 years old. It has an inventive mix of mazes, tricycle raceways, tunnels, etc. Open daily. $4 for children, adults free; 529–8499.

Hanna-Barbera Land is north of town (Holzwarth Road exit from I–45) and full of cartoon characters and kid entrancers like an indoor do-seum featuring computers and electronic games. Open Tuesday through Sunday, Memorial Day to Labor Day; weekends in spring and fall. $7.95. Information: 350–0914.

Mountain Park, at the intersections of the Southwest Freeway (U.S. 59 South) and the west loop (I–610), is amusement of a higher order. Based on the motivational and behavior theories of child psychiatrist Jean Piaget, it has special zones for music, dance, drama, gymnastics, role playing, etc.; a ballroom where kids dive and swim through 80,000 balls. Open year-round. $3 for children, $1 for adults; 668–4300.

Nathan's Physical Whimsical, inside the Sharpstown Mall (Southwest Freeway at Bellaire), is an indoor fun park with more than 20 rides and activities aimed at developing children's motor skills. Open daily. $4.50 for children, $1 for adults; 777–5437.

Rodeos are a Texas tradition that children love. During the summer the Future Farmers of America Club of Cy-Fair High School stages the **Cy-Fair Rodeo** every Friday night on Telge Road, just off U.S. 290 West in the northwest section of Harris County. For information: 373–0530 (Cy-Fair High School) or 373–0516 or 469–9005 (Carroll Grimm). Year-round, the **Round-Up Rodeo** runs full tilt in Simonton, 36 mi. west of Houston via FM 1093 (Westheimer). There's lots of action in the standard rodeo events, plus a calf-and-goat scramble for kids—you may even go home with a live souvenir of Houston. This indoor facility is air-conditioned, and an optional inexpensive barbecue dinner is served before the show. 346–1534.

A new **Children's Museum** was scheduled to open in the fall of 1985 at 3201 Allen Parkway; 522–1138.

The downtown area has several free delights for children. Just walking through the soaring lobby of the Hyatt Regency Hotel or riding its glass-enclosed elevators (one looks onto the lobby; the other, out onto Houston) is thrilling to the young. From the Hyatt it's easy to move into the labyrinths of the underground tunnel system. There's an ice-cream parlor hidden in there somewhere—follow the directional maps. Unfortunately, the **Houston City Library** is not connected to the tunnel system, but its Children's Room is worth seeking out. Story times are 10:00 A.M. on Thursday and 11:00 A.M. on Saturday, often with sign language for the hearing-impaired. Information: 224–5441. On the way out, pause in the brick plaza to smile at the bright red sculpture, *Geometric Mouse No. 2* by Claes Oldenburg—even children can figure out what this modern piece represents.

Just outside the west loop (I–610) the Galleria offers hours of exploring fun—kids love the souvenir and magic stores on the lower level of Galleria I—and ice skating at the Ice Capades Chalet; 626–1292. Older children thrive on a double-header science trip south of town to **NASA/Johnson Space Center** (see the *Museums* section, below), combined with a stop at **Armand Bayou** (see the *Tours* section, above) or a visit to the **Robert A. Vines Environmental Science Center,** an ecology-teaching facility of the Spring Branch School District (see the *Gardens* section, above). For children's theater see the *Stage* section, below.

The **Alabama-Coushatta Indian Reservation,** 93 mi. north of Houston, between Livingston and Woodville, has train and bus tours into the Big Thicket (see the chapter following the *Houston* chapter), a reptile garden, a replica of an Indian Village where the traditional crafts are demonstrated and explained, and a tribal-dance show. There are also a restaurant, camping, and a small lake where you can picnic, swim, and canoe. A historical drama, *Beyond the Sundown,* plays on summer evenings. Information and tickets: (409) 563–4391.

PARTICIPANT SPORTS. From fall to early spring, Houston's generally mild weather allows a variety of outdoor sports without much regard for the seasons. Summer's heat and humidity, however, can be overwhelming, particularly between 10:00 A.M. and 4:00 P.M. From mid-April through September, it is wise to hunt up an air-conditioned indoor facility or settle for some form of water recreation.

Although *runners* and *joggers* seem to sprout among the cars on many city streets, most folks run on trails along the bayous or in the parks. Special Exertrails combining a jogging course with exercise stations begin at the garden center in Hermann Park and at the tennis center in Memorial Park. There are similar Exertrails along Brays Bayou (on South Braeswood, between Stella Link and Buffalo Speedway in southwest Houston) and in MacGregor Park, 5225 Calhoun (southeast of downtown).

An extensive system of *hike-and-bike trails* links many of the bayous, parks, and business centers. Free detailed maps are available from the Houston Parks and Recreation Dept., 2999 S. Wayside (77023); 641–7530. *Bicycles* can be rented from Recycled Cycles Willowbend, 4122 Willowbend; 661–8352.

For a general listing of all current sport races and tournaments check the "Thursday Weekend Preview" section of the *Houston Chronicle* or the weekend section of the Friday *Houston Post.* The Sunday papers usually include an additional rundown on things to do. *Inside Running,* a local magazine on the newsstands, also lists marathons, fun runs, etc., by the month.

Ten *golf* courses are open for public play in the greater Houston area. Check with each regarding specific location, fees, tee times: Bear Creek Golf Course, 859–8188; Brock Park Golf Course, 458–1350; Glenbrook Park Golf Course, 644–4081; Gus Wortham Park Golf Course, 921–3227; Hermann Park Golf Course, 529–9788; Melrose Park Golf Center, 447–4434; Memorial Park Golf Course, 862–4033; Sharpstown Park Golf Course, 988–2099; World Houston Golf Club, 449–8384; and Stephen F. Austin State Park Golf Course, (409) 885–3613.

Although many private stables offer boarding and training, only a few offer *horseback riding* by the hour. Best bet: the Woodlands Equestrian Center, 292–3218.

Swimmers have their choice of 47 municipal pools operated by the city parks and recreation department. Not all are in "good areas," so caution is advised. For information: 641–7509.

The city parks-and-recreation department also operates three major *tennis* centers with outdoor laykold courts, shops, showers, instruction, etc. The MacGregor Tennis Center is southeast of downtown at 5225 Calhoun, 747–5466; the Memorial Drive Tennis Center is west of downtown at 1500 Memorial Loop Dr. in Memorial Park, 861–3765; and the Southwest Tennis Center is at 9506 S. Gessner, 772–0296. More than 80 public courts in various stages of repair are scattered around town.

If either *swimming* or *tennis* is a major sport for you, a best bet in Houston would be to look for a hotel that includes those recreations in its offerings.

Though opportunities are limited, *canoeing* is growing in popularity in Houston. Organized *float trips* to various bayous and creeks in the greater Houston area and to the Guadalupe, Rio Grande, and Medina Rivers can be arranged through several outfitters: Texas Canoe Trails, (512) 625–3375; River Safari, Inc., 528–2800; Guadalupe Canoe Livery, (512) 885–4671 or (512) 964–3189; and Whitewater Experience, 522–2848.

Locally, you can canoe on Buffalo, Armand, and Dickinson Bayous and both sail and canoe on Clear Lake. Rentals are available from River Safari, Inc., 528–2800; Gulf Coast Sailboats (Kemah), 334–1722; and Whitewater Experience, 522–2848.

Windsurfing is another popular water sport, particularly in Galveston Bay and on Clear Lake. Check those last numbers given for rentals. T-Marina, 61st St. and Offats Bayou in Galveston, has rentals for windsurfing, water skiing, sailing on small boats and catamarans, and paddleboating.

Although there are catfish in the bayous that thread through Greater Houston, serious *fishing* means a trip to Clear Lake and Galveston Bay or out into the Gulf. Information on marinas, charter party boats, etc., is available from the Clear Lake Area Convention & Visitors Bureau, 1202 NASA Road One (77058) (488–7676), and from the Galveston Convention and Visitors Bureau, 2106 Seawall Blvd., Galveston, TX 77550; (409) 763–4311.

Two Galveston party-fishing boats have toll-free Houston telephone numbers: Reel Fun Charters (deep sea fishing in the gulf) (771–4725) and Galveston Party Boats (bay fishing); 222–7025.

Both Lake Livingston and Lake Conroe north of Houston are known for their bass fishing. For a list of marinas and facilities on Lake Conroe, contact the Conroe Visitor & Convention Bureau, P.O. Box 2347, Conroe (77305); (409) 756–6644. For Lake Livingston, contact the Polk County Chamber of Commerce, 516 W. Church St., Livingston (77351); (409) 327–4929.

The fastest-growing sport in America is *racquetball,* and four Houston health clubs are open to guests: Continental Racquetball (in the 1960 area), 893–5146; Courts West Racquetball Club (Bear Creek area), 463–6815; and the Westchase Racquetball and Athletic Club (southwest), 977–4804.

SPECTATOR SPORTS. When the tides of fortune are running high for one of the city's three major professional-sport teams, it's standing room only at the games. When the *Houston Oilers* lost their NFL Super Bowl bid in the playoffs in 1980, they were welcomed home with a party that filled the Astrodome and spilled out into the parking lots. Good thing they didn't win—it would have immobilized the city.

The Astrodome is also home to the *Houston Astros* baseball team and the USFL Houston Gamblers during the spring and summer, and the *Houston Rockets* play NBA basketball at the Summit in Greenway Plaza.

On the collegiate level, most of the major schools field high-quality teams in all three sports, but football is king in Texas and draws the most emotion. For who is playing whom where, when you're in town, check the papers and call the school directly or call Ticketron or Ticketmaster (see the *Tourist Information* section, above). And don't pass up a chance to see a swim meet at the natatorium of the University of Houston, which has one of the best teams in the country year after year.

Celebrity tennis tournaments pop up several times a year at some swanky places, and both soccer and rugby are played on a non-pro basis on area fields. Professional wrestling is a year-round draw at the Coliseum downtown, and horse-racing fans can ride special buses east to Delta Downs in Vinton, Louisiana, for a day of playing the ponies; (800) 551–7142.

HISTORIC SITES. In addition to Allen's Landing and Sam Houston Park in the downtown area, there are several historical sites well worth a day's trip.

San Jacinto Battleground State Historic Park, 22 mi. southeast of downtown via TX 225 and technically in La Porte, marks the site where a ragged band of Texans led by Sam Houston defeated the mighty Mexican army led by Santa Anna and won independence for Texas in 1836. The 570-ft.-high San Jacinto Monument has the stirring story chiseled around its base and an excellent free museum inside (see the *Museums* section, below). The elevator ride to the top of the monument is $1.50 for adults, 50¢ for children. Pick up a free detailed map of the battleground at the museum and then wander among the oaks and old tombstones near the picnic grounds. Nearby, the *U.S.S. Texas* is open for tours daily, year-round ($2.00 adults, $1 children six through

17), and kids love climbing on the gun enplacements that flank this only surviving dreadnought-class battleship. Several picnic areas border the Houston Ship Channel and upper Galveston Bay, ideal for crabbing or bank fishing.

Sam Houston Memorial Park, in Huntsville, 69 mi. north of Houston via I–45, has two historic homes in which Houston lived, his law office, and an excellent museum on Texas history, all free and open daily from 9:00 A.M. to 5:00 P.M., year-round. For information: (409) 295–7824.

Washington-on-the-Brazos State Park, northwest of Hempstead, marks the site of the first constitutional convention, which created the Republic of Texas in 1836. None of the original buildings survives, but a replica of Independence Hall has an audio-visual show about the historic times in this tiny town, and the Star of the Republic Museum is a lodestone of Texana. A picket fence surrounds Barrington, home to Anson Jones, the fourth and last president of the Texas Republic. This trip is without equal in early April, when the fields flow away from the park in waves of wildflowers. All the above are open daily, 10:00 A.M. to 5:00 P.M., March through Labor Day; Wednesday through Sunday only the rest of the year. For information: (409) 878–2461. From Houston take U.S. 290 west through Hempstead to Chappell Hill. Turn north on FM 1155 to Washington. Chappell Hill also has several historic homes. Inquire at any of the stores on Main St.

Henkel Square is a collection of early Texas homes and buildings on the square in Round Top, a tiny hamlet in the hills between Houston and Austin. Funded by the Texas Pioneer Arts Foundation, Henkel Square has won national awards for its painstaking restorations, and docents lead visitors on detailed tours. Tickets are $2 for adults, $1 for students, and can be bought in the brightly painted Victorian building that used to be Round Top's drugstore. Open daily, 10:00 A.M. to 5:00 P.M., year-round except Thanksgiving and Christmas. This is a comfortable two-hour drive from Houston via U.S. 290 West and Texas 237 South.

Winedale is 4 mi. north of Round Top via FM 1457 and FM 2714 and, with careful timing, can be combined with a visit to Henkel Square. Now part of the University of Texas, Winedale is a rural farmstead that functions as a living museum. The two-story Sam Lewis house is furnished to the period and has unusual stenciling and ceiling frescoes. Around it are a smokehouse, a pioneer kitchen, and a barn where University of Texas English-department students perform Shakespeare on August-weekend evenings. In the back pasture is the rather elegant McGregor-Grimm House, a fine example of a pre–Civil War plantation home in cotton-rich Texas. Although Winedale's grounds are free and open daily, the buildings are open only on Saturday from 10:00 A.M. to 6:00 P.M. and on Sunday from noon to 6:00 P.M., with a small admission charge. There are often special events here, so check before you go; 278–3530.

MUSEUMS. As Houston's cultural consciousness has risen and expanded in the last decade, so have the quality and fortunes of its handful of museums, concentrated primarily in the Hermann Park–Montrose–Rice University area. A day's exploring can mix and match several to suit your personal interests. A listing of current special exhibits and traveling shows is published in numerous magazines and brochures (see the *Tourist Information* section, above).

The Museum of Fine Arts. The original physical core of this somewhat confusing building is a neo-classical rectangle, to which have been added a series of wings and galleries. Entrance is through the Brown Pavilion on Bissonnet, a contemporary horizontal arc of glass that completes an expansion designed by Mies van der Rohe. Pick up a map at the door to keep your bearings as you move through the various areas and exhibits. When you've saturated your appreciation level, the museum's small lunchroom serves some of the best salads and sandwiches in town.

Because much of the money for acquisition and expansion over the years has come from corporate or private philanthropic gifts representing differing motives and tastes, the collection covers a vast range of art history. Of note are the Straus Collection of Renaissance and eighteenth-century works, which includes *Temptation of St. Anthony* by Fra Angelico; the Beck Collection of Impressionist and Post-impressionist paintings by Daumier, van Gogh, Cassatt, Signac, Derain, Braque, Kandinsky, Bonnard, and Matisse; and the Samuel H. Kress collection of Italian and Spanish Renaissance works, among which is Bellotto's *The Marketplace at Pisa.*

At the opposite end of the spectrum are a fine collection of Remingtons; *Number 6, 1949,* by Jackson Pollock; *Two Women Before the Window* by Picasso; and significant oriental, pre-Columbian, African, and Oceanic art. Within the past five years the museum has been aggressively expanding its photography collection, a portion of which can usually be seen in the Lower Brown Mezzanine.

Significant sculpture including works by Calder and Rodin is scattered around the museum's shady backyard (the former front entrance), and a new sculpture garden will soon link the museum with its school, the *Alfred C. Glassell, Jr., School of Art* across Bissonnet. Small exhibits of high-quality student work are usually on display in this second building.

A guide to the entire collection is available in the museum's bookstore, along with a brief list of things you shouldn't leave without seeing. In addition, more than 20 traveling shows open here annually. Admission and parking are free. Open Tuesdays, Wednesdays, Fridays, and Saturdays 10:00 A.M. to 5:00 P.M.; Thursdays to 9:00 P.M.; Sundays 1:00 to 6:00 P.M. Try to catch the free 30-min. gallery talks by museum instructors at 1:30 and 2:00 P.M. on Wednesday and Sunday, September 1 through May 30. For information: 526–1361.

A third portion of the Museum of Fine Arts, *Bayou Bend,* is across town in the River Oaks residential area. This unusual Latin-Colonial home with its 14 oak-studded acres of gardens along Buffalo Bayou was the former home of one of the museum's great patrons, Miss Ima Hogg. Designed by noted architect John Staub, Bayou Bend was built in 1927 to house Miss Ima's extensive collection of American antiques. She gave both the collection and the home to the Museum of Fine Arts in 1965.

Miss Ima had a discerning eye and bottomless pocketbook, and the collection reflects both. One of the finest museums of its kind in the country, Bayou Bend is free but open for tours only by advance reservation, and there's often a wait of several weeks. If all else fails, the second Sunday of every month is open house through only the gardens and downstairs rooms, from 1:00 to 5:00 P.M. Closed March and August. For information: 529–8773.

The Contemporary Arts Museum. Diagonally across from the Museum of Fine Arts on the corner of Montrose and Bissonnet sits an aluminum-sheathed trapezoid. This is the somewhat "spacey" Houston home of the avant-garde in art, a most curious place. To the uninitiated, it seems the museum carries the "life is art, art is life" theme to new limits. A recent photo exhibition focused on Galveston gas stations, and an early display involved growing vegetables in a raised dirtbox. Do drop in and have your art consciousness raised—those in the know say the professional staff is doing an ever-improving job. Open Tuesday through Saturday, 10:00 A.M. to 5:00 P.M.; Sunday, noon to 6:00 P.M. There are free guided tours of the Upper Gallery exhibitions at 2:00 P.M. on Sunday, and the museum's shop has beautiful handcrafted gifts and inventive toys for children. 526–3129.

A few blocks away at the University entrance to the campus, the **Rice University Institute for the Arts** mounts extremely fine and varied exhibits, some from the de Menil collection. Free; open Tuesday through Saturday, 10:00 A.M. to 5:00 P.M.; Sunday, noon to 6:00 P.M. Closed June through August. For information: 522–0886.

A tiny jewel of a museum, **The Rothko Chapel,** is tucked away in a residential neighborhood at 3900 Yupon, between the 1300 and 1400 blocks of W. Alabama. Free and open daily from 10:00 A.M. to 6:00 P.M., this is a place to sooth the spirit and lift the heart through peace or meditation. The small octagonal room is lined with 14 huge monochromatic paintings by the late Mark Rothko, and the sculpture in the adjacent park, *Broken Obelisk* by Barnett Newman, comments on the life and sudden death of Martin Luther King. Beautiful in and of itself, this chapel is a good place to pause for more than a moment in your sightseeing. For information: 524–9839.

The University of Houston has two gallery-museums, the **O'Kane Gallery** on the downtown campus (across Buffalo Bayou via N. Main Street from the downtown business district), 221–8042, and the **Blauffer Gallery** on the main campus (entrance 5 off Cullen Blvd.), 749–1320. Both host changing exhibits in a variety of media. Call to see what's up.

Another small museum of interest to Americana fans is the **Museum of American Architecture and Decorative Arts** on the second floor of Moody Library at Houston Baptist University, 7502 Fondren (southwest). Free and open Tuesday through Thursday, 10:00 A.M. to 4:00 P.M.; Sunday, 2:00 to 5:00 P.M. For information: 774–7661, ext. 311.

Five other museums deal with life as lived rather than as perceived through art. The **San Jacinto Museum of Texas History** is in the base of the monument at San Jacinto Battleground State Historic Park (see the *Historic Sites* section, above). The museum is divided into two major rooms, one covering the Spanish-Mexican period of 1518–1835 and the other devoted to the Anglo-American settlement years of 1835–61. Free and open Tuesday through Sunday, 10:00 A.M. to 6:00 P.M. For information: 479–2431.

The **Houston Museum of Natural Science, Burke Baker Planetarium,** and the **Museum of Medical Science** share a wooded site at the north end of Hermann Park. One of the largest natural-science museums in the Southwest, the *Houston Museum of Natural Science* has everything from dinosaur skeletons to sea shells, including an excellent exhibit of Indian artifacts collected from Alaska to South America. The complicated story of oil is told in clear terms in the Hall of Petroleum Science and Technology, and important events in Lone Star past come to life in the Strake Hall of Texas History. The main-floor galleries of the new Frensley Wing often showcase important traveling exhibits. Best of all, this is a hands-on place. You are welcome to feel, examine, or manipulate anything that is not behind ropes or glass. For information: 526–4273.

Upstairs, the Harris County Medical Society welcomes you to the *Museum of Medical Science.* "Talking exhibits" explain human anatomy and physiology, and visitors can test their eyes, lung capacity, and heart. Graphic models follow the development of a fetus and the miracle of birth. The remaining life processes are explained by TAM, a transparent/talking mannequin. For information: 529–3766.

The *Burke Baker Planetarium* explores the universe ten times a week in its computerized theater, and the shows change with the seasons. By advance arrangement you can view the heavens through the 16-in. reflector of the Margaret Root Brown telescope. For information: 526–4273.

All three museums are open Tuesday through Saturday, 9:00 A.M. to 4:45 P.M.; Sunday and Monday, noon to 5:00 P.M.; and Friday from 7:30 to 9:00 P.M.

The words "Houston . . . the *Eagle* has landed" not only brought instant international recognition to the city on Buffalo Bayou, but they also announced the age of man in space. The **NASA/Lyndon B. Johnson Space Center,** south of Houston in the Clear Lake–Nassau Bay area, is headquarters for America's space program, and visitors see lunar rocks, rockets and spacecraft, training labs, and other examples of today's space technology.

NASA visits start at Space Park (alongside the parking lot) where three rockets are on display, including a giant four-stage Saturn V. Self-guided tours begin at the Visitor Center (Building 1) and continue through four other facilities; Mission Control Center (sign up for tours at the information desk as soon as you arrive); Mission Simulation and Training (you can walk through skylab and shuttle trainers); the Lunar Sample Building; and the Space Shuttle Orbiter Training. Plan on driving to the last two; it's a long walk. In all, the NASA experience requires about three hours and stamina. NASA is free and open daily except Christmas from 9:00 A.M. to 4:00 P.M. Information: 483–4433.

ART GALLERIES

From old masters to contemporary hand weaving, Houston's commercial art galleries serve a broad audience. Although scattered all over town, the majority are in the west sector, with several in the Galleria alone. Few specialize in any one form of art, but the following list may help you narrow the field to your particular interests. The best bet is to pick up a free magazine, *Art Happenings of Houston,* available at all the museums and galleries and at the guest-information counters of major hotels. Current exhibits are also listed monthly in *Houston City* magazine and *Texas Monthly,* and weekly in the local papers.

Archway Gallery, 2517 University Blvd., 522–2409, is a cooperative, exhibiting the better regional artists in all media, including Raku. The *Art League of Houston,* 1953 Montrose Blvd., 523–9530, also covers all media, with excellent juried or invitational shows at various times of the year. *Davis-McClain Galleries,* 2818 Kirby, 520–9200, exhibits contemporary and traditional realistic landscapes, paper works, and sculptures. *DuBose Gallery, Inc.,* 1700 Bissonnet, 526–4916, focuses on contemporary paintings and sculpture and is a favorite with leading interior decorators. *Harris Gallery,* 1100 Bissonnet, 522–9116, showcases the newest of Houston's artists with works on paper, paintings, and photographs. *Hooks-Epstein Galleries,* 1200 Bissonnet, 522–0718, focuses primarily on late-nineteenth- and early-twentieth-century European works on paper, paintings, and sculpture. *Meier Gallery, Inc.,* 2310 Bissonett, 526–2983, specializes in contemporary Impressionistic and abstract paintings, watercolors, and sculpture, with emphasis on regional artists. *Kauffman Galleries,* 2702 W. Alabama, 528–4229, handles new works in all media, from photography and lithography to painting and sculpture, by major international contemporary artists. *Meredith Long & Co.,* 2323 San Felipe, 523–6671, handles major contemporary American artists and fine nineteenth- and twentieth-century American paintings. *Moody Gallery,* 2015-J W. Gray, 526–9911, represents 15 contemporary regional artists working in painting, sculpture, and other media. *Watson/de Nagy & Co.,* 1106 Berthea, 526–9883, focuses on contemporary paintings and works on paper of young Houston artists. *Houston Center for Photography,* 1441 W. Alabama, 529–4755, is the showcase for area photographers.

MUSIC. All dimensions of the musical arts thrive in Houston wherever they can find public performance space. *Jones Hall* is the premier auditorium, but most of the musicals and stage shows play in the *Music Hall,* part of the Civic Center complex. The 1985–86 season should see completion of the new $65-million Gus W. Wortham Theater Center in that same area, adding two new theaters principally for the use of the Houston Grand Opera and the Houston Ballet. Tight stage space finds many productions moving to *Wortham Theatre* on the University of Houston's central campus year-round or to *Miller Theatre's* outdoor stage during the warm months. For current offerings, check the local newspapers, magazines, etc., as noted in the *Tourist Information* section, above. Best bet is the bimonthly *Performing Arts Calendar,* published by Arts for Everyone.

The *Houston Symphony Orchestra,* currently under the baton of Sergiu Comissiona, presents a full season of concerts from September through May in Jones Hall, often with internationally acclaimed artists in guest roles. During the summer the symphony presents a special Summer Festival and evening outdoor concerts in Miller Theatre in Hermann Park. For information: 227–ARTS.

Symphony musicians have formed two additional professional music groups, the *Houston Symphony Pops Orchestra,* which plays a six-concert season with guest conductors October through May in the Music Hall, and the *Houston Symphony Chamber Orchestra,* which performs a limited series. For information for both: 224–4240.

Popular music in a symphonic context is also the theme of the *Houston Pops Orchestra,* conducted by Ned Battista in six to eight performances annually, in either Jones Hall or the Music Hall. This is the only year-round pops orchestra in the world, and the second half of their concert "season" usually features internationally known guest artists such as Dinah Shore, Pearl Bailey, and José Greco. Information: 871–8300. *Texas Chamber Orchestra* performs chamber-orchestra and ensemble music in a six-concert series and sponsors some Saturday-afternoon children's concerts at the Museum of Fine Arts. For tickets and information: 974–6414.

Chamber music is also performed by the *Shepherd School of Music at Rice University,* 527–4933; the *University of Houston Central Campus Music Ensemble,* 749–1116; and the *Chamber Music Ensemble of the University of St. Thomas,* 522–7911, ext. 240. Some musicians within those groups specialize in baroque and Renaissance music of the twelfth through seventeenth centuries, as do the *Cambiata Soloists,* 462–3676 or 667–6351.

A variety of music is performed year-round in a series of concerts at *Festival Hill in Round Top.* Founded and directed by noted pianist James Dick, the Festival Hill programs are usually performed by guest artists on an outdoor stage under the stars of the rural Texas countryside. The April-to-August series is more intimate, often chamber music played in the parlors of the handsome old William Lockhart Clayton house. Gourmet dinners and overnight accommodations can (and must) be arranged in advance; (409) 249–3129. Ask directions when you call and plan on a two-hour drive from downtown Houston to get there.

The *Houston Harpsichord Society* gives five public concerts a year. For information: 461–5893. Music for love, not money, motivates the 70-member *Houston Civic Symphony* to give six free weekend concerts annually, often in the Brown Auditorium of the Museum of Fine Arts. Guest artists add to programs ranging from Bach to Stravinsky. For information: 682–6767.

Music lovers should also investigate the Rice University Concerts, 527–4911; the Christ Church Cathedral Concerts, 222–2593; the University of St. Thomas Concerts, 522–7911, ext. 240; and the University of Houston Concerts, 749–

3796. The Houston Baptist University School of Music, 995-3338 also performs at various locations in the Houston-Galveston area.

Chances are if a major musical show is playing in Houston, it has been produced either by the Houston Grand Opera (HGO), Theatre Under the Stars (TUTS), or the Society for the Performing Arts.

The *Houston Grand Opera*'s season and offerings know no limits. The basic series of six full-staged major operas ranges from the traditional scores of *Turandot* and *Rigoletto* to premieres of innovative works and feature internationally known singers in Jones Hall performances. The same management produces the Spring Opera Festival at Miller Theatre and five light-opera productions a year such as *Evita, Sugar Babies,* and *The Merry Widow.* HGO also brings in touring shows or creates fresh shows that open in Houston and then go on the road (*Porgy and Bess, Treemonisha,* etc.). Called by *Time* magazine "incontestably . . . the top performing-arts company in the South," HGO also sponsors the touring activities of the *Texas Opera Theatre* and the *Houston Opera Studio,* both of which give musical-theater programs or recitals in Houston at various times. HGO information: 222–ARTS or 546–0200.

Theatre Under the Stars presents guest artists and local professional singers in six major light-opera musicals a year, two of which are free productions each summer in Miller Theatre. The winter season plays in the Music Hall, and TUTS's December production of *Scrooge* has become a Houston holiday tradition. 622–1626.

The *Society for the Performing Arts* presents major cultural attractions from around the world in Jones Hall from September through June. Among their plums are the Houston premieres of both the Pittsburgh Symphony Orchestra and L'Orchestre de Paris conducted by Daniel Barenboim. For information: 227–1111.

Choral music is a Houston specialty all its own. The *Houston Symphony Chorale* (224–4240) gives concerts as well as accompanying the symphony upon occasion, and the *Houston Chamber Singers* (627–3609) have a full series featuring medieval to modern works. The four universities previously mentioned here also have choral groups; inquire at the numbers given.

The S.P.E.B.S.Q.S.A.—*Society for the Preservation and Encouragement of Barber Shop Quartet Singing in America*—is active here (497–3852), and the local *Gilbert and Sullivan Society* (627–3570) mounts full-stage performances of those favorites every summer.

DANCE. Most major American dance companies perform in Houston, courtesy of the Society of the Performing Arts. The *Houston Ballet,* in turn, tours throughout America, gaining a strong reputation for its varied repertoire and technical precision. Founded in 1955, it became a professional company in 1969 and presents five programs of four performances each in Jones Hall during its November-through-May season, often with international guest artists. The company traditionally performs *The Nutcracker* at Christmas. For information: 225–0271.

The *Greater Houston Civic Ballet,* under the direction of Margo Marshall, performs eight times a year, often showcasing new ballets by local and national choreographers. For information: 468–3670.

Young dancers in training perform with the *Allegro Ballet* (496–4670) in six concerts yearly. The American heritage is the focus of the *Southwest Jazz Ballet Company* (686–6299) in 50 performances each year, and contemporary dance is performed by *Space/Dance/Theatre* (630–7264), under the direction of James Clouser. The avant-garde in contemporary dance can be seen in the offerings of the *Houston Contemporary Dance Company* (521–2679).

STAGE. In theatre lingo, Houston is a great "break a leg" town. One of the three oldest professional resident repertory companies in America, the Nina Vance Alley Theatre, thrives here with a strong, almost year-round playbill, and nearly two dozen professional and fine amateur groups compete as smaller satellites.

From a humble first performance in a small room literally at the back of an alley in 1947, the *Nina Vance Alley Theatre* now plays in a $3-million downtown house that resembles a contemporary castle, with turrets and ramparts. Inside, two shows often run simultaneously, a major production in the 800-seat large theater and a more intimate show in the 300-seat Arena theater. In all, this professional company produces 20 shows with 500 performances each year. A special chiller-thriller mystery runs Thursday through Sunday during the summer, preceded by classic films of the same genre on Tuesday and Wednesday evenings. Downtown businesspeople enjoy the full one-act plays featured at Lunchtime Theatre (12:15 to 1:00 P.M.) during the October-June season. For the current play and ticket information, call the box office at 228–8421. Tickets bought between 12:00 noon and 1:00 P.M. on day of performance are half-price; a special student rate ($5.00–$5.50 is available 15 minutes prior to curtain.

The drama department of the University of Houston central campus produces a *Children's Theatre Festival* during July and August in the Wortham Theatre. For information: 749–3459. Children's theater is also the focus of *Theatre on Wheels* (953–1666) and the *Houston Youth Theatre* (520–9875). In addition, the Alley, *Marionette Playhouse* (376–5777), and the *Main Street Theatre* (524–6706) often stage productions for the younger set.

Students at the Houston International Theatre School (HITS) perform a two-week *Children's Theatre Jubilee* during the summer, featuring the New Mime Company and the Unicorn Players. For information: 861–7408.

Offering plays ranging from the avant-garde and experimental to classics and melodrama are the Chocolate Bayou Theatre, Box 270363 (77277), 528–0119; Country Playhouse, 12802 Queensbury, 467–4497; Main Street Theatre, 6256 Main, 524–6706; The Ensemble, 1010 Tuam, 520–0055; Stages, Waugh & Allen Parkway, 527–8243; and Theatre Suburbia, 1410 W. 43d, 682–3525.

Also, check what's playing at the *Arena Theatre,* 7322 Southwest Freeway (at Frondren) (777–1212), and at the *Tower Theatre,* 1201 Westheimer, (526–1709).

SHOPPING. Houston, with a population of more than three million people, offers shopping opportunities from probably the most exotic and wildly expensive merchandise in the world to budget items and flea markets. A drive through and around Houston, either on or off the freeways, reveals that one is never more than a minute away from a shopping area. These can range from a cluster of four stores on one block to vast full-service shopping centers and malls covering acres.

In the heart of downtown Houston from the 800 to the 1200 blocks on Main St., and on the avenues on either side of it, are department stores and specialty shops. Both *Foley's* and *Sakowitz's Number 1* downtown stores are on 9th and Main. Paid parking is possible within the area.

The new Park in Houston Center is the first major retail development to be built in downtown in a generation, a multi-story mall entered from San Jacinto, McKinney, and Lamar streets. Unfortunately, it is not connected to the city's underground tunnel system at this writing. To access those small shops, enter the tunnel labyrinth through the lobby of the Hyatt Regency on Louisiana St. The tunnels do not reach to Foleys or Sakowitz either, but they do connect most of the major bank and office buildings. The banks, in particular, supply maps for this weather-controlled shopping-and-eating adventure.

The most famous shopping area in Houston is *The Galleria* at Post Oak and Westheimer. In this L-shaped, three-level structure are two deluxe hotels, an Olympic-size skating rink, five major nationally known specialty stores, four theaters, 19 restaurants, a medical clinic, a private health club, and office facilities. The Galleria is noted for the quality of its stores, which include *Neiman-Marcus, Gumps of San Francisco, Fred Joaillier of Paris, Tiffany & Co., Mark Cross, Alfred Dunhill, Gucci, Cartier, Charles Jourdan, Ted Lapidus, Au Chocolat, Lord & Taylor, Frost Bros.,* and *W & J Sloan.* This list names but a few of the 259 businesses in the Galleria. Of course, you will find less-expensive stores there, with merchandise ranging from books and candles to luggage and cutlery. The Galleria has free parking.

On the third level is a medical clinic, where you can go through a thorough examination including all the necessary tests, and have the results by the end of the day. At press time this service cost $450 for the works.

Another shopping sector nearby and teeming with exclusive merchandise is on Post Oak between Westheimer and San Felipe. On Post Oak, facing Westheimer and the Galleria, is the *Sakowitz* Post Oak store, Houston's most famous home-owned specialty shop for men, women, and children. Continuing along Post Oak on the same side of the street, you will come to *Abercrombie & Fitch,* which specializes in imports and items for those who have everything (how does a miniature VW for children, which operates like a full-grown car, at $7,000, grab you?). The sportswear department will send you decked out as the chic-est gal or guy on the block to hunt elephant or shoot ducks. In the next block is *Saks Fifth Avenue,* with a bevy of shops that surround it in its own miniature Galleria, shops such as *Roberta of Italy, Courreges,* and the furrier *Szor Deiner.* At San Felipe—still on Post Oak—is yet another group of elegant stores that specialize in fine merchandise. But that's not all. On the opposite side of Post Oak are more clusters of boutiques all the way back to Westheimer.

Other shopping areas are sprinkled strategically about Houston. *Greenspoint,* the largest and newest mall, is near the Intercontinental Airport at the intersection of I–45 and North Belt.

The Village, near Rice University and the Medical Center complex, is a bit more than four blocks square, another area offering total shopping. It has more than 500 stores, restaurants, and business establishments in a wide price range. On Rice Blvd. you will find specialty shops selling exclusively British merchandise for example, or Scandinavian, though at 2415 Rice Blvd. you will find the last of the old 5 and 10s, *Variety Fair.* Variety Fair seems not to have stored any of its stock in more than 30 years, so they are bound to have exactly what you need, from Easter grass in July to sand pails in December. On the same block, right next door, is *Domicile,* where a marvelous collection of stuffed animals can be found, along with gift ideas from straw through crystal and back to fabrics. The Village is bounded by Rice and University Aves. on the north and south and by Kirby and Greenbriar on the east and west.

Other total shopping can be found to the west of Houston at *Town & Country* on the West Belt at Katy Freeway (I–10); *Memorial City* on Gessner and Katy Freeway; *Carillon West, Westwood, Northline Mall, Sharpstown* on Bellaire, and a few other centers that bear no name but have the stores to keep the shoppers happy.

To the south of the city are *Gulfgate, Almeda Mall, Almeda Square,* and *Baybrook Mall.* At Shepherd Dr. and Gray, the *River Oaks Shopping Center* consists of white and black art-deco buildings that house shops to service the extremely affluent neighborhood with art and antique auction galleries as well as more mundane shops. Off Shepherd at Hazard is a Cuban grocery and restaurant, with a Spanish-goods shop next door. On Shepherd at Alabama is *Cactus Records,* a record supermarket; if they don't have it or can't get it, it's unlikely it was ever on the market.

At 2423 Westheimer is a one-block clump of shops that includes ABBR. (it stands for abbreviation), which sells clothing for those ladies who are the size of little girls but don't want to dress like little girls. The large selection of sizes go from 00 to 14. On the same block is *The Empty Vase* at 2439 Westheimer, where giant hand-made silk flowers can be bought, along with other unusual gifts.

If it is flea markets you like, *The Common Market,* at 6116 Southwest Freeway (U.S. 59 South) (782–0391), and *Four Seasons Common Market,* at 4412 North Shepherd (697–4765), should have what you want. A branch of the famous outlet store, *Loehmanns,* 7455 Southwest Freeway (777–0164), offers high-quality merchandise at low prices, as does *T.J. Mandy,* 6100 Westheimer (781–7986) and 9864 Fondren (271–1084).

Typical Texas wear? Western style, of course. For the haute couture in boots, hats, and fashions, *Cutter Bill Western World* bills itself as "the ultimate western store." Highest styles. Highest prices. 5647 Westheimer at Chimney Rock, another shopping area; 622–5105.

For western wear that is as good if not as high styled or as high priced, try *Stelzig's Western Wear* downtown at 410 Louisiana; 223–4344.

Sears, Montgomery Ward, and *Penney's* are in many shopping centers. The White Pages can be helpful. If your eyeglasses need tightening or the car needs fixing, check the Yellow Pages.

Westheimer Road has an artsy area, too: east of the Galleria, between the 100 and the 1900 blocks. Here you can find neon sculpture, unusual cards, old movie posters, T-shirts, candles, leaded glass, paintings, wood and ceramic work, fancy writing paper. You can still get your hair cut for only $4.50 in the 1600 block; you can't miss the sign. And if you are in Houston in October, the Westheimer Art Festival is worth a visit here.

At Avondale and Westheimer are six or seven boutiques with the usual abundance of antique and flower shops. In the Galleria small, slender men can find imported Italian clothes to fit them at *Copperfield, Walker Jones, Leopold Price and Rolle. Norton Ditto* has handsome menswear both downtown and in the Post Oak area; *Spurs* on Post Oak also has women's fine western wear in the boutique across from Saks Fifth Avenue. Maternity clothes and bridal attire can be found in specialty shops in almost every shopping center. *James Avery's* gold and silver craftwork is available on Post Oak. Tex-Mex and Texas foods can be found in *Sakowitz* and *Neiman-Marcus.*

Recommended reading, from any bookstore: *The Underground Shopper—Houston,* $3.95, which lists bargain stores in every category. This includes furniture, saddles, antiques, and flowers. It lists things for the baby, the bath, the kitchen, and the garden, and it tells where the best bargains are. You may have to hassle the Houston traffic more than you'd like, but in the end you should have found a great treasure.

Special suggestion: Do not plan to walk from store to store unless you have no streets to cross. Be prepared to move your car to each different shopping area, even if it is nearby. Parking is free, and the traffic is too heavy to deal with on foot.

DINING OUT. Houston enjoys an abundance of fine restaurants, but it isn't always easy to find them. As is everything else in this city, the excellent eateries are widely scattered across more than 550 square miles, and they're often situated in the most unlikely places, since Houston has no zoning. There is nothing to keep your next-door neighbor from tearing down his house and putting up a gas station or, for that matter, a restaurant. So don't be surprised if you stumble across a gourmet dining room in a little bungalow on a residential side street. At the same time, you're just as likely to find such a spot in some seedy strip shopping center, wedged between a grocery and a drugstore. (Many restaurateurs who flocked to Houston during the oil boom like sharks drawn to blood have moved on to other waters. If you visited a couple of years ago, don't necessarily expect your favorite restaurant to still be here.)

Many first-time visitors to Houston assume that the only restaurants worthy of serious consideration are those specializing in barbecue and Mexican food.

Well, if a person were to have but one meal here, it would be a shame not to enjoy a plate of smoked brisket or some *tacos al carbón.* But these regional specialties represent only a fraction of Houston's culinary offerings. As the city's fortunes have risen over the past dozen years, so too have the fortunes of the canny restaurateurs who cater to the increasingly sophisticated tastes (with one eye on the increasingly ample bank accounts) of the local elite. But you needn't be loaded to eat well in Houston. For every high-priced haven of haute cuisine, there are dozens of down-to-earth diners and burger joints, not to mention the ever-growing number of moderately priced dining establishments that turn out consistently fine fare. Additionally, over the past half dozen years, the number of excellent ethnic eateries has burgeoned, imparting a welcome international flair to the local restaurant community. All together, these places are spreading Houston's reputation as a restaurant town. Surely, he who is tired of eating in Houston has simply lost his appetite.

Price classifications and abbreviations. The price ranges given for the listed restaurants are determined by the cost of an average meal for one person, including appetizer, main course with vegetables, and dessert. Drinks, tax, and tip are **not** included in our ranges and will add to your tab. The tax on meals in Houston is 6%. An *Inexpensive* designation means a meal should run less than $10; *Moderate,* $10 to $20; *Expensive,* $20 to $30; *Deluxe,* $30 to $40; and *Super Deluxe,* more than $40.

Abbreviations for credit cards are:

AE—American Express
CB—Carte Blanche
DC—Diner's Club
MC—MasterCard
V—Visa

Abbreviations for meal codes are:

B—Breakfast
L—Lunch
D—Dinner

Always call first to double check hours of operation. Call to reserve at most expensive, deluxe, and super-deluxe places. Check then on the dress code.

AFGHAN

Moderate

Khayyam 2727 Fondren (Southwest); 974–6977. At lunchtime or during the evening rush hour, a drive from downtown to this far-southwest restaurant may seem as arduous as a trans-Asian caravan by camelback, but it's worth the trek. Specializing in the cuisine of Afghanistan, Iran, and the Arabian Middle East, the kitchen turns out an array of unusual and very good lamb dishes, as well as several more familiar kabobs. The juicy chicken kabob is particularly good. A delicious homemade yogurt is a key ingredient in many of the specialties here. D, daily. AE, MC, V.

AMERICAN ECLECTIC

Expensive

Cafe Annie. 5860 Westheimer (west of Galleria); 780–1522. In the sophisticated surroundings of this strip shopping center restaurant, the menu features unusual combinations and sauces laced with inventive genius and a high respect for the best of fresh food. Quite simply, one of the best chef-owned spots in town. L, Tuesday through Friday; D, Tuesday through Saturday. AE, MC, V, DC.

Confederate House. 4007 Westheimer (Highland Village); 622–1936. Surely this is the best place in Houston to sample that celebrated Texas delicacy the chicken-fried steak. This method of cooking steak (breaded and deep fried) probably originated as the poor man's answer to weiner schnitzel and is a time-honored way of camouflaging bad meat in countless roadside cafés. But that's not the case at the Confederate House. Their chicken-fried steak is fabulous, as are all the other steaks at this genteel, clubby restaurant near the exclusive River Oaks neighborhood. Fried shrimp are also noteworthy, as are the onion rings and French fries. The extensive wine list is especially strong on Californias. And be sure to leave room for a wonderful southern-style dessert: pecan fudge balls. L, Monday through Friday; D, daily. All major credit cards.

Harvey's. 2049 Richmond (Montrose); 520–0238. This comfortable, residential-style restaurant has a rotating blackboard menu that often features an exceedingly tender filet of beef in bearnaise sauce. Other specialties include snapper with shrimp and crab meat, Texas lump crab meat, trout Florentine, and breast of chicken sautéed with artichokes and vecherin cheese. Desserts are sublime; try the apple mousse or the Queen Mother torte. Fresh flowers and classical music add to the cozy atmosphere in this converted house. L, Tuesday through Friday; D, Tuesday through Sunday; Sunday brunch. All major credit cards.

Rainbow Lodge. 1 Birdsall (near Memorial Park); 861–8666. Despite an eclectic menu ranging from pasta primavera to game birds, the food at this in-town hideaway can't compete with the eccentric decor, which manages to be elaborate and rustic at the same time. With its secluded location and whimsical architecture, the Rainbow Lodge seems right out of some fractured fairy tale—and it's charming. Sit in the glassed-in dining room, order the dependably good sautéed liver, and enjoy your view of the dense woodlands along Buffalo Bayou. You'll never believe you're in the middle of the nation's fourth-largest city. L, Tuesday through Friday; D, Tuesday through Saturday. All major credit cards.

The Warwick Sunday Brunch. Warwick Hotel, 5701 Main (museum area); 526–1991. Watching people strut their Sunday best at the Warwick has become a Houston tradition, but don't let the local swells distract you from the matter at hand: a glorious monument to culinary excess. Buffet tables bend under the weight of enormous ice sculptures that loom over huge platters of shrimp, oysters, crab claws, pâté, and more salads than anyone could reasonably hope to sample at one sitting. Quite a spread, but go easy—the next room has the cooked-to-order omelets, succulent roast beef, and a dessert table. The rich, dark coffee may be the best in town. Sunday brunch, 11:00 A.M. to 2:30 P.M. All major credit cards.

Moderate to Expensive

Ouisie's Table. 1706 Sunset Blvd. (Rice University area); 528–2264. Ignore the feeling that you've wandered uninvited into a private party and find out why those hordes of casually stylish people continue to jam this trendy spot near the Rice campus. The answer is on the blackboard: the everchanging menu usually includes steak, chicken, lamb, seafood, and a vegetarian dish, but some things are better than others. The real standouts are the cold entrées. L, Monday through Saturday; D, Tuesday through Saturday. AE, MC, V.

Shanghai Red's. 8501 Cypress (on the ship channel); 926–6666. This Rube Goldbergesque restaurant-cum-warehouse in the heart of the city's industrial district may be the ultimate theme restaurant. It's very silly and very, very popular (expect a wait even with reservations). The price may be high for standard "surf 'n' turf" fare, but the real reason to come here is to get a good look at the ship channel. Houston has a closed (fenced) port, so this is about as close as you'll get without signing on for a stint in the Merchant Marine. The view is not pretty, but it does have a certain commercial-industrial charm. L, D, daily. All major credit cards.

Inexpensive to Moderate

Charley T's. 3700 Buffalo Speedway; 960–9711. A grilled veal chop that will melt in your mouth is a recent addition to a fine collection of steaks, shrimp, and chops that has to be rounded off with Charley's famous homemade butterfinger ice cream topped with chocolate sauce. L, Monday through Friday; D, Monday through Saturday. All major credit cards.

Paradise Bar and Grill. 401 McGowan (near downtown); 522–9509. Welcome to paradise. This curious eatery on the southern edge of downtown has the feeling of a renovated speakeasy: dim lighting, no windows, ragtime music. But the best part is the food, which is inventively prepared, invariably fresh, and very reasonably priced. Lunch features deli specialties; dinner specials include the Paradise burger (stuffed with bleu cheese) and chicken Morocco, cooked with yogurt and spices over an open flame. Service is winningly earnest. L, D, Monday through Friday. No CB.

TGI Friday's. 5010 Richmond (Magic Circle), and other locations; 627–3430. Anyone familiar with Manhattan's Upper East Side will recognize this bright blue building near the Galleria as a clone of one of the world's most successful singles bars. Well, one needs nourishment before a night on the prowl, and Friday's fills the bill with a formidable menu. You'll need a speed-reading course if you plan to read the entire menu before ordering. Burgers, potato skins, omelets, and salads are quite good. L, D, daily. All major credit cards.

The Wine Press. 1962 W. Gray (River Oaks); 528–6030. Favored dishes at this quietly elegant little dining room include chicken breast Monterrey, artichoke beef, and fettucine with shrimp and white sauce. The fresh-fruit offerings make a very nice lunch, and as you would expect, they have a wide selection of wines. L, D, daily. AE, MC, V.

Inexpensive

Antone's. 807 Taft (near downtown), and other locations; 526–1046. Exemplary po'-boy sandwiches (sliced loaves of French bread loaded with Italian cold cuts) make this ethnic grocery a popular noon-hour spot with downtown office workers. Take it to go or enjoy it out back in dilapidated "po'-boy park." L, Monday through Friday; open until 6:30 P.M. during the week, 7:00 on Saturdays; hours at other locations may differ. No credit cards.

Black-eyed Pea. 2048 W. Gray (River Oaks), and other locations; 523–0200. This Dallas-based chain successfully mass produces southern home-style meals. Chow down on meat loaf, chicken-fried steak, fried catfish, and black-eyed peas at any of five locations around town. This food is better than your mama would want to believe. L, D, daily. AE, MC, V.

Chili's. 1952 W. Gray (River Oaks), and other locations; 528–6443. Another down-home sort of place, Chili's is a block or so down the street from the Black-eyed Pea (and, again, at other locations about town). The emphasis here is on burgers and, you guessed it, a bowl of Texas red, with or without beans. As a matter of necessity, the draft beer is very cold. L, D, daily. AE, MC, V.

Frenchy's. 3919 Scott (University of Houston area), and other locations; 748–2233. Despite appearances, this is not just another fast-food outlet. The spicy fried chicken is better than you'd ever imagine and puts the Colonel to shame. Don't bother with the greasy French fries—move right on to the savory beans and rice or the pungent dirty rice (rice cooked with liver). Crumble some corn bread into the bacony mustard greens and enjoy a taste of heaven. L, D, daily. No credit cards.

Fuddrucker's. 3100 Chimney Rock (Magic Circle) and other locations; 780–7080. Yes, it's an ugly name, but they happen to produce the number-one contender for best burger in Houston. The secret just may be the fresh meat. Inside this large tin building (it looks sort of like a gazebo of the Titans) you'll see the glassed-in meat locker housing huge sides of beef about to be ground, grilled, and slapped onto a fresh homemade bun. Help yourself to the lettuce, tomatoes, and other garnishes (avoid the gummy melted-cheese sauce) and enjoy your burger out in the beer garden with an icy longneck. Fuddrucker's also serves steaks, hot dogs, and wurst. And just try to leave without sampling one of those huge brownies. L, D, daily. AE, MC, V.

Goode Company. 4902 Kirby (Rice Village area); 520–9153. Look for fairly standard American fare with a regional twist: burgers, chicken, fajitas, and hot dogs grilled over mesquite. Onion rings and fries, of course. L, D, daily. No credit cards.

Hobbit Hole. 1715 South Shepherd (River Oaks); 528–3418. Vegetarian items dominate the menu at this pleasantly laid-back establishment, though burgers are available for unregenerate carnivores. The colossal egg-salad sandwich, adorned with sprouts, sunflower seeds, avocado, and tomato on whole wheat, is certain to expand your Middle Girth. Other sandwiches are equally memorable, and the iced herb tea is a pleasant alternative to Lipton's. L, D, daily. AE, MC, V.

Longhorn Cafe. 2536 Richmond (Montrose) and other locations; 528–1260. Enjoy chicken-fried steak and other Texas specialties in an airy down-home atmosphere. There's a real fine country-style breakfast that includes the best hash browns in town and big flaky biscuits with cream gravy for dippin'. Just ask for the BDB—Best Deal Breakfast. B, L, D, daily. All major cards.

Old Bayou Inn. 216 Heights Blvd. (Heights); 864–7021. The kitchen still grills up the best cheeseburger in Houston at this comfortable neighborhood tap room. Order a basket of homemade potato chips and an icy brew, and kick back for a spell. L, D, daily. AE, MC, V.

Paulette's Restaurant & Oyster Bar. 2905–B Westridge off South Main; 666–6142. As the name suggests, here is the home of the ultimate fried oyster. Have it as part of the seafood special and you will partake of the finest in Texas and Southern cooking. Don't miss the gumbo. It's an experience in itself. L, D, Monday through Saturday. AE, MC, V.

Treebeard's. 315 Travis (Market Square, downtown); 225–2160. If you've never sampled Louisiana red beans and rice, get in line. This airy, cafeteria-style restaurant on Market Square serves up what's probably the best commercial version of this Cajun specialty to be found west of the Sabine River. L, D, Monday through Friday. AE.

Vie de France. 5085 Westheimer (Galleria II); 840–7227. Tromping around the Galleria for the afternoon can be wearisome. This bakery near Marshall Field turns its fresh French loaves into sumptuous sandwiches that will keep you on your feet for another round of conspicuous consumption. Try the roast beef, or a piece of quiche with soup or salad. The chocolate-and-almond croissants, by the way, are nearly irresistible. L, D, daily. No credit cards.

BARBECUE

Inexpensive

Gabby's. 9401 S. Main (Astrodome area), and other locations; 661–0957. Though Gabby's is a chain operation, the place has the look and feel of an old boardinghouse, which is fine by the patrons here, since the barbecue is a darn sight more acceptable than the victuals turned out by most chain restaurants. Not the best barbecue in town, but it'll do. L, D, daily. No credit cards.

Goode Company. 5109 Kirby (Rice Village); 522–2530. The walls of this chowhouse are so laden with Texana—from steer heads to tractor seats to rodeo posters—that it could damn near double as a junk shop. But the most authentically Texan thing about the place is the constant ching of the cash register. (The taped music places a close second.) Barbecued chicken is the best of the smoked meats here. The beans are the best in town. The pecan pie is the best in the world. That's a fact. L, D, Monday through Saturday. No credit cards.

Green's Almeda Barbecue. 5404 Almeda (near the Medical Center); 528–5501. This is barbecue with soul. While the sausage links may be too greasy for most palates, the ribs are sure to make a true believer out of anyone. For a "light" meal, try the chopped-beef sandwich. It's so greasy—and so good. L, D, Monday through Saturday. No credit cards.

John's Barbecue Stand. 1402 Crockett (near downtown); 223–5671. If Gabby's is masquerading as an old-time barbecue place, this is the real thing. John's has been around so long, some of the regulars even look smoked (you'll recognize them by the brown paper bags they tote in to the back tables). Smoked brisket and links are perfectly respectable here, but the best choice is either the ribs or (even better) the barbecued pork, which is relatively hard to find in Texas. The finely shredded cole slaw is a favorite among many good side dishes. B, L, D, Monday through Friday. No credit cards.

Luling City Market. 4726 Richmond (Magic Circle); 871–1903. Roy Jeffrey cooks *the best* barbecue in Houston right here. Roy learned how to smoke meat at the original Luling City Market in Central Texas, an area that's justly famous for its good barbecue. And now that Roy has forsaken Central Texas, plenty of barbecue-loving Houstonians hope he'll never go home. The ribs are rich and succulent; the mildly spicy links plump and moist; the lean beef brisket a sheer marvel. Ask the cutter to slice you some "outside" beef, the dark brown crusty part. The smoky taste reveals the secret of truly good barbecue—it doesn't need sauce. Nonetheless, you'll find a bottle of Roy's piquant sauce on every table, just in case you care to liven things up a bit. As if all that weren't enough, the beans, cole slaw, and potato salad are exemplars of their kind, there's a full bar, and iced tea refills are free. L, D, Monday through Saturday. AE, MC, V.

Luther's. 1100 Smith (downtown), and other locations; 759–9748. Another good chain operation, Luther's has outlets at half a dozen spots around town serving up your standard Texas-style beef barbecue with all the fixin's. The location near the main library is convenient if you're anywhere downtown. L, D, daily; downtown location closed weekends. No credit cards.

Matt Garner's. 138 West Gray (near downtown); 527–8488. The original 4th Ward establishment on this site burned several years ago. It was a classic East Texas-style barbecue joint. The rebuilt Matt Garner's has an expanded menu that includes burgers and baked potatoes. It might not be as authentic, but we're glad it's back. L, D, Monday through Saturday. AE, CB, DC.

Otto's. 5502 Memorial at Reinecke (near Memorial Park); 864–2573. Otto's is a sentimental favorite among Houston barbecue aficionados, but that sentiment is backed up by years of good eating. The brisket is consistently moist and flavorful. Try it sliced on a sandwich with a side order of slaw topped with sliced jalapeños (which you serve yourself)—it's the classic Houston lunch. L, D, Monday through Saturday. No credit cards.

CHINESE

Expensive

Uncle Tai's Hunan Yuan. 1980 Post Oak Blvd. (Magic Circle); 960–8000. There's still a restaurant of the same name on New York's Upper East Side, but Uncle Tai is in the kitchen of his Houston outpost (which is now his headquarters). Since his arrival several years ago, the Uncle has secured his reputation here with such Hunanese specialties as stir-fried duck with young ginger, scallops with garlic sauce, and hot-and-sour fish broth. L, D, daily. AE, DC.

Moderate to Expensive

Dong Ting. 2727 Fondren (southwest); 527–0005. San Hwang, the owner of this handsome Hunan restaurant, is perhaps the most engaging host in Houston. He'll not lack for dinner guests as long as his kitchen continues to turn out such delectable dishes as lion's head (crab and pork meatballs) and Hunan peasant's delight, a blissful union of twice-cooked bean curd and pork with green onions. House specialties may be had at lunch for a reduced price, accompanied by hot-and-sour soup or salad, and rice. Peking dust, mingled layers of dried crushed chestnuts and whipped cream, is an ethereal dessert. L, Monday through Friday; D, Monday through Saturday. All major credit cards.

Inexpensive to Moderate

Shanghai East. 5015 Westheimer (Galleria); 627–3682. Another New York transplant, this Szechuan restaurant on the third level of the Galleria serves such provincial specialties as twice-cooked pork, shredded beef, and chicken with peanuts. L, D, Monday through Saturday. All major credit cards.

Inexpensive

Lucky Inn. 912 St. Emanuel (Chinatown); 228–1522. When it's the middle of the night and suddenly you've just got to have some chicken with snow peas or sweet and sour pork, this is the place. Lucky Inn has dependably good Cantonese fare, and it has it until 10:00 P.M. on weekdays and 3:00 A.M. every weekend. You can also get a good cheap lunch cafeteria-style on weekdays. L, D, daily. AE, MC, V.

DELICATESSEN

Inexpensive

Butera's. 5019 Montrose (museum area); 523–0722. With an ample dining room and tables out front under an awning, Butera's lines 'em up and packs 'em in every weekday at noon. A variety of sandwiches are made each day, but if you don't see what you want on the counter, just ask and they'll make it for you if the ingredients are on hand. The real calling card here is the wide selection of soups (occasionally overspiced) and salads (often underspiced). Try the green-bean salad with tomato and onion or the broccoli-cauliflower combo. Butera's has a wide selection of imported beers and wines at reasonable prices. L, daily; D, Monday through Friday till eight. AE, MC, V.

New York Coffee Shop. 9720 Hillcroft (southwest); 723–8650. Expatriate New Yorkers flock to this pleasant coffee shop on weekend mornings to enjoy lox, eggs and onions, hot bagels with cream cheese, and other well-prepared deli-style favorites. It may be a long drive home, so pick up some bagels to go on the way out. B, L, daily. No credit cards.

Nielsen's. 4500 Richmond; 963–8005. Also 4500 Montrose (museum area); 520–7475. The Richmond location is new for this old friend, and you will keep coming back to this old-style deli for the tasty corned-beef sandwiches and creamy potato salad. If you're in a hurry, pick up one of the boxed lunches (a sandwich and a half, potato salad, brownies, and pickles). Richmond: 7:00 A.M. to 6:00 P.M. weekdays, 8:00 A.M. to 4:00 P.M. weekends; Montrose: 10:00 A.M. to 6:00 P.M. daily. No credit cards.

FRENCH-CONTINENTAL

Deluxe to Super Deluxe

La Reserve. Four Riverway, in the Inn on the Park (Magic Circle); 871–8177. La Reserve has established its reputation as one of Houston's very best dining spots, particularly for *nouvelle cuisine.* This elegant establishment also offers one of the best deals in the city: *Le Grand Menu.* You get seven courses—a selection of the chef's specials of the day, including two appetizers, two entrées (in smaller-than-normal portions), a salad, a cheese, and dessert. The pheasant mousse and sweetbreads are grand, and try the Napoleon when the pastry wagon comes around. L, Monday through Friday; D, Monday through Saturday. All major credit cards.

Le Restaurant de France. 400 Dallas, in the Hotel Meridien (downtown); 759–0202. This was the first of the *serious* hotel restaurants in Houston. If the name didn't give you a clue, food *is* taken very seriously here. But taste the gorgeously arranged buttery lobster salad and you'll see why. This is food that commands respect. The *nouvelle* sauces are miraculous; the duck dishes, especially the terrine, altogether distinguished. If you come on an expense account, you'd better clinch the deal or be on very good terms with your accounting department. *Prix-fixe* meals are offered. L, Monday through Friday; D, Monday through Saturday. All major credit cards.

Tony's. 1801 S. Post Oak (Magic Circle); 622–6778. Tony's has long had a reputation as the best restaurant in Houston. It just may be, though in the past few years it's acquired some stiff competition (Le Restaurant de France, for instance). Still, this is the place to dine if you hope to parley with the powerful, hobnob with the *haut monde,* blend with the big shots. Of course, it helps if you *are* a powerful big shot. The regular patrons get extremely attentive service, and it has on more than one occasion been at the expense of those outside their elite circle. That rather large caveat aside, a meal at Tony's can be exceptional. The secret to a superior meal? Dispense with the menu and ask your captain for his suggestions; several very good pasta dishes don't even appear on the menu. In fact, any unlisted special is likely to be just that—special. If it all becomes a bit overwhelming, remember: The grilled veal chop is stupendous, and the ambrosial raspberry soufflé would get a banker into heaven. L, Monday through Friday; D, Monday through Saturday. All major credit cards.

Deluxe

Maxim's. 3755 Richmond (Greenway Plaza); 877–8899. This eccentrically luxurious restaurant has been a local favorite for years, first downtown but more recently in the suburban climate of Greenway Plaza. The style of cooking is French Creole, and the most notable specialties are the crab dishes. Try the Charlie Bell salad made with lump crab meat, or the delicious crab meat with brown butter. L, Monday through Friday; D, Monday through Saturday. All major credit cards.

Expensive

Brennan's. 3300 Smith (near downtown); 522–9711. No longer connected to the famous New Orleans French Quarter restaurant of the same name, Brennan's has a pleasing *vieux carre* atmosphere. Unfortunately, the food is not always up to expectations, but the simple dishes, such as steak Diane, are fairly dependable. On Saturdays, the jazz brunch adds to the New Orleansy flavor. L, Monday through Friday; D, daily; Brunch, Saturday and Sunday. All major credit cards.

Café Moustache. 4702 Westheimer (Magic Circle); 621–6281. First-rate omelettes are a specialty at this attractive bistro near the Galleria. Crepes, quiche, and steak with very good *pommes frites* are other popular items on the menu. The management is considerate enough to provide chamber music and copies of *The New York Times* at the Sunday brunch. L, D, Monday through Saturday; Brunch, Sunday. All major credit cards.

Chez Eddy. 6560 Fannin (Medical Center); 790–6474. Who says French food can't be good for you? In the heart of the Medical Center, this elegant restaurant features low sodium–low fat *nouvelle cuisine.* The fruit-and-yogurt dessert creations are better than anything this healthful has any right to be. L, Monday through Friday; D, Monday through Saturday. AE, MC, V.

Fuad's. 6100 Westheimer (southwest); 785–0130. This quasi-plush restaurant offers a number of Lebanese specialties along with the more conventional Continental fare. Veal à la Fuad—in a cream sauce with artichokes—is a notable feature of the menu. L, Monday through Friday; D, daily. All major credit cards.

GERMAN

Inexpensive

Bavarian Gardens. 3926 Feagan (Heights); 861–6300. This German beer hall serves up hearty renditions of wiener schnitzel, sauerbraten, and various sausages. Side dishes include formidable potato pancakes and zesty red cabbage. The resident oompah band does its most interesting work with cowbells and the large, mournful-sounding alp horns. During Oktoberfest (all month long) the outdoor *Biergarten* is packed with singing, swaying, dancing revelers. L, Monday through Friday; D, Monday through Saturday. No CB.

INDIAN

Inexpensive to Moderate

India's. 5704 Richmond (southwest); 266–0131. Houston is blessed with several fine Indian restaurants; this is one of the best. Tandoori chicken, boneless chicken *tikka,* and *nan* (a delicious flat bread) are among the treats that come from the clay tandoori oven. Other noteworthy specialties: *rogan josh* (lamb cooked in yogurt) and *sag paneer* (an amazing and wonderful sort of creamed spinach cooked with large chunks of a mild white cheese). Weekdays, enjoy an all-you-can-eat buffet at lunch for $6.95. L, D, daily. All major credit cards.

Taj Mahal. 8328 Gulf Freeway (southeast); 649–2818. Situated in an area not known for its stellar restaurants, the Taj Mahal is a great place to stop for dinner on your way out to Gilley's if you're interested in a real transcultural experience. The food is excellent, with a menu very similar to India's (the owner of India's and some of the kitchen staff are Taj Mahal alumni). The lunch buffet is a real bargain at $5.95. L, D, Tuesday through Sunday. All major credit cards.

ITALIAN

Moderate to Expensive

Damian's. 3011 Smith (near downtown); 522–0439. This welcome addition to Houston's growing list of good Italian restaurants won't disappoint. For starters, sample the *Gnocchi Verde* (spinach dumplings with tomato and cream sauce) or the *Calamari Fritti* (fried squid). The *Taglierini BRV*—white, red and green pasta topped with cheese, mushrooms and zucchini—may be the perfect Italian dish. Popular entrees include *valigetta* (a suitcase of veal scallopini stuffed with fontana cheese and eggplant) and *involtini di pollo* (breast of chicken stuffed with Italian sausage and sauteed in wine). L, Monday through Friday; D, Monday through Saturday. All major cards.

D'Amico. 2407 Westheimer (near River Oaks); 524–5551. Veal and fish are very good at this restaurant, but the real forte is the pasta dishes. Straw and hay, green and white fettucine in a subtle cream sauce, is highly pleasing. Tortellini alla Genovese, delicate stuffed pillows of green pasta in a cream sauce with peas and prosciuto, is exquisite. Obviously, this is not a spaghetti house. Pasta dishes are designed as first courses; the portions will be a bit dainty for most appetites if that's all you order (though larger portions may be had). The dessert cart? Delightful decadence on wheels. Service ranges from snooty to rude, but with food this good, that's usually just a minor annoyance. L, Monday through Friday; D, nightly. All major credit cards.

Moderate

Nino's. 2817 W. Dallas (Montrose); 522–5120. A popular neighborhood restaurant, Nino's draws a large lunchtime crowd from nearby downtown. Standard Italian dishes are generally the best bet: Spaghetti with tomato sauce, meat sauce, or simply butter and garlic is dependably good; the hearty lasagna is tasty and filling. This is not food of great distinction, but most days it fills the bill very well, *grazie.* L, Monday through Friday; D, Monday through Saturday. All major credit cards.

Inexpensive

Allegro. 2407 Rice Blvd. (Rice University area); 528–2409. This bakery in the Rice Village has become a real hot spot among the city's yuppies, and not without cause. The outdoor tables are just right for lingering over croissants and coffee. A menu of more substantial cold plates and salads offers sustenance for extended afternoons of people watching. The mint chicken salad in half a cantaloupe is a standout. L, daily; D, Tuesday through Saturday. AE.

Italian Gardens. 7500 Bellaire (in the Sharpstown Center, southwest); 995–0778. Who would believe that good cooked-to-order Italian food could be turned out just as quickly as burgers and fries? Well, they do it at this Sharpstown fast-food counter. As you step up to place your order, you'll notice a machine turning out fresh pasta; you have a choice of spaghetti or fettucine. Move on to the salad bar, and by the time you're finished loading up your bowl, the pasta is ready to serve with your choice of sauce: tomato (spicy or mild), meat, meatball, clam, mushroom, or marinara. L, daily; D, Monday through Saturday. No credit cards.

Lalo's Pizza. 6060-A W. Bellfort (southwest); 995–5312. An Argentine pizza place? One visit is all it takes to convince even the most skeptical. All pizza joints should be this good. Try Lalo's special (sliced ham, double cheese, olives and sweet red peppers) or the Sugazzeta (onions, olive oil and double cheese). You'll go home a beliver—this is the best pizza in town. If you're in an adventurous mood, try the appetizer called Matambre. The primary ingredients are lean roast beef and garlic. Now you know what makes the gauchos so tough. L, Tuesday through Saturday; D, Tuesday through Sunday; no credit cards.

MEXICAN

Inexpensive to Moderate

Armando's. 1811 S. Shepherd (Montrose); 521–9757. Though it's right next door to a Taco Bell, the food at this pleasant restaurant is light-years away from your basic burrito and beans and is about as close as Mexican cooking gets to being light and healthful. The menu has expanded to include steak and shrimp, but Armando's made its reputation with a variety of inventive chicken dishes. The chicken enchiladas are ever popular, and with good reason. The location is right across the street from the Comedy Workshop. L, Monday through Friday; D, Monday through Saturday. All major credit cards. It even has valet parking, surprising for a restaurant with prices so reasonable.

Merida. 2509 Navigation (north side), and other locations; 227–0260. Taking its name from the capital of Yucatán, Merida specializes in the cuisine of that southeastern region of Mexico. Order special No. 1, *cochinitas pibil,* a marinated pork roast, served with rice, black beans, onions, and soft flour tortillas. L, D, daily. All major credit cards.

Ninfa's. 2704 Navigation (north side), and other locations; 228–1175. Ninfa's is a treasured Houston institution. Every Houstonian over the age of four knows the stirring tale of how the widowed Mama Ninfa and her five children turned their struggling northside cantina (formerly a tortilla factory) into a prosperous statewide restaurant empire. They didn't do it by mouthing corny homilies about the American Dream, but by developing an extensive, creative menu.

Tacos al carbón (aka *tacos a la Ninfa*), charbroiled beef wrapped in soft flour tortillas, are marvelous and made the place famous, but that's just the beginning. Some of the specialties here will forever disabuse epicurian snobs of the faulty notion that Mexican food is just a greasy, lowborn novelty. *Pechugas de pollo,* savory, marinated chicken breasts, are light but very satisfying. Tender chunks of deep-fried pork, called *carnitas,* served with sour cream and an explosive green chile sauce, are equally hard to pass up. Stay away from the Tex-Mex items, crispy tacos and such—they're fine, but you can get that sort of thing anywhere—and stick with Mama's special dishes, some of which aren't even on the regular menu. Ask your waiter about *alambre abrigado,* a sort of shish kebob of beef, ham, onions, peppers, and tomatoes chopped and rolled into flour tortillas; or *queso al suizo de pechuga,* tortillas stuffed with chicken and melted Swiss cheese. If you'd care to sample the *chilpanzingas,* ham and cheese turnovers with a fiery afterburn, give the kitchen a day's advance notice so they can prepare the special corn-meal mixture that's needed. But one of the best things here is free and arrives on your table as soon as you sit down—fresh, hot tortilla chips served with little pitchers of red and green sauces. The green sauce is a creamy miracle, the possible ingredients of which offer a subject for continuing debate. Ninfa's no longer has the cachet of the out-of-the-way eatery known only to the cognoscenti, but it's impossible to keep food this good a secret. L, D, daily. All major credit cards.

Primo's. 519 Rosalie at Smith (near downtown); 528–9158. Also 77 Harvard at Washington (Heights); 862–0766. Tex-Mex items abound on the menu, but the reason to eat at Primo's is the best Mexican-style steak in town. Called *fajitas,* this marinated skirt steak is thick, juicy, and comparatively tender. (This is never a particularly tender cut of meat, and in many restaurants it is served dry and rather tough.) The *carne guisada,* stewed chunks of beef in a spicy tomato sauce, is also quite good. L, D, daily. AE, MC, V.

Spanish Village. 4720 Almeda (near the Medical Center); 523–1727. This restaurant is in a somewhat marginal neighborhood but continues to draw large and festive crowds for both lunch and dinner. The food is greasy but quite tasty and filling. The cheese-and-onion enchiladas are classics. L, D, Tuesday through Saturday. No credit cards.

Tila's Cantina. 616 Westheimer (Montrose); 520–6315. The combination of fresh ingredients and inventive recipes gives Tila's real flair. The Mexican/New American Cuisine is served up in an art deco-ish building with a great view of the notorious Westheimer strip. L, Tuesday through Sunday; D, daily. AE, MC, V.

Inexpensive

Cortes Meat Market and Delicatessen. 2404 W. Alabama (Kirby); 522–7771. This tiny lunch counter–dining room between trendy Montrose and exclusive River Oaks serves up generous plates of sturdy Mexican food, including beef tips with rice and beans, Tampico crepes with lobster sauce and guacamole, and beef or bean tacos. This is also a popular spot on weekend mornings for Mexican breakfasts. B, L, Tuesday through Sunday; D, Tuesday through Friday. No credit cards.

The Last Concert. 1403 Nance (north side); 226–8563. This really is one of those places where you don't go for the food. Your choice is simply between the large dinner and the small dinner, neither of which is that great (the cold Mexican beer and tortilla chips seem a reasonable alternative). No, the reason you go there is because it's one of those quaint, unmarked little dives where you actually knock on the door to get in and they check you out through a peephole. Tell 'em Juan sent you (just kidding). A note of caution: This is in a fairly rugged neighborhood. L, Tuesday through Friday; D, Tuesday through Saturday. No credit cards.

MOROCCAN

Moderate to Expensive

Casablanca. 14025 Memorial (Memorial); 531–9060. This well-decorated restaurant surely seems authentic: You sit on the floor and eat with your fingers. (Yes, there is a belly dancer.) Main-course selections include quail, shrimp, veal, lamb *cous-cous,* and a commendable Cornish hen served with preserved lemon or a honey-and-garlic sauce. All meals have five courses and include soup, marinated vegetables, and *b'stilla,* a delicious, flaky pastry filled with chicken and nuts and dusted with confectioner's sugar. D, Monday through Saturday. AE, MC, V.

SEAFOOD

Expensive

San Jacinto Inn. San Jacinto Battleground; 479–2828. A trip to the San Jacinto Inn will teach you a lot about Texans. How we came to be? Tour the battle grounds; this is where we won independence from Mexico. How we got so rich? Check out that maze of refineries along the road as you drive out here from in town. Why we stay here? Finish your dinner of fresh Gulf seafood and fried chicken and see if you feel like moving. Meals are served family-style in this huge, airy dining room. The quantity of food tends toward the excessive, but that's Texas. L, Sunday; D, Tuesday through Sunday. All major credit cards.

Moderate to Expensive

Bayou City Oyster Company. 2171 Richmond; 523–6640. Fresh oysters on the half-shell are just the start of a fine meal here. Or maybe you would prefer an unusual version of oysters Rockefeller loaded with bacon but little spinach. There are grilled seafood dishes as well. L, D, daily. All credit cards accepted.

Don's. 3009 S. Post Oak (Magic Circle); 629–5380. The large numbers of people packed into the oyster bar and waiting for a table at Don's should tip you off: This restaurant serves some of the best seafood in town. The Louisiana-style specialties include seafood gumbo, crawfish étouffée, fried catfish, and stuffed shrimp. For such a noisy, crowded place, Don's is awfully comfortable, thanks largely to the very friendly service. L, D, daily. All major credit cards.

Magnolia Bar and Grill. 6000 Richmond (southwest); 781–6207. Enjoy a dozen fresh oysters shucked to order while you make up your mind. It's not easy choosing among the Cajun seafood dishes. Crawfish are available in season (December through June), but don't forget the frog legs, shrimp and soft-shelled crab. L, D, daily. All major cards.

Moderate

Captain Benny's Half Shell. 7409 S. Main (between the Medical Center and the Astrodome), and other locations; 795–9051. There are no tables in this tiny boat-shaped building, so elbow your way up to the bar and holler out your order for a dozen of the best oysters in Houston, fresh from Matagorda Bay. And if you've never tried catfish, please don't miss this chance. You'll wonder how anything with whiskers could taste so good. L, D, Monday through Saturday. No credit cards.

Mr. Whipple's from South Louisiana. 5621 Beechnut near Hillcroft (in the Maplewood Shopping Center, southwest); 771–2968. Cajun cooking is the attraction at this curious little place. Try the hot boiled shrimp, the oyster loaf (a French loaf scooped out and stuffed with fried oysters), and the fried catfish. L, D, Monday through Saturday. AE, DC, MC, V.

Inexpensive

Glatzmaier's Seafood Market. 809 Congress (on Market Square downtown); 223–3331. This noisy, cafeteria-style fish house is a fun lunch spot, especially when Big Joe Danza is over in the corner pounding on the piano. When things quiet down, the atmosphere in this antique room with its churning ceiling fans is remindful of a lazy afternoon in some French Quarter oyster bar. Generous plates of fried fish with a crispy corn-meal batter draw long lines every weekday. The broccoli with cheese and "Mama's potatoes" may just be the best steam-table vegetables ever. L, Monday through Friday. No credit cards.

STEAK

Deluxe

Brenner's. 10911 Katy Freeway (northwest); 465–2901. This homey little steakhouse on the I–10 East access road (take the Wilcrest exit about a dozen miles west of downtown and make a U-turn back toward the east) is pretty special. It serves the best steaks in Houston, and perhaps the world (partisans of Ruth's Chris Steakhouse will probably give you an argument). But the crispy-chewy German-fried potatoes with onions or the tart homemade Roquefort dressing alone would be reason enough to bestow world-class honors on Mrs. Brenner's kitchen. Service is very friendly. The woodsy dining room overlooks a peculiarly charming backyard diorama, which blocks out the view of the freeway. This may be the perfect Houston restaurant. L, Tuesday through Friday, and Sunday; D, Tuesday through Sunday. All major credit cards.

The Palm. 6100 Westheimer (southwest); 977–2544. This Houston version of the famous New York restaurant naturally serves up incredible steaks. The lobsters are large enough to be frightening, especially since you pay by the pound. L, Monday through Friday; D, daily. All major credit cards.

Ruth's Chris Steakhouse. 6213 Richmond (southwest); 789–2333. This New Orleans–style steakhouse is quite popular with people in the oil business, as evidenced by all the oil-company logos that adorn the place. Most steaks (as well as the side dishes) are large enough to feed two people. Feel free to divide an order or ask for a doggie bag. L, Monday through Friday; D, Monday through Saturday. All major credit cards.

Moderate

The Hofbrau. 1803 Shepherd (Heights); 869–7074. A local incarnation of an Austin institution, this funky steakhouse is something of a shrine for University of Texas graduates, apparently fulfilling some spiritual need between pilgrimages to the real thing. The steaks, cooked in lemon butter, may not be all that tender, but they are quite flavorful. And besides, this is a lot of fun. L, Monday through Friday; D, daily. AE, MC, V.

Steak and Ale. 5000 Richmond (Magic Circle), and other locations; 965–0351. A chain operation with outlets all over town, Steak and Ale serves decent steaks, prime rib, and lobster, but we mention it primarily because it's convenient. There was a time when they didn't serve ale, but that little problem of faulty advertising has been corrected since the Molson brewing company of Canada began distributing their products in the Lone Star State. L, Monday through Friday; D, daily. All major credit cards.

Inexpensive

Texas Tumbleweed. 1007 N. Gessner and other locations; 464–9507. Decent steaks cooked over mesquite and live country and western music are the primary draws at this chain establishment. L, Monday through Fridays; D, daily. AE, MC, V.

THAI

Inexpensive

Renu's. 1230 Westheimer (Montrose); 528–6998. Rated one of the best new restaurants of 1981 by *Esquire* magazine, this ambitious neighborhood favorite in the Montrose area continues to please, and educate, a devoted clientele. Favored dishes include: chicken with basil; tiger cries, morsels of rare beef to be dipped into a smoldering green chile sauce; *pad thai,* a wonderfully complex noodle dish that is more sweet than spicy; and *sate,* delicious little skewerfuls of pork, beef, or chicken served with a piquant peanut sauce that George Washington Carver would have been proud to claim. L, Tuesday through Friday; D, Tuesday through Sunday. All major credit cards.

Thai Pepper. 2049 W. Alabama (Montrose); 520–8225. This attractive newcomer is giving Renu's some healthy competition. Deep-fried cheese rolls served with a sweet sauce for dipping are an unusual appetizer. The lime beef, an incendiary salad of marinated beef, lettuce, tomatoes, onions, and peppers tossed in a spicy sauce is guaranteed to wake up your taste buds. Cool off with some coconut ice cream for dessert. L, Monday through Friday; D, daily. AE, MC, V.

VIETNAMESE

Inexpensive

Mai Que. 4404 W. Holcombe (near the Medical Center); 663–6544. Mai Que (pronounced "My Way") has dozens of Vietnamese specialties from which to choose on its menu. The noodle dishes are particularly good. The Vietnamese Muzak is definitely an acquired taste. L, D, Tuesday through Sunday. All major credit cards.

Viet Nam Kitchen. 2929C Milam (near downtown); 520–7106. This pleasant restaurant on the southern edge of downtown offers a varied and extensive Vietnamese menu. Some very good dishes are quite inexpensive, such as the *bun thit nuong* (charcoal broiled pork with vermicelli) and the *bun bo xao* (vermicelli with beef). Summer rolls (called *goi cuon*), shrimp, pork, vegetables, and vermicelli rolled in rice paper, make a nice appetizer for two. By all means have the iced French coffee for dessert. L, D, daily. MC, V, AE, DC.

Vietnam Restaurant. 3215 Main (near downtown); 526–0917. Imperial rolls and spring rolls, served with a cool plate of sliced cucumber, lettuce, mint, and other greens are just right for a light snack or as an appetizer. The crab dishes are among the proprietor's recommended specialties. L, D, daily. AE, MC, V.

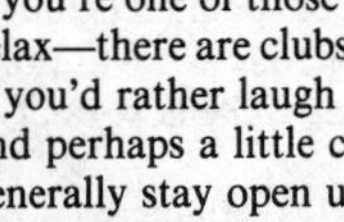

NIGHT LIFE. Houston's nightly entertainment choices are many and diverse. Our best-known night spot is certainly Gilley's, the honkytonk immortalized by the movie *Urban Cowboy.* Gilley's and the other country-and-western joints listed here provide entertainment and atmosphere that don't exist in many parts of the country; they're a part of our regional identity. But if you're one of those people who for some curious reason hates country music, relax—there are clubs aplenty that feature rock 'n' roll, jazz, disco, even comedy if you'd rather laugh than listen. Or if you're simply in search of a quiet drink and perhaps a little conversation, you'll find that as well. Bars and nightclubs generally stay open until 2:00 A.M., but a surprising number close at midnight; call and check if you plan to be out late. Many take credit cards, but again, call first if you want to avoid depleting your cash reserves. And remember: It may be a long drive back to your hotel, and it's a tough town in which to catch a cab should you find yourself a victim of intemperance. So watch your intake—you want to call the boss in the morning to tell him that he just acquired a new subsidiary, not that he needs to wire bail money.

COUNTRY-AND-WESTERN DANCE HALLS

Bill Mraz Ballroom. 835 W. 34th (North Heights); 862–5990. A Czechoslovakian dance hall with a dance floor the size of a basketball court. Sunday evenings are for country-and-western music; Saturdays for polkas and waltzes from the Bill Mraz Orchestra. Charmingly old-fashioned: You can ask a stranger's date for a dance without starting a fight.

Boomers. 1122 Uvalde at I-10 (east side); 451–2955. This dance hall on the east side of town has a DJ to spin your favorite Mexican music. It's still country and western—but *Mexican* country and western now.

Boot Kicker's Country Ball Room. 1231 South Gulf Freeway (I–45), League City; 338–1641. Live country music Friday and Saturday, with some of the area's better performers. Bring friends; there is room for 1,600.

Cow Palace. 12888 North Freeway (airport area); 876–9498. Not far from Intercontinental Airport and large enough to double as a good-sized hangar, this country-and-western disco has been known to bring in a live act on occasion.

Dance Town USA. 7214 Airline Drive (north side); 697–2083. Open Wednesdays, Fridays, and Saturdays, Dance Town sells beer, wine, and setups; BYOB if you want something stronger. Very good local recording artists, such as Mundo "You're in Love with the Wrong Man" Earwood and Dick "Go to Hell Ayatollah" Allen and the River Road Boys.

Gilley's Club. 4500 Spencer Highway, Pasadena; 941–7990. *Urban Cowboy* may have cast the national spotlight on this sprawling honkytonk (it once billed itself as the world's largest, an honor now claimed by Billy Bob's in Fort Worth), but Gilley's was a legend in these parts long before John Travolta learned to two-step. Aside from the busloads of tourists, things haven't changed that much. The atmosphere is remindful of a carnival or county fair; more people are lookin' for love than are lookin' for a fight, and some folks even bring the kids. You can still ride the mechanical bull, be a real man at the punching-bag machine, and play pool, pinball, and video games. Or you can dance to excellent music provided by some of the biggest names in country music. It's most fun when Mickey Gilley and his sidekick Johnny Lee take the stage (a fairly rare occurrence these days). Gilley is a topflight performer, travels with a fine band, and seems to enjoy strolling around the club chatting with fans between sets. As large as Gilley's is (about five acres), it gets crowded to the point of claustrophobia when popular fellas like Jerry Jeff Walker or Willie Nelson are in town. The latest addition to the Gilley's empire is a rodeo arena right next door to the club.

Hitching Rail. 12407 Robert E. Lee (northeast); 458–8811. Hunkered down by the C. E. King Parkway (the road to Lake Houston—call for directions), this dilapidated open-air hall is about as rustic as they come. The band will never make it to the Grand Ole Opry, but if you're out this way (about 25 mi. northeast of downtown, on the edge of the piney woods), check out this slice of Texana. Open Tuesday through Sunday.

Johnny Lee's Club. 7325 Spencer Highway, Pasadena; 479–9185. Now that Johnny "Lookin' for Love" Lee has quit his job in the house band at Gilley's and become a big star, he's gone down the street and gotten his own club. And it's a good one; much more intimate than Gilley's, Johnny's books rock-'n'-roll as well as country-and-western music. (And grateful boy that he is, Johnny is still found on occasion playing that big place down the street that gave him his start.)

Papa Blakely's. 21602 FM 1093 (west side); 342–9641. Head way out Westheimer (which becomes Farm Road 1093), and 7 mi. past Highway 6 you'll spot this big little house on the prairie off to your right. Unless it's raining, they've got the whole backyard for dancing. Open Wednesday through Sunday.

POP/ROCK/FOLK

The Ale House. 2425 W. Alabama (Montrose); 521–2333. This extremely casual music club offers everything from New Wave to funk, jazz fusion to rockabilly.

Anderson Fair. 2007 Grant at Welch (Montrose); 528–8576. Time stopped in 1967 at this Montrose-area institution. This home for aging hippies provides a stage for local folkies and touring legends such as Dave Van Ronk and Houston's own Townes Van Zandt.

Cardi's. 5901 Westheimer (southwest); 789–4111. Houston's self-proclaimed "one-stop-rock-shop," Cardi's draws a good-time crowd of working folk out to enjoy loud live music. Some nights you can get beer for a nickel before 9:00 P.M.

Caribana. 2413 Rice Blvd. (Rice University area); 524–6903. Houston's first reggae club brings those Jamaican rhythms to this sedate university area.

Fitzgerald's. 2706 White Oak at Studewood (Heights); 862–7580. Originally a Polish meeting hall, Fitzgerald's is host to some of the best up-tempo rock and blues on the Gulf coast and regularly features the New Orleans sounds of the Neville Brothers, the Nuevo Wavo music of Joe King Carasco, and such dissimilar types as fiddler Vassar Clements and New Wave instrumentalists the Raybeats. The stage acts perform upstairs. Downstairs is a comfortably time-worn neighborhood bar.

The Parlor. 2402 Mandell (Montrose); 529–8069. A comfortable tavern with interesting carved-wood walls and soft folk music. Sunday is amateur night. Wednesday is Irish night and very informal—bring your instrument if you think you can cut it.

Paul Berlin's Club. 6130 Richmond; 266–5696. Return to the days of the Big Bands, the jitterbug, the swing, and musical spoons. Sixteen-piece bands play Friday and Saturday, when a cover charge of $5.50 is charged. Open Tuesday through Saturday afternoons and evenings.

Rockfeller's. 3620 Washington (Heights); 861–9365. Housed in a grand old bank building, this can be the best music room in town if you choose your seat properly. Pay the few extra dollars to reserve a table downstairs in the center of the room. Some seats off to the side have an obstructed view; the sound is unpredictable in the balcony. This is *the* club for touring musicians. The diverse lineup runs from jazz to bluegrass and has in the past featured Stephane Grapelli, Buddy Rich, Flora Purim, the Pointer Sisters, David Grisman, Ricky Skaggs, Doc Watson, Jose Feliciano, Harry James, Herbie Mann, Dizzy Gillespie, Roy Orbison, Doc Severinson, Riders in the Sky, Delbert McClinton, and scores of others. The crowd here can be inattentive and overtalkative, which is annoying when you've paid up to $15 cover. There is a full bar.

Texas. 6106 Fairdale (southwest); 780–7034. Dance to country-and-western, rock, and pop music at this southwest-area nightspot. They have barbecue on Sundays.

JAZZ

Baxter's. 907 Westheimer (Montrose); 527–0595. Local and regional jazz bands play for a well-turned-out crowd at this tiny club on the Westheimer strip.

Cody's. 3400 Montrose (Montrose); 522–9747. About 2½ mi. from downtown, this glassed-in room and roof terrace atop a 10-story building offers the best view in town of Houston's changing skyline. It's also been home at one time or another for two of Houston's best young jazzmen: pianist Paul English and saxophonist Kirk Whalum. No cover; two-drink minimum. A fairly casual dress code (no sneakers, jeans, or T-shirts) is rather strictly enforced.

The Metropol. 1007 Waugh Drive (Montrose); 524–9840. The Metropol started out as a private club, but that idea didn't go over so well in egalitarian Houston. These days, anyone can drop in between Wednesday and Sunday to listen to Scott Gertner's contemporary danceable jazz.

DISCO/DANCING

The Copa. 2631 Richmond at Kirby (near Greenway Plaza); 528–2250. This shopping-center club has a mixed clientele of gay and straight dancers. Disco and rock 'n' roll blare from a very expensive sound system.

Fitzgerald's. 2706 White Oak; 862–7580. Rhythm and blues, new wave rock, and good times roll in this stylish club that gives no elbow room. Local and regional talent give great performances to enthusiastic crowds.

Fizz. 6400 Richmond; 789–7707. Video screens battle laser shows for your attention as the heavy rock beat goes on and the dancers writhe. Older folks will no doubt get dizzy here, but the yuppies and younger love it.

Mother's. 2775 Fondren (southwest); 782–6111. A DJ spins a selection of top-40 tunes that keep things moving on two dance floors. Mother's has plans to book some national bands.

Night Moves. 12845 Westheimer (west side); 497–2501. Much larger than you'd imagine from its shopping center facade. The dance floor is enormous—there's more than enough room for everyone to get serious about dancing to the country music.

Harrar's. 428 Westheimer (Montrose); 526–2895. This worthy Ethiopian restaurant transforms itself into a disco from 11:00 P.M. to 2:00 A.M. every night but Monday. The sound system packs a lot of punch for such a small place.

Numbers. 300 Westheimer (Montrose); 526–6551. This large disco on the Westheimer strip is something of an old established landmark in the heart of Houston's gay community. New wave music is the theme here.

Window. Westin Galleria Hotel, 5060 W. Alabama (Galleria II); 960–8100. On the 24th floor of the Westin Galleria Hotel, this rooftop hot spot caters to a very well-dressed bunch of young professionals. Though technically a private club, hotel guests are granted complementary membership. A one-night membership can be had for $5.

HOTEL AND PIANO BARS

Bistro Vino. 819 W. Alabama at Roseland; 526–5500. Windows of this old stucco home surround you as soft piano music soothes you in the setting of a French and Italian bistro and bar. An easygoing but elegant setting is topped with good food, served Monday through Friday.

The Black Swan. Inn on the Park, 4 Riverway (Magic Circle); 871–8181. This is just one spot in which to enjoy a drink in the elegant Inn on the Park, tucked away in its own quiet corner of one of the city's most rapidly developing areas. One may also imbibe at the Palm Court or the adjacent lobby piano bar.

Brittany Bar. Warwick Hotel, 2001 S. Post Oak (Magic Circle); 961–9300. Most of the public spaces in this I. M. Pei–designed hotel have a feeling of monastic simplicity, but this wood-paneled bar tucked off an interior court has an almost pub-like atmosphere.

Chaucer's. Plaza Hotel, 5020 Montrose (museum area); 524–3161. In the basement of the Plaza Hotel, this is a good place to relax after a round of museum touring and gallery hopping. Unlike most of Houston's hotel bars, this one is very casual.

City Lights. Stouffer's Hotel, 6 Greenway Plaza East; 629–1200. Who says it's lonely at the top? Join the gang at this watering hole on the roof of Stouffer's. Unfortunately, the view of southwest Houston is blocked in some directions by taller buildings.

La Colombe d'Or. 3410 Montrose (Montrose); 524–7999. This "European"-style hotel and restaurant occupies the old Fondren mansion. The Fondrens were one of the founding families of the Humble (now Exxon) Oil fortune. The atmosphere and the prices may be far from humble in both the wine bar and the Cognac lounge, but the selection of wines and Cognacs is indeed extensive.

Hunt Room. Warwick Hotel, 5701 S. Main (museum area); 526–1991. The bar of Houston's most traditional hotel; drinks are also served by the piano in the lobby.

The Irish Pub–Kenneally's. 2111 S. Shepherd; 630–0486. It is what its name says it is: a fine bar with dark wood, and brogue floats through the air. The live music is, of course, Irish. Open daily and no cover.

Le Nautille. Hotel Meridien, 400 Dallas (downtown); 759–0202. Partitioned off from the rest of the lobby with attractive carved limestone panels, this swanky little corner features a pianist on Saturday evenings.

Pierre's. Adams Mark Hotel, 2900 Briarpark at Westheimer (southwest); 978–7400. You'll find this hotel piano bar on the western edge of town featuring jazz sometimes, depending on who's playing.

The Roof. Westin Oaks Hotel, 5011 Westheimer (Galleria); 623–4300. On the 21st floor of the Westin Oaks Hotel, this is just the spot to hide out when the rigors of shopping become too much. If you're lucky, you might catch Kirk Whalum, Houston's hot young saxophone genius.

Shamrock Pub. Shamrock Hilton, 6900 Main at Holcombe (Medical Center area); 668–9211. Stop by for a drink and enjoy a stroll around this giant hotel. It was built in the late '40s by oilman Glen McCarthy, upon whom Edna Ferber based the character Jett Rink in *Giant* (played by James Dean in the movie).

Spindletop. Hyatt Regency, 1200 Louisiana (downtown); 654–1234. What booming Sun Belt city could live without a John Portman–designed hotel with a revolving bar on top? The downtown construction boom has eliminated the panoramic views in many directions, so drinkers now must content themselves with views of towering workaholics in the office buildings that surround the hotel.

Terrace Cafe. Four Seasons Hotel, 901 Austin (downtown); 650–1300. This handsome room trimmed in polished brass and etched glass serves a good drink and has entertainment by a jazz combo, sometimes the Rob Landus Trio.

Westheimer Pub. 9003 Westheimer (southwest); 784–4638. A large piano bar on the outer reaches of Westheimer Rd. that often features a three- or four-piece jazz combo.

COMEDY CLUBS

Comedy Showcase. 12260 Gulf Freeway (southeast, near Almeda Mall); 947–0823. Local and regional standup comics perform every night but Monday.

Comedy Workshop & Comix Annex. 2105 San Felipe at Shepherd (Montrose); 524–7333. The first and best of Houston's comedy clubs features original musical revues in the cabaret. Next door at the Annex standup comics do their stuff. Weekends are reserved for the pros. Earlier in the week, the old hands try out new material and fledgling funnymen find out that sometimes comedy is no laughing matter.

Laff Stop. 1952A W. Gray (River Oaks); 524–2333. This well-appointed club in the River Oaks Shopping Center hosts touring professional comics—not the big names, but the young Turks who are just breaking on to the talk shows. Magicians are also featured on occasion.

BARS. An appropriate place to start a Houston bar tour is **downtown** Market Square, *La Carafe,* 813 Congress (229–9399), occupies the oldest commercial building in town. It's been a stage-coach stop, an Indian trading post, and a brothel, though today your pleasures are limited to beer, wine, and an excellent jukebox with selections from most everyone from Piaf to Blondie. Across the square is *Warren's Inn,* at 316 Milam (226–9362). Warren's, too, has an entertaining, if somewhat eccentric, jukebox selection (Ed Ames! Cheryl Ladd!), but is best known for a curious affliction: a plague of bats. Really. But that was several years ago; the strangest creatures to hang out there recently have been the Urban Animals, a fierce-looking but fairly benign roller-skating gang. Among the more traditional bars in the downtown area are *Fat Ernie's,*

behind the Hyatt Regency at 500 Dallas (658–1802), and the bar at *Brennan's*, 3300 Smith (522–9711), which has a quiet New Orleansy courtyard and serves a well-prepared sazerac cocktail or milk punch.

A few miles to the northeast of downtown, across the bayou, are two notorious ship-channel bars. The *Athens Bar and Grill*, 8037 Clinton (675–1644), dispenses large volumes of retsina and good Greek food to homesick Greek sailors and the rest of a motley crew that enjoys belly dancing and jovial rowdiness. Right around the corner, at 2327 McCarty, is *Harbor Lights* (673–9221), a beacon for thirsty sailors and certifiable eccentrics since 1931. (If the lady dancing next to you has a tattoo, try not to gawk.) The decor includes a map showing Nevada whorehouses. This isn't the sort of neighborhood where you're likely to need such a map, but be careful unless you're really a tough customer.

MONTROSE

To the west of downtown, south of the bayou, is the Montrose neighborhood, which is often compared to New York's Greenwich Village. (The resemblance is more philosophical than physical.) Home of hipsters, gays, young professionals, blacks, chicanos, and rednecks, Montrose is the most diverse and tolerant of the city's neighborhoods. In the heart of this cultural melting pot is *Grif's Shillelagh Inn*, 3416 Roseland (528–9912). More than just another Irish bar, Grif's is the unofficial headquarters of Houston's most avid sports fans. After big games, you'd almost think you were in the locker room. Another Montrose-area taproom that's more than just another Irish bar is *Birraporetti's*, 1997 W. Gray (529–9191), in the River Oaks Shopping Center. It's an Irish bar that happens to be in the middle of an Italian restaurant. You try to figure it. Around the corner, behind the River Oaks Theater, is an unmarked door beneath a fire escape at 2006 Peden. This is *Marfreless* (528–0083), a lovers' hideaway full of cozy couches in secluded nooks. Taped classical music adds to the romance. Across W. Gray, still in the River Oaks Center, is the *Wine Press*, 1962 W. Gray (528–6030), where you can enjoy wine by the bottle or by the glass, a wide selection of beers, and any brand of Scotch you can name. Over on the south side of the neighborhood, *Zimm's*, a wine bar at 4319 Montrose (529–4600), offers more than 200 different wines and daily wine specials by the glass for those who wish to sample the grape in moderation. This, along with a few neighboring establishments, is the closet thing in Houston to a sidewalk café.

ICE HOUSES

Houston does have a traditional sort of drinking establishment not unlike the sidewalk café, but most of them have been around longer than the sidewalks. Ice houses are the humble forerunners of the convenience store (7-11 started out as an ice house) and date from the days when people bought big chunks of block ice to cool the icebox. On hot days the thoughtful proprietors of these establishments started a tradition by keeping a few bottles of beer on ice for thirsty customers. Refrigerators ruined the market for block ice, but there's still no better way to cool a brew, as any knowledgeable Texan will gladly tell you. You'll recognize an ice house by the open garage doors across the front that let in the breeze, usually a few picnic tables scattered around the yard, and perhaps a horseshoe game in progress out under the oaks. Though sober-minded prigs may look upon this noble institution and see only an all-day picnic for alcoholics, right-thinking people have widely hailed the ice house as the poor man's country club. One of the best is the *West Alabama Ice House* (528–9342), conveniently situated in the Montrose at 1919 W. Alabama, but you'll find others in any of the city's older neighborhoods. Near Rice University, at 2349 Bissonnet, is *Munchies* (528–3545), an ice house with a cosmopolitan twist: imported beer and live chamber music. Only in Houston.

THE GALLERIA AREA

If you'd prefer a more up-to-date spot to pursue your pleasures, head west to the Galleria area, where you'll find the greatest concentration of singles bars in the city. Behind the Galleria, in the 5000 block of Richmond, is the Windsor Plaza Shopping Center. At one end, you'll find *Friday's,* 5010 Richmond (627–3430), offering scores upon scores of specialty drinks at the raised bar in the center of the restaurant ("The better to see you, my dear"). At the far end of this strip center is *Cooter's,* 5164 Richmond (961-7494), which entertains a fun-loving crowd with ladies' nights on Mondays and Wednesdays, and two-for-one drinks on Tuesdays. Happy hour runs all the way from 3:00 to 9:00 P.M. during the week. Toward the center of the strip is *The Acapulco Bar,* 5050 Richmond (626–5990), which might remind you of your vacation in Cancun—though the management requests that you not wear your flip-flops. Nearby, you'll find *Faces,* 5134 Richmond (871–8780), which bills itself as a video dance club. The dance floor is backed by a 15-by-15-ft. screen that shows rock video tapes. And you might just find yourself the star of the video screen. Other area hot spots include: *Rialto,* 5351 W. Alabama (840–9720), a concept in singles bars called "adult playpen" (Remember those mobiles in your playpen? Look for motorcycles hanging from the ceiling); and *Remington Bar and Grill,* 4608 Westheimer (850–0451), a pueblo-style building where an upscale gang of singles mingles. A big farther afield, you'll find *Todd's,* 7901 SW Freeway (777–2527), one of Houston's oldest singles bars which attracts a young crowd with a DJ and top-40 format; and *Fizz,* 6400 Richmond (789–7707), immediately recognizable by the fake palm trees out front and distinguished by its late night breakfast extravaganza from 2:00 to 4:00 A.M. (The dress code is casual, but leave your faded jeans—"designer jeans preferred"—at home, along with your sandals, tennis shoes and shorts.) For gentlemen with no interest in meaningful relationships there's Houston's most notorious strip joint, *Caligula XXI,* 2618 Winrock (974–3867). The ladies at Caligula are skilled practitioners of a regional specialty known as couch dancing. How to describe couch dancing? Well . . . it's not for the germ conscious.

Southwest Houston probably has more bars per square mile than any other part of the city; naturally, not all of them are geared toward real or imagined couplings (though you never know where the magic will strike). *Houlihan's Old Place,* 1800 S. Post Oak (621–1740), is conveniently next door to one of Houston's first-run moviehouses and offers free hors d'oeuvres during happy hour, including an oyster bar on some days. Another popular happy-hour spot is a country-and-western disco called *San Antone Rose,* 1641 S. Voss at San Felipe (977–7116). Instead of a mirror ball above the dance floor, look for a lighted wagon wheel. The records, of course, are more likely to be by Waylon and Willie than by Donna Summer. But if you've had it with bars that follow one trend or another, drop in to the *Dark Horse Tavern,* 5706 Richmond (781–0322), a resolutely untrendy spot with more of a neighborhood feel than most of the bars in this part of town. A couple of blocks up the road you'll find the *Richmond Arms,* 5921 Richmond (977–8635), an English-style pub where Houston's expatriate Brits gather to throw a few darts. If you'd like to wind up the evening with even more of an "international" flair, venture on out to the 10000 block of Westheimer, where you'll discover the Carillon West Shopping Center, a Houston developer's vision of a quaint European village (complete with bell tower). Here you'll find *Sherlock's Baker Street Pub,* 10001 Westheimer (977–1857), and *The Great Caruso,* 10001 Westheimer (780–4900), where you can drink and dine while a troupe entertains with Broadway show tunes and light opera.

Still undecided? You can always pick up a six-pack and drive around. At the *Beverage Barn,* 9204 Richmond, between Fondren and Gessner (783–2407), you can drive the car right through the store and grab whatever you need, from milk to beer to a pint of your favorite. Cheers.

GALVESTON

by
FRANCES KAY HARRIS

Frances Kay Harris, a member of the Society of American Travel Writers, has been Travel Editor of the Galveston Daily News *for more than a decade and a half and does a daily forty-five-minute radio show that deals largely with travel. A longtime resident of Galveston, she is a graduate of the University of Texas and has been an actress on Broadway.*

Galveston Island has been a family resort as far back as the days when the Karankawa indians used to pile the wife and kiddies into their canoes and paddle the two miles from the mainland to hunt deer and fowl and to fish on the beach. At least, this is what they were doing in 1528, when the Spaniards first discovered the island.

As time passed, despite the overabundance of snakes, the rumors that the Karankawas were fond of human flesh, and the fact that the island lay in the path of virulent storms, it still attracted many folks from many flags.

In 1817 Jean Laffite established a full camp in Galveston, using it as a base during his privateering days. Privateering differs from pirating in that the privateer is authorized by his government to seize enemy ships, whereas a pirate is in business for himself and takes his loot indiscriminately. Laffite is reputed to have been a true patriot and not the villain some histories have made him out to be. It is still believed by some local optimists that he might have left a bit of his treasure buried under Galveston sands. A plaque marks the place where his house is believed to have been.

Although the island lived under only five flags (the French didn't make any effort to occupy the area), Galveston was active in shucking the rule of the Spanish, then of Mexico, and it assisted in the Texas War of Independence. Once the Republic of Texas was established in 1836, the city of Galveston applied for a charter.

In 1839 Michael B. Menard drew up plans for a city. The design makes it very easy to get around in Galveston to this day. All the streets running east and west are labeled alphabetically (Avenues B, C, etc.), and those going the mile and a half between the Gulf of Mexico to the south and Galveston Bay in the north are numbered.

A great deal of Galveston now dates from no earlier than the 1900 storm. In September of that year an unheralded hurricane and giant tidal waves almost demolished this thirty-two-mile-long sandbar. When the disaster was over, more than six thousand people were dead, the port was destroyed, and most of the island's buildings were rubble.

Nevertheless, the islanders rebuilt Galveston. A seventeen-foot concrete seawall was constructed to protect the city from the wave action of the Gulf. Behind this bulwark, with sand dredged from surrounding channels and bayous, the entire town was raised, from seventeen feet at the south-end side to about six feet near the bay. This included streets, pipes, and houses. It was a mammoth undertaking but proved as effective as hoped when in 1915 an even more powerful storm swept over Galveston and relatively few (275) lives were lost.

The first seawall was less than four miles long. Over the years it has been lengthened, until today it extends for more than ten miles from the east end of the island. It is the longest continuous sidewalk in the world.

Galveston has several names. It is called Treasure Island, thanks to Jean Laffite, and the Oleander City because every street and most yards have many bushes of the single-, double-, and triple-petaled blossoms, ranging in colors from an almost blue-white, through yellows, through a great variety of pinks, to deep reds. During April and May the entire city is ablaze with these brilliant blooms. Yet another name for Galveston is the Port and Playground of the South, because of the shipping business the city enjoys and because it is a resort offering much to see and do for the entire family.

Many visitors come to Galveston to take advantage of the rich fishing grounds. Free and commercial fishing piers reach out into the waters of the Gulf; surf fishing is very big on the beach; those who prefer deep-sea fishing in the bay and out into the Gulf can join party fishing boats or charter private yachts or smaller craft. Fishing tackle can be rented, bait bought, and the necessary Texas fishing licenses purchased at bait stores, at the commercial piers, or in the county courthouse. (Offshore fishing does not require a license.)

The beaches of Galveston are equally attractive to visitors. Texas beaches are almost all free to the public. At both ends of the island cars may drive to the water's edge on the sand, though in other areas this is not permitted, in the interest of safety. Certain sections of the beach are designated surfing areas. Some of the beach is patrolled; other parts have lifeguards in attendance at certain times. Both free and paid parking is available. Steps from the top of the seawall down to the beach are strategically spaced along the entire length. It is possible to park free on the boulevard and walk down to the sand.

Exploring Galveston

To get the most out of your visit to Galveston, make your first stop the American National Insurance Company's ANICO Tower at 19th and Market streets. This is Galveston's "skyscraper"; it rises 365 feet above Moody Plaza, just one block from the Strand. The observation area and archives are available to the public only through The Heritage Tour Service, provided by the Galveston Historical Foundation; tel. 762–TOUR. On a clear day one can see not only the layout of the city, but also more than thirty miles in all directions.

On the north side of the island, from 9th Street to 41st, is the harbor, which can accommodate more than a hundred vessels at one time. To the east is the University of Texas Medical Branch, which incorporates, in just the few blocks between 4th and 11th Streets and the Strand and the post office (Avenue E), the University of Texas Medical School (1881; oldest in the state), John Sealy Hospital, the Shriners Burns Institute, Graves Psychiatric Hospital, Ziegler Tuberculosis Hospital, St. Mary's Hospital, the Child Care Center, the Marine Biomedical Institute, the Learning Center, and the Texas Department of Corrections Hospital.

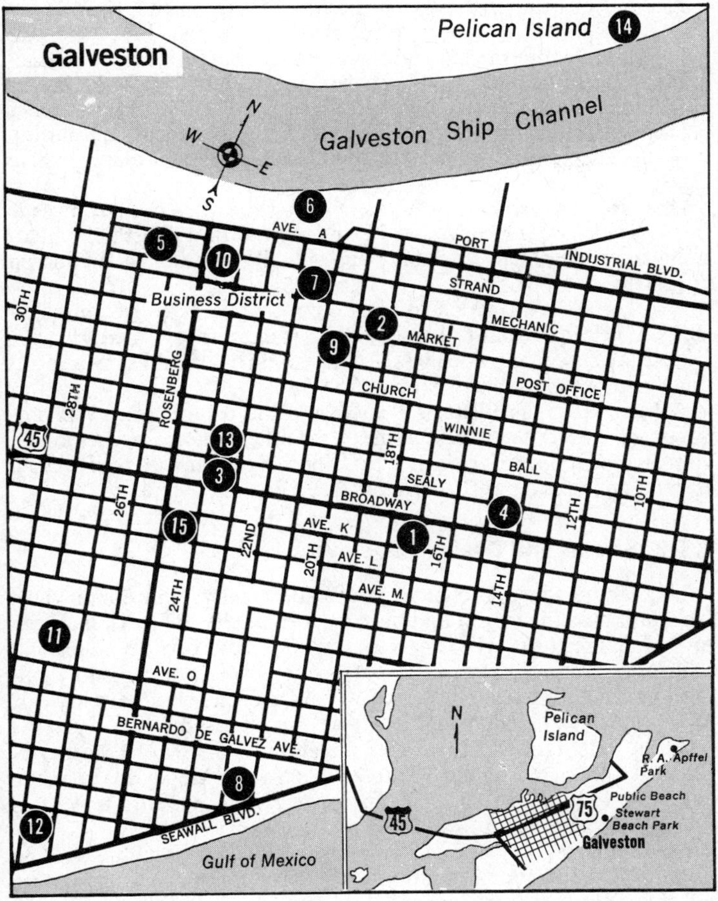

Points of Interest:

1) Antique Dollhouse Museum
2) American National Insurance Co. Tower
3) Ashton Villa
4) Bishop's Palace
5) Center for Transportation and Commerce
6) The Elissa
7) Galveston Arts Center
8) Galveston Convention and Visitors Bureau
9) Grand Opera House
10) Historic District
11) Kempner Park
12) Menard Park
13) Rosenberg Library
14) Seawolf Park
15) Sweeney-Royston House

Another orientation experience is the Treasure Island Tour Train. This is a pink, surrey-topped series of open cars pulled by their "engine" through both the old and the new parts of Galveston. The train goes through residential neighborhoods, where several historical homes are pointed out, passes the "Mosquito Fleet" at Pier 19, where an inner harbor is home for more than a hundred small fishing boats and shrimp trawlers, then wends its way to the Galveston Yacht Basin, where pleasure craft from all over the state are moored.

One other sightseeing trip will not only show the city, but provide transportation: "The Galveston Flyer," a motorized replica of an old-fashioned trolley, runs frequently and will allow you to get off and on at specific stops.

Another great attraction to Galveston is its large collection of restored nineteenth-century homes. Walk or drive through the Historic District. Maps are provided by the Galveston Historical Foundation at the Visitor's Center, 2016 Strand; 765–7834.

Ashton Villa, the Bishop's Palace, and the Samuel May Williams house are open to the public. Some of the other restored houses are on view at special times during the year. For more details see the *Practical Information* section on *Historic Sites and Houses,* below.

The Strand and Seawall Boulevard

The Strand, once known as the Wall Street of the South when Galveston was the largest and most important city in Texas, has been revived and restored. The iron-front buildings have been repainted and refurbished. The old stores and warehouses are now occupied by cultural and business establishments. Most are open seven days a week, offering marvelous opportunities to eat, browse, and buy.

At the foot of the Strand, at 25th Street, is the Center of Transportation and Commerce, a railroad museum at Shearn Moody Plaza, in the old Santa Fe train station. No expense has been spared to make this railroad museum one of the finest in the country.

Galveston's 1877 "tall ship," *The Elissa,* at Pier 22, is within walking distance of the Strand. A children's playground with its own miniature tall ship adjoins that museum. Tours include a film of the restoration project.

Seawall Boulevard is the avenue that fronts the Gulf of Mexico. On the south side is the seawall; on the north, between 4th Street in the east end and 95th Street in the west, are most of the hotels, motels, and condos in Galveston.

Along the north, or land, side of Seawall Boulevard are many restaurants, souvenir shops, and establishments where you can rent skates, surfboards, pedal surreys, and bikes by the hour or the day.

Activities and Amusements

The entire island is geared for family fun and entertainment. Stewart Beach Park, on the east beach at the foot of Broadway Boulevard, has a complete bathhouse, various rides, arcades, two water slides, and a miniature golf course.

Sea-Arama Marineworld is located at 91st Street and Seawall Boulevard. This is an entertainment complex not only for children. It features professional sea- and land-animal shows, water revues, and fine aquatic displays. To "do" Sea-Arama properly should take about three hours.

Entertainment is year-round in Galveston. During the summer the historical drama *The Lone Star,* by Paul Green, alternates with Broadway favorites at the Mary Moody Northen Amphitheater at Galveston Island State Park, FM 3005 at the 13-Mile Road. The Strand Street Theater, Galveston's only repertory theater, always has something on the boards. The Galveston Symphony Orchestra presents regular and pop concerts throughout the year. Dance programs and visiting artists also play Galveston. For times and places check with the Galveston Convention and Visitors Bureau, in the Moody Civic Center at 21st and Seawall Boulevard, where most convention activities are held; 763–4311.

Take a free ferry ride. The Texas Department of Highways and Public Transportation provides free ferry service between Galveston and Point Bolivar. The ferry connects with Highway 87 on the Bolivar Peninsula of the Texas mainland. The round trip should take about forty minutes. On summer weekends expect a 2 to 3 hour wait to board in your car. A more practical idea would be to park your car on the Galveston side, in the lot near the ferry landing, then walk aboard. The ride is smooth and colorful. The ferry passes small shrimpers and large cargo vessels from all over the world. Sometimes schools of porpoises accompany the ferry; seagulls always follow it. The ferry runs twenty-four hours a day.

Galveston offers something for everyone, from birdwatching and bowling to zooming down water slides. Rent a sailboat or motor craft, or water ski from Washington Park at 61st and Offats Bayou, where the boat launch is. Tennis and golf packages are offered by several of the hotels and motels. Ride a horse, or fish, or walk along the top of the seawall or on the sand down at the water's edge. Or just lie in the sun.

PRACTICAL INFORMATION FOR GALVESTON

HOW TO GET THERE. There are three ways to get to Galveston Island: two by land and one by sea.

By car or bus from Houston, Galveston is a 50-mi. drive on Interstate 45, over the double causeway into the heart of the city. At the western tip of the island a toll bridge spans San Luis Pass. This is for traffic to and from the southwestern Gulf coast.

Highway 87 crosses East Galveston Bay. This route from Port Arthur and the northeast-Texas mainland requires transport by a ferry operated by the Texas highway department between Point Bolivar and Galveston Island.

The driving times to Galveston from other cities, in hours, are: Corpus Christi 4; Houston 1; Dallas 6; San Antonio 5.

Bus. Transportation Enterprizes, 765–7731, operates service between Galveston and Houston.

Cruise ship. Several cruise lines use the port annually between mid-December and the end of March. Check with your travel agent.

Airport limousine. The Galveston Limousine Service runs shuttle vans between Galveston and Hobby Airport and Houston Intercontinental Airport approximately every hour and a half. The schedules and rates are listed in the clearly designated waiting areas at both airports. The elapsed time between destinations can range from one and a half to two hours.

Galveston has no train service and plane service comes and goes. Ask your travel agent to check.

TELEPHONES. The area code for Galveston is 409. You do not need to dial the area code if it is the same as the one from which you are dialing. However, it will be necessary to dial "1" first if you are dialing outside the city to the other 409 areas. Information for Galveston is 1411; information for outside the city is 1–555–1212. An operator will assist you on person-to-person, credit-card, and collect calls if you dial "0" first. If you are seeking information for a toll-free "800" number, dial 1–800–555–1212.

HOTELS AND MOTELS. There are many hotels, motels, and condominium suites to accommodate the tourists, but none can offer more than in-house swimming pools and temporary permission to play golf at the country club. Mobile-home parks and campgrounds are situated at both the east end and the west end of the island.

Hotel rates are based on double occupancy, European Plan (no meals). Categories, determined by price, are: *Expensive,* to $150; *Moderate,* $40 to $85; *Inexpensive,* $18 to $35. Most of the hotels are on Seawall Boulevard.

Flagship Hotel. 2501 Seawall Blvd.; 762–8681. On the beach side of the boulevard, the hotel is built on a steel pier that extends out over the Gulf of Mexico. Every room has a view of the sea and the city from its own balcony. Full-service facilities. The view is worth the stay. *Expensive.*

Marriott Hotel Galvez. 2024 Seawall Blvd.; 765–7721. A white, wedding-cake-type structure originally built in 1910. It faces the Gulf—as do most of its rooms—and is conveniently situated across from the Moody Civic Center. Full hotel services. No charge for children under 12 in the same room. Rates vary, depending on the time of year. *Expensive.*

The San Luis on Galveston Isle. 53rd and Seawall Blvd. 244 deluxe rooms, all with balconies overlooking the Gulf. Two restaurants, family plans available. *Expensive.*

Tremont House, 2300 Ship's Mechanic Row (one block off the historic Strand). 125 deluxe rooms and suites. Elegant. *Expensive.*

Hotel chains are represented by the following:

Airport Resort Inn, nr. Galveston Municipal Airport.

Econo Lodge, 61st near the Blvd.

Gaido's Motor Inn, 3800 Seawall Blvd.

Holiday Inn, one near the Yacht Basin and Medical complex in the east end, the other on the beach at 50th and Seawall Blvd.

Key Largo, 54th and Seawall Blvd.

Motel 6, 74th and Broadway on I-45 north side.

Quality Royal, 54th and Seawall.

La Quinta Motor Inn, 1402 Seawall Blvd.

Ramada Inn, 50th and Seawall.

Republic Inn, 61st and I-45 on south side.

There are many other motels. For extensive information ask the Visitor's Bureau at 21st and Seawall Blvd., 763–4311, for their brochure listing accommodations and prices. Reservations are recommended during the summer. In the winter many of the hotels and motels have rooms from $20 to $40. Vacation packages are offered year-round.

For longer stays and larger accommodations, several condominiums rent their rooms and suites by the day, by the week, and for even longer.

By the Sea, 7310 Seawall Blvd.; **Casa del Mar Hotel Condominiums,** 6102 Seawall Blvd; **Islander East Condominium,** off Seawall Blvd. on the east end of the island, on the sand at 0915 East Beach; **Victoria Condotel,** 6300 Seawall Blvd.; **The Galvestonian Condominium,** 1401 East Beach Blvd.; **Seascape Condominium,** 10811 San Luis Pass Rd.

On the other hand, if you would like to rent a house by the week or month, **Jamacia Beach,** 737–1044, **Pirates Beach** and **Pirates Cove,** 737–2771, and **Sand 'N Sea Properties,** 737–2556 and **Sea Isle,** 737–2750 all at the west end of Galveston, have such available.

Galveston now has seven bed-and-breakfast homes, or inns. Central information, and for reservations: 1805 Broadway; 762–0854.

GETTING AROUND. The city bus system is not satisfactory for tourist destinations; a car is a necessity to get around Galveston. If you did not bring your own car, rental cars are available from Avis, Budget, Hertz, National, and Thrifty in Galveston. See the Yellow Pages for offices and phone numbers. Taxis are plentiful; check the Yellow Pages and call for pick-up.

TOURIST INFORMATION. The *Galveston Convention and Visitors Bureau,* 21st and Seawall Blvd. (763–4311), is in the Moody Civic Center building, the site of most conventions and many civic and social events. It is open daily in the summer but closes on Sunday the rest of the year. It has a collection of free brochures, booklets, pamphlets, and listings of the sightseeing opportunities in Galveston. Of special interest is "So Much More to See and Do," which lists almost everything available to the visitor, and "Galveston Island Accommodations," in which the locations and rates are cited.

The *Strand Visitors Center,* 2016 Strand (765–7834), run by the Galveston Historical Foundation, is open seven days a week from 10:00 A.M. to 5:00 P.M. It has a fine collection of free information especially relating to the projects of the Foundation. Audio walking tours by portable cassette recorder are available. The center has a 24-page activity and guide book for children entitled *Strand Discovery Tour,* for $2. In this same center, arrangements may also be made to do a self-guided, taped tour. The guidebook and the tour are highly recommended.

Galveston Chamber of Commerce, 315 Tremont (23d St.; 763–5326), will also answer inquiries.

RECOMMENDED READING. *The Underground Guide to Galveston,* $4.25 at the Galveston Historical Foundation's Strand Visitors Bureau at 2016 Strand or at the Book Bag at 2301 Strand. You may order in advance from Aurora Press, P.O. Box 2181, Galveston, TX 77553. This 43-page booklet is full of suggestions on shopping spots, attractions, restaurants, and clubs and entertainment. The quality of the establishments is rated.

The Children's *Strand Discovery Tour* is now available at the Strand Visitors Center, 2016 Strand (765–7834) for $2. This 24-page activity book offers youngsters a fun-filled, easy-to-follow exploration of the Strand, the wharves, and the downtown area. Actually, no family should be without it. See the free film *Galveston–The Golden Age of the Gilded Isle* by Robert Cozens.

TOURS. The *Treasure Island Tour Train* departs from 21st and Seawall Blvd. alongside the visitors' bureau at specified hours during the year. Call 765–9564 or 744–1826 for schedules. Five trips go daily during the summer and two a day the rest of the year. The tours are of 1½ hour's duration, with commentary, passing through 17 mi. of old and new Galveston. The "train" consists of open cars, pink no less, with a fringe on top; 64 passengers can be accommodated.

The train rides along Seawall Blvd., passing the remains of Fort Crockett, which lived through two wars—though no shots were ever fired at it or from it in anger. It glides through typical neighborhoods, the historical district, the downtown business section, the Strand, and into the medical complex. (The University of Texas Medical Branch occupies more than 80 acres and comprises 53 buildings.)

It would be a good idea to take this tour before you begin sightseeing on your own; it will give you a clear idea of where everything is. Adults: $3.50; children 12 to 3: $1.75; kiddies 2 and under: free.

The Galveston Flyer, a trolley (really a bus designed to look like a trolley), leaves from 24th St. and Seawall Blvd., on the hour, from 9:00 A.M. to 5:00 P.M. daily. It makes stops at Ashton Villa at 24th and Broadway, at the Center for Transportation and Commerce, the railroad museum at 25th and Strand, continues down Strand to the visitors' center at 2016 Strand, remains on Strand to the east end, returns to Seawall Blvd., and makes the Galvez Hotel the last stop before beginning the run over again. Cost is $3.75 for adults; $2 for children. You may get on and off at your convenience at no additional charge. The tour is narrated.

Sightseeing Galveston Island by sea is also possible, at 10:00 A.M., 2:00 P.M. and 7:00 P.M. daily from June through September. The *Buccaneer,* at Pier 18 (763–5423), takes visitors on the two-hour narrated tour. She has a comfortable lounge, a snack bar, and a sun deck. Her journey passes the Mosquito Fleet and the inner harbor, where the fishing boats and shrimp trawlers return with their catches. More than 100 craft call this harbor home base. To see them at their best be at Pier 20 around sunset, when many boats come in. The *Buccaneer* points out Galveston's docks, the shipyards, Pelican Island, the Coast Guard station, the Galveston Jetties and the Galveston Yacht Basin. Adults: $5; children under 12: $3.

The Colonel, a 150-foot long paddlewheeler does tri-daily, narrated historical tours of the Galveston Bay harbor area. Evening: seafood dinner and jazz cruises. Call 763–4900 for times and prices.

Tours in Other Areas. A worthwhile off-the-island trip is a visit to NASA, 30 mi. northwest on I–45 at the Johnson Space Center in Clear Lake City, on NASA Rd. 1. It is open to the public from 9:00 A.M. to 4:00 P.M. daily. Guided tours are available if you make previous reservations; (713) 483–4321. Ask at the visitors center information desk for self-guided tour maps.

The *Lunar and Planetary Institute* is also in this area, at 3303 NASA Road One. Advance tour arrangements are necessary. Call 486–2180 between 8:30

A.M. and 5:15 P.M. weekdays. Drive west on I–45 to NASA Road One; take the off ramp, turn right, and stay on that road until you come to the space center. Direction signs abound.

SEASONAL EVENTS. The *Rainbow Festival on the Strand,* formerly called the Galveston Shrimp Festival, is held annually. It offers special entertainment events on the Strand. Arts and crafts and international foods are for sale. On Sunday the traditional blessing of the shrimp fleet boat parade is held. The shrimp trawlers are elaborately decorated and compete for recognition and honor. The blessing is done by several of the local clergy, who pray for a safe and productive harvest.

On the second and third weekends in May, the *Historic Homes Tours* are conducted. This is a project of the Galveston Historical Foundation. The tour features private homes that are not otherwise open to the public.

Mardi Gras is celebrated with parades and festivities during the week preceding Ash Wednesday. This year the dates are Feb. 2–10.

The *Dickens Evening on the Strand* is really a weekend. During those two days on the first weekend in December the Strand re-creates an authentic Victorian holiday street scene. This outstanding winter event is sponsored by the Galveston Historical Foundation. Call 765–7834.

PARKS. At the eastern end of Seawall Blvd., down the ramp and on the sand, is *Apffel Park,* on Boddecker Dr. The park has boat-launching facilities, jetty and surf fishing, bait camps, restaurants, a recreation pavillion with concessions and gift shops.

Stewart Beach Park, 4th St. on the sand, has a complete bathhouse, an amusement park with rides, a skating rink, a miniature golf course, and water slides. See the *Children's Activities* section, below, for hours and prices.

Menard Park, between 28th and 27th Sts. and Ave. Q and Seawall Blvd., a small, block-square park, has a recreation building with restrooms, a large picnic area, and five concrete tennis courts—which are free; just come out and wait your turn.

Sea-Arama Marineworld is a unique family-entertainment complex featuring professional shows and attractions. Free parking. See *Children's Activities,* below, for details.

Galveston County Beach Pocket Park #1 is at 7½ Mile Rd. on FM 3005. This has picnic areas, playgrounds for children, showers, restrooms, and a boardwalk to the beach. Parking is $2.

Two miles west, at 9½ Mile Rd., is *Galveston County Beach Pocket Park #2,* and at the 11-mile road is park #3. Same facilities as Park #1. Parking at #2 and #3: $3.

Farther west, at 13 Mile Rd., is *Galveston Island State Park.* This beautiful 2,000-acre tract stretches from the Gulf to the bay. Ideal for birdwatching, it features nature trails. It has both day and overnight facilities. Hookups for trailers and RVs are available.

Seawolf Park on Pelican Island (cross the bridge at 51st) features picnicking, fishing facilities, and two World War II vessels to visit. See *Children's Activities,* below, for times and charges.

Two other quiet, cool areas are *Central Park,* a block-square area in front of the county courthouse at 21st and Winnie (Ave. G), offering nothing but a moment's respite between sightseeing sprints; and, at 27th and Ave. O, the *Garten Verein,* where a 12-sided Victorian building will catch your eye. The building is not open to the public except for special occasions.

CAMPING. *Galveston Island State Park* is on 13 Mile Rd., 6 mi. southwest of the Galveston city seawall, on FM 3005. This 2,000-acre park spans the width of the island from the Gulf to the bay. Recreational and natural features of the park include swimming, fishing, beachcombing, birdwatching, and nature trails along the 1.6 mi. of sandy beach—as well as camping.

Camping: 150 sites with water and electrical hookups; each has a shade shelter, picnic table, and cooking grill; restroom and shower nearby. $6 a night.

Screened shelters: 10 shelters, 9 by 12 ft.; electrical outlet; light and picnic table inside; water and cooking grill outside. $8 a night.

There is a group trailer area of 20 sites, with water and electrical hookups; restroom and showers nearby. $6 a night.

There are also picnic sites with shade shelters, picnic tables, and cooking grills, with a restroom and showers nearby. No reservations needed, and no charge for this amenity other than the entrance fee of $2 per day per vehicle that applies unless the visitor has an annual or restricted annual entrance permit or a parklands passport.

If you plan to stay, reservations will be accepted up to 90 days in advance for the overnight sites if you call (409) 737–1222 between 8:00 A.M. and 5:00 P.M. or write to the park at Rt. 1, Box 156A, Galveston, TX 77551.

East Beach Travel Park; (409) 763–2296 or CB Channel 15, KFZ 1970. At 021 Seawall Blvd., down on the sand east of Ferry Rd. This section is clean and properly maintained, with 24-hour security. Call for costs. Open seven days a week from 6:00 A.M. to midnight; general store, laundry, immaculate restrooms, hot and cold showers, souvenir shop, game room.

Mobile-Home Parks are: Gulf View Trailer Park, 5800 Seawall Blvd.; 744–9193 and Bayou Haven, 6310 Heards La., off 61st St.; 744–9148.

Camping overnight on the sand beaches is permitted only in specified areas. Safety is the concern here. At the extreme end of West Beach near the San Luis Pass bridge is a licensed campground. Trailers and recreational vehicles are also welcome there.

BEACHES. State law forbids Texas beaches to be closed to the public. All 32 mi. of Galveston Island's beachfront is open. At certain times of the year automobile traffic is not allowed on the sand in specific areas, in the spirit of safety. There are many free places to park within a short walking distance to the water and many commercially-operated beach parks that charge for parking and amenities. The farther west one drives the less crowded the beaches become.

Commercially-operated beach parking areas provide various degrees of concessions, beach-apparatus rentals, bathhouses, sanitary facilities, and security. The Galveston County Sheriff's Department provides lifeguard protection in designated areas. Signs clearly indicate where surfing is permitted. The Galveston Park Board of Trustees, is responsible for the cleanup of the public beaches; a $200 fine for littering is enforced.

Across Seawall Blvd. from each hotel are stairs leading down to the sands. Again, this is not a private beach. It is a convenience for the guests at the hotels who don't want to drive to the beach. A car is necessary to reach the beaches not at your doorstep, since city public transportation is not scheduled for tourists.

PARTICIPANT SPORTS. There is a wide range of activities open to those who wish to take part in the action. Seawall Blvd., which extends to over 10 mi. of continuous sidewalk—the longest in the world—presents an ideal **walking, jogging, skating, and bikeriding** expanse. Single- and 10-speed bikes, as well as surrey-type pedal vehicles, are available for rental at numerous locations along the boulevard between 6th and 20th Sts. At Beach Bike Rental the surreys cost $7 an hour.

Surfing is permitted along specifically designated areas of the beach. Several spots on the beachfront rent surfing equipment by the hour or by the day.

Water-skiing lessons are given at Washington Park, near the boat launch, on Offats Bayou and 61st St.

Horses to be ridden along the beach can be rented at the Sandy Hoof Stables, 11118 W. Beach, between 7 and 8 Mile Rds. off FM3005. See *Children's Activities,* below.

Tennis. Menard Park, between 27th and 28th Sts. and Ave. Q and Seawall Blvd., has five free concrete courts. The Galveston Racquet Club, 83rd and Airport, 744–3651, charges nonmembers for instruction and use of the courts.

Golf. Galveston has two 18-hole courses. Pirates Golf Course, 1700 Syndor Lane, west of Stewart Rd., is a public course. The Galveston Country Club, 9 mi. farther west on Stewart Rd., 737–1776, is private but extends reciprocal privileges if you belong to another golf club or if you are staying at a hotel or condominium that offers golf packages.

FISHING. Galveston Island is famous for its fishing opportunities, and no wonder. More than 52 varieties of fish swim in the temperate waters on and surrounding Galveston Island. Angle from free and commercial piers, wade into the surf, drop a line in the inlets and bays, join a party fishing-boat excursion for bay and deep-sea action, or charter your own small craft for more privacy.

If you opt for fishing from the piers that extend into the Gulf, you will find free piers on the seawall at 10th, 17th, 27th, 29th and 61st. Sts. The rock groin jetties at the entrance to the harbor at the east end of the island are also free.

The commercial piers are beyond the Flagship Hotel at Seawall Blvd. and 25th, at 91st St., and at Seawolf Park on Pelican Island. Well-stocked bait-and-tackle shops, at which refreshments can also be bought, will be found on the commercial piers, where the cost to fish is $2.00 for adults and $1.00 for children. If you rent a rod it will be another $3.00, and you'll have to leave a $10.00 deposit. Bait is $2.50. These piers are open 24 hours. A state fishing license is required for those aged 17 to 65. Licenses may be bought on the piers and at any bait camp or sporting-goods store. Some convenience stores sell them, as does the Galveston County Courthouse. See the Yellow Pages under "fishing bait" to expedite matters.

Party boats provide the easiest way to do your deep-sea fishing. It is wise to make reservations as soon as you know when you intend to go. These boats go into the bay or the Gulf. They have all the necessary equipment designed to make your day a success; all the tackle and bait are provided, sonar locates the fish, and the crew is helpful and courteous. (Anti-seasickness pills are recommended for Gulf trips.) The trips are usually of 12-hour duration, departing at 8:00 A.M. Rates are $43 on weekdays and $53 weekends for the *New Buccaneer.* The *Jean Laffite* costs $11 a person for 4-hour bay-fishing excursions. All these boats belong to Galveston Party Boats, Inc., at Pier 18; 763–5423.

Texsun II (762–8088) has private boats for charter, at Pier 19. Sukeba Services at the Galveston Yacht Basin (763–1046) and Reel Fun Charters at 400 Strand (762–8629) do too.

You will find more boat charterers in the Yellow Pages, and the Convention Bureau's pamphlet entitled "So Much To Do and See."

Seawolf Park on Pelican Island charges $2 to fish from the pier. The Galveston Island State Park at 13 Mile Rd. west on the island includes fishing privileges in the daily $2-a-car fee.

CHILDREN'S ACTIVITIES. Galveston has developed its well-earned reputation as a family resort with several installations that will keep the children occupied and delighted for hours.

Sea-Arama Marineworld, 91st and Seawall Boulevard, 744–4501, is open daily at 10:00 A.M. All the shows and attractions operate every day until dark. To see the several live shows and all the exhibits and displays should take about three hours. There is a snack bar on the ground level, and other opportunities to buy ice cream or cold drinks in other spaces. Don't miss the great performing dolphin shows and sea lion shows. Exotic birds and snakes also perform. A water-ski show and more than 20 Killers of the Deep should not be missed. Adults: $8.95; $5.50 for children 4 to 12; those younger are admitted free. The entire family will enjoy this unique educational-entertainment complex.

Seawolf Park on Pelican Island, 744–5738, is on the site of what once served as the quarantine station through which all immigrants passed as they came into the port of Galveston. Today a three-level pavilion offers a magnificent view of the harbor. Tables and chairs are strategically placed for dining and picnicking convenience. To the east is the *Selma,* a World War I concrete ship that went aground and sank. Many fishermen drop their lines off this ship. At the pavilion snack bar, hot food and cold drinks can be bought for a picnic overlooking the harbor, where small sailboats and huge cargo vessels glide by. A 380-ft. fishing pier enables the anglers to bring in flounder and trout while the children cavort in the imaginative playground. Two vessels are on exhibit: the U.S.S. *Cavalla,* one of World War II's most distinguished submarines, and the U.S.S. *Stewart,* a World War II destroyer. The park is open dawn to dusk. Prices are $3 for parking; $2 for the tour of both ships. To get to Seawolf Park take Broadway (Avenue J and also I–45) to 51st St. Turn north, cross the bridge, and continue straight down the main road until you reach the park, about 10 min. from 51st.

Stewart Beach Park, at the foot of Broadway on the sand in the east end of Galveston, 765–5023, is the most developed of several municipal beach parks.

Parking during the week, Monday through Friday, from 8:00 A.M. until 6:00 P.M., and on Saturdays and Sundays from 6:30 A.M. to 8:00 P.M., costs $3 per car, truck, or van. The closing date for the park is October 31 each year; it opens again on February 16—though the beach itself is accessible year-round.

The bathhouse facilities' hours are the same as above, and the cost is $1.00 per person, $1.50 for a locker, good all day.

Connected with Stewart Beach are *Sky Rapids,* 762–1993, open from 10:00 A.M. until dark, daily. The *Watercoaster* has the same hours.

Bumper Boats and the *Roller Skate Track* are open 10:00 A.M. to 7:00 P.M. during the week and 10:00 A.M. to 10:00 P.M. on weekends.

The *Go Carts,* open 9:00 A.M. to dark daily.

The Peter Pan Golf Course, which is open from 8:00 A.M. until there are no more customers, costs $3 for 18 holes and $4.50 for 36.

There are snack bars selling food and cold drinks. The beach is near for swimming. Chairs and umbrellas are for rent at the water's edge. Lifeguards are on duty.

West End Attractions—which means beyond 61st St.—include (at presstime):

Aqua Raceway, open from 10:00 A.M. to 8:00 P.M.; $4 for 8 min.

The *Sandy Hoof Stables,* 11118 West Beach, 737–2782, is open 8:00 A.M. until 6:00 P.M. You can hire a horse and ride along the beach, $6 an hour. Phone first.

The *Sir Goony Miniature Golf Course,* 8910 Stewart Rd., 744–9172, is open from 10:00 A.M. to 10:00 P.M. An 18-hole game costs $1.50. There are also an electronic game room and a concession stand.

HISTORIC SITES. Downtown adjacent to the harbor is the *Strand.* The section of the Strand along the equivalent of Ave. B, from 20th to 25th Sts., was once known as the Wall Street of the Southwest. It was Galveston's financial center in the last century, and in this neighborhood big business flourished in shipping, insurance, and banking. Today the Strand contains one of the finest concentrations of nineteenth-century iron-front commercial buildings in the United States. It has been designated a national historic landmark, and many medallions of the Texas Historical Commission can be seen on both sides of the street.

The Strand is being returned to its former glories. The nineteenth-century iron-front buildings have been painted and restored; once-empty stores now house eating places, boutiques, businesses, night spots, art galleries, artisans' studios, and an old-fashioned candy factory. The area between 20th and 25th is lighted as it was before the 1900 storm (a time from which almost everything in Galveston is dated)—by gas. For further information call at the Strand Visitors Center at 2016 Strand, 765–7834, or write to the Galveston Historical Foundation, P.O. Drawer 539, Galveston, TX 77553.

Also downtown, three blocks north of The Strand, is the 1894 *Grand Opera House* at 2020 Postoffice (Ave. F). During its era, "The Grand" was known as the Palace of the Southwest, presenting outstanding performances in drama, opera, music, and dance. Celebrities such as Sarah Bernhardt, Lillian Russell, Anna Pavlova and the czar's Imperial Russian Ballet, William Jennings Bryan, Otis Skinner, and John Philip Sousa and his band graced that stage. Galveston was not only one of the busiest ports in the nation, but a cultural center as well.

The theater became a cinema, saw hard times, and eventually closed its doors. Now the Grand has been acquired by the Galveston County Cultural Arts Council and has been restored to its former magnificence. The Grand is a functioning concert hall, fully heated and air-conditioned. It is home to Galveston Arts' nine-month-long Performing Arts Series, featuring symphonies, operas, ballets, and more, as well as concerts by touring troupes and local companies such as the Galveston Symphony. Rock, country-and-western, and bluegrass musicians also appear onstage, particularly during the summer. For information call Galveston Arts at 763–6459.

Worth a visit too is *St. Joseph's Church,* 2206 Avenue K. It is a simple frame structure with a rich Victorian Gothic interior. It was built by German immigrants in 1859. The church has been restored and is being developed into an ecumenical museum to display the city's religious history. The GHF has tour information; 765–7834.

HISTORIC HOMES

The citizens of Galveston are aware that their city has more than 500 structures of historical significance. In fact, Galveston is reputed to have more nineteenth-century homes in good condition than any other city in the country.

Many of these sturdy houses have been restored to their former splendor and are private residences, but some are open to visitors.

One of the most elegant is *Ashton Villa,* 2328 Broadway (762–3933). Built in Italianate style before "the war" (in this case the Civil War), this three-story mansion is surrounded by spacious lawns and towering shade trees. The house is made of bricks fired on the island, and it is completely furnished and restored to its antebellum beauty. Tours begin in the restored carriage house with a multimedia presentation, *The 1900 Storm.* This 12-min. documentary tells of Galveston before the turn of the century, the unpredicted 1900 hurricane, its impact on the island, and the remarkable recovery by Galvestonians. Well-informed volunteer docents take visitors through the house, recounting the history of the lives led there. Children of all ages love the miniature dollhouse. Times: weekdays, 10:00 A.M. to 3:30 P.M.; weekends, noon to 5:00 P.M.; closed Tuesdays, September to May. Admission charged.

The Bishop's Palace, 1402 Broadway (762–2475), was officially opened on January 1, 1893. It was designed by Galveston architect Nicholas Clayton and took seven years to build. During the 1900 storm this limestone-and-granite house provided shelter for hundreds of homeless victims. The owners built this lavish mansion with an eye to entertaining. It is said that they had as many as 1,000 guests at a time. In 1933 the house was sold to the Catholic diocese, the present owners, as a residence for the bishop, though it was rarely used for that purpose. It is open to the public from noon until 4:00 P.M. daily. There is an admission charge: $2.50 for adults, $1.50 for teenagers, and 50¢ for those under 12. This house is the most widely known architectural attraction in Galveston, and it is ranked among the top 100 homes in the United States for architectural significance.

A block west of Ashton Villa, at 2428 Broadway, is the castle-like building known as *Open Gates.* The 1889 home of the George Sealys was designed by Stanford White and made of Belgian half-brick in Roman style. The house is now owned by the University of Texas Medical Branch and is being restored for use as a conference center.

Yet another area of preservation of 40 blocks of Galveston's beautiful residential historical sector reaches from Broadway to Market and from 11th to 19th Sts. Structures within this East End Historical District cannot be changed without consent of a city board. This district has been designated a national historic landmark and is listed on the National Register of Historic Places. A map depicting this area can be picked up at the Strand Visitors Center at 2016 Strand. This will help you with a self-guided tour by car, bicycle, or foot.

Three other houses are worth a visit:

The *Samuel May Williams Home,* 3601 Ave. P (or Galvez), is one of the oldest buildings on the island. It was a prefab, built in Maine and shipped to Galveston in 1839. It is now restored, even to the authentic furnishings, and is open to the public. The Galveston Historical Foundation will give times; 765–7834. Admission: $2.50, adults; $2, senior citizens; $1.75, students and military.

J.R. Smith House. 2217 Broadway (765–5121). Open for daily tours. Also offers six elegantly furnished guest rooms for B&B.

The *Syndor-Powhatan House,* 3427 Avenue O (763–9374), is the headquarters for the Galveston Garden Club. It was built in 1847, is completely restored and furnished; open for tours only on Tuesdays. Call first. Admission charged.

MUSEUMS. When we speak of museums in Galveston we do not mean giant ethnic, anthropological, or astronomic enterprises. The historic homes and the restored Strand area, which are designated as national historic landmarks, are living museums, and some are open to the public. Galveston has several other installations that serve as museums. Although the time spent within their confines has a cultural aspect, "entertaining" and "fun" might be more descriptive of your visit to any or all of them.

The Center for Transportation and Commerce. This is a first-rate five-acre museum at the foot of historic Strand and Rosenberg (25th) Sts., in the Shearn Moody Plaza. The museum was completed in mid-1982. It took four years and $5.5 million to create this, one of the finest, most unusual museums in the world.

A parking lot at the museum's front door (behind the main building) accommodates 200 cars. The entrance is into and through an 1875 depot, complete with telegrapher's table, ticket window, pot-bellied stove, and the sounds heard in train stations of that era. Innovative audio-visual techniques present the history of Galveston, from those days in the early 1500s when the Karankawa Indians began to trade with the islanders to what the city is today. A working HO-gauge miniature railroad is the heart of an exhibit of the activities of the port of Galveston. The focal point of the museum is the People's Gallery, "A Moment Frozen in Time—1932" in the original train-station waiting room. This gallery consists of 39 life-sized models in monochromatic white plaster, all in positions of motion and all authentically attired. Outside on the four once actively used train tracks is a collection of 35 railcars, four steam locomotives, baggage and boxcars, a Pullman, a parlor car, a caboose, and the *Anacapa,* a deluxe 1929 private railcar. Adults, $4; children, $2. Open daily all year. Call 765–5700 for information.

The Elissa. A towering survivor of the Age of Sail, this ship is ranked as Texas' number-one tall ship. The *Elissa* is berthed at Pier 22 adjacent to the Strand. A film, public tours, and exhibits tell her story. The *Elissa* is the oldest ship in Lloyds Register of Shipping and is the third-oldest merchant ship afloat. This 430-ton, 160-ft., square-rigged sailing ship was built in Scotland in 1877. In 1883 she brought cargo into the port of Galveston. She has sea-traded around the world and changed hands and names several times, once even becoming a smuggler's vessel. In 1975 the Galveston Historical Foundation bought her, and completely restored her to be fully operational. Tickets may be purchased at Pier 22, or at the Strand Visitors Center, 2016 Strand; 765–7834. $3.50, adults; $2.50, children.

The ANICO Tower. Galveston's tallest building, where from the observation level one can see over 35 miles in all directions. Only seen with the Heritage Tour Service. Call 762–TOUR for specific information.

The Rosenberg Library. The first library in the state—and one of the finest—is at 823 Tremont (23d St.) (763–8854). It contains artifacts and pictures of early Galveston and Texas history. The library has an extensive collection of rare books and documents. The several art galleries within the building have continually changing exhibits. It has a vast collection of large-type books. Open Monday through Saturday.

The Antique Dollhouse Museum. 1721 Broadway, 762–7289, house a rare collection of dolls from all over the world in a restored pre-Civil War cottage; open daily (except Sundays October through March). $3 for adults, and $2 for children.

Galveston County Historical Museum. Newly opened. 2219 Market St. (766–2340). Offers a variety of programs and exhibits. Free.

THE ARTS, THEATER, MOVIES. *The 1894 Grand Opera House,* 2020 Postoffice, has been restored. The resurrection of this theater, which once presented the top stars from around the world, is the site for solo entertainment, group concerts, and presentations of drama and the dance. For information on events, and self-guided tours, call 763–6459.

The Strand Street Theatre, 2317 Mechanic (Ave. C), is Galveston's only professional repertory company. Presentations include musicals, drama, comedy, and classical works. For information on current show and prices, call 763–4591.

The Dance Center, 2118 Strand (upstairs), offers a wide range of dance classes and a monthly dance concert. It also hosts visiting dance companies. Call 763–5713.

Galveston Arts Center, 202 Kempner (22d St.); 763–2403. Scheduled exhibits, classes in dance, theater, music, creative writing, ceramics, pottery, painting, weaving, drawing, printmaking, photography, and filmmaking. Usually fully booked. Some classes are single presentations; others are done in a series.

The Galveston Symphony Orchestra. Now in its sixth year, it is composed of local talent, with the conductor from the Houston Symphony Orchestra. The orchestra presents several fine symphony concerts and some pops concerts each season. Check the local paper for programming.

The *Mary Moody Northen Amphitheater.* In the Galveston Island State Park, 12 mi. west of the city; 737–3442. The Lone Star Historical Drama Association presents two smashing outdoor musicals from late June through August. *The Lone Star,* a historical drama, and Broadway musicals—*Hello Dolly* this season—alternate. Performances are at 8:30 P.M. Go early to the Amphitheater Chuckwagon Restaurant, open 5 to 8 P.M., for barbecue before the show. A souvenir shop is also open.

Movie theaters. Galvez Mall, 61st and Broadway (I–45), has Cinema I, II, and III.

SHOPPING. Downtown, between 21st and 23d Sts. on Postoffice (Ave. E), is an outdoor pedestrian mall. Eibands, Galveston's complete department store; Walgreens, Walter Pye, a specialty shop for men; the Victoria Market, a collection of boutiques in a remodeled building, and other stores line both sides of the street.

On the Strand between 20th and 25th Sts. are boutiques, eating places, jewelers, craft shops, and art galleries.

To the east end of Galveston, on the Strand from 4th to 6th Sts., is the Port Holiday Mall, a shopping center across from the Holiday Inn and the University of Texas Medical Branch. The Fair, a branch of a chain of Texas specialty shops, is the anchor, and a supermarket, a restaurant, and several small stores occupy the lower level. All air-conditioned. Free parking. Near the Galveston Yacht Basin and Yacht Club.

At the west end of Galveston, 6402 Broadway (Ave. J, also I–45), is another covered, air-conditioned shopping center known as the Galvez Mall. This is the largest mall in Galveston and offers total shopping. A hairdresser, three cinemas, and a cafeteria are among the many businesses and boutiques here.

Safeway supermarket and Eckerd (general merchandise and drugs) hold down a two-block row of stores at Ave. S between 59th and 61st Sts.

Along the beachfront, on Seawall Blvd., extending from 6th to 91st Sts., are souvenir shops that sell T-shirts, bathing suits,sunning lotions, caps, visors sun hats, shells straw items, and everything typically found at resorts to tempt the tourist. Two piers, which extend over the beach and Gulf waters at 2201 and 2215 Seawall Blvd., have a complete stock of such merchandise.

In the Strand area you will find stores selling a great selection of merchandise. Boutiques featuring clothing for all ages and sizes, designed for fun and/or elegance, are numerous. You'll find candles, jewelry, shells, antiques, scents and toiletries, art, cookies, books, gourmet groceries, and Christmas decorations. The Old Strand Emporium, 2112 Strand (763–9445), open seven days a week, 10:00 A.M. to 6:00 P.M., is a delicatessen, sandwich shop, and gourmet grocery with a wine cellar. They sell coffee beans and will custom grind them to your order. Go for lunch; stay to shop. La King's Confectionary, 2323 Strand, is an old-fashioned candy store that makes its own merchandise, and you can watch them do it. There is also an old-fashioned soda fountain where banana splits of days of yore, and Cokes flavored with your favorite taste, can brighten your life. They also serve sandwiches. Tuesday through Saturday, 10:00 A.M. to 6:00 P.M.; Sunday, 1:30 to 6:00 P.M. Another Galveston "must."

DINING OUT. Galveston is famous for its seafood—not surprising, considering that it is an island in the Gulf of Mexico. Some of the restaurants featuring fish are diversified enough to have meat and fowl on the menus. Some are known for their methods of preparation: fried, broiled, grilled, sautéed, smothered in fancy sauces, or boiled and served cold. Galveston offers a large selection of restaurants for the most discerning palates.

Because Galveston is a resort that also caters to quick eaters on holiday, the fast-food franchises are well represented on all the main thoroughfares: Broadway (I–45), Seawall Blvd., 61st St. between Broadway and the Boulevard—and there is a cluster off 61st St. and Ave. S (Stewart Rd.). These are all inexpensive.

The price classifications and abbreviations below are based on an average three-course dinner for one person for food alone; beverages, tax, and tip would be extra. *Inexpensive* means less than $5; *Moderate* means between $6 and $10; *Expensive* is up to $25 and maybe more.

Credit cards are usually accepted. Visa and MasterCard are the most popular, but if you have another one, ask. Travelers checks are not too welcome but may possibly be cashed. Out-of-town personal checks will do only if you have a major credit card.

Most of the restaurants listed here are open for lunch and dinner even if they close early. It is a good idea to check times, since they alter with the seasons.

We have not listed every restaurant in every category. The listings below are just a selection of places enjoyed by the locals. The Visitors Bureau at 21st and Seawall Blvd. has a list of other dining opportunities, as do the Yellow Pages, which are more extensive.

CONTINENTAL

Clary's. 8509 Teichman Rd., 740–0771. *Expensive.* West end; (Across from Galveston News Building. West on Broadway [I–45], off at 83d, under the freeway and right on Teichman's Rd.). Noted for seafood prepared in a variety of ways; steaks are top quality. If you don't like heavy seasoning, say so when you order. Make reservations if you don't want to stand in line. All credit cards.

The Wentletrap. 2301 Strand, downtown in the historical district; 765–5545. *Expensive.* This restaurant has a long and varied menu and an even longer wine list. Specialties of the house often depend on the fish caught in island waters that day. The meats are top grade (delicious and tender), and the chef is justly proud of his sauces and seafood concoctions. The restaurant is in the 1871 T. J. League Building, which has been handsomely restored to create a relaxed ambience and Old World elegance. Open seven days a week for lunch, cocktails, and dinner. Reservations are recommended for dinner. So are coat and tie. All credit cards.

Café Torrefie. 2126 Strand, downtown; 763–9088. *Moderate.* Not usually as expensive as The Wentletrap—but it can be. This restaurant is in a restored bank building. In fact, for special occasions, dine in the old vault. Relaxed ambience. Reservations are recommended. All credit cards.

The Merchant Prince in the Tremont House is noted for its nouvelle cuisine. *Very expensive.* Reservations not necessary. All credit cards.

SEAFOOD

Gaido's. 3818 Seawall Blvd., on the beachfront; 762–0115. *Moderate to Expensive.* Gaido's has the reputation for the finest stuffed flounder ever prepared by human hands. Everything prepared to your special order. MC, V.

Hills Pier 19. 20th and Wharf; 763–7087. Downtown, a block north of the Strand, on Galveston Bay. *Moderate to Expensive.* The food is acquired cafeteria-style, but the location is what counts. Above the restaurant, on two broad open decks, are tables where one can dine after selecting the food, which is prepared right before your eyes. Watch the fishing boats and shrimp trawlers come home at twilight, or the big cargo vessels and tankers on their way out of the port. This is the most exciting view in town. The food is good but may be expensive, though there are inexpensive lunch specials. Seven days a week, 11:00 A.M. to 7:00 P.M.

Shrimp & Stuff #1. 3901 Ave. O; 763–2805. An informal and *inexpensive* place to take the kiddies. Nothing elegant, but the food is tastefully prepared and not greasy. **Shrimp & Stuff #2,** 68th and Stewart Rd., west of 61st St., is also *inexpensive* and a family-style operation. They have also expanded to hamburgers, roasts, and chicken.

ETHNIC RESTAURANTS

Mario's Flying Pizza. 2202 61st Street; 744–2973. *Moderate.* Italian. Makes the best Fettucini Alfredo this side of the Atlantic. And their pizzas and other pastas are also superb. Family style; closed Mondays.

Tong's Happy Buddha. 2827 61st St.; 744–5774. Chinese food, well prepared and pleasantly served. A family restaurant. Lunch is *inexpensive;* dinner is *moderate.*

Corella's Corral. 2528 61st street, west end; 744–9138. *Inexpensive.* The Mexican meals here are not too highly seasoned, although the staff will supply you with the hot stuff if you prefer that spicy taste. Family style. Monday through Saturday, 10:00 A.M. to 8:45 P.M.

MISCELLANEOUS

Le Paysan, 2021 Strand, calls itself a French Bakery cum French Cafe. From breakfast through lunch and tea to dinner. *Inexpensive to moderate.*

Fullen's Waterwall. 2110 Strand; 765–6787. *Inexpensive.* Features a solarium and a 35-foot-wide waterwall. Gourmet hamburgers and fried foods; wine and beer.

The Warehouse. 101 14th St., east end, one block north of the Strand; 765–9995. *Inexpensive.* Typical Texas barbecue of ribs or chicken; huge hamburgers, and always fresh French fries. 10:00 A.M. to 8:00 P.M.

The Old Strand Emporium. 2112 The Strand; 763–9445. *Inexpensive.* Any delicatessen delicacies you desire can be eaten here or wrapped to travel.

HOTEL DINING ROOMS

Marriott's Hotel Galvez, the *Flagship, La Quinta,* the *San Luis,* the *Tremont House,* both *Holiday Inn,* and *Gaido's Motor Inn,* along with many of the other motels, have coffee shops and/or gourmet dining rooms. The prices range from expensive to moderate and, in some cases, inexpensive, depending on where you are and what you order.

NIGHT LIFE. Galveston—so far as night life is concerned—is no Paris or Manhattan, or Houston for that matter. If you do feel the need to get out on the streets at night, there are plenty of bars, lounges, beer parlors, and nightclubs here. However, their popularity shifts rapidly, and by the time you read this book, many of the places listed would be out of business or might have moved—so we won't try to list them now.

The best bet for the visitor is to try word-of-mouth recommendations at the time of the visit. Another good idea would be to stick to the hotel and motel lounges, which remain pretty stable; popular night spots include the bar at the restored Marriott's Hotel Galvez, 21st and Seawall Blvd., and the *Lookout Lounge* at the Flagship Hotel, Rosenberg (25th St.) and Seawall Blvd. Both feature live popular music for dancing. The Holiday Inn at 600 Strand also features live music in its *Mariner Lounge,* as does the San Luis. The Tremont House has a pianist nightly in the lobby-lounge.

The *Wentletrap Restaurant,* 2301 Strand (see *Dining Out*), has a jazz pianist evenings, and *Café Torrefie,* 2126 Strand (see *Dining Out*), features a variety of musical offerings from jazz to folk to modern country.

There is live music for dancing at the *Balinese Room,* 2101 Seawall Blvd., and—for those visitors who missed live country-and-western music in Austin and aren't too dandified—there is *Jim's Country and Western Club,* 504 Seawall Blvd., 763–0356, with country classics, both live and recorded, seven days a week, after 9:00 P.M. Cover charge.

CORPUS CHRISTI AND THE COASTAL BEND

The Texas Riviera

by
DOROTHY McCALEB

Dorothy McCaleb, a resident of the Texas coastal bend for more than twenty years, is a researcher and writer for the Corpus Christi Convention and Tourist Bureau.

This 50-mile wide arc of subtropical land is rapidly developing into a lively resort area with new luxury hotels, condominiums, restaurants and recreation facilities.

Corpus Christi wraps her arms around Corpus Christi Bay, reaches south to include the Padre Island National Seashore, then stretches north to bring in the Aransas National Wildlife Refuge.

This is the coastal bend of Texas, or "The Texas Riviera," lying almost directly across the Gulf of Mexico from Tampa–Saint Petersburg, Florida.

This is where the birds come for the winter. Some fly on to Central, or even South, America, but thousands stay in the area. Audubon Society Christmas bird counts come to as many as 165 species. One avid amateur birder counted 158 species one day in April (spring migration) in a few square miles.

The mainland is fortunately blessed with barrier islands—Padre, Mustang, and San Jose—which protect it from storm surges.

Statistics say the average temperature is 71.2 degrees Fahrenheit. To arrive at that average takes many summer afternoons when thermometer readings soar into the 90s, then some January and February nights when the warning is to protect tender vegetation because a light freeze may be expected. Another blessing is almost constant afternoon and evening breezes off the Gulf, which cool off summer nights and warm up winter afternoons. The humidity is lower than farther up the coast.

Corpus Christi has a land area of 116.5 square miles and a water area of 275.5 square miles—the city is 70 percent water. The bright Texas sun shining down on that is what gives the city its title of "The Sparkling City by the Sea." After dark, city lights produce the same effect, especially when seen from the air or from Harbor Bridge.

It was in 1519 that Alonzo Alvarez de Pineda, while charting the entire Gulf coast, reportedly discovered "a beautiful bay." The discovery came on the feast day of Corpus Christi (Body of Christ), so he named the waters Corpus Christi Bay.

For three centuries, missionary priests, adventurers, explorers, traders, and refugees roamed the immense area. Legends still persist that buccaneers left treasure buried in the sands of the islands.

Not until 1839 and 1840 was a trading post established, by Captain Henry Lawrence Kinney (near what is now 401 North Broadway). He called it Corpus Christi—still a notably unique name for a city.

About that time, Irish settlers established homes along the banks of the Nueces River. They and the native Mexicans lived together peacefully (not so, the Indians). Early settlers joined in creating the Republic of Texas, then later in helping it become a state. General Zachary Taylor camped where Artesian Park is now, waiting for the Mexican War to begin. There were Union bombardments along the shores during the Civil War. The chamber of commerce and the tourist bureau have a list of historic markers in the area. La Retama Library, downtown at Mesquite and Peoples, has an excellent local-history room

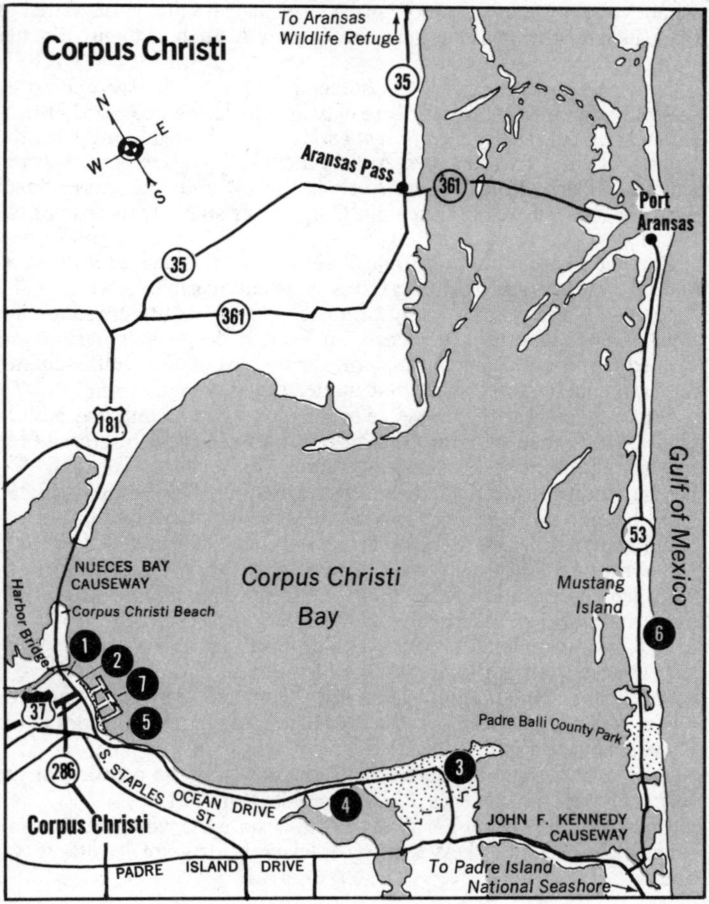

Points of Interest:

1) Bayfront Arts and Sciences Park, including the Corpus Christi Museum, Art Museum of South Texas, and Harbor Playhouse
2) Bayfront Plaza Auditorium and Convention Center
3) Corpus Christi Naval Air Station
4) Corpus Christi State University
5) Memorial Coliseum
6) Mustang Island State Park
7) T-heads and L-head Marina (off Shoreline Blvd.)

where you may browse or borrow. A new central library was slated to open in late spring, 1986, near the County Courthouse and Blucher Park.

Now this beautiful city is the home of well over 250,000, according to 1985 estimates. Nearly half are classified as Hispanic (mostly Mexican-American). *Dies y seis de septiembre* is celebrated along with the Fourth of July. The so-called Anglos include Irish, German, French, English, Czech, Polish, and Greek heritages, and lots more. Small percentages are Black or Orientals. Corpus Christi is a truly cosmopolitan city.

Partly because of the subtropical climate, the lifestyle is informal, as well as gracious and friendly. Dress is usually casual.

Corpus Christi didn't really begin to take on its present character until a series of things happened. In 1926, a deep-water harbor was opened in this natural port. It is now the deepest on the Gulf and ninth largest in the country. And first in cleanliness!

Water Street was the first edge of the city. Then landfill was built in front of it. Famed sculptor Gutzon Borglum designed the steps of the seawall—built in 1939–41—with ramps (now called "L" and "T" heads), leading down to land areas for recreation. The seawall is 12,300 feet long and 14 feet high, with a 20-foot-wide sidewalk atop it.

On March 12, 1941, a naval air station was dedicated at the south end of the city, followed by the Corpus Christi Army Depot. Here navy fliers are trained, and military helicopters are repaired and sent out all over the world. The graceful Harbor Bridge, replacing an old lift bridge, was completed in 1956. The city was on its way.

If the bayfront is the pretty face of the city, Padre Island Drive is its backbone. And Padre Island Drive did not even exist until the 1960s. Residential, business, and industrial growth on both sides of the Drive has been rapid.

A face-lift to the northern end of the city was the creation of the Bayfront Arts and Science Park, completed in 1981.

Corpus Christi is not a walking town, despite the wonderful seawall sidewalk. The city is best seen on a leisurely drive of less than two hours.

A Drive along the Bay

Starting anywhere along Shoreline Drive (say, at the end of I-37), go north past the Bayfront Plaza Convention Center and Auditorium (home of the Corpus Christi Symphony). The Art Museum of South Texas will be on your right, with the Harbor Playhouse nearby, facing the Corpus Christi Museum.

Drive to the port entrance, under the south leg of Harbor Bridge, to watch the big ships from all over the world enter and leave port.

Then back to Shoreline for a long, lovely drive south. Soon the boulevard becomes Ocean Drive. That complex of buildings you will pass at Ayers Street is Spohn Hospital. Notice the interesting carillon in front of First Baptist Church in the 3100 block.

After a short causeway, you will come to the island campus of Corpus Christi State University. Past the university, at the end of Ocean Drive, is the north gate of the naval air station, which is not open to general visitors, except Thursdays at 1:00 P.M. for guided bus tours.

On the way back, take time to notice the lavish homes in many styles of architecture and the subtropic landscaping. When you get to Cole Park, stop and walk out to the end of the fishing pier for a beautiful view, a favorite of photographers.

Corpus Christi's financial district is up on a bluff, around Broadway and Leopard Street—hence its being referred to as "uptown." The Central Business District is called "downtown."

Aransas Pass and Port Aransas

Another popular drive is the 74-mile "Loop." Go north over the Harbor Bridge and the Nueces Bay Causeway to Aransas Pass by way of State Highway 35. Conn Brown Harbor there is the home of hundreds of picturesque shrimp boats and, increasingly, of services for offshore oil drilling. Visit the Seaman's Memorial Tower; its crucifix is made of driftwood.

Then, for Port Aransas, out to the ferry landing (free; twenty-four hours) on State Highway 361. Watch the dolphins cavort around the ferry.

Drive through Port Aransas to the beach. Stop to see the exhibits at the University of Texas Marine Sciences Institute. Drive along the beach (a rare treat) to an access road—1 or 1A—that will take you to Park Road 53. Head south, passing Mustang Island State Park.

Continuing left at the intersection with Park Road 22, onto 22, you may drive farther south to the national seashore. Or take a right turn at the intersection, go over the Kennedy Causeway and along Padre Island Drive, making a right at Ennis Joslin Road, to get back to Ocean Drive leading into town again.

Rockport-Fulton and the Aransas Wildlife Refuge

In Rockport, on the coast about ten miles north of Aransas Pass on Route 35, an established artists' colony has been joined by large condominium complexes. A stroll along downtown's Austin Street, parallel to the waterfront, will take you past boutiques, art galleries, and shell shops, ending at the yacht basin. Fulton Beach Road, which veers off Route 35 and is more or less parallel to it, leads past many beautiful homes to the newly restored Fulton Mansion. Throughout this area there are numerous RV parks and other accommodations for "Winter Texans."

Continue on Route 35 over the Copano Bay Bridge to the turnoff to Austwell. Turn right and follow signs to the entrance to the Aransas National Wildlife Refuge, seventy-five miles north of Corpus Christi. The refuge is known to birdwatchers around the world, primarily because it is the sole winter resting-place for the whooping cranes. These rare birds spend their summers in Alberta, Canada, coming to the refuge here in October and staying through March. A boat tour of the refuge leaves Sea Gun Marina in Lamar Wednesdays, Fridays, Saturdays, and Sundays from October through April; the tour lasts four hours and is the best way to see the refuge and especially the whooping cranes. (See *National Parks* in the *Practical Information* section, below.) There is a viewing tower by land access, with telescopes. The refuge is also home to thousands of deer, wild turkeys, javelina (wild pigs), bobcats, and more.

Kingsville and the King Ranch

No trip to Texas would be complete without a visit to a real ranch. How about the most famous: the King Ranch. The visit will consist of your driving in a twelve-mile loop through part of the ranch, and there is a brochure available. Visitors cannot roam free on the ranch, and there are no overnight accommodations. Stop at Joe Cotton's in Robstown (S.H. 44 and U.S. 77) for real Texas barbecue, served on butcher paper.

From Corpus Christi, take State Highway 44, then go south on U.S. 77 to Kingsville. The Kingsville Visitors Center, 101 North Third St., P.O. Box 1562, Kingsville, TX 78363; 592–8516, will tell you how to reach the ranch gates west of the city on State Highway 141. In Kingsville, also visit the John E. Conner Museum at Texas A and I University: weekdays, 10:00 A.M. to 5:00 P.M.; Sundays, 2:30 to 5:00 P.M.

Corpus Christi and the Coastal Bend are not what many expect of Texas. It has beautiful seacoast, fine weather most of the year, wild areas—and yet it is one of the fastest-growing parts of the state, an area whose star is rising. Truly "The Texas Riviera."

PRACTICAL INFORMATION FOR CORPUS CHRISTI AND THE COASTAL BEND

HOW TO GET THERE. Most tourists come to Corpus Christi and the Coastal Bend by car. Or to save time, they fly down and rent a car at the airport. Buses and private boats are the two other types of entry.

By car. I–37 out of San Antonio brings you right into Corpus Christi, ending at Shoreline Drive. An alternate is U.S. 77 to I–37—or turn off at Sinton onto U.S. 181. Or take U.S. 181 at San Antonio, about 145 mi.

From Houston, U.S. 59 to U.S. 77. Or "Hug the Coast" on State Hwy. 35, over Copano Bay Bridge, through Fulton, Rockport, and Aransas Pass to Gregory, where 35 merges with U.S. 181, about 220 mi.

From the west and the "Valley" (Rio Grande), enter Corpus Christi by State Hwy. 44, which you pick up at Robstown from U.S. 77 or at Alice, by U.S. 281, from 144 to 166 mi.

All are lovely rides when the spring wildflowers (5,000 species in Texas) are in bloom.

The driving times to Corpus Christi from other cities, in hours, are: Brownsville–South Padre Island, 3½; Houston, 4; San Antonio, 3.

By air. Corpus Christi International Airport is served by six airlines: *American, Continental, Eastern, Texas National, Southwest* and *United.* There are no flights across the border, but the "International" is kept in the title anticipating resumption of direct flights to Mexico.

The airport—newly redecorated with a larger baggage area, more parking and a new restaurant, and lounge and VIP rooms—is off State Hwy. 44. An airport limousine is available; hotels and motels send pickup cars.

Rental cars available at the Airport are Avis, Budget, Hertz, and National, and, nearby, Dollar and Thrifty.

Private planes fly into Corpus Christi International Airport frequently. Also smaller ones land at the Aransas County Airport, north of Rockport. Aransas Pass and Port Aransas have public paved landing fields, with fuel pumps, hangars or tie-downs.

By bus. *Greyhound Bus Lines.* Terminal in Corpus Christi, 819 N. Broadway, uptown on the bluff. Buses from Houston, San Antonio, and the Valley.

Trailways Bus System. 701 N. Chaparral, downtown. San Antonio to Corpus Christi. Houston via Victoria or State Hwy. 35. Also from the Valley.

By boat. You can sail your yacht across the Gulf of Mexico to the Corpus Christi Ship Channel, then to the City Marina. There is a waiting list for slips; temporary dockage is hard to get. Check with the marina office, on the Lawrence Street T-Head; 882–7333.

Smaller craft can easily be piloted down the Intracoastal Waterway, past Copano, Aransas, and Redfish Bays into Corpus Christi Bay—but you might enjoy stopping at any of the many marinas along the way.

TELEPHONES. The area code for Corpus Christi and the coastal bend is 512. You do not need to dial the area code if it is the same as the one from which you are calling. Information (Directory Assistance) is 1411 locally or, from outside the 512 area, (512) 555–1212. To place a long-distance call outside the locality, dial 1 (one) plus the number or, if it is to a number outside the 512 area, 1 plus the area code plus the number. Ambulance within the City of Corpus Christi is 882–5571, and Police are 882–1911.

HOTELS, MOTELS, AND CONDOMINIUMS. Accommodations in and near Corpus Christi are hotels, motels (sometimes called inns), and, increasingly, "condos." These are condominium units privately owned by individuals or corporations, and placed in a "rental pool" when the owners do not wish to use them. There is no single source for condo booking; call the Tourist Bureau or the chambers of commerce (see *Tourist Information,* below).

Condos owe their popularity with tourists to the convenience of a fully equipped kitchen, a dining area, and two or more queen-size beds. Such a "home away from home" for a family or small group will not have all hotel services, however.

There are no hostels in the area and no tourist homes, but there is a bed-and-breakfast service and plenty of camping (see below).

Our selection of facilities offered is grouped by location and, within each, by rates. Special seasonal, weekly, monthly, or weekend rates are common. Often there is no charge for children in the same room, and there are frequently senior-citizen discounts. Credit cards are generally accepted.

All accommodations listed are air-conditioned and have free parking. Double-occupancy rates are classified as: *Expensive;* \$63–\$95. (the highest rates are not called Deluxe, since informality, not elegance, prevails here); *Moderate;* \$41–\$62; *Inexpensive,* up to \$40.

CORPUS CHRISTI BAYFRONT

The Hershey. *Expensive.* 900 N. Shoreline (78401), 887–1600. Opened early 1985. 486 guest rooms, balconies. Indoor/outdoor pool. Health club, racquetball courts, sundeck, game room, gift shop, nightclub. Two waterfront restaurants.

Holiday Inn—Emerald Beach. *Expensive.* 1102 S. Shoreline (78401); 883–5731. Private beach, heated pool, sundeck. Holidome Fun Center. Triton's Trumpet Restaurant. Lucy's Club. Children and pets welcome.

Marriott. *Expensive.* 707 N. Shoreline (78401); 882–1700. 350 guest rooms, all with balconies. Indoor/outdoor pool, recreation room. Two restaurants, nightclub.

La Quinta Royale. *Moderate.* 601 N. Water (1 block from Shoreline) (78401); 888–4461. Rooftop pool, coffee shop. Tour and charter boat service in lobby. Dining, dancing, and entertainment at La Vista Royale, with a superb view of bay.

Sheraton Marina Inn. *Expensive.* 300 N. Shoreline, P.O. Box 1661 (78403); 883–5111. Redecorated in 1984. Near yacht clubs. Tennis, pool. Brass Tack restaurant/bar on first floor. Horizon Club on top with dining, dancing, live entertainment.

I–37 NEAR THE AIRPORT

Hilton Inn. *Moderate.* 6255 I–37 (at Corn Products Rd.) (78409); 289–0600. Pool, tennis, putting green. Lounge and restaurant. Tramp Steamer Club with dancing and entertainment. Special weekend rates.

La Quinta Motor Inn. *Moderate.* 5155 I–37 (at Navigation Blvd.) (78408); 888–5721. Pool. Children and pets welcome. Restaurant adjacent.

CORPUS CHRISTI BEACH

Best Western-Sandy Shores Inn & Resort. *Moderate to expensive.* 3200 Surfside (on beach) (78403); 883–7456. Pool. Saunas. Superb view from restaurants. Calypso nightclub. Recently expanded.

Koronado Hotel. *Expensive.* 3615 Timon Blvd. (78402); 883–4411. Rebuilt 1981. Kitchens. Pool. Private balconies. Game room, laundry. No pets.

Villa Del Sol Hotel Condominium. *Expensive.* 3938 Surfside (78402); 883–9748. Kitchens. Pools. Sleep 6. Spectacular view of bay and city.

NORTH PADRE ISLAND

Holiday Inn–North Padre Island. *Expensive.* Windward Drive on the Gulf. P.O. Box 18179, Corpus Christi, TX 78418; 933–8041. Private beach, pool. Game room. Lounge. Oliver's Restaurant, entertainment.

PORT ARANSAS

The Dunes Condominium. *Expensive.* 1000 Lantana Lane (on the Gulf at Horace Caldwell Pier), P.O. Box 1238, Port Aransas, TX 78373; 749–5155. In summer a 3-day minimum; winter rates. Pool, tennis.

Island Retreat. *Moderate for hotel rooms.* P.O. Box 637, Port Aransas, TX 78373; 749–6222. A condo. On the Gulf. Pools, tennis, playground.

Port Royal. *Expensive.* On the Gulf. Box 1526, Port Aransas, TX 78373; 749–5011. Condos, 1–3 bedrooms. Pool, tennis, volleyball. Lovely grounds. Restaurant due in 1986.

Tarpon Inn. *Moderate.* 200 E. Cotter, Port Aransas, TX 78373; 749–5555. Since 1886. Historic marker in front. Redecorated. Two long porches overlooking the "flats." Famous for tarpon scales lining lobby wall. Good dining, bar.

Three-day minimum in summer and deposit sometimes required. Get full list from Port Aransas Chamber of Commerce (see *Tourist Information.*).

ROCKPORT-FULTON

The area abounds in parks for travel trailers and RVs. "Winter Texans" stay one to seven months. Rockport Chamber of Commerce has lists (see below, *Tourist Information*).

Sandollar Resort. *Moderate.* Fulton Beach Rd. (entrance also from State Hwy. 35), Star Rte. 1, Box 30, Rockport, TX 78382; 729–2381. Efficiencies. Also 76 spaces with full hookups. Two pools, playground. Laundry. Restaurant. Lighted pier, marina.

Sea Gun Resort. *Moderate.* State Hwy. 35, 9 mi. north of Rockport on Copano Bay. Star Rte. 1, Box 85, Rockport, TX 78382; 729–2341. Motel rooms and condo cottages. Pool, playground, tennis, laundry, restaurant, bar, marina with snack bar, games. Home of the *Whooping Crane* boat. 400-ft. lighted fishing pier.

Village Inn Motel. *Inexpensive.* 503 N. Austin, Rockport, TX 78382; 729–6370. Close to beach, harbor, shopping. Kitchenettes. Pool. Children and pets welcome.

HOW TO GET AROUND. The area is so spread out, with attractions all over the place (and the city's public transit leaves much to be desired), it is recommended you rent a car unless you came in one—or have friends to show you around.

There are, however, several taxi services—all with radio-directed, air-conditioned cabs and 24–hour service—for short drives. See the Yellow Pages.

Car-rental agencies, at the airport, are listed below. (To call toll free, dial 1–800–555–1212 and ask for the toll-free number of the agency you desire.)

Avis, Airport: 289–0073; 101 N. Shoreline: 883–5108
Budget, Airport: 289–0434; 800 N. Water: 888–8211
Hertz, Airport: 289–0777
National, Airport: 289–1515
Thrifty, 1928 N. Padre Island Dr.: 289–0041

A taxicab from the airport to bayfront should cost $10 to $12, metered. There is also a limousine service between the airport and downtown, leaves after flights and on call. Also pickups. Price $6. Call 289–0191.

City bus service is poor but a good way to see part of town not usually encountered and see how the people live and work. For information, call 882–1722. Fare is 50¢ for adults, 25¢ for children 6 to 12 and for Senior Citizens. Children five or under, free.

TOURIST INFORMATION. There is lots of help in the Corpus Christi area, both for before you arrive and for after you get there. Requests for specific information, as well as general information, are honored by:

The Corpus Christi Area Convention & Tourist Bureau, 1201 North Shoreline, P.O. Box 2664, Corpus Christi, TX 78403; 882–5603.

Corpus Christi Chamber of Commerce is next door to the bureau—they share a large lobby—but its mailing address is P.O. Box 640, Corpus Christi, TX 78403; 882–6161.

Aransas Pass Chamber of Commerce, 452 Cleveland Blvd., Aransas Pass, TX 78336; 758–2750.

Port Aransas Chamber of Commerce, 421 W. Cotter, P.O. Box 356, Port Aransas, TX 78373; 749–5919.

Rockport Area Chamber of Commerce, near the ski basin, State Hwy. 35, P.O. Box 1055, Rockport, TX 78382; 729–6445 and 729–9952.

Rockport-Fulton Tourist Association. Paws and Taws Bldg., Fulton Beach Rd., P.O. Box 1482, Rockport, TX 78382; 729–2388.

All are open weekdays from 8:30 or 9:00 A.M. to 5:00 P.M. and closed Saturdays and Sundays—except the Corpus Christi Tourist Bureau, which is also open 8:30 A.M. to noon Saturdays. Closed holidays.

SEASONAL EVENTS. Every locality has its own *annual* appropriately named festival; including Seafair in Rockport Columbus Day Weekend, Shrimporee in Aransas Pass, a late weekend in October. The *Sparkler,* a free publication of the Corpus Christi Area Convention & Tourist Bureau, found in your hotel rooms and at the bureau office, lists events for the month of issue, with full details.

The "Weekend" section of the *Corpus Christi Caller-Times* is included in all the Friday editions. It offers up-to-date information on what's going on.

CORPUS CHRISTI

End of **April** into **May:** *Buccaneer Days,* a 10-day festival with music and sport contests, carnival, fireworks, and illuminated night parades. On the bayfront and throughout the city; free.

First Sunday of Buc Days: *Art Jamboree.* Hundreds of artists in all media show works day-long. Food and drink booths. Special children's section. South Bluff Park. Free shuttle buses from courthouse parking lot. Small admission.

Weekend in mid-**July:** *Texas Jazz Festival,* featuring visiting stars. The preceding week there are jazz sessions throughout the city. Jazz Cruise on the Bay Friday or Saturday night (admission). Jazz Mass at the Cathedral or Holy Cross Church, 1109 N. Staples, Sunday 11:00 A.M. The Jazz Festival itself is at Memorial Coliseum, 1:00 to 8:00 P.M.; free.

End of **September-October** weekend: *Bayfest,* an annual family festival (an outgrowth of the Bicentennial celebration). The accent is on ethnic foods, arts and crafts, and historic exhibitions. There are three stages for music and dancing. Children's section. Biergarten. Marathon races. Water sports. 50 booths with interesting foods and drinks. On five blocks of Shoreline Drive, from I–37 to Art Museum; free.

December: *Christmas Tree Forest* at the Art Museum of South Texas. The Corpus Christi Symphony with guest soloists presents Handel's *Messiah* at the Bayfront Plaza Auditorium, 4:00 P.M. the second Sunday; free. At Christmastime all boats are decorated for the holiday with lights.

FISHING TOURNAMENTS IN PORT ARANSAS

July. *Deep Sea Roundup* (after Independence Day weekend). Around the Gulf and bay. Attracts more than 600 contestants. Full week of activities around the municipal docks and the Civic Center.

Mid-July. *Outboard Motor Tournament.* Hundreds of boats using only outboard motors compete for trophies.

There is a fishing tournament almost every weekend from June to September. Get full list of dates and sponsors from Port Aransas and Aransas Pass Chambers of Commerce (see *Tourist Information*).

TOURS. Wherever you make your temporary home in the coastal bend, it's an easy day's trip to attractions elsewhere. If you are not driving yourself, there are tours by land and water.

Gray Line Tours of Corpus Christi, Suite 105, 101 N. Chaparral, P.O. Box 224, Corpus Christi, TX 78403; 882–2011. Narrated sightseeing tours in Corpus Christi and to Padre Island and Port Aransas. Nite Life Party. From $6 for adults.

Fun Time Tours, 601 N. Water (at La Quinta Royale), Corpus Christi, TX 78401; 854–3257. Special tours and neighboring city tours.

BY BOAT

Captain Clark's Flagship. Peoples Street T-Head on the bayfront; 884–1693 and 643–7128. Mailing address: 311 Seco, Portland, TX 78374. A luxury, triple-decker, 400–passenger paddlewheeler. Air-conditioned main deck, snack bar; restrooms. Harbor and Bay trips; day and moonlight cruises with live bands and dancing. Charters available. Day trips: Adults $4; under 12, $2. Nights: Adults, $5 and $6.

Check with the tourist bureau, 1201 N. Shoreline, 882–5603, for other tours or cruises.

BEACHES. Gulf beaches in Texas are open to the public; cars may even be driven on them in specified lanes. Exceptions are Mustang Island State Park and the Padre Island National Seashore, which have paved roads and parking areas. There is no public transportation to these beaches, however.

Padre Island stretches for miles from Corpus Christi before you reach the national seashore (see *National Parks* below). Immediately to the north of Padre Island is Mustang Island. (See Mustang Island State Park under *State Parks.*).

Padre Balli Park. Nueces County, Park Rd. 22, north Padre Island; 933–8121. Swimming, picnicking. (See also *Camping,* below.)

J. P. Luby Youth Park. Has pavilion and surfers' pier at Access Road 3A-I from Park Road 53.

Port Aransas County Park. Extends to jetties (good fishing); 749–7116. Special surfing and swimming areas. Restrooms, showers. Ranger and first-aid stations. (See also *Camping*).

Corpus Christi Beach. (Oldtimers still call it North Beach.) Within the city limits. Go over Harbor Bridge, taking the first exit from Corpus Christi at Timon Blvd., and turn off at any street. This 200 ft. wide stretch of restored beach extends nearly 1.5 mi. No driving allowed on this bay beach. Parking areas are lit and paved. Swimming and picnicking, new restrooms. Convenient to downtown, with a fine view of the city's new skyline.

Magee Beach. On Shoreline Dr. downtown in front of Memorial Coliseum. Concession stand at breakwater; lit for night fishing. Park on Shoreline or at parking lot and walk down the steps of the seawall.

Cole Park. Ocean Dr., close to downtown. Nature created a small beach at the north end of this man-made park. Playgrounds, picnic tables, restrooms. Not recommended after dusk. Excellent new lighted fishing pier. Nearby Amphitheater where band concerts are held Sundays during the summer.

Rockport Beach. Off State Hwy. 35 at yacht basin. This long spit of land has swimming on one side, waterskiing and boating on the other. The water is shallow for a long way out. Picnic kiosks. Restrooms.

Fulton Beach. Off State Hwy. 35. A small swimming area at new fishing pier. Restrooms.

San Jose Island. (Formerly St. Joseph's Island.) Undeveloped. Accessible only by jetty boat from Port Aransas: Woody's Sports Center, at The Gateway, Port Aransas, Texas 78373; 749–5252. Don't miss the last boat back! Eight trips every day. The fare is $6 for adults, $3 for children.

NATIONAL PARKS. The U.S. Department of the Interior manages two large areas in the coastal bend: under the National Park Service, Padre Island National Seashore; under the Fish and Wildlife Service, Aransas National Wildlife Refuge.

Padre Island National Seashore. Superintendent, 9405 S. Padre Island Dr., Corpus Christi, TX 78418; 937–2621. For surf and driving conditions, 949–8175; ranger station, 949–8173. Park Rd. 22.

The only national seashore in Texas occupies 80.5 miles of the slim barrier island that stretches 113 miles along the Gulf, from Corpus Christi to Brownsville, with an area of about 237,600 acres. (There is a man-made channel-break in the island about two-thirds of the way down.)

Malaquite Beach is for day use. The Pavilion there, damaged by Hurricane Allen in 1980, is barely functioning. A new facility is in the planning and funding stage. Paved parking lot on the land side. No driving on the beach. Camping is permitted on the beach corridor seaward of vegetation or dunes, for a mile at north end of the seashore and for a 5–mi. stretch beginning at the end of the paved road. There is a paved camping area 1 mi. south of the ranger station (½ mi. north of Malaquite): fresh drinking water, rinse-off showers, restrooms, dump station, picnic tables. Camping fee, $4 a night. No electric or water hookups.

From the northern entrance to the park, a conventional car may be driven for 8.5 mi. on hard-surfaced road, then 5.5 mi. on the beach—no farther unless you have a four-wheel-drive, since you'll get stuck in the soft sands. Jeep rentals or tours are available at Foy's Beach Rentals, 10001 S. Padre Island Drive, Corpus Christi, TX 78418; 937–4001.

To get to the seashore from Corpus Christi, go all the way out S. Padre Island Dr. to Park Rd. 22 (over the J. F. Kennedy Causeway). Pick up a detailed map, information on the day's weather, and tide reports at the superintendent's office, 9405 South Padre Island Dr.; 937–2621.

Driving from Port Aransas, use Park Rd. 53 to Park Rd. 22. Visit the ranger station inside the park for information. Free summer programs by park naturalists.

Aransas National Wildlife Refuge. P.O. Box 100, Austwell, TX 77950; 286–3559. Established in 1939. All the world knows it as the winter home of the last free flock of whooping cranes (there from October 15 to April 15)—75 at last count.

To get there by car, take State Hwy. 181 to State Hwy. 35. Continue through to Aransas Pass, Rockport-Fulton, and over Copano Bay Bridge. About 20 mi. farther, a large sign will direct you to turn right for Austwell and the refuge. The entrance is 16 mi. farther. You are welcome to drive in at sunrise but must leave by sunset.

Stop at the new visitors' center, open 8:00 A.M. to 5:00 P.M., year-round. Sign in—87,000 guests do every year. Pick up maps and leaflets on the birds, mammals, amphibians, and reptiles in the refuge. Climb to the top of a 38 ft. viewing tower. Picnicking. Drive a 16-mi. loop.

To see the whooping cranes close up, a trip by boat is recommended. The *Whooping Crane,* at Sea Gun Resort, north end of Copano Bridge, Hwy. 35, makes birding trips from October 20 to April 10, Wednesday, Friday, Saturday, and Sunday, leaving at 1:30 P.M. and returning at 5:00 P.M. Adults, $12; children under 10, $8. Take binoculars. Sea Gun Resort, Star Rte. 1, Box 85, Rockport, TX 78382. Call 729–2341; ask for the marina.

The *Scat Cat* out of Fisherman's Wharf, Port Aransas, also makes birding trips, January, February, and March. Call 749–5448 for days, times, and rates.

STATE PARKS. There are three large state parks in the coastal bend—one entirely within the city limits of Corpus Christi. For information in advance, write Texas Parks and Wildlife Dept., 4200 Smith School Rd., Austin, TX 78744. If already in the area, Region 5 headquarters is at 715 S. Bronte, State Hwy. 35 south of stop light in Rockport; 729–2315.

Mustang Island State Park. P.O. Box 326, Port Aransas, TX 78373; 749–5246. Only a few years old, this well-kept 3,704-acre park, right on the Gulf, is only 14 mi. south of Port Aransas on Park Rd. 53. Camping, with water, electricity, trailer dump station, showers, restrooms. Swimming and picnicking area.

Goose Island State Park. State Hwy. 35 to 12 mi. north of Rockport to Park Rd. 13; 729–2858. Stop to see "Big Tree." 307 acres. Camping, recreational hall with group facilities. Water, electricity, restrooms, showers, boat ramp, trailer dump station, and swimming. 1,620-ft. fishing pier.

Lake Corpus Christi State Park. Near Mathis. I–37 to State. Hwy. 359. P.O. Box 1167, Mathis, TX 78368; 547–2635. Screened shelters. Campsites with electricity, water, restrooms, showers, picnicking. Fresh-water fishing. Groceries. Boat ramp.

All Texas state parks have an entrance fee, $2 per day per car. Annual entrance permits are $8; $15 for entry to all parks. Seniors enter free.

SPORTS. The mild climate makes sports a year-round activity. Even swimming in the Gulf may be enjoyed from April to November. Corpus Christi is known as "that tennis town in Texas." Regional NCAA championship matches are played here.

Golf. *Corpus Christi Golf Center.* Public. On Old Brownsville Rd; 883–3696. 18 holes, par 72. Fees: $4 weekdays, $6 weekends and holidays.

Oso Golf Course. Municipal. 5601 S. Alameda; 991–5351. 18 holes, par 70. Fees: $4.25 weekdays, $5.25 weekends.

Guest privileges may be obtained at the Corpus Christi Country Club, Naval Air Station, Padre Isles Country Club, Pharaoh's Country Club, and River Hills Country Club.

Tennis. *H. E. B. Tennis Center.* Municipal. 1520 Shely (off Ayers St.); 888–5681. Pro shop, 24 lighted courts. $1.25 per player for 1½ hours, daytime; $1.75, nights.

South Bluff Tennis Center. 502 King St. (in South Bluff Park); 883–6942. Seven lighted courts. Same rates as H. E. B.

Private facilities at Corpus Christi, Padre Isles, and Pharaoh's Country Clubs and the T-Bar-M Racquet Club extend guest privileges.

Many hotels and condos in Corpus Christi, Port Aransas, and Rockport have fine tennis courts for guests.

The Bay is perfect for **wind surfing** as well as **sailing,** and a 20-ft.-wide sidewalk along the Shoreline seawall invites **skaters.**

There is a **bicycle** path along Ocean Drive and there is great **jogging** along the Shoreline seawall and out along Ocean Drive. Swantner Park features tests for heart performance.

Sailing. Corpus Christi Yacht Club, on the L-Head, and the Bay Yacht Club, on the Lawrence St. T-Head, are home ports for sailboats of all sizes. Rental sailboats or cruises by sail may be obtained at the Peoples St. T-Head.

Swimming. See *Beaches, National Parks,* and *State Parks.* Almost all hotels and motels have swimming pools, many heated for all-year use.

FISHING. The deep blue waters of the Gulf of Mexico off Mustang and Padre Islands yield game fish—often of record size—such as sailfish, blue and white marlin, and tuna, as well as tarpon, jewfish, jack crevalle, dorado (dolphin), gafftop, sheepshead, black drum, and pompano. Red snapper are brought in all year. Kingfish (king mackerel) and ling (cobia) are caught in late summer.

The bays are fished all year from piers and jetties as well as by boat, for redfish and speckled trout (by sportsmen only), sand trout, and flounder.

Local people drop a line at the barge dock (next to the art museum) in Corpus Christi or at the Channel View parks, one at each end of Harbor Bridge. They also go out on the lighted breakwater at Magee Beach and the pier off Cole Park and Oso Pier (the only one with a small fee). In winter they let out sail lines along Ocean Drive.

Fishermen try the Gulf surf. A favorite place are the jetties, both south and north, at the ship channel in Port Aransas. There is also a new pier at the end of Station St.

Conn Brown Harbor in Aransas Pass is lined with fishermen in winter after a "norther" blows in. Up the coast are many private and motel piers. Fulton Beach, for example, has a new public pier.

A license is necessary, with few exceptions. These are obtainable at most tackle-and-bait shops, convenience stores, and sporting-goods stores. Texas residents may buy a license good from September 1 to August 31 of the next year for $8.00. A temporary 14-day sportfishing license for Texas residents is now $5.00. Nonresidents pay $7 for 5 days, $15 for a year.

Special Note: *Horace Caldwell Pier,* Port Aransas County Park, and *Bob Hall Pier,* Padre Balli Park, were destroyed by Hurricane Allen in 1980. New concrete piers, 1200 ft. long, with 160-ft. T's, lighted, with fish-cleaning tables, concession stands, restrooms, and even wheelchair ramps, are now open at both sites. Entrance fee of 50¢ per person; $1.00 for each fishing device.

PARTY ("HEAD") BOATS

Star Trek. Peoples St. T-Head, Corpus Christi; 883–5031 (nights, 991–3143). Fishing trips at 7:30 A.M. and 2:00 P.M. and 6:00 P.M. daily. There are also several other smaller party boats and charters at this T-Head.

Deep Sea Headquarters, next to the ferry landing, P.O. Box 388, Port Aransas; TX 78373; 749–5597 and 881–8202. *King Fisher,* 65 ft.; daily trips.

Dolphin Dock, 404 W. Cotter, Port Aransas, TX 78373; 749–6624. *Dolphin; daily trips.*

Fisherman's Wharf, 1 Tarpon St., P.O. Box 387, Port Aransas, TX 78373; 749–5448 or 888–8093. *Scat Cat* and *Wharf Cat* (catamarans). Trips to "Snapper banks," to Gulf or bays, half day and all day. Also to the Aransas National Wildlife Refuge in January, February, and March. Also charters.

CHARTERS

Deep Sea Charter Association. 10 fast, privately owned and operated vessels. At Deep Sea Headquarters (see above).

Sport Center, 847 N. Alister, P.O. Box 717, Port Aransas, TX 78373; 749–5271. Capt. Rick Corn; 749–6458.

HUNTING. The bays and estuaries around Corpus Christi attract migratory waterfowl. Many, of course, alight in the refuges. Dove, quail, and deer are taken south and west of this area. For duck and goose hunting, a Texas stamp is now required, along with a license and a federal stamp from a post office. Sporting-goods stores and convenience stores carry the stamps and issue licenses. For regulations, write or call Texas Parks and Wildlife, 714 S. Bronte, Rockport, TX 78382; 729–2315.

Sea Gun Marina. Star Route #1, P.O. Box 85, Rockport, TX 78382. Call 729–2341 and ask for the marina. Private duck blinds, boat service, guides, game cleaning and packing.

Redfish Bay Marina. Causeway to Port Aransas, State Hwy. 361, P.O. Box 380, Aransas Pass, TX 78336; 758–2632. Guide, boat and motor rentals.

CAMPING. There are camping spots all over the area—but no camping is allowed on the T-Heads or in city parks. Good facilities are provided at the Padre Island National Seashore (no electrical hookups), Mustang Island State Park, Goose Island, and Lake Corpus Christi State Park. (See listings in *Parks,* below.)

Camping ranges from a makeshift shelter on the Gulf beaches to elaborate RVs with air conditioning and color TV.

Nueces County Padre Balli Park, Park Rd. 22, north Padre Island; 949–8121. 70 sites, $7 a night. Water, electricity, hookups, showers. Laundry and waste site. Maximum length of stay is three nights. Beach camping, $4 a night for up to six people; 50¢ for each extra.

Nueces County Park at Port Aransas, on Mustang Island; 749–7116. Same facilities. Length of stay, 14 nights. Special surfing and swimming areas.

The ranger station at each park is open all year, 24 hours a day.

Puerto del Sol Travel Trailer Park, 5100 Timon Blvd, north end of Corpus Christi Beach; 882–5373. Waterfront sites, pull-throughs. All hookups. Restrooms, showers, laundry. Fishing, swimming. Open all year. Rates $14 daily for two. Weekly and monthly rates.

Ancient Oaks KOA, 1222 S. Bronte (State Hwy. 35), Rockport, TX 78382; 729–5051. October 1 to Labor Day. Pool, recreation room, playground. 1 mi. to beach, fishing. Tenters are welcome summer and holidays, 50 sites. 104 RV sites. Rates: $10 for 2, $1 for each extra. $1.50 daily for AC or heating. Weekly and monthly rates.

For full list of campsites and trailer parks, contact the tourist bureau or chamber of commerce in the desired location. (See *Tourist Information,* above.)

CHILDREN'S ACTIVITIES. All those Corpus Christi beaches (see the *Beaches* section, above) are ideal playgrounds for children. But do watch them carefully, even when a lifeguard is on duty. Guard against too much sun, also.

Corpus Christi Museum. 1900 N. Chaparral (in Bayfront Arts and Science Park); 883–2862. Having started out as a junior museum, now, after celebrating its silver anniversary, it is recognized as one of the finest small museums in the country and is the only general museum in South Texas.

South Wing—geology, anthropology, natural history. The Hall of Marine Science includes exhibits from the Gulf of Mexico. "Touch" tables, aquariums, art gallery. Then go across a wide mall with gift shop, etc., to the North Wing.

North Wing—Exhibits on life in Corpus Christi in the early 1900s. P. T. Barnum Room, just for laughs. The Front Porch has entertainment—music and dancing—Saturdays and Sundays, 2:00 P.M. Saturdays kids enjoy a trading post, treasure hunts, and special movies. Open 10:00 A.M. to 5 P.M., Tuesdays through Saturdays, 2:00 to 5:00 P.M., Sundays. Closed Mondays and Christmas Day. Plenty of parking. Free.

Surreys by the Sea. Pedal a surrey with fringe on top along water's edge. $8 an hour; 1–3 people. Two locations on seawall, Corpus Christi. 887–8715.

MUSEUMS. Corpus Christi boasts two nationally known museums, facing each other in the Bayfront Arts and Science Park.

Corpus Christi Museum. 1900 N. Chaparral, Corpus Christi, TX 78401; 883–2862. The largest in South Texas. A general museum—though especially strong in natural history—famed for presentation of exhibits for all ages. (See also the *Children's Activities* section, above). Beautifully landscaped. Entrances and parking on Water or Chaparral streets. Open Tuesday through Saturday, 10:00 A.M. to 5:00 P.M.; Sunday, 2:00 to 5:00 P.M. Closed Monday and Christmas Day. Free.

Art Museum of South Texas. 1902 N. Shoreline Dr., Corpus Christi, TX 78401; 884–3844. The beautiful building, designed by Philip Johnson, has three levels and almost 30,000 sq. ft. of space. Its location on Corpus Christi Bay is superb. Every visitor should see this building. The museum features painting and sculpture and visiting collections. Local residents don't seem to like the abstract works as well as they do the building. Its small permanent collections are not often shown. There is an auditorium where art films are shown. Good museum shop. Worth a visit—perhaps whatever is being shown will appeal to you. But don't miss the Christmas-tree forest if you're here in December. Open Tuesday through Saturday, 10:00 A.M. to 5:00 P.M.; Sunday, 1:00 to 5:00 P.M. Closed Monday. Free.

Heritage Park. 1600 block N. Chaparral. Cluster of restored historic homes open on Tuesday, Wednesday and Thursday mornings. Example: **Sidbury House,** classic example of Victorian architecture.

Museum of Oriental Cultures (formerly the Japanese Museum). 426 S. Staples (at Agnes), Corpus Christi, TX 78401; 883–1303. An outstanding collection of Oriental art, including a huge collection of Hakata dolls, cloissonné, and lacquerware. Models of shrines and palaces. Open 10:00 A.M. to noon and 1:00 to 4:00 P.M., Monday through Friday; 2:00 to 5:00 P.M., Sunday. Closed Saturday. Admission is $1 for adults, 35¢ for students, and 25¢ for children under 12.

DINING OUT. Dining along the Texas Gulf Coast means seafood, of course. Also Mexican, (at least Tex-Mex), Italian, and Oriental food, steaks, and barbecue. Selected restaurants are listed by locality, then price. Seafood places here often serve steaks, and vice versa. Corpus Christi is not New Orleans or San Francisco, but you'll enjoy the food—and the lower prices.

Ratings are based on the price of a full dinner for one, excluding tax, tip, and alcoholic beverages. *Inexpensive,* less than $7; *Moderate,* to $17; *Expensive* to $30.

CORPUS CHRISTI

Wayward Lady. *Moderate to expensive.* Elegant four–story, floating restaurant. Offers dining on three levels, with prices progressively more expensive as you ascend to the third deck with its tuxedo–clad waiters. AE, CB, DC, MC, V.

Captain Boomer's. *Upper moderate.* A floating barge at the Peoples St. T Head; 882–8341. Seafood, from local shrimp and "catch of the day" to live lobsters (flown in). Oyster bar. Not cordon bleu but a friendly atmosphere and a nice view of the bay. AE, CB, DC, MC, V.

The Torch. *Upper moderate.* 4425 S. Alameda; 992–7491. Since 1957. First choice for steaks, charcoal broiled. Seafood specialties. Original salad dressings. Excellent service. Pleasant but uninspiring surroundings. Open Monday through Saturday, 5:00 to 11:00 P.M. Closed Sundays and holidays. AE, CB, DC, MC, V.

Luciano's. *Moderate.* 1618 S. Staples (near Six Points); 884–1832. This family has been serving a large selection of Italian dishes since 1948. Old Country atmosphere. Imported and domestic wines. Open for lunch, Monday–Friday,

11:00 A.M. to 2:00 P.M. For dinner Monday through Thursday, 4:30–10:30 P.M.; Friday and Saturday, 4:30 to 11:00 P.M.; Sunday, 3:00 to 10.00 P.M. Major credit cards.

Water Street Oyster Bar. *Moderate.* 309 N. Water (behind Sheraton Marina); 881–9448. Stand-up oyster bar, table seating. Patio, bar. New and popular. Who would think this was previously a transmission shop?

Sam's International *Inexpensive to Moderate.* Moved to 525 S. Staples, near Oriental Museum, South Bluff Park, 882–5833. Latin dishes (Spanish, Mexican, etc.) include arroz con pollo and fillet of fish Veracruzana. Order Valenciana paella in advance. The menu changes daily. Open 11:30 A.M. to 2:30 P.M. for lunch; 5:30 to 9:00 P.M. for dinner. Closed Sundays. MC, V

Luby's Cafeterias. Two locations; see the Yellow Pages. Excellent cafeteria food. L, D daily. No credit cards.

Old Mexico. *Inexpensive.* 3329 Leopard at Nueces Bay Blvd.; 883–6461. A variety of Mexican dishes—many you have never heard of. Home of the puffy taco. A child's plate is available. Open Tuesday through Saturday; 11:00 A.M. to 9:30 P.M. Closed Sunday and Monday. AE, MC, V.

PORT ARANSAS

The White Marlin. *Upper moderate.* Cotter St. at Ferry Landing; 749–4500. Really fresh shrimp and fish—they send out their own boat. Lavish salad bar. Oyster bar with entertainment. Open seven days, 5:00 to 10:00 P.M. Special lunch includes food, a mug of beer or large glass of wine, tax and tip, Monday–Saturday, 11:30 A.M. to 2:30 P.M., $6. MC, V.

Seafood and Spaghetti Works. *Moderate.* Alister at Ave. G; 749–5666. Nowhere but in Port A would you find a good restaurant in a dome next to a Texas Twister water slide! You can't miss it. Food delights may be Italian, seafood, whatever. Salad bar. Beer, wine. Open seven days, 5:00 to 9:30 P.M. AE, MC, V.

ROCKPORT-FULTON

Schrenkeisens. *Expensive.* Fulton Beach Rd. and Broadway (at the city limits of Fulton); 729–3332. This is where you go locally for a gourmet-Continental meal. For example, Colorado lamb, veal dishes, red snapper, fine pastries. Wine list to match. Flowers at the tables. Piano bar. Special Saturday and Sunday brunch, 11:30 A.M. to 2:00 P.M., $10. Open all year. Summer, 6:00 to 10:00 P.M., weekdays; to 11:00 P.M. Friday and Saturday. Winter, open 6:30 P.M. AE, MC, V.

Charlotte Plummer's Seafare. *Inexpensive to moderate.* Fulton Beach Rd. at the yacht basin; 729–1185. "The Little Fisherman's Wharf of the Gulf Coast." Meals are served "shipboard style." New ownership, still popular. Breakfast 7:00 to 11:00 A.M. Regular menu, 11:30 A.M. until the kitchen closes at 9:30 P.M. Closed Monday. No credit cards.

NIGHT LIFE. Bars, usually called "lounges," sometimes "cantinas," are to be found all over the Corpus Christi area. Almost all restaurants have bars, or at least serve beer and wine (except cafeterias and fast food places, of course).

Night life has brightened considerably with dining and dancing, and often live entertainment, in the major hotels (see "Weekend" special section of *Friday Caller* and *Times* for who's performing where and when).

Some popular hotel spots are: *Reflections* and *Hightide* in the Hershey; *Bentley's* in the Marriott; *Horizon Club,* atop the Sheraton Marina Inn; *Lucy's,* in the Holiday Inn–Emerald Beach; *The Tramp Steamer Club,* Hilton Inn; *Calypso Room,* Best Western-Sandy Shores; *Oliver's,* Holiday Inn, North Padre Island.

Also notable are:

Cooper's Alley. Gaslight Square; 888–4141. Very popular with young professionals. Good bar. Seafood. Also weekend brunches. Open 7 days, 11:00 A.M. to 2:00 A.M. Cover Fri. and Sat. Also in Port Aransas.

Cantina Santa Fe. 1011 Santa Fe; 884–1756. 11:00 A.M. to 2:00 A.M., Mon.–Sat.

Doc Holliday's. 5820 S. Staples; 993–0528. 8:00 P.M. to 2:00 A.M., Tues.–Sat. A madhouse when spring breakers arrive.

Silver King Bar. In Tarpon Inn, Port Aransas. Quiet jazz.

Western Palms. 4448 Ayres; 852–9062, reservations. All ages for country-western dancing. Pizza. Beer. BYOB. 6:00 P.M. to 2:00 A.M. $3 cover, except until 7:00 P.M. Tues.–Fri.

DALLAS AND FORT WORTH

The Metroplex

By
KAREN ARRINGTON JORDAN

Karen Arrington Jordan, a member of the Society of American Travel Writers, is Travel Editor of the Dallas Morning News, *having previously been an assistant travel editor for the paper, an editor with the* Abilene *(Texas)* Reporter-News, *and an editorial intern with the Southwest Bureau (Dallas) of the* Wall Street Journal. *A native of the Texas Gulf coast, she is an alumna of Texas A & M University (College Station).*

Parts of the Practical Information section were produced by Elizabeth Logan, dining critic of the Dallas Morning News *and a frequent contributor to* D *(Dallas) magazine and* Houston City *magazine.*

If you've heard of Dallas—and TV producers are certain you have—you've also heard it is "a city that never should have been." There is no major waterway (Dallas's version of the Trinity River is little more than a nuisance), and there are no natural resources. Dallasites—more than a few, incidentally, chuckle that the TV show "never should have been"—have made the city what it is today, the nation's 7th largest (a few shy of 1 million) and a center of commerce, banking, insurance, and transportation.

For "a city that never should have been" there certainly are car- and planeloads of people who want to come to the Metroplex, a metropolitan statistical area including also Fort Worth, the Mid-Cities, and encircling towns, and suburbs, with a total population of 2.975 million —a 25 percent increase over 10 years ago. These visitors want to play, and many want to stay. Now the country's third leading convention, market, and tradeshow city, Dallas is also among the nation's top three cities in million-dollar businesses, fashion markets, and film and video, and among the top four in the recording industry. Some 400 of the 500 largest industrial corporations listed in *Fortune* have representatives, divisions, subsidiaries, or affiliates in the Metroplex.

Dallas works. It's more business than talk, not only from finance to fashion, but also from airport to architecture, from sports to churches. If not the most colorful city around, it certainly is clean and cultural.

The Southwest's banking center, Big D is home to more insurance companies than any other U.S. city; more than 125 firms serve the oil industry here. Dallas firms sell more Dale Carnegie courses and more Rolls-Royces than any other city in the Southwest and, for cooling down from a hard day at the office, more Coors. One statistic that fits the stereotype: Dallas has more Cadillacs per capita than any major city outside the Arab world. The world's fourth busiest airport, Dallas–Fort Worth, is bigger than the island of Manhattan and, naturally, is the country's largest landing strip. Any glossy photograph of the glassy Dallas skyline—and likewise of neighbor-to-the-west Fort Worth's—is out of date by the time it comes back from the developer. Any older buildings left standing—after wrecking crews clear a space for a new hotel, office, or apartment building—are being renovated.

The downtown's "signature" building is perhaps the 50-story Reunion Tower, adjacent to the Hyatt Regency at 300 Reunion Boulevard.

Vehicular traffic fades, for the most part, with the sun's setting on a hectic business day in both downtown Dallas and Fort Worth—the exceptions being nights of concerts and, in Dallas, professional basketball games. The pedestrian and the touring motorist have the areas to themselves; but for that reason—and as in most major cities—nighttime is not the wisest time for a visitor to take in the downtown landmarks of either city. Except for downtown hotels, most businesses

Points of Interest

1) Adolphus Hotel
2) Concert Hall (Planned)
3) Convention and Visitors Bureau (in the Chamber of Commerce)
4) Dallas Centre Complex
5) Dallas Hilton
6) Dallas Memorial Auditorium and Convention Center
7) New Dallas Museum of Art (Arts District under dev.)
8) Farmer's Market
9) Greyhound Terminal
10) Hyatt Regency Hotel
11) JFK Memorial Plaza
12) Majestic Theater
13) Municipal Building
14) Neiman-Marcus
15) New Arts Theater
16) Old City Park
17) Plaza of the Americas
18) Public Library
19) Reunion Tower
20) Texas School Book Depository
21) Thanksgiving Square
22) Trailways Terminal
23) Union Station
24) Visitor Information Center

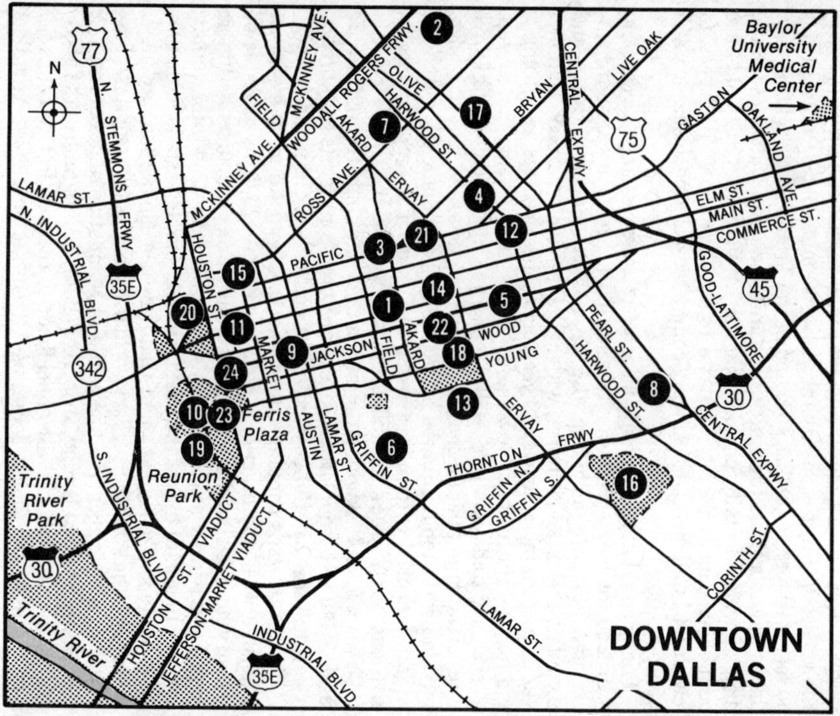

are closed. And John Neely Bryan's Cabin, John F. Kennedy Memorial Plaza, Dealey Plaza, and Union Station, all in the revitalized west end of Dallas's business district, are more safely visited by the light of day—especially on a best-of-both-worlds Saturday or Sunday.

At day's end, Dallasites desert downtown, mostly for points north, especially to the restaurant and club scenes of Greenville Avenue, parallel to and just east of Central Expressway (U.S. 75)—the road to Richardson and Plano—and near Southern Methodist University (in Highland Park) and NorthPark Shopping Center; the Bachman Lake area of Northwest Highway, northwest of Love Field; and Addison, a Far North Dallas suburb bounded by popular Prestonwood Town Center shopping mall. If Dallas shoppers are not "charging it" at NorthPark or Prestonwood, chances are they've found a parking spot at the multilevel Galleria or nearby at Valley View Mall, both in an area between Dallas Parkway and Preston Road on LBJ Freeway (Loop 635), a fifteen-mile drive north via the Dallas North Tollway from downtown.

Points east of downtown Dallas lead to the Texas State Fair Grounds, which includes the Cotton Bowl and myriad museums, and on to Mesquite and northeast to Garland. White Rock Lake Park—a haunt of joggers, bicyclists, lakeside fishermen, sailors, and picnickers—lies to the northeast of downtown in the East Dallas–Casa Linda residential sections of town.

Equidistant from downtown on U.S. 35E are Marsalis Park and Zoo to the south in Oak Cliff and Dallas Market Center to the north-northwest. In the latter direction, Stemmons Freeway leads to Farmers Branch, Carrollton, and Lewisville, but football fans and Muppet lovers take the Texas 183 exit off north 35E west to suburban Irving, home of Texas Stadium and Sesame Place. The south entrance to Dallas–Fort Worth Airport is "just down the road a piece"; the north entrance is accessible from both Texas 114 (the road to Grapevine) and the western extension of Loop 635.

A fifteen- to twenty-minute drive west of downtown Dallas—or east of downtown Cowtown (Fort Worth)—along I–30 (also known as the Old Dallas–Fort Worth Turnpike), the Metroplex's greatest concentration of theme and amusement parks is centered in Grand Prairie and Arlington: Six Flags Over Texas, Arlington Stadium (home of baseball's Texas Rangers), WhiteWater, Wet 'n Wild, Southwest Historical Wax Museum, International Wildlife Park, Texas Sports Hall of Fame, and the Fire Museum of Texas.

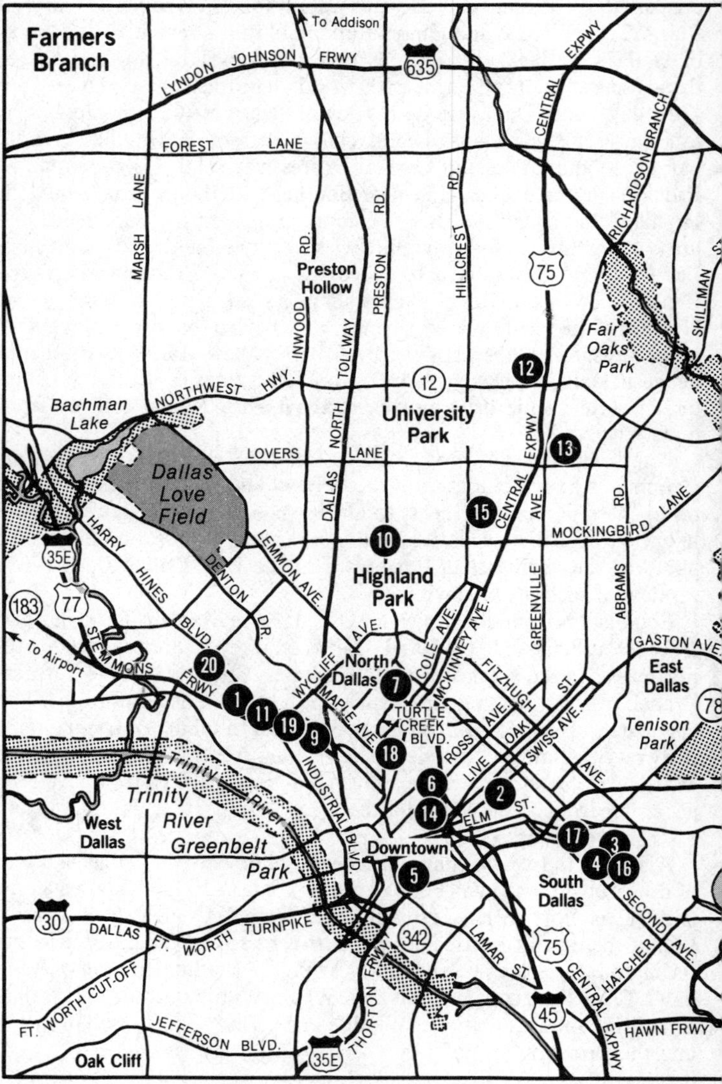
Farmers Branch
To Addison
LYNDON JOHNSON FRWY
635
CENTRAL EXPWY
FOREST LANE
RICHARDSON BRANCH
MARSH LANE
INWOOD RD.
Preston Hollow
PRESTON RD.
HILLCREST RD.
75
SKILLMAN
Fair Oaks Park
NORTH DALLAS TOLLWAY
NORTHWEST HWY.
12
Bachman Lake
University Park
LOVERS LANE
Dallas Love Field
GREENVILLE AVE.
ABRAMS RD.
MOCKINGBIRD LANE
HARRY HINES BLVD.
LEMMON AVE.
DENTON DR.
Highland Park
35E
183
77
To Airport
STEMMONS FRWY
COLE AVE.
MCKINNEY AVE.
GASTON AVE.
East Dallas
WYCLIFF AVE.
North Dallas
FITZHUGH
MAPLE AVE.
TURTLE CREEK BLVD.
ROSS AVE.
LIVE OAK ST.
SWISS AVE.
Tenison Park
78
Trinity River
Trinity River Greenbelt Park
INDUSTRIAL BLVD.
West Dallas
ELM ST.
Downtown
South Dallas
30
DALLAS FT. WORTH TURNPIKE
342
SECOND AVE.
LAMAR ST.
HATCHER
FT. WORTH CUT-OFF
THORTON FRWY
45
CENTRAL EXPWY
HAWN FRWY
JEFFERSON BLVD.
Oak Cliff
1
2
3
4
5
6
7
9
10
11
12
13
14
15
16
17
18
19
20

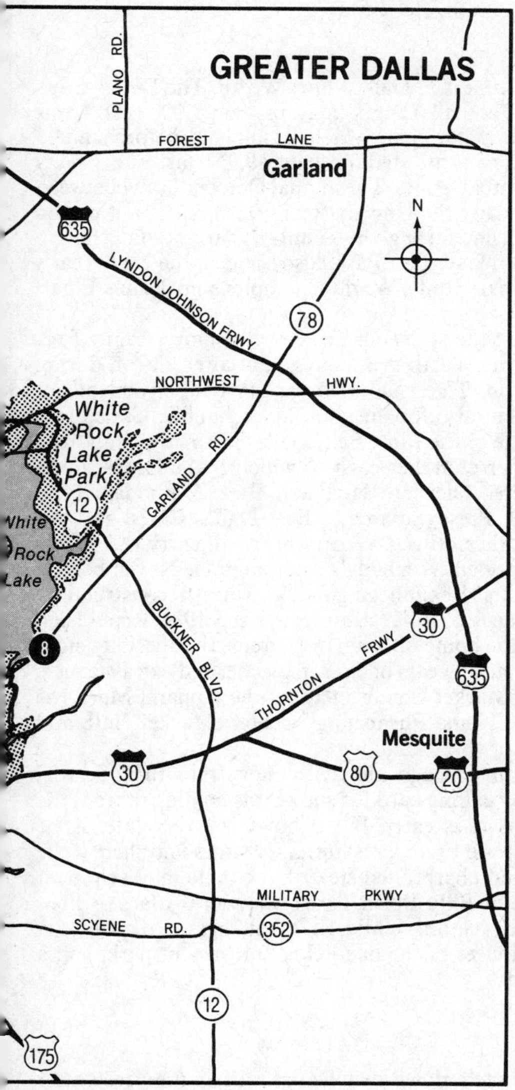

Points of Interest

1) Apparel Mart
2) Baylor University Medical Center
3) Cotton Bowl
4) Dallas Health and Science Museum
5) Dallas Memorial Auditorium and Convention Center
6) New Dallas Museum of Art (Arts District under dev.)
7) Dallas Theater Center
8) DeGolyer Estate
9) Furniture Mart
10) Highland Park Shopping Center
11) Market Hall
12) NorthPark Center
13) Old Town Mall
14) Plaza of the Americas
15) Southern Methodist University, including McFarlin Auditorium
16) State Fair Park, including the Dallas Museum of Natural History, Science Place/Southwest Museum of Science and Technology, Age of Steam Railroad Museum, Dallas Aquarium, Hall of State, Civic Garden Center, and Music Hall.
17) Texas State Fair Grounds
18) Theatre Three
19) Trade Mart
20) University of Texas Health Science Center

Serious Sports

Sports are also big business in Dallas–Fort Worth. The Dallas Cowboys of the National Football League play in the 65,000-seat Texas Stadium in Irving, the majority of which is sold out beforehand to *season*-ticket holders. The same stadium held 49,953 just a few years ago for a *high school* football game. The annual October brawl between the University of Texas and the University of Oklahoma is not played in Austin or Norman, but during the country's largest state fair in Dallas's Cotton Bowl, in State Fair Park, also scene of the New Year's Day extravaganza. Lamar Hunt's World Championship Tennis Finals are in Dallas as well.

The safest time to jog the streets or drive on the cloverleafing freeways around Dallas–Fort Worth is Sundays right after kickoff during the Cowboys' fall season. The usual 3:00 P.M. start is convenient not only for national TV, but also for the churchgoing public. Sometimes referred to as the Buckle of the Bible Belt, Dallas is home to hundreds of faiths—including four churches each of which is the largest in its denomination anywhere. They are Highland Park Methodist, First Baptist, Highland Park Presbyterian and East Dallas Christian.

Dallas is known in other veins, too. It forever will carry the stigma of being the site of President Kennedy's assassination, November 22, 1963. Home of Texas' first Republican governor since Reconstruction, former Gov. Bill Clements, Dallas also hosted the 1984 Republican Convention. Dallas is the home of Neiman-Marcus, the specialty store that in 1987 will celebrate 80 years of class, panache, and extravagance. The Texas-size Dallas Market Center includes the Apparel Mart, the Decorative Center, the Home Furnishings Center, Market Hall, and the World Trade Center.

Though windier than Chicago and with more rain than Seattle, Dallas's weather is a big calling card for snowbirds coming in from the northern climes. Dallas rises early, but it bows out very late: After dinner at, perhaps, a classic French restaurant (visitors find there *is* life after chili, barbecue, and charbroiled steaks), a couple may skip over to Fort Worth to take in Billy Bob's Texas, the world's largest honkytonk. Residents and visitors—children of all ages—frequent Six Flags Over Texas, a pioneer of the one-ticket amusement park, and a variety of other spreads.

Art to Art

Except at the major hotels, downtown Dallas rolls up the streets after 7:00 P.M., when the cultural scene lights up elsewhere. While Fort

Worth wins accolades for three world-class museums—the Amon Carter, Kimbell, and Science and History—Dallas makes headlines in the arts of symphony, opera, ballet, and theater, and especially the promising futures of each. In mid-1982 Dallas voters approved a $247-million bond issue, which included $28.6 million for a new concert hall in the new downtown Arts District and $18 million to renovate more than a half dozen buildings, including museums, at State Fair Park. The same year Dallas opened its new $40-million downtown library and, in early 1984, the $40 million Dallas Museum of Art, in the Arts District.

John Neely Bryan founded Dallas—named for Vice-President George Mifflin Dallas—in 1841 when he set up a trading post on the banks of the Trinity. But "culture" came to Dallas in 1855 with a party of 200 French, Swiss, and Belgians intent on founding a utopia. It's not certain what they thought they would find in the area to complement their efforts. They failed, but the scientists, artists, naturalists, writers, and musicians on the scene had dignified a frontier city.

Artists, writers, and musicians still call Dallas home, and along with their white- and blue-collar cohorts, they live in all corners of sprawling Dallas and its thriving suburbs and neighbors (don't let the names fool you: Plano, Grand Prairie, Mesquite, Farmers Branch), and in Oak Cliff, a scenic section of South Dallas where it's again becoming fashionable to live.

Friendly Rivalry

According to a study made by the University of Texas Graduate School of Business, Dallas, Houston, and Austin, in that order, are the most popular destinations when Texans travel within their state. (Fort Worth finished behind San Antonio and Galveston.) But a more interesting note is that, according to another study, Dallasites on the average travel to Houston, 250 miles to the south, more often than they do the 20-plus miles to Fort Worth on the other end of the Old Dallas–Fort Worth Turnpike (now I–30). The two cities are so close, yet so far apart.

Fort Worth, a city of 400,000, and Dallas have grown because of their persevering, industrious residents and, in some ways, despite them. Somewhere between Dallas and Fort Worth the line between east and west is drawn. Or, as the late Oklahoma humorist Will Rogers once put it: "Fort Worth is where the West begins and Dallas is where the East peters out." There has always existed a friendly rivalry between the two cities, but just how friendly depends upon whom you ask. Though competitive down to the latest concert or nightclub, the two

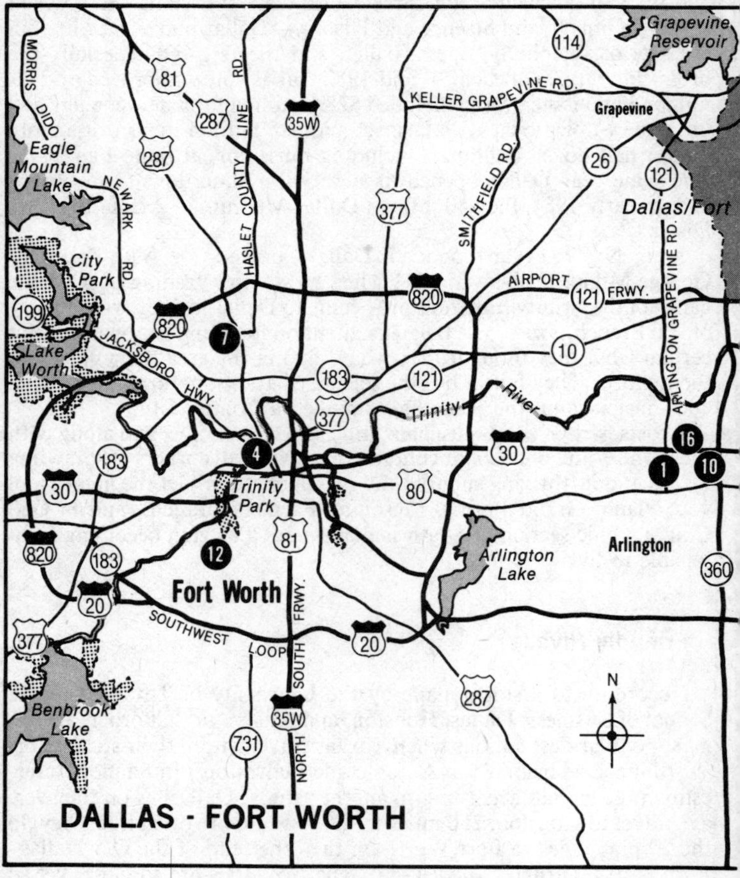

Points of Interest

1) Arlington Stadium
2) Dallas Love Field
3) Downtown Dallas
4) Downtown Fort Worth
5) The Galleria
6) International Wildlife Park
7) Meacham Field Municipal Airport
8) Prestonwood Town Center

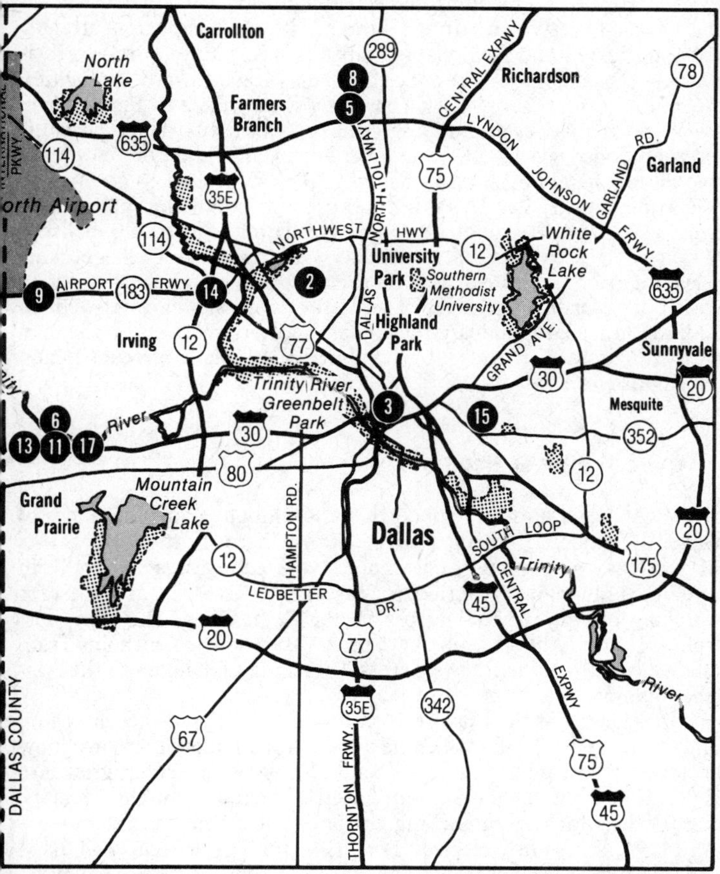

9) Sesame Place
10) Six Flags Over Texas
11) Southwest Historical Wax Museum
12) Texas Christian University
13) Texas Sports Hall of Fame
14) Texas Stadium
15) Texas State Fair Grounds
16) Wet 'n Wild
17) WhiteWater

have cooperated on planning and economics more than once—witness the Dallas–Fort Worth Airport—though it didn't happen overnight.

Sophisticated and fashionable Dallas is in a hurry; Fort Worth is more laid back. A well-dressed city, Dallas leans toward formalities; clean jeans and a jacket are accepted most anywhere in Fort Worth. But because most every building (and parts of many theme parks) is air-conditioned because of the summer heat, Dallas and Fort Worth are two cities where a businessman might take *off* his coat to go outside.

During World War II, both cities grew in population and wealth because of the defense industries, chiefly relating to airplanes, helicopters, and other such military products. After the war, Dallas became a leading producer of electrical and electronic equipment and, along with Fort Worth, a producer of aircraft and missile parts as well. In addition to its cattle-industry headquarters, Fort Worth is on the map with the aircraft, grain, and oil industries and as a mercantile and distribution center.

Where the West Begins

Though never a fort, Fort Worth was eventually named in honor of General William J. Worth, a Mexican War hero. Fort Worth got its start in 1849 as a military encampment protecting area settlers from Indians. Built on bluffs overlooking the Trinity River, it was perfect for watching over the sprawling prairie for Comanches. The view west from the Trinity bluffs soon changed to cattle on the Chisholm Trail, as cowboys drove their herds across Texas and Oklahoma to the Abilene, Kansas, stockyards.

Fort Worth was their last stop on the way north and their first stop on the way home during the cattle drives. A section of downtown, now occupied mostly by the Tarrant County Convention Center, grew into Hell's Half Acre, a shoot-'em-up haven of saloons, gambling houses, and brothels for the fun-seeking cowboys after their drives.

In 1876, Fort Worth elected "Long Hair Jim" Courtright as marshal and told him to keep peace in town but not to chase off the cowboys—or their money. Fast with his guns, he was an honored Civil War veteran and had toured with Buffalo Bill Cody's Wild West Show. With Hell's Half Acre calmed down but still stomping, Fort Worth saw many famous visitors, among them Doc Holliday, Wyatt Earp, and Butch Cassidy and the Sundance Kid. (A gambler himself, Courtright was gunned down on Main Street in 1887 by White Elephant saloon owner Luke Short, a retired cowboy.)

The *New York Daily Chronicle* reported in 1882: "Fort Worth is cosmopolitan. It has the rush and energy of a frontier town with strange contrasts of nationality. It smacks of Mexico and New York. Broadway and ranch brush against one another."

Real Cowtown

Soon the railroads were stretching west into Fort Worth and the city entered into its boom-town stage. The Fort Worth Stockyards, second in size only to Chicago's, and several meatpacking houses sprang up at the turn of the century. The town soon earned its other nickname, Cowtown. Longhorns and other cattle filled the stockyards, and buffalo skins were brought in from West Texas for shipment north and east. Rodeos and stock shows became the order of the day. They're still on the scene today, in fact, at Will Rogers Memorial Center and in the revitalized Stockyards area.

After the turn of the century, Fort Worth still had its cowboys, cattle, and Hell's Half Acre but was no longer a frontier town. It was receiving national attention. Established on the city's West Side during World War I, Camp Bowie was an enormous army training facility for 100,000 soldiers. Shortly after the Armistice was signed in 1918, Camp Bowie finally shut the door on Hell's Half Acre. J. F. Cantrell began cleaning up Fort Worth himself, so to speak, by opening the nations' first washateria in 1934.

There was no oil discovered in Fort Worth, but there might as well have been. Hundreds of thousands of barrels of black gold headed for Fort Worth, which had twenty-two refineries by 1922. Oil companies' headquarters came to the city and with them lots of money. Big buildings sprang up in Fort Worth. Now the Hyatt Regency, the historical fourteen-story Hotel Texas—where John F. Kennedy spent his last night—was the direct result of oil money, as well as being the tallest building in Fort Worth in 1921. The city is still headquarters for hundreds of oil and oil-related industries, including exploration development, wildcatters, petroleum equipment, and refining.

A slice of Fort Worth's present downtown facelift, Sundance Square, with its turn-of-the-century architecture, features restaurants, shops, and nightspots in low-rise buildings. The downtown rebirth includes three new luxury hotels and six new trolley-style buses serving the downtown area, the Stockyards north of downtown, and the museum complex to the west.

Downtown Fort Worth is bounded by I–30, I–35W and the more scenic Trinity River, which makes a better name for itself in Cowtown, especially along Trinity and Forest Parks to the west and southwest. These parks are home to Fort Worth's celebrated Botanic and Japanese gardens and zoo, aquarium, and Log Cabin Village, respectively. Texas

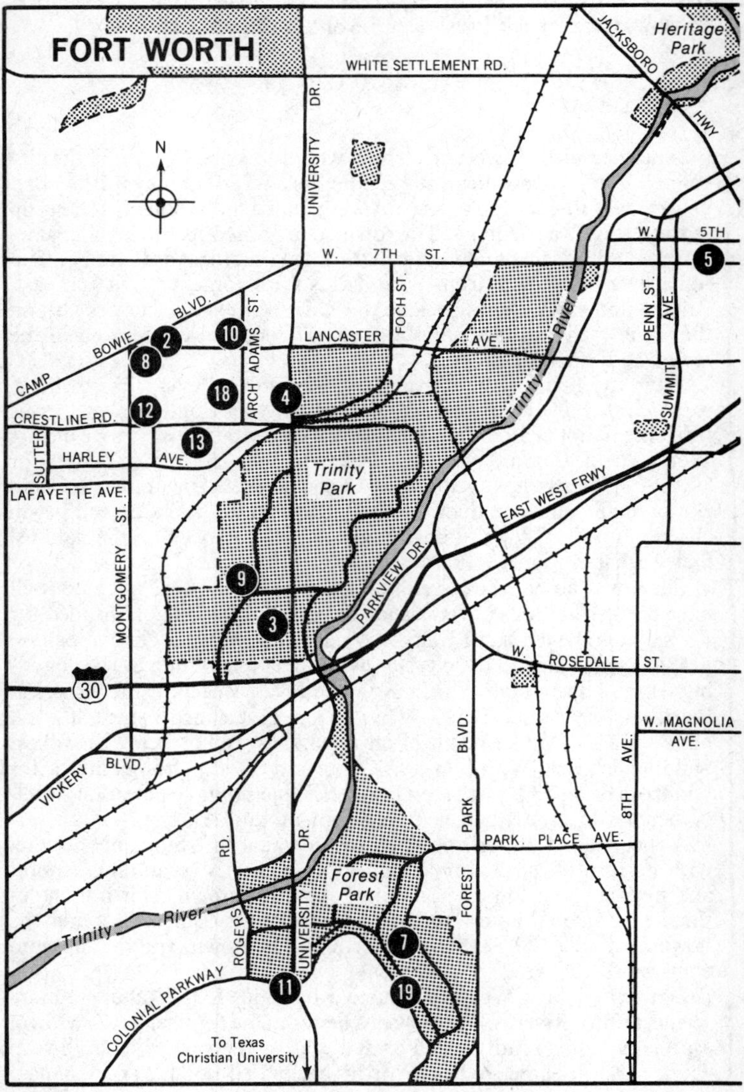
FORT WORTH
N
Heritage Park
JACKSBORO HWY
WHITE SETTLEMENT RD.
UNIVERSITY DR.
W. 5TH
W. 7TH ST.
5
CAMP BOWIE BLVD.
2
8
10
ARCH ADAMS ST.
LANCASTER AVE.
FOCH ST.
PENN. ST.
SUMMIT AVE.
Trinity River
18
4
12
CRESTLINE RD.
13
SUTTER
HARLEY AVE.
LAFAYETTE AVE.
Trinity Park
EAST WEST FRWY
PARKVIEW DR.
MONTGOMERY ST.
9
3
30
W. ROSEDALE ST.
W. MAGNOLIA AVE.
VICKERY BLVD.
FOREST PARK BLVD.
8TH AVE.
PARK PLACE AVE.
ROGERS RD.
UNIVERSITY DR.
Forest Park
Trinity River
7
19
11
COLONIAL PARKWAY
To Texas Christian University

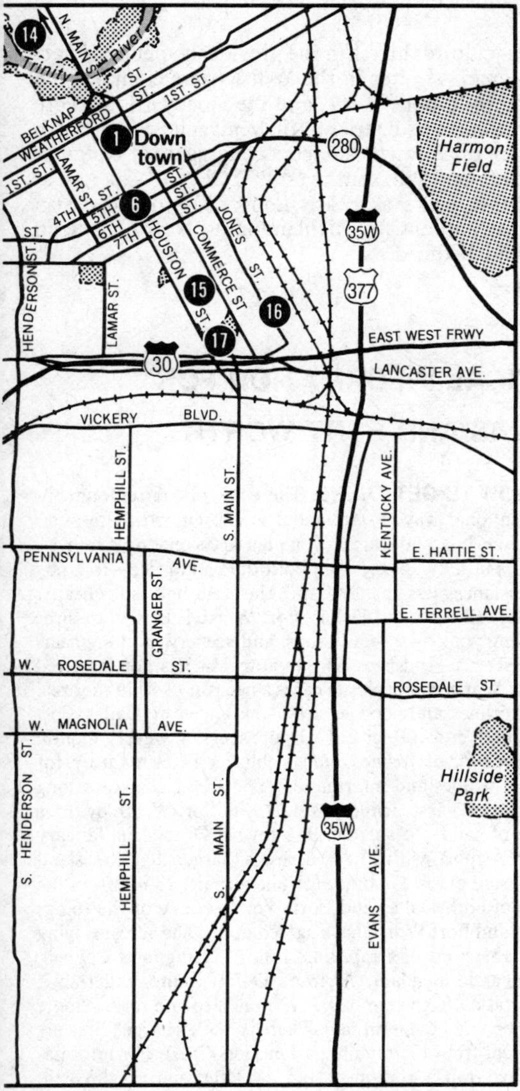

Points of Interest

1) Americana Hotel
2) Amon Carter Museum
3) Botanic Garden
4) Casa Manana
5) Cattlemen's Museum
6) Convention and Visitors Bureau
7) Forest Park Aquarium
8) Fort Worth Art Museum
9) Japanese Garden
10) Kimbell Art Museum
11) Log Cabin Village
12) Museum of Science and Technology
13) Southwestern Exposition and Fat Stock Show Buildings
14) Stockyards
15) Tarrant County Convention Center
16) Train Station
17) Water Garden
18) Will Rogers Memorial Coliseum
19) Zoological Park

Christian University and Amon Carter Stadium are several more blocks south.

West of Trinity Park, culture thrives in the previously mentioned art museums and Casa Manana theater in the Will Rogers complex. On the wilder side of town, Billy Bob's Texas and the Stockyards area are ten minutes north of the business district in the rejuvenated area north of downtown. Outside of downtown, shoppers congregate at Ridgmar Mall, west on I–30; at Hulen Mall, southwest of TCU on I–20; and at Northeast Mall, northeast on Texas 121 at Loop 820—in and near a sea of suburbs known as Haltom City, Richland Hills, North Richland Hills, Hurst, Euless, and Bedford.

PRACTICAL INFORMATION FOR DALLAS AND FORT WORTH

HOW TO GET THERE. There are, of course, four conventional ways to get about in the United States: car, plane, bus, and train. If you plan to travel long distances, it is usually cheaper—in both time and price—to go by plane than by rail. For distances less than 300 mi., the train or bus is cheaper and may be faster, too. But rail service to Dallas–Fort Worth is limited to three times a week. As for calling your own shots, stops, and scenery, nothing beats a car—especially around Texas. And because public transit has not mastered the expansive Dallas–Fort Worth Metroplex, a car is a necessity within the area.

By air. Because new airlines and services are being added at Dallas–Fort Worth (midway between both cities) Regional Airport seemingly every month, travelers should consult the *Official Airline Guide,* published twice monthly, for the most current airline schedules and information. The area has come a long way since 1919, when America's first airline was started in Fort Worth by three men to fly gift packages of candy to surrounding towns. Opened in January 1974, Dallas–Fort Worth Airport, with 17,800 acres, is "larger than the island of Manhattan," as Texans are quick to point out. The airport, 17 mi. from the central business districts of both Dallas and Fort Worth, is one of the things highly competitive Dallas and Fort Worth have agreed upon. The acreage, lying within the boundaries of the cities of Grapevine, Euless, Irving, and Coppell, was mostly low-yield farm and ranch land. Airtrans, D–FW's automatic transit system, provides transportation from terminal to terminal, to and from remote parking areas, and to the on-site hotel (Amfac). There is a 50¢ charge (quarters only) to use Airtrans, except from the remote parking lots (free). For information on Surtran, the surface transportation system to Dallas and Fort Worth, see the *How to Get Around* section, below.

The approximate flight times to Dallas–Fort Worth Airport from these Texas cities are: Austin, 50 minutes; Brownsville-Harlingen, 1½ hours; El Paso, 2½; Houston, 1; and San Antonio, 1. The approximate flight times from these U.S. cities are: Atlanta, 2 hours; Miami, 4½; New Orleans, 1½; Phoenix, 2; Chicago, 2½; Denver, 1½; Las Vegas, 2½; Los Angeles, 3; New York, 4; San Francisco–Oakland, 3; Seattle, 3½; Washington, D.C., 3; Anchorage, 8; and Honolulu, 7. Flight time from Mexico City is 2½ hours; Toronto, 3; London, 10; Frankfurt, 11, and Tokyo, 14.

Discounts are offered by many airlines to members of families traveling together. Thirty-day excursion fares, youth fares for college students, and special low fares (on a standby basis) for members of the armed forces are also offered by many airlines. Most of the fares have certain restrictions, such as requiring the traveler to make the trip during certain times of the week, principally to avoid those days when traffic is heavy. Discounts change frequently; savings can range from 15 to 45% over regular coach fare, so check with a travel agent or airline for the exact rates.

For more information on the Dallas–Fort Worth Regional Airport, write P.O. Drawer DFW, Dallas–Fort Worth Airport, TX 75261.

By bus. Both *Trailways,* with corporate headquarters in Dallas, and *Greyhound* (Phoenix) offer extensive, competing route systems and schedules. Travelers from all U.S. areas can find easy access to the Dallas–Fort Worth Metroplex. Check with a travel agent or a nearby Trailways or Greyhound office for details on special tours and unlimited travel passes offering Dallas–Fort Worth as a destination, turnaround, or brief stop. The great distances involved in travel to and around Texas could make these passes very advantageous. In downtown Dallas, the Trailways bus terminal is at 1500 Jackson St., the Greyhound terminal at Commerce and Lamar. In downtown Fort Worth, the Trailways bus terminal is at 901 Commerce, the Greyhound terminal at 1005 Commerce. Numerous other terminals are used in and around both cities, including the Mid-Cities and other suburban areas.

By train. Amtrak services both Dallas (653–1101) and Fort Worth (336–1010) on a limited schedule. The Amtrak Eagle Route originates in Chicago and stops in Dallas three afternoons a week (Monday, Wednesday, and Saturday) before going southward to San Antonio, where connections are available to Los Angeles. The return trip arrives in Fort Worth each Tuesday, Friday, and Sunday afternoon on its route eastward to Dallas and eventually Chicago. Because of the layover, train travel between Dallas and Fort Worth alone is obviously not a popular means of transportation. Consult a travel agent or Amtrak for details on excursion- and family-fare structures, and discounts for senior citizens and the handicapped. The Amtrak passenger station in downtown Dallas is at Union Station, 400 S. Houston (at Young); in Fort Worth, at 15th and Jones.

By car. Whether in the traveler's own vehicle or a rental, the easiest access to and around the Metroplex is by car. Major attractions in Dallas and Fort Worth are spread throughout the area, and the two cities are 28 mi. apart on either end of the Old Dallas–Fort Worth Turnpike—now officially I–30 with free access. Interstate highways—I-35E (north-south through Dallas) and I–35W (north-south through Fort Worth), I–30, and I–20—connect Dallas and Fort Worth to the rest of the country.

The approximate drive times to Dallas–Fort Worth from these Texas cities are: Austin, 3½ hours; Brownsville-Harlingen, 10; El Paso, 11; Houston, 5; and San Antonio, 5.

Most major car-rental companies have outlets at the Dallas–Fort Worth Regional Airport, Dallas Love Field, and numerous locations in and around Dallas, Fort Worth, the Mid-Cities, and the suburbs. For reservations, refer to these toll-free numbers: *Avis,* (800) 331–1212; *Budget,* (800) 527–0700; *Dollar Car Rental,* (800) 421–6868; *Hertz,* (800) 654–3131, and *National,* (800) 328–4567.

TELEPHONES. The area code for Dallas County is 214; for Tarrant County (Fort Worth), 817. The following cities and suburbs are **214:** Dallas, Grand Prairie, Irving, Farmers Branch, Carrollton, Lewisville, Renner, Addison, Richardson, Plano, Garland, Wylie, Rowlett, Mesquite, DeSoto, Duncanville, and Cedar Hill. The following cities and townships are **817:** Fort Worth, Richland Hills, North Richland Hills, Haltom City, Grapevine, Euless, Hurst, Bedford, Arlington, Mansfield, Crowley, Benbrook, and Cresson.

You do not need to dial the area code if it is the same as the one from which you are dialing. Local directory assistance in either city is simply 1411. An operator will assist you on person-to-person, credit-card, and collect calls if you dial "0" first. From outside the 214 area-code region, directory information for Dallas can be obtained toll-free by dialing 1–214–555–1212. From outside the 817 area-code region, directory information for Fort Worth can be obtained toll-free by dialing 1–817–555–1212. In either case, ask the operator if the party you need to call has a Metro number that can be dialed free from anywhere in the Dallas–Fort Worth Metroplex. Dial 1–800–555–1212 to see if there is an 800 toll-free number for the business you want to reach.

EMERGENCY NUMBERS. In Dallas proper: *emergency* ambulance, police or fire, 744–4444; Parkland Hospital, 638–1800. In Fort Worth proper: *emergency* ambulance, 335–4357; fire 332–2131, and police, 335–4222. John Peter Smith Hospital, 921–3431. Or, dial "0" for Operator, and ask the person's help in connecting you immediately with the appropriate agency. Please note that these are for *emergency* use only.

HOTELS AND MOTELS in Big D (from Oak Cliff to Far North Dallas), Fort Worth, and the Mid-Cities and D–FW Airport areas cater to a wide variety of tastes and pocketbooks. We offer only a selection of convenient hotels and motels. New facilities are opening almost every month, and many others are undergoing expansions, additions, or restorations. Dallas is the third most popular convention, trade, and market-show city in the country, so be sure to reserve your rooms as soon as your travel plans are set.

A free publication from the Dallas Convention & Visitors Bureau (see *Tourist Information,* below) lists dozens of discount packages offered by some of the city's most luxurious hotels, as well as modestly priced accommodations. Many packages are geared around the weekend or sporting events. For more information on lodging in the Fort Worth area, contact the Fort Worth Convention and Visitors Bureau (see *Tourist Information*). With rare exceptions, all lodgings in the Metroplex are air-conditioned, and most have swimming pools. Rates may be higher during the State Fair (October) and Cotton Bowl week (New Year's Day and the week preceding). Most hotels near Six Flags charge higher rates when the park is open daily (summer). Weekend rates at some hotels are lower.

Hotel rates are based on single occupancy in a regular double-bed room. Categories determined by price are: *Super Deluxe,* $110 and up; *Deluxe,* $90 to $109; *Expensive,* $80 to $89; *Moderate,* $70 to $79; *Inexpensive,* $60 to $69; and *Basic Budget,* less than $60. All rates are subject to change with inflation. All hotels are in alphabetical order by price category and represent only a sampling.

D–FW AIRPORT/MID-CITIES AREA

Deluxe

The Mandalay Four Seasons Hotel. 221 S. Las Colinas Blvd. at Texas 114, in Irving's Las Colinas Urban Center; (214) 556–0800. 10 minutes from D–FW Airport, 5 minutes from Texas Stadium, 15 minutes from downtown Dallas. 27-story. Opened in summer 1982. Three restaurants, including Enjolie, and two clubs.

Expensive

Amfac Hotel and Resort. In the center of D–FW Airport; (214) 453–8400; The world's largest airport hotel, with 1,450 rooms in two towers. Eight restaurants, five bars. Bear Creek Golf and Racquet Center.

DFW Hilton. 1800 Hwy. 26E, north entrance to DFW Airport; (817) 481–8444. Opened 1983. Free shuttle service. 400 rooms. Health club. Conference center.

DFW Marriott. 8440 Freeport Parkway, north entrance to DFW Airport; (214) 258–4800. Seven minutes from airport. Free shuttle service. Opened October 1982. Two restaurants, two clubs, indoor/outdoor pool, exercise room, whirlpool and sauna.

Sheraton Grand Hotel. Texas 114 at Esters, just north of D–FW Airport; (214) 258–4900. Opened October 1982. Restaurant, two lounges.

Moderate

Holiday Inn–D–FW Airport North. 4441 W. Highway 114, Irving; (214) 255–7147. Extensively remodeled. Restaurant, bar.

Inexpensive

Holiday Inn Six Flags. 903 N. Collins Ave., Arlington; (817) 261–3621. Restaurant, bar.

Holiday Inn–Texas Stadium. 1930 E. Airport Freeway (Texas 183); (214) 438–1313. Restaurant, bar.

Ramada Inn. 700 Lamar E., Arlington; (817) 265–7711. Restaurant, bar.

Ramada Inn–Airport. 120 W. Airport Freeway, Irving; (214) 579–8911. Near Texas Stadium. Restaurant, bar.

Rodeway Inn and Conference Center. 833 N. Highway 360, Arlington, near Six Flags Over Texas and Arlington Stadium; (817) 265–8241. Restaurant, two lounges.

Sheraton-Safari. 402 Safari Parkway, on I–30, Grand Prairie; (214) 263–4421. Adjacent to amusement parks and museums. Restaurant, club.

Basic Budget

Best Western Tom Penny Inn–Irving. 2200 E. Airport Freeway (Texas 183), Irving; (214) 438–6666. Near Texas Stadium. Restaurant.

Fiesta Motor Inn. 1000 E. Division, Arlington; (817) 461–2171. Near restaurant.

Flagship Inn. 601 Ave. H East, Arlington, near Six Flags Over Texas and Arlington Stadium; (817) 640–1666. Formerly Inn of Six Flags. Restaurant, club.

Holiday Inn–D–FW Airport South. 4440 W. Airport Freeway (Texas 183), Irving; (214) 399–1010. Recently remodeled. 408 rooms. Three restaurants, two bars. Health club.

Quality Inn–Arlington. 1601 E. Division, Arlington; (817) 261–2300. Restaurant, bar.

La Quinta–D–FW Airport. 4105 W. Airport Freeway (Texas 183), Irving; (214) 252–6546. Near Sesame Place. Bar, 24-hour restaurant next door.

Turnpike Motor Lodge. 2001 E. Copeland, Arlington; (817) 461–1122.

DALLAS AREA

Super Deluxe

The Mansion on Turtle Creek. 2821 Turtle Creek Blvd.; (214) 559–2100. On 4½-acre estate on the tree-lined creek of the same name. 129 rooms and 14 suites. Two dining areas, including the elegant Mansion on Turtle Creek Restaurant.

Plaza of the Americas. 650 N. Pearl Blvd., downtown; (214) 747–7222. Trusthouse Forte property. On the west side of three towers connected by an atrium with shops, restaurants, offices, and an ice rink. Two restaurants, including Cafe Royal (French), and three bars.

Deluxe

Adolphus Hotel (Amfac). 1321 Commerce St., downtown; (214) 742–8200. $45-million restoration complete. Built by brewer Adolphus Busch in 1912, marketed now as "a beautiful lady with a past." Spacious rooms. Three restaurants, including the celebrated French Room; three bars.

Crown Plaza–Holiday Inn. 4099 Valley View Lane, at LBJ Freeway (I–635) at Midway; (214) 385–9000. Luxury inn. Atrium. Three restaurants, two lounges, including Isadora's.

Dallas Marriott-Park Central. 7750 LBJ Freeway (I–635) at Coit Road; (214) 233–4421. Near Olla Podrida shopping. Totally renovated. Restaurant, two lounges.

Doubletree Inn. 8250 N. Central Expressway (U.S. 75) at Caruth Haven; (214) 691–8700. In Campbell Centre. Near the Greenville Avenue restaurants and clubs and NorthPark and Old Town shopping. Two lounges, including Cirrus, and restaurant.

The Fairmont. Ross at Akard, downtown; (214) 748–5454. Texas' 5-star hotel. 600 rooms in two towers. Three restaurants, including the elegant Pyramid Room and the Venetian Room for dinner shows, and two bars.

Granada Royale Hometel. 2727 Stemmons Freeway (I–35E); (214) 630–5332. All-suite hotel near Market Center. Restaurant, bar.

Hyatt Regency Dallas. 300 Reunion Blvd., southwest downtown, next to Reunion Tower and across the street from Reunion Arena; (214) 651–1234. 19-floor atrium. 1,000 rooms. Three restaurants, three bars.

The Lincoln Hotel. 5410 LBJ Freeway (I–635) at Dallas Parkway; (214) 934–8400. In Lincoln Centre. 522 rooms. Opened summer 1982. Four restaurants, two lounges.

Loews Anatole Dallas. 2201 Stemmons Freeway (I–35E), in Market Center; (214) 748–1200. A trio of glass pyramids covers two atria of trees and tapestries. 27-story adjoining tower. 1,620 rooms (145 suites). 19 restaurants and bars.

The Melrose Hotel. 3015 Oak Lawn Ave., just northwest of downtown; (214) 521–5151. A small hotel built in 1924. Totally renovated. Restaurant.

The Registry. 15201 Dallas Parkway, in the Quorum, at Belt Line Road; (800) 527–1690 for reservations, or (214) 386–6000. Four restaurants, three lounges. 570 large rooms, including 40 suites. Adjacent to Prestonwood Town Center and Sakowitz Village Shopping.

Sheraton–Park Central. 12720 Merit Drive, near LBJ Freeway (I–635) at Coit Road, near Olla Podrida shopping; 385–3000. Opened December 1982. 560 rooms. Three restaurants, three lounges.

The Westin Hotel. 13340 Dallas Parkway at LBJ Freeway (I–635), in the Galleria; (214) 934–9494. 440 rooms. Opened December 1982. Three restaurants, lounge.

Expensive

The Bradford Plaza. 302 S. Houston St. at Jackson, downtown, opposite both courthouse and Union Station; (214) 761–9090. Refurbished. Restaurant, lounge.

Dallas Hilton Inn. 5600 N. Central Expressway (U.S. 75) at Mockingbird Lane; (214) 827–4100. Midway between downtown and LBJ Freeway (I–635), near Southern Methodist University. Three restaurants, including Trader Vic's and Harper's, and three bars.

The Hilton–LBJ. 4801 LBJ Freeway (I–635) at Inwood Road; (214) 661–3600. Near Galleria shopping. Restaurant, bar.

The Regent. 1241 W. Mockingbird Lane at Stemmons Freeway (I–35E), 5 minutes from Love Field; (214) 630–7000. Two restaurants, bars.

Sheraton-Dallas. Live Oak at Olive Street, downtown; (214) 922–8000. Reopened in 1983 after $45-million renovation. Three restaurants, three bars.

The Summit. 2645 LBJ Freeway (I–635) at I–35E; (214) 243–3363. Convenient to both D–FW and Love Field airports. Two restaurants, including Gabriel's, and a club.

The Wyndham at the Dallas Market Center. 2222 Stemmons Freeway; (214) 631–2222. Opened January 1983. 542 rooms. 30 guest stories. Two restaurants, four lounges.

Moderate

Brookhollow Inn. 7900 Brookriver Dr., Mockingbird at Stemmons; (214) 688–1010. All suites. Richardson and Arlington properties, too.

Dallas Hilton. 1914 Commerce St., downtown, near Convention Center; (214) 747–7000. 746 rooms. Five restaurants and bars.

Harvey House Hotel. 7815 LBJ Freeway (I–635) at Coit Road; (214) 960–7000. Near Olla Podrida shopping. Rooms surround six courtyards. Restaurant, club.

Marriott Market Center. 2101 Stemmons Freeway (I–35E), in Market Center; (214) 748–8551. 418 rooms. Two restaurants, two bars.

Sheraton Inn–Mockingbird West. 1893 W. Mockingbird Lane, near Love Field; (214) 634–8850. Expanded facilities. Restaurant, club, including Las Vegas–style entertainment.

Twin Sixties Inn. 6060 N. Central Expressway (U.S. 75), near Mockingbird Lane; (214) 691–3600. Near Southern Methodist University. Restaurant, bar.

Viscount Hotel. 4500 Harry Hines Blvd. (U.S. 77); (214) 522–6650. In Market Center. Restaurant, bar.

Inexpensive

Executive Inn. 3232 W. Mockingbird Lane, near Love Field; (214) 357–5601. Restaurant, bar.

The Grenelefe. 1011 S. Akard St., just south of downtown, near Convention Center; (214) 421–1083. Small hotel. Restaurant, bar.

Holiday Inn–Downtown. 1015 Elm St., downtown; (214) 748–9951. Restaurant, lounge.

Holiday Inn–Central. 4070 N. Central Expressway (U.S. 75); (214) 827–0881. Restaurant, bar.

Holiday Inn–Market Center. 1955 Market Center Blvd.; (214) 747–9551. Restaurant, lounge.

Howard Johnson's–Central. 10333 N. Central Expressway (U.S. 75) at Meadow Road; (214) 363–0221. Near NorthPark shopping. Restaurant, bar.

Quality Inn–Market Center. 2015 Market Center Blvd.; (214) 741–7481. Restaurant, bar.

Ramada Hotel Dallas (formerly LeBaron Hotel). 1055 Regal Row at John Carpenter Freeway (Texas 183), across Trinity River from Texas Stadium; (214) 634–8550. Two restaurants, three clubs.

Sheraton Inn–Northeast. 11350 LBJ Freeway (I–635) at Jupiter Road; (214) 341–5400. Restaurant, bar.

Stoneleigh Terrace. 2927 Maple Ave., just north of downtown; (214) 871–7111. Restaurant and bar.

Basic Budget

Best Western Inn–LBJ. 8051 LBJ Freeway (I–635) at Coit Road; (214) 234–2431. Near Olla Podrida shopping. Lounge, with restaurant next door.

Best Western Market Center. 2023 Market Center Blvd., across from Market Center; (214) 741–5041. Restaurant, bar.

Best Western Red Bird Inn. 4023 S. Walton Walker Blvd.; (214) 339–3121. Restaurant, bar.

Holiday Inn–Northwest. 1735 S. I–35E, Farmers Branch; (214) 242–6431. Restaurant, bar.

Howard Johnson's–East. 7201 Ferguson Road; (214) 328–4681. Restaurant nearby.

Howard Johnson's–Stemmons. 3111 Stemmons Freeway (I–35E); (214) 637–0060. Restaurant, bar.

Non-Smokers Inn. 9229 Carpenter Freeway (Texas 183); (214) 631–6633. Near Texas Stadium. Restaurant nearby.

NorthPark Inn and Convention Center. 9300 N. Central Expressway (U.S. 75), between Park and Walnut Hill lanes; (214) 363–2431. Near NorthPark shopping. Restaurant and coffee shop.

Park Cities Inn. 6101 Hillcrest Ave., opposite Southern Methodist University; (214) 521–0330. Restaurant nearby.

Plaza Hotel. 1933 Main St., downtown; (214) 742–7251. Restaurant, bar.

La Quinta–North Central. 4440 N. Central Expressway (U.S. 75) at Henderson-Knox; (214) 821–4220. Restaurant nearby.

La Quinta–NorthPark. 10001 N. Central Expressway (U.S. 75) at Meadow Road; (214) 361–8200. Near NorthPark shopping. Restaurant.

La Quinta Northwest–Farmers Branch. 13325 Stemmons Freeway (I–35E) at Valley View; (214) 620–7333. Restaurant nearby.

La Quinta-Regal Row. 1625 Regal Row, off Stemmons Freeway (I–35E); (214) 630–5701. Restaurant nearby.

La Quinta–Richardson. 13685 N. Central Expressway (U.S. 75) at Mid-Park Road; (214) 234–1016. Restaurant nearby.

Ramada Inn–Farmers Branch. 13333 Stemmons Freeway (I–35E), Farmers Branch; (214) 241–8521. Restaurant, bar.

Rodeway Inn–Market Center. 2026 Market Center Blvd.; (214) 748–2243. Restaurant nearby.

Rodeway Inn–North Central. 4150 N. Central Expressway (U.S. 75) at Fitzhugh; (214) 827–4310. Restaurant nearby.

Tropicana Inn. 3939 N. Central Expressway (U.S. 75), near downtown; (214) 526–8881. Restaurant, lounge.

Valley View Inn. 6101 LBJ Freeway (I–635) at Preston Road; (214) 387–2525. Near Valley View shopping. Restaurant, bar.

FORT WORTH AREA

Expensive

Americana Hotel–Tandy Center. 200 Main St., downtown; (817) 870–1000. In the middle of historic district. Connected to Tandy Center shopping. 510 rooms. Two restaurants, three bars.

Moderate

Fort Worth Hilton Inn. 1701 Commerce St., downtown, near I–30; (817) 335–7000. Across from Water Gardens and near Convention Center. Two restaurants, bars.

Hyatt Regency Fort Worth. 815 Main St., downtown; (817) 870–1234. Across from Convention Center. Building formerly the famous Hotel Texas. Totally redone. 530 rooms. Two restaurants, three bars.

Inexpensive

Green Oaks Inn. 6901 West Freeway; (817) 738–7311. Next to a golf course. Restaurant, bars.

Holiday Inn Midtown. 1441 S. University Drive; (817) 336–9311. Rest., club.

Ramada Inn Central. 2000 Beach St; (817) 534–4801. Two restaurants, bar.

Basic Budget

Best Western Fort Worther. 4213 South Freeway; (817) 923–1987.

Best Western Kahler West Branch Inn. 7301 West Freeway; (817) 244–7444. Formerly Best Western Tom Penny Inn. Near a restaurant.

Best Western Metro Center Hotel. 600 Commerce St., downtown; (817) 332–6900. Restaurant, lounge.

Best Western Park Central Inn. 1011 Throckmorton St., downtown; (817) 336–2011. Restaurant.

Days Inn. Las Vegas Trail, in White Settlement; (817) 246–4961. Restaurant.

Days Inn–Felix Street. 812 E. Felix St., (817) 926–9211. Restaurant.

Drummers Inn–North. 2520 N.E. 28th St.; (817) 624–3104. Restaurant.

Holiday Inn–Northeast. Junction of Texas 183 and I–820, Hurst; (817) 284–9461. Restaurant, club.

Motel 6. 6401 Airport Freeway, Haltom City; (817) 834–3851.

La Quinta. 7888 I–30; (817) 246–5511.

Quality Inn South. 4201 South Freeway; (817) 923–8281. Restaurant, bar.

Rodeway Inn. 1111 W. Lancaster; (817) 332–1951. Club.

South Loop. 6328 South Freeway; (817) 293–5333. Near a restaurant.

HOW TO GET AROUND. Airport. Dallas–Fort Worth Regional Airport is about 17 mi. from the central business districts of both Dallas to the east and Fort Worth to the west and, depending upon traffic, a 20- to 35-minute drive in either direction. LINK buses meet flights frequently (ticket counters are adjacent to baggage-claim areas in all airline terminals) and transport passengers until late evening to Dallas's Union Terminal downtown (400 S. Houston at Young), North Dallas Terminal (LBJ and North Central Expressway), and Love Field (7 mi. north of downtown) and to major downtown hotels in either Dallas or Fort Worth for $8 one-way, $15 round-trip. For more information, phone 790–0441 in Dallas. Taxis are metered (about $20 to either downtown Dallas or Fort Worth, plus tip, and a 50¢ surcharge for each additional passenger). Getting from terminal to terminal and in and out of the airport can be a motorist's dream. But the 30-minute drive between the airport and downtown Dallas can prove much longer if attempted around the time of a Dallas Cowboys football game. City streets are usually deserted at game time, except on or near both Texas 183 and 114, the south and north routes, respectively, from D–FW Airport to Dallas and two of the byways running right by Texas Stadium. Multilingual information at the airport: 574–4420. Helicopter service information (NorthPark Inn Helicopter, Dallas): 363–2431.

Dallas transportation. Dallas Transit System (101 N. Peak, 827–3400 main office, 826–2222 for route information) operates citywide air-conditioned buses, with 24-hour service on major routes (50¢ exact change for first zone, more for second and third zones). The downtown Hop-A-Bus shuttles (25¢ exact change) operate during business hours Monday through Friday, a bus calling at each Hop-A-Bus stop every 12 minutes. Two routes are available: The Blue Route (downtown library and City Hall) and the East-West Main St. Red Route. Commuters and visitors weary of downtown parking-garage prices (upwards of $10 a day) can use Park & Hop: Park all day in Lot E at Reunion Arena (southwest corner of downtown) for $1 and receive tickets good for round-trip rides to and from the central business district. Certain designated buses, equipped with wheelchair-lift service, serve some routes to major hospitals, clinics, and centers for the handicapped. Dallas Transit Bus Charters require 3-hour minimum and a 48-hour notice. Taxis (most air-conditioned) are metered ($1.30 for the first 1 mile, $1 for each additional mile, and 50¢ surcharge for each additional passenger). Several major taxicab services make pickups downtown, at major hotels and airports, and by phone from almost any location.

Fort Worth transportation. City Transit Service of Fort Worth, or simply Citran (2304 Pine, 870–6200), operates Fort Worth's air-conditioned buses, with daily service 6:00 A.M. to 9:00 P.M. on major routes (75¢ exact change, except in the downtown "free zone"). Three major areas of Fort Worth—downtown, the North Side Stockyards, and the four major museums—are served by the "trolley" trails. The trolleys are actually specially decorated buses with yellow trim and lettering, wooden bench seats, and brass railings, at the same fare rate. Trolley brochures with complete maps of all trails are available at the Fort Worth Chamber of Commerce, the museums, and several establishments in the

Stockyards area, including the visitor-information center at 123 E. Exchange Ave. The Tandy Subway, another free ride, is the only privately owned subway in the world and Texas' only subway. The 7-minute ride runs about 1 mi. from a parking lot in the north of downtown to the Tandy Center. Taxis (most air-conditioned) are metered ($1.30 initially to first quarter-mile, $1 for each additional mile, and 50¢ surcharge for each additional passenger). Several taxicab services make on-street pickups downtown, at major hotels and D–FW airport, and by phone from almost any location.

By car. An automobile, whether your own or a rental one, is a necessity for taking in the Dallas–Fort Worth Metroplex (see *How to Get There,* above). Hint to drivers: Do not be confused by the oft-used terms "turnpike" and "tollway" in the Metroplex. What was the Dallas–Fort Worth Turnpike, running east and west between the two central business districts, is now part of I–30, and no toll is charged; the Dallas North Tollway, running north and south just northwest of downtown Dallas to I–635 (LBJ Freeway), has doubled its toll to 50¢ to help finance an extension north.

On foot. A hint to walkers: As a safety precaution, both Dallas and Fort Worth police are quick to fine jaywalkers on downtown streets. Pedestrians should cross streets only in designated walks with the appropriate green signal light. Dallas has no subway system, but **Underground Dallas** affords downtown pedestrians the opportunity to park, shop, lunch, and bank without venturing out into the heat or cold. Entrances to the network of corridors may be found at the First International Building, One Main Place, and First National Bank for one segment, and Thanks-Giving Square and Republic Bank for another. The Underground is closed on Sunday and open only until 1:30 P.M. on Saturday.

TOURIST INFORMATION. Dallas. For free information, brochures, and booklets on Dallas and environs, contact the Dallas Convention & Visitors Bureau, Dallas Chamber of Commerce, Information Dept., 1507 Pacific Ave., Dallas, TX 75201; (214) 954–1482. Hours are 8:30 A.M. to 5:00 P.M., weekdays. Walk-ins may find the chamber's other information center more accessible: The Dallas Visitors Information Center at Union Station (400 S. Houston St. in the southwest corner of downtown; (214–747–2355) is open 9:00 A.M. to 5:00 P.M. daily.

Fort Worth. For free information, brochures, and booklets on Fort Worth and environs, contact the Fort Worth Convention & Visitors Bureau, 700 Throckmorton, Fort Worth, TX 76102; (817) 336–8791. The office is open 8:30 A.M. to 5:00 P.M. weekdays.

Mid-Cities. For more information on the Mid-Cities area, especially on theme parks and amusement centers and accommodations, contact the Arlington Convention & Visitors Bureau, City of Arlington, P.O. Box A, Arlington, TX 76010; (817) 265–7721, and the Grand Prairie Chamber of Commerce, 306 W. Main, Box 1227, Grand Prairie, TX 75051; (214) 264–1558.

Other sources. The Friday editions of the three major daily newspapers—the *Dallas Morning News,* the *Dallas Times Herald,* and the *Fort Worth Star-*

Telegram—offer reams of information on local and area attractions, as do the monthly magazines *D* and *Texas Monthly.* The *Dallas Morning News* offers arts and entertainment information via a recorded telephone message: "Artsline, 385–1155," is operated 24 hours a day by the Dallas Arts Combine with assistance from the City Arts Program. It details activities and events on a rotating basis for more than 50 Dallas cultural organizations. The recording provides specific information on local music, dance, and theater events, free public performances, galleries, museums, and touring shows.

SEASONAL EVENTS. January. The *Cotton Bowl Classic and Parade,* usually staged New Year's Day in Dallas, draws a national TV audience. Revelers and families line the downtown streets for the free morning parade. And in early afternoon, football fans fortunate enough to secure tickets converge on the Cotton Bowl in State Fair Park (2 mi. east of downtown) for the bowl game between the Southwest Conference champion and another highly ranked college team. The only continuously held livestock show in the United States since 1896, the extravagant *Southwestern Exposition, Fat Stock Show, and Rodeo* warms Fort Worth, usually late-month and early February, with a combination of contests, rodeos, cowboys, carnivals, parades, and of course, people-watching.

February. The *Quaker State Open* tournament in Grand Prairie hosts the professional bowlers' tour. Amateur boxers compete in *Golden Gloves* tournaments in Fort Worth and Dallas, and runners hoof through the streets of Fort Worth for the *Cowtown Marathon.*

March. Dallas is the scene of the *Southwest Sports and RV Show* and a stop on the *Virginia Slims women's tennis* circuit at Moody Coliseum, and *Dallas Grand Prix. Cow Town Goes Green* on St. Patrick's Day.

April. Major-league baseball, of the American League's *Texas Rangers* variety, is uncorked early in the month (through early October) at Arlington Stadium, midway between Dallas and Fort Worth. Strollers and motorists take to the sidewalks and streets, especially along stately Turtle Creek in Dallas, to admire the *spring blooms* at their height around Eastertime. Lamar Hunt's *World Championship Tennis Finals* are staged in Dallas's Reunion Arena in late April or early May. And Traders' Village in Grand Prairie hosts a *Western Days Celebration and Rodeo.*

May. The first weekend of the month, *Mayfest* in Fort Worth's Trinity Park offers arts and crafts, live entertainment, folk songs and dances, children's activities, sports and games, and lots of food. The Metroplex enjoys two stops on the Professional Golfers Association tour, the *Byron Nelson Classic,* now at Las Colinas in Irving, and the *National Invitation Tournament* at Colonial Country Club in Fort Worth. The Swiss Avenue Historical District, just east of downtown Dallas, holds its *tour of homes.* Dallas's *Artfest*— an event sponsored Memorial Day weekend at State Fair Park by 500 Inc., an organization that has donated more than $1 million to Dallas arts organizations—includes a juried art show, arts and crafts displays, and continuous entertainment.

June. The revitalized stockyards area north of downtown Fort Worth gets an added shot in the arm the second weekend with the *Chisholm Trail Round-up.* A parade, a trail ride, rodeos, historical tours, a chili cookoff, armadillo races, square dancing, street dances, and mock western gunfights commemorate the Chisholm Trail cattle drives from South Texas through Fort Worth to Abilene, Kan., in the late 1880s. Summer in both Dallas and Fort Worth is open season for *theater, musicals,* and *concerts.* Among the offering are: The Dallas Symphony Association's 10–week *Starfest at Park Central,* with big-name stars all along the musical scale; musicals, from Dallas's State Fair Park Music Hall to Fort Worth's celebrated Casa Manana in Amon Carter Square; and *Shake-speare festivals* under the stars. June, July, and August are also the height of traffic on area *lakes* and in *theme parks and amusement centers.*

July. *Fireworks* shows on the Fourth of July light up the skies from Dallas's Cotton Bowl to various parks and lakes throughout the Metroplex.

August. Football fans dig out the binoculars and dust off the stadium seats for the *National Football League exhibition season* at Texas Stadium, but they really get serious in . . .

September, when the *Dallas Cowboys* begin their *de rigueur* march to the National Football Conference playoffs. Area universities—including the Southern Methodist Mustangs, the Texas Christian Horned Frogs, the North Texas Mean Green, and the UT–Arlington Mavericks—take to their respective gridirons too. Fort Worth circles the last weekend for *Pioneer Days* in the Stockyards area for a carnival, a street shootout, handicrafts displays, a street dance, and a parade.

October. The *State Fair of Texas,* the biggest of its kind in the country, explodes with 17 days of entertainment, including a midway, exhibitions, contests, a rodeo, and a Broadway musical. State Fair Park is also the scene of the annual football battle between the University of Texas (Austin) and the University of Oklahoma (Norman) in the Cotton Bowl, also the stage for other college and high school games during that stint. Usually staid downtown Dallas rolls up its sleeves for *Cityfest,* a carnival of the arts. Public spaces and building lobbies are backdrops for musical productions, arts and crafts exhibits, ensembles, films, and demonstrations. Fort Worth reserves the first weekend for *Oktoberfest* at Tarrant County Convention Center, as the Symphony League's festival fills the arena and exhibit halls with a family-oriented schedule. Also on the calendar are the Dallas *Neiman-Marcus Fortnight,* an international salute to products from afar, *A Taste of Dallas's* best victuals, and the season tipoff at Reunion Arena (through spring) for the *Dallas Mavericks* of the National Basketball Association.

November. Runners and fast walkers take to the streets of downtown Dallas on Thanksgiving morning for the YMCA *Turkey Trot.*

December. The *White Rock Marathon,* takes place around and near this East Dallas lake. It's beginning to look a lot like Christmas early on as giant *Christmas trees* adorn both cities. And, looking like towering Yuletide presents from afar, downtown buildings in Fort Worth are outlined in lights.

FREE EVENTS. *Artsline 385–1155* is a hotline detailing activities and events of more than 50 Dallas cultural organizations on a rotating basis, including arts and entertainment, music and dance, theater and free public performances, galleries and museums, touring shows, and others. It may be dialed 24 hours a day. Many events are free.

Regularly scheduled events in the area that are free to the public include parades—especially New Year's Day for the Cotton Bowl; in late January for the Southwestern Exposition, Fat Stock Show, and Rodeo (Fort Worth), and in October for the State Fair of Texas. Also, Shakespeare festivals in summer, city festivals in spring and fall, Neiman-Marcus Fortnight in October (Dallas), sidewalk and park symphonies, and several ballet performances during the year.

Most public parks, lakes, gardens, museums, and some historical sites charge no admission. See also *Participant Sports,* below.

TOURS. Dallas City Tours. *Gray Line* (4110 S. Lamar, Dallas, TX 75215; 824–2424), offers a variety of tours in and around the city. The latest sampling of tours includes Dallas All Around the Town, Dallas Then and Now, Southfork Ranch and J. R.'s Dallas, Dallas A to Z, and—for groups of 30 or more—Texas BBQ and Billy Bob's Texas, Six Flags Over Texas, Dallas After Dark, Dinner Theater and Beyond, Fort Worth–Where the West Begins, and A Day at a Texas Ranch. For prices, seasons of availability, and reservations, contact Gray Line. Tours may be boarded at these downtown locations: Dallas Hilton, 1914 Commerce; the Adolphus, 1321 Commerce; Holiday Inn, 1015 Elm St; Fairmont Hotel, Ross and Akard; Loew's Anatole and Marriott Market Center; and Hyatt Regency, 300 Reunion Blvd. Call for schedule.

Ed Smith Tours offers many of the same itineraries, including Southfork Ranch. For information contact the company at 4447 North Central Expressway, Suite 440, Dallas, TX 75206; 559–2790.

American Tours gives general city tours and custom-designed tours of Dallas and Fort Worth. $20 per hour per group. Call (214) 745–8939.

Silver Cloud Tours offers three-hour excursion tours of historical landmarks and Dallas architecture. Call (214) 521–1664 for group rates and information.

Fort Worth City Tours. *Gray Line* (1111 W. Lancaster, Fort Worth 71602; 429–7563), shows the best of Fort Worth and environs. Tour sites include the Water Gardens, Tarrant County Convention Center, the Stockyards area, Billy Bob's, Chisholm Trail, Botanic Gardens, downtown, major art museums, Scott Theatre, and—in or near Dallas—the Southfork Ranch, Texas Stadium, downtown, JFK Memorial, Neiman-Marcus, Market Center, and—in or near Arlington—Six Flags Over Texas, American Airlines Academy, Arlington Stadium, and the Southwest Historical Wax Museum. For prices, seasons of availability, reservations, and gathering points, contact Gray Line.

The *North Fort Worth Historical Society* offers group tours of the Stockyards area, including visits to local shops, clubs, a cattle auction, and others. Rates vary with group size. Contact the society in the Stock Exchange Building, 131 E. Exchange Ave., Suite 115; 625–5082.

Other tours, inbound reception operators. For complete, up-to-date listings of tour and imbound reception operators in the Dallas area, write the Dallas Chamber of Commerce, Convention & Visitors Bureau, 1507 Pacific, Dallas, TX 75201; 954–1482. In the Fort Worth area, contact Fort Worth Convention & Visitors Bureau, 700 Throckmorton, Fort Worth, TX 76102; (817) 336–2491.

PARKS. Visitors may expect to see a sprucier **State Fair Park** in years to come. In 1982 an $18-million plan was approved by voters to renovate more than a half dozen buildings and to prepare the grounds for the Texas sesquicentennial celebration in 1986. Site of the State Fair of Texas for 17 days each October, Fair Park offers 273 acres of entertainment, culture, and recreation just 2 mi. east of downtown Dallas via I–30. Begun in 1904, the complex now houses several museums (see *Museums,* below) either city operated or directed by private, nonprofit organizations, while all other facilities are managed throughout the year by the State Fair of Texas. Most facilities are open daily to the public, except during the fair. Science Place–Southwest Museum of Science and Technology $1.00/50¢ (428–8351), Civic Garden Center (428–7476), Aquarium (428–3587), Texas Hall of State (421–5136), or Museum of Natural History (421–2169). The Age of Steam Railroad Exhibit (361–6936) charges $1.50 for adults, 75¢ for children.The midway, with its nostalgic wooden roller coaster, is open weekends during the summer and, naturally, during the fair. State Fair Coliseum and the Cotton Bowl also are within the park. The Music Hall stages the Dallas Summer Musicals and the Metropolitan Opera, and the bandshell is site of the summer Shakespeare Festival. For information on what's happening at Fair Park, call 565–9931.

White Rock Lake. This Dallas lake is popular for sailing, picnicking, fishing, jogging, biking, hiking, people watching, and admiring mansions—including the late H. L. Hunt's on the west side. Bounded by Garland Road, Buckner Boulevard, and Northwest Highway in East Dallas, this city park is free. For information, call 321–2125. For more information on White Rock and other area bodies of water, see the *Lakes* section, below.

Old City Park, just south of downtown Dallas, features several restored buildings of the 1840s to 1910; see the *Historic Sites* section, below.

Thanks-Giving Square is an oasis of grassy park, trees, and a chapel in the heart of downtown Dallas at the intersections of Bryan, Pacific, and Ervay. As business and traffic are negotiated at a frantic pace a few feet away, brownbaggers relax with associates at lunchtime amid the crimson crape myrtles of summer. The bells of thanksgiving may be heard during the noon hour weekdays and each half hour on weekends, recalling the reason for the park. Opened in 1977 to mark the 200th anniversary of the American Thanksgiving tradition, the square and its quiet chapel have been developed by the private interfaith Thanks-Giving Square Foundation. Philip Johnson designed the chapel, a white cube of Italian marble on a circle of red granite, and, inside, Gabriel Loire's stained-glass ceiling draws visitors' attention upward. Various religious and national holidays are observed throughout the year in services and programs. Open weekdays, 9:00 A.M. to 5:00 P.M.; weekends and holidays, 1:00 to 5:00 P.M. For information and schedules, call (214) 969–1977.

Fort Worth Nature Center and Refuge. 10 mi. northwest of downtown, via Texas 199 (the Jacksboro Highway) to Buffalo Road. Maintained by the city's parks and recreation department, this 3,400-acre wildlife habitat also offers a marked nature trails, fishing, picnicking, and a visitor center. The wide variety of native habitats range from prairie and cross-timber forest to a lotus-marsh lake and river. Designated a national natural landmark, the center provides guided tours for prescheduled groups as well as many activities for the drop-in visitor. Naturalists in the Hardwicke building can answer questions. The nature center accepts native animals for rehabilitation and release. As many as 700 animals—some injured or orphaned, or rejected wild-animal pets—are cared for each year. A small herd of buffalo is maintained on a 50-acre range, as are several tame deer and a prairie-dog town. Open daily, 8:00 A.M. to 5:00 P.M. weekdays and 9:00 A.M. to 5:00 P.M. weekends. Free. For guided-tour reservations for groups of 10 or more, call (817) 237–1111.No overnight camping is allowed.

Woodsy **Trinity and Forest Parks** off University drive in Fort Worth afford a beautiful drive or bicycle trip along the clear fork of Trinity River. The area includes parklands, pool, casting pool, a zoo, rides, a miniature train and **Trinity Park Duck Pond,** where feeding the ducks is encouraged. Admission to the parks is free.

ZOOS. The **Fort Worth Zoological Park,** at 2727 Zoological Park Dr., off University Dr. south of I–30, has earned its wings and stripes. Its more than 850 species are housed in arrangements such as a rain forest of tropical birds, an African Diorama, and the James R. Record Aquarium and Herpetarium. The latter features one of the largest reptile exhibits in the world and houses a substantial variety of fresh- and saltwater fish and invertebrates, in addition to seals and sea lions. The Fort Worth Zoo Education Complex offers programs at 1:00 and 3:00 P.M. on weekends, its multimedia theater featuring an elaborate sound system. The zoo opens daily at 9:00 A.M.; closing hours vary. Adults $2, children $1.50, 25¢ and free, depending on age. Call (817) 870–7050 for more information. The **Forest Park Train,** with its 5-mi. jaunt lasting 45 minutes, is the world's longest miniature-train ride. From the entrance to the zoo, it runs summer months, Monday through Friday, 10:00 A.M. to 5:00 P.M., and Saturday and Sunday, 10:00 A.M. to 6:00 P.M. The rest of the year, Saturday and Sunday only, 10:00 A.M. to 4:00 P.M. All ages, 60¢. Call (817) 923–8911.

The 50-acre **Dallas Marsalis Zoo,** at 621 E. Clarendon Dr. in Oak Cliff south of downtown, offers more than 2,000 mammals, reptiles, and birds, but its prairie-dog village near the entrance can keep many visitors distracted for at least a half hour. Breathing room at the small zoo is on the drawing boards:

$18.4 million has been committed by voters to expand the zoo and create a new African-exhibit area. The zoo is open daily May through August, 9:00 A.M. to 6:00 P.M., and the rest of the year, until 5:00 P.M. Adults $2, children age 6–11 $1.25; parking $1.00. Call (214) 946–5154 for information.

Dallas Aquarium: See the *Museums* section; below.

International Wildlife Park: See the *Theme Parks* and *Amusement Centers* section, below.

Fort Worth Nature Center and Refuge: See the *Parks* section, above.

GARDENS. The 114 acres of the **Fort Worth Botanic Garden,** off I–30 at University, offer 150,000 plants of more than 2,000 species. The majority of the tree-shaded (150 varieties) growths are a result of the garden's own seed and cuttings. Among the more than 200,000 guests a year are many blind visitors strolling through the Fragrance Garden. The garden of roses—some 4,000—is the site of many special events, especially weddings. The garden was built and landscaped during the Depression by 750 men, many working for meal tickets; the flagstone walks and shelter houses cost a mere $4,500. The project took 4,000 tons of rock. The garden, free to the public, is open daily, 8:00 A.M. to sundown. Call 870–7686 for information.

The 7½-acre **Fort Worth Japanese Garden** in a corner of the Botanic Garden is a pleasant switch from the gravel pit and garbage dump formerly on the site. Built in the early 1970s, the garden offers a Meditation Garden, a Moon Viewing Deck, a Pagoda, and strolling gardens. Five bridges, three big pools, and authentic lanterns also adorn the landscape. The garden is open Tuesday through Friday, 10:00 A.M. to 4:00 P.M.; Saturday, 10:00 A.M. to 5:00 P.M., and Sunday, 1:00 to 5:00 P.M. (closed Monday). Summer hours (May 1 through Labor Day) are Tuesday through Saturday, 9:00 A.M. to 7:00 P.M., and Sunday, 1:00 to 6:00 P.M. The last ticket is sold 1 hour before closing. Adults $1, children under 12 free with adult (no more than five children per one adult). Special tours can be arranged for adult groups of 10 or more in advance. Call 870–7685.

The **Fort Worth Water Gardens,** 4.3 acres of south downtown real estate at I–30 and Main Street, draw thousands of visitors each year, in addition to the attention given them by movie companies (including the one that made *Logan's Run*), TV producers, dancers, singers, and brides. Philip Johnson and John Burgee of New York designed the park, built (a few hundred feet from the Chisholm Trail used 100 years ago) by the Amon G. Carter Foundation and presented to the city in 1974. Visitors can stand 38 ft. below ground level to experience 1,050 gallons of water per minute rushing down 710 feet of wall around the Active Water Pool, and nearby sheets of water flow silently down 22-ft. walls into a moat surrounding the Quiet Water Pool. The aerated-water pools use 40 nozzles to spray circular patterns over the pool. Though the plaza is open free 24 hours daily, water is activated from 9:00 A.M. to 11:00 P.M.

The **Dallas Civic Garden Center,** 1st and M.L. King Jr. Blvd., in State Fair Park, was begun in 1938. Its Tropical Garden Room houses tropical plants, a waterfall and pool with aquatic plants and tropical fish. The contemporary gardens outside include an herb-and-scent garden and, remarkably, a Shakespeare garden. Some displays include Braille. Lectures and seminars are commonplace at the center, open free Monday through Friday, 10:00 A.M. to 5:00 P.M., and Saturday, Sunday, and many holidays, from 12:30 P.M. Call 428–7476 for information.

On 22 acres of rolling woodlands overlooking White Rock Lake in East Dallas, the **Dallas Arboretum and Botanical Society** provides a natural setting for visitors to meet horticulturists and other garden enthusiasts. For more information, contact the society, 8617 Garland Road, (214) 327–8263.

THEME PARKS AND AMUSEMENT CENTERS. The Dallas–Fort Worth area is a "big spread" for the first-time visitor trying to maneuver cloverleafing freeways and endless roads, some known by three and four names apiece. So the centrally located concentration of theme parks and amusement centers in Arlington and Grand Prairie is a blessing. The only problem is that once little Johnny sees one, he'll want to see them all.

Between Dallas and Fort Worth along I–30 (also known as the old Dallas–Fort Worth Turnpike) are:

Six Flags Over Texas. 2201 Road to Six Flags, near Arlington Stadium, in Arlington. Texas' top attraction, Six Flags has drawn more than 50 million visitors from around the world since it opened its doors in 1961. Situated 20 minutes from both downtown Dallas and Fort Worth, the park offers more than 100 rides, shows, and attractions on its 205 acres. The six flags flying above the entrance commemorate the days when Texas was under the countries of Spain, France, and Mexico, when it was a Republic, when it briefly was part of the Confederacy, and now as a state in the United States. A separate part of the park is devoted to each flag.

Some of the more celebrated attractions include: the $2.1 million Cliffhanger—the first total freefall ride gives riders the sensation of stepping off the top of a 9-story building; the Texas Chute Out, a 200-ft. parachute drop; Judge Roy Scream, the huge wooden roller coaster; the Shock Wave, the longest, tallest, fastest double-loop roller coaster anywhere; the 300-ft. high oil derrick, with views, from the top, of both downtown skylines; the log flume, where passengers are guaranteed to cool off, and the narrow-gauge railroad encircling the park.

The park is always undergoing improvements and additions. One of the latest is Roaring Rapids river ride. On land formerly devoted to LaSalle's Riverboat Adventure and about half the area originally known as Skull Island, huge circular rafts carry a dozen passengers each through a rapids effect created by tons of water forced over specially designed contours in the 1,440-ft.-long river's concrete bed. Another addition has been Air Racer—biplanes circling a 14-story tower.

The Southern Palace features full-scale musical revues with 5 hours of shows throughout the day. During selected summer nights, the park features fireworks shows and, in the 5,000-seat Music Mill Amphitheater, top-name entertainment in concert. Six Flags pioneered the one-price ticket: At this writing, $14.95 for adults, $7.95 for children under 42 inches tall, and free for children age 2 or younger. Two-consecutive-day tickets are available. The park is open weekends in the spring and fall, with daily operation in the summer (the park opens at 10:00 A.M.; closing times vary widely). Call ahead (214) 640–5050.

Wet 'n Wild. Just across the street from Six Flags, one of the newest additions to the Dallas-Fort Worth theme-park crowd is a (somewhat enlarged) copy of another Wet 'n Wild in Orlando, Florida. The 47-acre park offers its visitors the chance to splash, slide, ride, float, paddle, dive, and, if you look sharp, swim.

Fifteen rides are offered, among them the Kamikaze Waterslide (a six-story, 300-foot long slip down into a pool), the Banzai Boggan (a watery roller coaster), the Corkscrew Flume, and, for the more leisurely minded, the Lazy River and the River Raft Ride.

There's food on sale—the usual poolside snacks (hamburgers, hot dogs, pizza, etc.)—and picnic areas, if you want to enjoy your meal on solid ground.

The park is open for weekends only in May and September, 10:00 A.M. to 6:00 P.M. During June, July, and August, it's open all week, 10:00 A.M. to 9:00 P.M. (10:00 P.M. weekends). Admission is $11.25 for adults, $9.75 for kids 3–12. Under 3, swim free. Parking is free, and there's shuttle-bus service to and from the park from many of the area hotels. (817) 265–3013.

WhiteWater. 701 E. Safari Parkway (I–30 and Belt Line), in Grand Prairie. One of America's largest water parks opened in 1982 at a cost of $9 million. The investment shows. This 27-acre oasis—with a water surface area of 1½ acres—a few feet off the interstate features: a 4-ft. wave pool (without the undertow and sea creatures) the size of a football field; the 50-ft.-tall, 275-ft.-long White Lightning waterslide on which swimmers can reach speeds in excess of 30 m.p.h.; an inner-tube rapids; a pool for little squirts all to themselves; six twisting body flumes; cable rides; an ordinary (all things are relative in Texas) pool with slides; a bank of video games; outdoor carpeting and chaise longues. In all, some 2.5 million gallons of water are filtered every 4 hours—for numbers nuts, that's enough to fill 62,500 bathtubs.

All ages let down their guard here: Grown people jump out of the rides' receiving pools, running to get back in line. They are the same businessmen in three-piece suits you passed downtown yesterday. A staff of 60 Red Cross–certified lifeguards makes certain enthusiastic swimmers use every precaution, and a registered nurse is on duty at all times. Swimmers may arrive in their swimsuits or choose to change clothes in the free, clean facilities. Lockers are available for $2 a day. A gift shop sells swimsuits and such for visitors who forget theirs. Rafts may be brought in free or rented for $2 each. Guests are free to bring their own ice chests of food and soft drinks (no alcohol or glass), and they may buy nachos, pizza, hot dogs, ice cream, and soft drinks at the park. Parking is free, and the gates close when the park reaches a capacity of 6,000. The park is open during the summer, usually 10:00 A.M. to 10:00 P.M., and during September, 10:00 A.M. to 7:00 P.M. Adults, $9.95; ages 4 to 11, $8.50; under 4, free. After 5:00 P.M., the price is $6.95. Group rates are available. Call (214) 263–1999 for information. Location in Garland, too: 840–0600.

Wax Museum of the Southwest. 601 E. Safari Parkway (I–30 at Belt Line), in Grand Prairie. Some 180 famous personalities are depicted in 80 wax scenes in this museum, the largest of its kind in the Southwest. Displays include the heroes of the Alamo, the gun battle at the O.K. Corral, Bonnie and Clyde, President John F. Kennedy, and the life and Last Supper of Jesus Christ. Also on display are collections of rare antique guns and weapons, barbed wire, pre-Colombian art, Indian artifacts, Western art, and restored examples of early transportation. The museum is home for the American Cattle Breeders Hall of Fame, a tribute to some of America's best cattle and cattle breeders. Open daily year-round (except New Year's Day, Thanksgiving, and Christmas). Hours are: Memorial Day to Labor Day, 9:00 A.M. to 8:00 P.M.; the rest of the year, Monday through Friday, 10:00 A.M. to 5:00 P.M.; and Saturday and Sunday till 6:00 P.M. The box office closes 1 hour before scheduled closing. Adults, $4.95; ages 4 to 11, $3.95. Call (214) 263–2391 for information.

International Wildlife Park. 601 Wildlife Parkway (off I–30 and Belt Line), in Grand Prairie. Featuring one of the best collections of exotic wildlife in the country, this drive-through park is home to more than 2,000 animals, including rhinos, hippos, zebras, giraffes, elephants, ostriches, camels, and cape buffalo. They can be viewed roaming freely in their natural settings as visitors drive their own automobiles, windows down, through the animal preserve. Most visitors allow 1½ to 2 hours to meander along the paved roads within the 350-acre park. The Entertainment Village features a children's petting zoo, boat rides, and special animal shows and exhibits including elephant rides. All rides, shows, and attractions are included in the single admission price. The park is open daily, Memorial Day to Labor Day, 9:30 A.M. to 6:30 P.M., (last car admitted), and during September, 10:00 A.M. to 5:00 P.M. In October and November, weekends only. Admission is $8.95 per person. For information on special group discounts, call (214) 263–2203.

Texas Sports Hall of Fame. 401 E. Safari (I–30 at Belt Line), in Grand Prairie. One of the state's newest sports attractions, the $4.5-million Texas Sports Hall of Fame is a hero worshiper's heaven. The 29,000-square-ft. hall honors 130 and counting of Texas' most outstanding sports heroes in electronic and computerized exhibits. Among those lauded in the nation's only state sports hall of fame are such names as Tom Landry, Byron Nelson, A. J. Foyt, Willie Shoemaker, Babe Zaharias, Don Meredith, Rogers Hornsby, Lee Trevino, Randy Matson, Doak Walker, and Bobby Morrow. The two-level hall emphasizes nostalgia, with the extensive collection of sports memorabilia displayed against a backdrop of authentic period settings spanning 100 years of Texas history. Professional teams in Texas include Dallas Cowboys and Mavericks; Texas Rangers; Houston Oilers, Rockets, and Astros; and San Antonio Spurs. Open year-round. Hours are: Memorial Day to Labor Day, 10:00 A.M. to 7:00 P.M., daily.; rest of the year, 10:00 A.M. to 5:00 P.M., weekdays, and 10:00 A.M. to 6:00 P.M. weekends. Adults, $3; ages 4 to 12, $1.50. Special rates available for groups of 10 or more. Call (214) 263–4255 for information.

In Dallas:

State Fair Park. 2 mi. east of downtown via I–30. The Midway is open daily the two and a half weeks of the State Fair of Texas in October, and weekends

April through Labor Day. Tickets must be purchased for the rides, but admission to grounds and picnic areas is free when the fair is not in session. (See the *Parks* section, above.)

Open in summer, **Sandy Lake Park,** I–35E north to Sandy Lake Rd., sports a large pool, pony and stagecoach rides, miniature golf, paddle boats, game fields, and picnic facilities. Admission. Call (214) 242–7449 for information and hours.

RANCH EXPERIENCES. Dallas and Tarrant Counties represent the largest concentration of horses—some 65,000—in the nation. At this writing there are more than 20 stables and horseback-riding facilities in the Metroplex open to the public. Check the Yellow Pages of either city for the stables closest to your day's activities.

From Fort Worth's revitalized Stockyards to rodeos (see the *Spectator Sports* section, below) from Mansfield to Mesquite, the visitor to Dallas–Fort Worth area chasing his image of the West and its cowboys will not be *too* disappointed.

The **Big D Ranch,** about a half hour south of downtown Dallas, is a working cattle ranch on over 600 acres of rolling countryside. In addition to catering parties on the ranch, Big D offers an authentic 1880s Old West town with shows, rides, saloon, casino, stunts, and more. Open weekends, 10:00 A.M. to 8:00 P.M. $7.95 for adults, $6.95 for children. Off I–45 nine miles south of the I–635 intersection; exit 268 onto Malloy Bridge Road. P.O. Box 400907, Dallas, TX 75240; (214) 225–8191.

The **West Fork Ranch** at Fort Worth is operated by the Murrin Bros. Land and Cattle Co. For information or reservations, write them at Stockyards Station, P.O. Box 4130, Fort Worth, TX 76106, or call (817) 624–1101.

The **KowBell Ranch** affords youngsters the opportunity to ride horseback, take hayrides, go fishing, and even participate in a calf-roping scramble. Open to the public every Wednesday from June through August, the ranch is southeast of Fort Worth on Texas 157, 8 mi. south of I–20. For information call (214) 477–3092. Call five days ahead for reservations.

CHILDREN'S ACTIVITIES. Vast layouts such as *Six Flags Over Texas, WhiteWater,* and *International Wildlife Park,* to name just a few in the area (See *Theme Parks and Amusement Centers,* just above), can keep a child content from sunup to sundown—if he lasts that long. If the pocketbook calls for activities on the lighter, sometimes quieter side, both Dallas and Fort Worth offer good to excellent zoological parks, each for $2 or less. The *Fort Worth Zoological Park* is the starting point for the 5-mi. *Forest Park Train,* the world's longest miniature-train ride (60 cents). The *Fort Worth Museum of Science and History,* offering natural-history displays and a planetarium, is the largest educational museum for children in the country. A new feature at the museum is a mammoth Omni-Max theater (projection with a 360-degree view); $4 for adults, $2.50 children under 12. Call 732–1631 for information. The area proffers an array of miniature golf courses, go-kart tracks, coin-operated game arcades, city swimming pools (summers only) and smaller amusement parks, such as *Penny Whistle Park,* 10717 E. Northwest Highway at Plano Road; (214) 348–8297. Check the Yellow Pages of both Dallas and Fort Worth for locations closest to your "headquarters." (Also, see the *Parks, Zoos,* and *Museums* sections here.)

LAKES. Texas boasts a total of 6,300 sq. mi. of lakes and streams, surpassed only by Alaska. Interestingly enough, Caddo Lake, on the Louisiana line, is the only large natural lake. The Lakes Trail, one of 10 state-designated Travel Trails guiding motorists to major points of scenic, historical, and recreational interest throughout much of Texas, practically encircles the Dallas–Fort Worth North Texas area. As on other trails, the route generally avoids crowded freeways and interstates. Folders are available from the Texas tourist bureaus (the closest to Dallas–Fort Worth are Denison on U.S. 75/69 and Gainesville on U.S. 75/I–35) or by writing the State Department of Highways and Public Transportation (see *Facts at Your Fingertips* at the front of this book). Fort Worth and Tarrant County have the most lakes of any city and county in Texas; they are: Eagle Mountain, Benbrook, Lake Worth, Grapevine, and Arlington.

There are numerous lakes in the surrounding communities and countrysides, most with facilities for swimming, boating, fishing, camping, and picnicking. Check the Thursday sports sections of the *Dallas Morning News, Dallas Times Herald,* and *Fort Worth Star-Telegram* for up-to-date fishing reports on North and East Texas lakes. Fishing licenses are available at sporting-goods stores. For current information about area lakes, call (214) 670–4995.

Following is an alphabetical offering. (Some facts and figures courtesy of the Texas Highway Department, Travel and Information Division.)

Lake Arlington. 2,275 acres in southwest Arlington off Loop 303. Owned and operated by the city. Popular for boating, sailing, and waterskiing. Facilities for boaters and fishermen. White and black bass. Municipal and commercial parks.

Bachman Lake. Small lake in northwest Dallas on Northwest Highway (Loop 12) near Love Field. Popular for afternoon or weekend picnics, jogging, bicycling, roller-skating. Paddle boats for rent. No waterskiing. Near a restaurant-and-nightclub strip.

Lake Benbrook. 3,770 acres 10 mi. southwest of Fort Worth in Benbrook on Lake Shore Drive off U.S. 377. A Corps of Engineers impoundment on the clear fork of the Trinity River. Lakeside parks with picnic facilities, camping and trailer areas, restrooms, drinking water, boat rentals, launching ramps, fishing supplies, snack bar. Waterskiing, horseback riding, swimming, golf. Fees for some areas. Call 292–2400 for information.

Eagle Mountain Lake. 8,500 acres 12 mi. northwest of Fort Worth on west fork of Trinity River. All water sports. Trailer areas, restrooms, snack bars, boat rentals, launching ramps, fishing supplies. Fishing good year-round, with schooling white bass in spring.

Lake Granbury. 8,500 acres at De Cordova Bend on the Brazos River. 103-mi. shoreline. Parks, camps, service facilities.

Lake Grapevine. 7,380 acres 25 mi. northeast of downtown Fort Worth, 25 mi. northwest of downtown Dallas near the city of Grapevine. A Corps of Engineers reservoir. 60-mi. shoreline. Campsites, picnic areas, boat ramps, marina service, swimming, fishing supplies. Golf. Call 481–4541 for information.

Lake Lavon. 22,000 acres about 10 mi. north of Rockwall. A Corps of Engineers reservoir. Four parks with hookups for campers. Day-use parks, motorcycle trail, park (Caddo) especially for handicapped. Boat ramps, marina services, swimming beaches, duck hunting in specified area.

Lake Lewisville. 23,280 acres about 25 mi. north of downtown Dallas off I–35E. Formerly called the Garza–Little Elm Reservoir. A Corps of Engineers reservoir. Popular with area residents for water sports. A dozen public parks. Marinas, boat rentals, launching ramps, fishing, supplies, swimming, waterskiing, sailing, camping, trailer and picnic areas.

Mountain Creek Lake. 2,940 acres in southwest Dallas near the Dallas naval air station and Grand Prairie. Popular for fishing, boating.

Lake Ray Hubbard. 22,745 acres 10 mi. east of Dallas on east fork of the Trinity River. Owned by city of Dallas for municipal water supply and recreation. Lakeside marinas, camps, housing developments. Excellent fishing and boating.

White Rock Lake. Scenic lake in northeast Dallas, accessible off Garland Road (Texas 78) and Northwest Highway (Loop 12). Popular for sailing and fishing. Lakeside picnic and park facilities. No waterskiing. (See also the *Parks* section, above.)

Lake Worth. 3,247 acres 9 mi. northwest of Fort Worth on Texas 199. Scenic vistas along Meandering Drive. Popular for boating, waterskiing, sailing. Parks and picnic areas. (See also the "Fort Worth Nature Center" entry in the *Parks* section, above.)

Some of the lakes worth a 90-minute drive from Dallas-Fort Worth include:

Lake Texoma. 89,000 acres on the Texas-Oklahoma line on the Red River. One of the largest reservoirs in Texas. Shoreline of 580 miles. Scenic coves and inlets. This popular Corps of Engineers lake draws more than 9 million visitors a year. 57 modern campgrounds, scores of trailer parks, 110 picnic areas, 100 shelter buildings, 80 boat ramps. Marinas and luxury resorts. All types of boating activity. Some of best fishing in the nation: black bass, crappie, white bass, plus lunker catfish. Information available at south end of the dam on U.S. 75A.

Lake Tawakoni. 36,700 acres east of Dallas. Sabine River Authority reservoir. 200-mi. shoreline spreads over three counties. Marinas, camps, parks on wooded shores. Boat ramps, designated water-ski areas. Good fishing in countless coves and inlets. More than 5 sq. mi. of submerged-timber prime habitat. Information at north end of Iron Bridge Dam off FM 47 south of Point, Texas.

Cedar Creek Lake. 33,750 acres southeast of Dallas. This popular North-Central Texas recreation area supplies Fort Worth's water. Amid post oaks and pines. Campsites, picnicking areas, excellent fishing, swimming, boating.

Lake Whitney. 15,760 acres on Brazos River south of Fort Worth. A Corps of Engineers impoundment. More than 4 million visitors a year. Numerous campsites, marinas, parks, recreation areas, housing developments. Fishing good in sheltered coves and inlet. Depths ranging to 100 ft.; popular with scuba divers. State Park on its eastern edge.

Possum Kingdom Lake. 19,800 acres west of Fort Worth. Lakeside resorts and camps. Favorite with swimmers, scuba divers, boaters, fishermen. Woodlands surround lake. State Park on the southwestern shore.

CAMPING. The 106-acre Texas "flea market" called **Traders Village,** at 2602 Mayfield Road in Grand Prairie, includes a recreational-vehicle park open every day of the year. For more information on availability of the 130 hookups, call (214) 647–8205. You'll never be lonely here on the weekends, when everything imaginable is bought and sold Saturday and Sunday from 8:00 A.M. to dusk. Hundreds of booths and stalls feature collectible treasures, and craftsmen show off their skills and wares. The village also houses an antique carousel, children's ride, a restaurant, and concession stands. Among the many special events during the year is the Prairie Dog Chili Cook Off & Pickled Quail Egg World Championship. For information and selling space at Traders Village call (214) 647–2331.

Arlington KOA. Midway between Dallas and Fort Worth, just off I–20 (exit 449, 1½ miles north on Hwy. 157). 150 sites and trailer storage. Swimming pool, recreation room, other facilities. In Mid-Cities area near Six Flags, etc. (817) 461–0601.

See also the *Lakes* and *State Parks* sections here.

STATE PARKS. One of the best sources of information on Texas' state parks can be found in a folder, appropriately titled *Texas State Park Information,* available from Texas tourist bureaus (the closest to Dallas–Fort Worth are Denison on U.S. 75/69 and Gainesville on U.S. 77/I–35) or by writing the Texas Parks and Wildlife Department, 4200 Smith School Road, Austin, TX 78744.

The parks department maintains some 80 state parks as scenic attractions, recreational areas, and historic sites. No hunting of any kind is permitted, although fishing is, and boats, fishing licenses, and supplies are normally available. The folder breaks down each state park as to the availability of camping, screened shelters, group facilities, campsites with electricity and sewage, campsites with water and electricity, restrooms, showers, cabins, picnicking, groceries, fishing, swimming, waterskiing, boat ramp, museum/exhibit, historic structure, day-use only, group trailer, trailer dump station, nature trail, and miscellaneous.

Some of the state parks in the Dallas–Fort Worth area are: **Acton,** burial site of Davy Crockett's wife, near Granbury; **Bonham,** home of Sam Rayburn; **Cleburne; Dinosaur Valley,** near Glen Rose; **Eisenhower** and **Eisenhower Birthplace,** at Denison; **Fort Richardson,** at Jacksboro; **Governor Hogg Shrine** at Quitman; **Lake Mineral Wells; Lake Whitney; Possum Kingdom** near the town of Caddo, and **Tyler.**

With a state park on its eastern edge, **Lake Whitney** (15,760 acres on the Brazos River near Hillsboro) draws more than 4 million visitors a year to its campsites, marinas, parks, and recreation areas. Fishing is reported excellent in sheltered coves and inlets. Depths ranging to 100 feet are popular with scuba divers.

Woodland-surrounded **Possum Kingdom Lake** (19,800 acres west of Fort Worth) attracts its share of scuba divers too. Lakeside resorts and camps are favorites with swimmers, boaters, and fishermen alike. The state park is on the lake's southwestern shore.

PARTICIPANT SPORTS. As evidenced by its growth, Dallas–Fort Worth does not sit still for long periods. Neither do many of the sports-minded residents, and visitors to the area can benefit from the expansive offering of facilities—in addition to the hot-summer and mild-winter conditions. People in great numbers can be seen fishing (see the *Lakes* section) and playing golf, tennis, softball, and racquetball. They run (the White Rock Marathon, Cowtown Marathon, and Turkey Trot are here), jog (witness Dr. Kenneth Cooper's famous Aerobics Center), and go boating, sailing, waterskiing, and wind surfing. They ice skate, roller-skate, ride horses, cycle, bowl, take in local gun ranges, and sweat it out in numerous health clubs. And they can be seen soaking up the sun at White Rock and Bachman Lakes on either end of Northwest Highway in Dallas, at Trinity and Forest Parks in Fort Worth, and at area swimming pools and lakes.

Public **golf** courses in Dallas include: *Tenison,* 3501 Samuell Blvd., 823–5350; *Stevens Park,* 1005 N. Montclair, 946–5781; *Cedar Crest Park,* 1800 Southerland, 943–1004, and *L. B. Houston,* 11223 Luna Rd., 869–1778.

Fort Worth has: *Meadowbrook,* 1815 Jensen Rd., 457–4616; *Pecan Valley,* Benbrook Lake, 249–1845; *Rockwood,* 1851 Jacksboro Hwy., 624–1771; *Sycamore Creek,* 2423 E. Vickery, 535–7241, and *Z. Boaz,* 3200 Lackland Rd., 738–6287. *Grapevine,* below Grapevine Dam, is rated highly among the many courses.

Tennis. With 22 outdoor and five indoor courts, Fort Worth's *Mary Potishman Lard Tennis Center* (3609 Bellaire Dr., on the TCU campus; 921–7808 or 921–7960) is open Monday through Friday, 9:00 A.M. to 10:30 P.M., and Saturday and Sunday, 9:00 A.M. to 9:30 P.M. The *McLeland Tennis Center* (1600 W. Seminary; 921–5134), with 16 outdoor courts, is open Monday to Friday, 9:00 A.M. to 10:00 P.M., and Saturday and Sunday, 9:00 A.M. to 9:00 P.M. To reserve any of 200 Dallas city-park tennis courts, call 428–1501 between 8:15 A.M. and 5:15 P.M. no more than a day ahead of time.

At this writing there are more than 20 stables and **horseback-riding** facilities in the Metroplex open to the public. Check the Yellow Pages of either city for the ones closest to your activities. **Ice skating** is available at Prestonwood Town Center (Dallas Parkway at Belt Line) and the Galleria (Dallas Parkway and Loop 635), both in Far North Dallas; Plaza of the Americas in downtown Dallas, and Tandy Center in downtown Fort Worth.

Popular **bike** paths in Dallas are found at: Bachman Lake, 3.08 mi., 3500 W. Northwest Hwy.; White Rock Lake, 9.08 mi., 8300 Garland Rd.; Crawford Park, 2 mi., 8700 Elam Rd.; Kiest Park, ½ mi., 3000 S. Hampton Rd.; Netherland Park, ¼ mi., 5700 Meaders La. at Netherland, and Singing Hills Park, ½ mi., 1010 Crough Rd. For information or maps, call 670–4027.

SPECTATOR SPORTS. Dallas–Fort Worth takes no off season from sports. The hottest ticket in town, the Dallas Cowboys of the National **Football** League, light up Texas Stadium in Irving from August exhibition games through, in most seasons, January's playoffs. The Texas Rangers of the American League West invade the **baseball** diamond at Arlington Stadium on the old Dallas–Fort Worth Turnpike (I–30) from April through early October. Shuttle-bus service is available to both stadiums; contact team offices (Cowboys, 214–369–3211; Rangers, 817–273–5222) for more information.

The Dallas Mavericks of the National **Basketball** Association play from early autumn to late spring at Dallas's downtown Reunion Arena, also site of the WCT Finals in April or May. The Willow Bend **Polo** and Hunt Club in Plano (call 214–248–6298 for schedule) opens some of its matches to the public.

The Mesquite Championship **Rodeo,** (214) 285–8777, at I–635 and Military Parkway in Mesquite, kicks every Friday and Saturday night from April through September. Steve Murrin runs Fort Worth's Cowtown Rodeo, (817) 624–1101, March through May (performances every Saturday night) and from the last weekend in September (during Pioneer Days) through mid-November. Its arena, the historic Cowtown Coliseum in the Stockyards area, opened its doors to the public in 1908 and staged the world's first indoor contest rodeo in 1917. In Mansfield, southeast of Fort Worth, the KowBell Rodeo (214) 477–3092 is the country's only year-round indoor rodeo, with performances every Saturday night. The group of buildings that make up the Will Rogers Memorial Center in Fort Worth plays host, at various times of the year, to horse shows, boxing and wrestling matches, rodeos and auto shows, in addition to other community events. Rodeos also are a big attraction at the Southwestern Exposition, Fat Stock Show, and Rodeo in Fort Worth in late January and early February.

Wrestling is on tap every Friday night at the Sportatorium in Dallas and every Monday night at Will Rogers Coliseum. Weekend **auto races** are staged at various tracks throughout the Metroplex, from Kennedale to North Richland Hills, Mansfield, Grand Prairie, Carrollton, and Mesquite.

In addition to other college-sports programs, several universities compete on the **college gridiron,** including the Southern Methodist Mustangs and Bishop

College Tigers in Dallas, Texas Christian Horned Frogs in Fort Worth, University of Texas at Arlington Mavericks, North Texas Mean Greens in Denton, and Austin College Kangaroos in Sherman. The annual clash between the University of Texas at Austin and the University of Oklahoma is staged in the Cotton Bowl the second Saturday in October. The Cotton Bowl Classic, usually staged New Year's Day in Dallas, pits the Southwest Conference football champion against another highly ranked team at State Fair Park.

The Quaker State Open in Grand Prairie in February hosts the professional **bowlers'** tour. The Virginia Slims women's **tennis** circuit comes to Dallas (Moody Coliseum) in March, followed by the men's World Championship Tennis Finals (Reunion Arena) in late April or early May. The Metroplex enjoys two stops on the Professional **Golfers** Association tour, the Byron Nelson Classic at Las Colinas in Irving, and the National Invitation Tournament at Colonial Country Club in Fort Worth.

A tour of **Texas Stadium,** home of the Dallas Cowboys and the SMU Mustangs, is available at the Irving facility Monday through Friday, 10:00 A.M. and 2:00 P.M., and Saturdays, Sundays, and holidays, 11:00 A.M., 12:30 P.M., and 2:00 P.M. (no tours on games days). The tour begins between gates 10 and 1 and includes the press box, Stadium Club, playing field, locker room, and gift shop. Adults, $1.50; children under 12, $1. Getting into the stadium can be tricky: Take I–35 north from downtown, exit left to Texas 183, take the Loop 12 North exit, then pull into the stadium's gate-1 parking lot. Call Texas Stadium, (214) 438–7676, for information. Free parking.

The $4.5 million Texas Sports Hall of Fame in Grand Prairie honors 130 of Texas' most outstanding sports heroes via electronic and computerized exhibits; see the *Theme Parks and Amusement Centers* section, above.

HISTORIC SITES. The **Fort Worth Stockyards** area, North Main and Exchange Ave., retains the flavor of the Old West many visitors come to Fort Worth to see. But make no mistake, the revitalized North Side is real; it just has a few new coats of paint, an attractive river walk, and now the world's largest honkytonk. This is Cowtown, complete with restaurants, saloons, art galleries, western-wear stores, and special shops selling apparel and merchandise of the historic cattle era. There are even a bootmaker and a tattoo parlor. The Stockyards and Cattlemen's Exchange conducts livestock auctions Monday through Thursday, and working cowboys put on rodeos at the Cowtown Coliseum, scene of the world's first indoor rodeo.

Surrounded by a 14-square-block City Center project that includes the Americana Hotel and two tall towers, **Sundance Square,** at Main and Houston, Fort Worth, has returned a portion of downtown Fort Worth to the turn of the century. The restoration—with restaurants, specialty shops, art galleries, a western-art museum, and other businesses accented by bricked sidewalks, landscaping, and period-style lampposts—is named for Butch Cassidy and the Sundance Kid, who used the city's Hell's Half Acre as their hideout around 1900.

Restored **Thistle Hill,** 1509 Pennsylvania Ave. at Summit, is the last remaining mansion of the rich cattle barons. Open Monday through Friday, with tours hourly 10:00 A.M. to 3:00 P.M. and Sunday, 1:00 to 4:00 P.M. (closed Saturday). Admission is $2. For more information call (817) 336–1212.

The **Will Rogers Statue** in front of the Will Rogers Memorial Center (3400 W. Lancaster, Fort Worth) depicts the legendary humorist and actor astride his horse Soap Suds.

The Fort Worth Park and Recreation Department's collection of seven architecturally and historically significant Texas log structures dating from 1850 to 1860 makes up the **Log Cabin Village Historical Complex** at 2301 Rogers Road. Men and women dressed in costumes demonstrate pioneer crafts and produce for sale, in the gift shop, stone-ground cornmeal from the grist mill, hand-dipped candles, handwoven material, quilts, and corn-shuck dolls. The 7.6-acre location is in tree-shaded Forest Park at the corner of University Dr. and Log Cabin Village La. The village is open Monday through Friday, 8:00 A.M. to 4:30 P.M. (except Thanksgiving, Christmas, and New Year's Day); Sat. noon to 4:30 P.M., Sun. 1:00 to 4:30 P.M. Adults, $1.00; children, 35¢. For information call (817) 926–5881. Nearby, **Van Zandt Cottage** (Lancaster at University Dr.) was once used as a stopping place by both stagecoach passengers and cattlemen. It now is restored and furnished with antiques of the same period.

DALLAS

Chosen as the relocation site for endangered historical structures by the Dallas County Heritage Society, **Old City Park,** 1717 Gano St. at St. Paul, is a 12-acre "museum" of architectural and cultural history juxtaposed against the skyline of Dallas. Life in North Central Texas between 1840 and 1910 is depicted in: Millermore, the largest remaining antebellum home in North Central Texas, plus a railroad depot, a general store, a doctor's office, a smoke house, a merchandise store, and nearly 25 other period structures. Brent Place Restaurant, (214) 421–3057, is open for lunch, and a gift shop sells old-timey objects. Also on the grounds are a church and a bandstand, popular settings for weddings; restrooms; and a popcorn vendor. The grounds are staffed by volunteers and open free, sunup to sundown. A fee is charged to tour the museum buildings (adults, $4; senior citizens, $2; children 6 to 12, $2), Tuesday through Friday, 10:00 A.M. to 4:00 P.M., and Saturday and Sunday, 1:30 to 4:30 P.M. (closed Monday). The park location was first a buffalo trace, then an Indian campground. Call (214) 421–7800 for information.

Downtown Dallas's historical plaza—bounded by Elm, Market, Commerce, and Record Sts.—features two markedly different structures. The **John Neely Bryan cabin** (1841), substantiated as the residence of the first Dallasite, was made of handhewn logs chinked with clay. It also served as Dallas's first courthouse in the 1850s.

A note for photographers: You can dramatize the contrast of old and new in Dallas by snapping a photograph of the Bryan cabin, "Old Red" stone courthouse, and futuristic Reunion Tower—all in the same frame. Stand on the north side of Elm Street and look southwestward.

Across Main Street from the Bryan cabin in the **John F. Kennedy Memorial Plaza,** some 200 yards from where the president was assassinated on Nov. 22, 1963, stands a 30-ft. white cenotaph designed by Philip Johnson. Rarely a day goes by that tourists don't congregate here to reflect—and, in **Dealey Plaza,** two blocks to the west on Houston Street, to stare up at what was then called the Texas Schoolbook Depository Building on Elm, whence the fatal shots are said to have been fired.

Just north of here begins the **West End Historic District,** bounded by Woodall Rodgers, Elm, Record, and Lamar streets. This area of warehouses, some dating to the early 1900s, is undergoing a revitalization to draw companies and people back to the area. Trendy restaurants and night spots continue to open. The nearby renovated Brewery complex offers still more chic eateries and bars. Among other West-End historical structures is **Union Station** (1916), restored to its original beaux-arts style of Texas architecture. It houses Amtrak passenger service, a visitor information center, and, upstairs in the Grand Hall, a restaurant complex. While in the area, visitors should rise above it all via a glass elevator to the observation deck 50 stories up in the geodesic dome of **Reunion Tower.**

After years of neglect, portions of **Oak Cliff,** more than 100 square miles of south Dallas real estate, are being restored. Beautiful hills, bluffs, and tree-lined streets were the setting, between 1890 and 1930, for distinguished homes of Dallas's socialites and politicians. Efforts are being made to preserve existing neighborhoods, such as in the Winnetka Heights Historic District and its 850 homes bounded by Davis, 12th, Polk, and Rosemont. Today, Oak Cliff is home to 100 parks (including the zoo), 40 city pools and sports fields, two municipal golf courses, two country clubs, an airport, and three colleges (Bishop, Dallas Baptist, and Mountain View).

Listed in the *National Register of Historic Places,* **Swiss Avenue** is a historic neighborhood of homes just east of downtown Dallas. Tours of homes are held in early May.

DeGolyer Estate. 8525 Garland Rd., also listed the *National Register of Historic Places,* comprises 43 acres on the shores of White Rock Lake in East Dallas. Filled with English and Spanish antiques, the mansion is open for guided tours. The estate hosts a variety of cultural and educational programs during the year, in addition to free concerts in the formal gardens. Call (214) 324–1401.

Available at the Visitors Information Center in Union Station, 400 S. Houston St. in downtown Dallas, the *Dallas County Heritage Trails Map* is invaluable to the history buff chasing the Dallas of yesteryear. The folder was a Bicentennial project of the Dallas County Commissioners Court and was compiled by the Dallas Historical Commission and Heritage Trails Map Committee.

LIBRARIES. Every major city has a library, even a system of them. And most visitors usually don't need—or want—to be pushed in the direction of one. They can get their fill of books and bindings at home, thank you. But oh, Bennett Cerf, if you could see Dallas now! The famous publisher once described the Dallas Public Library as the world's worst. But he died in 1971, barely a year after plans began to build a new central facility.

In the spring of 1982, one of the most modern libraries in the nation opened to the tune of $40 million in downtown Dallas across from City Hall. The new library at 1515 Young St., which replaces the Commerce Street location, now houses 2 million volumes (over and above the capacities of branch facilities) and accommodates some 3,000 readers in reading nooks and balconies. Visitors are quickly impressed with the cable-TV studio, computers, theater, exhibit hall, listening rooms, library store, and snack bar.

Though it's *only* the seventh-largest city in the nation, Dallas has a library system that in terms of the number of books available for residents ranks fourth among the 10 largest cities in the country.

MUSEUMS. For a city its size, Fort Worth has an exceptional complex of four major museums—three art, one science and history. This cultural district, within a four-square-block area less than 2 mi. west of downtown, has been rightly called the Acropolis of the Southwest. All buildings are within easy walking distance, accessible to the handicapped, and open free, in most cases, to the public. Dallas has fine museums too, the largest group of them being within State Fair Park, 2 mi. east of downtown.

FORT WORTH

Amon Carter Museum, at 3501 Camp Bowie, owes its beginnings to its namesake, the prominent Fort Worther. First introduced to the painting and sculpture of Charles M. Russell (the famous "cowboy artist" of Montana) by humorist Will Rogers, Amon G. Carter was convinced that the artist portrayed the true American West. In 1935 he borrowed money to buy nine Russell watercolors, and the founder and publisher of the *Fort Worth Star-Telegram* continued to collect western art until his death in 1955. Carter's will instructed that a museum be built to house his collection. And today the museum's collection of Frederic Remingtons and Charles Russells remains one of the most acclaimed anywhere. Philip Johnson designed the building, which opened in 1961, built of native Texas shellstone. Ten more intimate galleries open from the main gallery. The museum also houses a large reference library, a theater, and a bookstore.

The collection of American painting, sculpture, and photography is complemented by exhibitions and programs. The permanent collection also features works by Winslow Homer, Martin Johnson Heade, Seth Eastman, Jasper Cropsey, Alert Bierstadt, Thomas Morn, John Mix Stanley, and Frederick Church.

Several examples of early 20th-century painting and sculpture are also found in the collection, among them works by Georgia O'Keeffe, John Martin, Stuart Davis, Ben Shahn, Charles Scheeler, Marsden Hartley, and Arthur Dove. Open Tuesday through Saturday, 10:00 A.M. to 5:00 P.M., and Sunday, 1:00 to 5:30 P.M. (closed Monday). Tours Tuesday through Saturday begin at 2:00 P.M. Group tours must be scheduled with the tour coordinator at least two weeks in advance. Call (817) 738–1933.

Sid Richardson Collection of Western Art. 309 Main St., Sundance Sq.; (817) 332–6554. This new one-room museum also features Remington and Russell. Tues.-Fri. 10:00 A.M. to 5:00 P.M.; Sat. 11:00 A.M. to 6:00 P.M.; Sunday 1:00 to 5:00 P.M.

Fort Worth Art Museum. 1309 Montgomery. Founded in 1901 as an art gallery in one room of the old public library by a group of patrons, it has evolved into a distinguished collection of 20th-century art. The collection has grown from its first acquisition of George Inness's *Approaching Storm* in 1904 to a collection including more than 3,000 works. Acquisitions in the late 1950s focused on modern masters, including Lyonel Feininger, Henri Matisse, Leonard Baskin, and Hans Hoffman.

The museum began to gain national and international recognition in the late 1960s and early '70s with the purchase of Picasso's *Suite Vollard* and *Femme Couchee Lisant* and the presentation of a Picasso exhibition jointly organized with the Dallas Museum of Fine Arts (now the Dallas Museum of Art). The museum's collection includes significant works by Frank Stella, Clyfford Still, Donald Judd, Joseph Cornell, Mark Rothko, and Morris Louis. Specially commissioned pieces include major works by Robert Irwin, Robert Rauschenberg, and Red Grooms. In addition to exhibitions, other activities include lectures, slide programs, symposia, film series, adults' and children's programs, video and film productions in the public schools, scholarly publications, and arts programs. Open Tuesday, 10:00 A.M. to 9:00 P.M.; Wednesday through Saturday, 10:00 A.M. to 9:00 P.M. Call (817) 738–9215.

Fort Worth Museum of Science and History. 1501 Montgomery. Begun in 1941 at the Children's Museum, the Fort Worth Museum of Science and History has grown from two rooms in an elementary school to the largest museum of its kind in the Southwest. Its 88,000-sq.-ft. facility contains seven exhibit galleries, the largest museum school in the country, and the **Noble Planetarium.** The museum's collection of more than 100,000 specimens and artifacts ranges from fossils to computers. The collection also provides materials for the Museum School. During museum hours, area schoolchildren (more than 50,000 each year) attend curriculum-coordinated programs in science, history, and astronomy featuring hands-on contact with the teaching collection. In addition to the planetarium show and special light and sound production *Laser Magic,* the museum has a 30,000-sq.-ft. *Omni-Max Theater.* The special film projector creates images that visually surround the audience and carry it to the depths of the ocean and the far corners of the universe. The museum is open Monday through Saturday, 9:00 A.M. to 5:00 P.M., and Sunday, 2:00 to 5:00 P.M. The museum is free. Noble Planetarium shows usually charge :2. Infants may not be admitted. The Laser Magic show ($3) is given Friday and Saturday, 7:30, 9:00, and 10:30 P.M., and midnight, and Sunday, 7:30 and 9 P.M. The Omni-Max has 35 showings weekly; $4.50 for adults, $2.75 for children under 12 and seniors 65 and over. Call (817) 732–1631 for information on all museum facilities.

Kimbell Art Museum. 3333 Camp Bowie. Only into its second decade, the Kimbell is already famous for its collection of the world's art, ranging from the prehistoric to early 20th century, and the innovative building that houses it. The collection sweeps across most areas of European art, from prehistoric sculpture to Picasso, with a strong representation of old masters. The museum also has excellent examples of Oriental sculpture, screens, scrolls, and ceramics; pre-Colombian objects; and African sculpture. Artists represented include Cussio, El Greco, Rembrandt, Rubens, Goya, Gainsborough, Velazquez, Monet, Cezanne, and Matisse.

Often called the architect's masterpiece, the building was the last design personally completed by the late Louis I. Kahn. It has received top awards for design and construction, lighting, and engineering, as well as for its barrier-free facilities. Through the years the Kimbell has mounted numerous important touring exhibitions, ranging from the heralded *Impressionist and Post-Impressionist Paintings from the U.S.S.R.* to the record-setting showing of *The Great Bronze Age of China* to *The Votive Tradition: Treasures of Buddhist Sculpture from Japan.* Also *Chinese Ceramics: 1620–1683.* The museum is active in lecture programs, film series, children's classes, concerts, and special tours.

The Kimbell is administered by a private foundation established by the late Fort Worth industrialist Kay Kimbell. Upon his death in 1964, he left his entire fortune to the foundation to build the museum to house and expand his collection. His widow joined his will, leaving her share of the community property to the same ends. Facilities include a 180-seat auditorium, a regional conservation center, a bookstore, a superb art library (by reservation only), and a buffet service open for luncheons. Open Tuesday through Saturday, 10:00 A.M. to 5:00 P.M., and Sunday, 1:00 to 5:00 P.M. Call (817) 332–8451.

The Western Company Museum. 6100 Western Place at I–30. Uses geology, chemistry, physics, and astronomy in presenting liquid petroleum and natural gas within a perspective of the makeup of the universe and through a microscopic study of molecular structures. An American-history presentation, with a view into the future, centers on the Industrial Revolution and driving forces of energy. Multimedia techniques include rig sounds, motion, light, cinema projection, voice, and photomural backgrounds. Situated within the headquarters of the Western Company of North America ("If you don't have an oil well, get one"), the museum is open Monday through Friday, 8:30 A.M. to 4:30 P.M. Call (817) 731–5751.

Cattlemen's Museum. 1301 W. 7th. Provides history and artifacts on the growth of the cattle industry from the 1800s to the present. Visitors learn the story of the industry from the evolution of the first American beef animal—the Texas longhorn—to the trail drives north to provide beef for the rest of the nation. Exhibits tell the story of the role of the woman in the beef industry as well as of the battles the cattle raisers have fought with fever ticks, natural disasters, and, most importantly, the rustler. It also tells the story of the origination of the brand inspector and the organization of the group that first employed him—the Texas and Southwestern Cattle Raisers Association. Included are all the tools of the cowboy's trade, from revolver to spurs, from branding iron to barbed wire. The museum presents short videotapes of the history of the older Texas ranches, including the Burnett Estates, the Waggoner Ranch, and the King Ranch. Adjoining the museum is the Cattle Raisers Memorial Hall. Open Monday through Friday, 8:00 A.M. to 5:00 P.M. Free. Call 332–7064.

Exhibits and displays at the **Pate Museum of Transportation,** on U.S. 377 14 mi. southwest of Fort Worth near Cresson, feature antique, classic, and other special cars, military aircraft and artifacts, a railroad car and artifacts, and a Navy mine sweeper boat, to name some. Open Tuesday through Sunday, 9:00 A.M. to 5:00 P.M. Free. Call (817) 332–1161, ext. 323.

Tandy Archaeological Museum, A. Webb Roberts Library, Southwestern Baptist Theological Seminary. Study of early Biblical periods. Permanent collection of artifacts uncovered at Tel Batash-Timnah, Israel. Tours available on request. Free. (817) 923–1921. Monday to Friday, 8:00 A.M. to 5:00 P.M.

DALLAS

The Dallas Museum of Art, formerly the Museum of Fine Arts, moved in early 1984 from State Fair Park to its new Edward Larrabee Barnes–designed building in the new Arts District, in northeast downtown at 1717 N. Harwood in late October 1983. The new museum is the result of one of the largest capital campaigns ever organized in the city. The drive gained wide public awareness several years ago during a major traveling exhibit, Pompeii AD 79. Voters later approved $25 million in bonds for the new building, to be matched by $15 million in private donations. Actual donations exceeded $20 million, and $25 million in new art was pledged from private collections. The museum facade is of huge blocks of Indiana limestone.

The permanent collection of 19th- and 20th-century American and European, pre-Columbian, African, classical, Impressionist, and Oriental works is bolstered by 10 to 12 temporary exhibitions each year. Featured in the permanent collection are works by Matisse, Gauguin, Wyeth, Courbet, and Picasso. Facilities include an extensive art library, a restaurant, a sculpture garden, and a children's gallery. Open Tuesday through Saturday, 10 A.M. to 5:00 P.M., (Thursday till 10:00 P.M.), and Sunday, from noon. Free. Call (214) 922–0220.

Dallas's largest concentration of museums is within State Fair Park, 2 mi. east of downtown:

The Dallas Museum of Natural History, at the entrance to the park, presents 54 natural habitats authentically re-created and furnished with actual specimens of 90-million-year-old fossil fish, and the Closeups Room allows visitors to handle and inspect new or special specimens. The museum also sponsors periodic environmental exhibits, lectures, and field trips. Open Monday through Saturday, 9:00 A.M. to 5:00 P.M., and Sunday, from noon. Free. Call 421–2169.

Since its founding in 1946, what is now called **The Science Place/Southwest Museum of Science and Technology** has become an outstanding resource center and educational showcase. Major traveling exhibits have included the record-breaking Ice Age Art exhibit and the Dreamstage exhibit—a portrait of the sleeping brain. Permanent exhibits expound on the human anatomy and health, as well as electronics, banking, and transportation. The first solar-powered airplane is here. Open Tuesday through Saturday, 9:00 A.M. to 5:00 P.M., and Sunday, from noon. $1.00 adult, 50¢ child. Planetarium shows at scheduled times ($1). 428–8351.

The Age of Steam Railroad Museum, a venture of the Southwest Railroad Historical Society and the State Fair of Texas, represents a collection of historical freight and passenger cars and engines from 1900 to 1950. A collection of railroad locomotives is on a siding of the Missouri-Pacific track adjacent. Open Sundays, 11:00 A.M. to 5:00 P.M. Adults $1.50; children 75¢.

The Dallas Aquarium features 340 species of amphibians, reptiles, and native freshwater, tropical, and cold-water fish. Feeding times open to the public are: tropical freshwater and marine fish, Monday through Friday at 9:00 A.M., and native freshwater, Monday, Wednesday and Friday at 3:00 P.M. Open Monday through Saturday, 9:00 A.M. to 5:00 P.M., and Sunday from noon. Free. 428–3587.

The Art Deco **Hall of State,** in the center of the park, was created to honor the Texas Centennial of 1936. It tells the story of Texas through thousands of historical objects and costumes. The hall also features a series of temporary exhibitions and has a growing publications program. Open Monday through Saturday, 9:00 A.M. to 5:00 P.M., and Sunday, 1:00 to 5:00 P.M. (The lower floor houses the Dallas Historical Society Research Center.) Free. 421–5136.

A turn-of-the-century fire station, **Old Tige's Dallas Firefighters Museum,** at 3801 Parry Ave., features an 1884 horse-drawn steam pumper and antique alarm bells. Call 821–1500. Free, but donations are accepted.

The Biblical Arts Center, at 7500 Park La. at Boedeker near NorthPark Center in North Dallas, features early-Christian architecture and biblical and secular art. The 30-minute light-and-sound biblical presentation includes the 124-by-20-foot oil painting *The Miracle at Pentecost.* Shows start at half-past the hour, with the last presentation beginning at 4:30 P.M. Open Tuesday through Saturday, 10:00 A.M. to 5:00 P.M., and Sunday, from 1:00 P.M. Adults $3.50 ages 6 to 12 $1.75, and under 6 free. Call 691–4661.

On the campus of Bishop College in Oak Cliff, the **Museum of African-American Art and Culture** is the only center of its kind in the Southwest, recognizing the contributions of black Americans. Founded in 1974, the museum (3837 Simpson-Stuart) offers a collection of modern and traditional works, as well as traveling exhibitions and musical performances. Free. Call 372–8000.

The International Museum of Culture, 7500 W. Camp Wisdom Road, Dallas; (214) 298–3331, focuses on contemporary cultures of the world, with dioramas, displays, and audio-visual shows. Tues.–Fri. 10:00 A.M. to 5:00 P.M.; Sat. and Sun., 1:30 P.M. Closed Mon.

MUSIC. Dallas voters said yes in 1982 to a bond issue that will eventually give citizens a new concert hall to join the Museum of Art as the second resident of the newly born Arts District, a neighborhood on the northern edge of downtown, southeast of the Woodall Rodgers Fwy. between St. Paul and Routh (pronounced "Ruth") Sts. The future home of the **Dallas Symphony Orchestra** as well as a center for other musical and educational events, the new concert hall has pledges from private contributors to finance 40 percent of the costs. Architect I. M. Pei was commissioned to design the $28.6 million concert hall, and Russell Johnson is responsible for acoustical engineering. Presently, the DSO shares the Fair Park Music Hall with numerous events, including the Civic Opera (see below) and Dallas Ballet (for the *Nutcracker*), meaning its season, beginning in September, is suspended until January in order to free the Music Hall for the October State Fair and the November opera season. In summer, the Dallas Symphony's 10-week award-winning Starfest series at Park Central brings in big-name stars all along the musical scale. Concert-goers bring their picnic suppers and blankets for an evening under the stars on Coit Road between Forest Lane and LBJ (I–635). The symphony played to its first audience in 1900. Today it is made up of 86 musicians who perform every week of the year under the leadership of Eduardo Mata. The full season includes several musical series featuring classical and pops performances, appearances with the Dallas Opera, sidewalk concerts, youth concerts, and performances for the handicapped. Call 692–0203 for ticket information.

The **Dallas Civic Music Association** presents five to six programs each season, between September and May, in McFarlin Auditorium on the SMU campus. Since its founding in 1930 it has presented an annual series of outstanding musical artists to the community. The **Dallas Chamber Music Society** hosts concerts featuring music ensembles of international repute, with performances each winter at SMU. For information on the **Dallas Classic Guitar Society's** fall season at SMU, call 343–3709.

The **Dallas Jazz Society** sponsors an annual salute to Duke Ellington in April, as well as other special concerts.

The **Fort Worth Symphony Orchestra** performs in concert from late September or early October through May at the Tarrant County Convention Center Theatre. For information call 921–2676. The **Texas Little Symphony** is well tuned in Fort Worth from October through March. For information on concerts and locations call 921–2676. Fort Worth is also the home of the internationally touring, Grammy-winning **Texas Boys Choir.**

The **Johnnie High Country Music Revue,** is a fast-paced, quality country-music variety show presented every Saturday at 8:00 P.M. at Fort Worth's Will Rogers Auditorium, 3301 W. Lancaster. A part of country music since childhood, Johnnie High has auditioned more than 5,000 acts in the last eight years for his weekly show. Call 332–0909 or 481–4518 for information.

Arenas drawing the big-name concerts in Dallas are Reunion Arena, SMU's McFarlin Auditorium, and the Dallas Convention Center, and, in Fort Worth, the Tarrant County Convention Center. Some are staged outdoors at the Cotton Bowl.

OPERA

The **Fort Worth Opera,** Texas' longest continuing opera company, will enter its 40th season in 1986. In addition to productions staged during the season at Tarrant County Convention Center Theatre, the opera has formed an educational adjunct, the **Southwestern Opera Theater,** which plays annually to 20,000 schoolchildren in the Metroplex. For ticket information on the season, which begins in November, call 731–0833.

Having celebrated its 25th anniversary in 1981, the **Dallas Opera** offers four productions from late October or early November through late December at the Music Hall in State Fair Park. For years the only place in America where Maria Callas would perform, the Dallas Opera afforded Franco Zefferelli, Joan Sutherland, and Montserrat Caballe their American debuts. Call 747–8600 for Majestic Theatre performance information. Box office, 871–0090.

The **High Noon Opera** stages performances in downtown Dallas and in shopping centers and schools. Information can be gotten by calling 747–8600.

For almost 40 years, the **Dallas Grand Opera Association** has brought the New York Metropolitan Opera to Dallas. Four operas are presented each spring in the State Fair Park Music Hall. For ticket information call 691–7200.

DANCE. Its season highlighted by a holiday production of the *Nutcracker,* the **Dallas Ballet** company each year stages four repertory productions. In addition to its Ballet Under the Stars, a series of free park performances in Dallas and 15 more on tour in the Southwest and Mexico, the company also performs in schools and hospitals. Founded in 1975 by the late George Skibine, Dallas Ballet also supports the Dallas Ballet Academy, which trains many of its professionals. Call 744–4430 for information on performances presented from October through March at the superbly renovated Majestic Theatre downtown.

The first professional black dance company in Dallas, the **Dallas Black Dance Theatre,** employs a repertoire of jazz, contemporary, and classical ballet. Situated on the campus of Bishop College in conjunction with the South Dallas Academy, the company trains dancers from preschool ages through adult. Call 371–1170 for information on performances. Also keeping Dallas on its toes are the *Dallas Metropolitan Ballet, Dancers Unlimited,* and the *Krassovska Ballet Jeunesse of Dallas* on the SMU campus.

The **Fort Worth Ballet** opens its season in October as well, at Tarrant County Convention Center Theatre. Call 921–6998 for performance information.

STAGE. Dallas is the center of most of the theatrical activity in the Metroplex. The $1 million **Dallas Theater Center,** at 3636 Turtle Creek Blvd., contains the only public theater designed by Frank Lloyd Wright. The grand Kalita Humphreys Theater and intimate Down Center Stage, with performances ranging from Shakespeare to modern, opened in 1959. A breeding ground for world-renowned talent, the Dallas Theater Center has brought along such playwrights as the late Preston Jones, whose *A Texas Trilogy* premiered in Dallas, went on to set box-office records at the Kennedy Center in Washington, D.C., and won a Golden Apple Award on Broadway. Call 526–8857 for information.

Theatre Three, at 2800 Routh in the Quadrangle, was founded in 1961 by Norma Young and Jac Adler. Featuring the new as well as classics, today's performances range from children's plays to musicals, comedies, and dramas. This theater in the round seats approximately 250. Several TV and film stars got their starts here, including Morgan Fairchild and Ronnie Claire Edwards. Call 871–3300 for information.

Dallas Repertory Theatre, now in its own building at NorthPark, turns in five productions each year. Casting is done through open auditions, with Equity members performing leading roles. Call 369–8966 for information.

The **Dallas Summer Musicals** are staged at State Fair Music Hall, 1st Ave. and Parry in State Fair Park. Broadway and Hollywood stars perform in 8 to 10 shows. Since its first season in 1941, the musicals have presented such historic moments as Gene Kelly's return to the stage after 33 years and the musical-comedy debuts of Donald O'Connor, Patti Page, and Rock Hudson. Productions range from one-man shows, such as Rich Little, to full musical productions, such as *A Chorus Line.* Call 691–7200 for information. With as many as 17 performances, a **Shakespeare festival** also is produced on the grounds of Fair Park in June.

Southern Methodist University in Dallas is home to the **Margo Jones Theatre** and the **Bob Hope Theatre.** The latter is the site of of the U.S.A. Film Festival, an annual series highlighting U.S. films and filmmakers and honoring guest directors with film retrospectives. For more information call 692–2573.

In addition to performances by the resident acting company, **Stage No. 1, Greenville Avenue Theatre,** 2914 Greenville, in Dallas, hosts other performing arts. Call 760–9542.

New Arts Theatre, at 301 N. Market at Ross, opened New Year's Eve, 1980, in downtown Dallas's West End Historic District. Its repertoire ranges from the works of Texas playwrights to Tennessee Williams to Shakespeare. Call 761–9064.

Built in 1921 as the headquarters of the Interstate Theatre chain, the baroque movie palace called the **Majestic Theatre,** 1925 Elm, featured famous vaudeville acts and movies of the days. After the theater was donated to the city of Dallas, funds were raised through a bond issue and private subscription to restore the building. Local dance, opera, theater, and concert agencies, as well as touring productions, use the multipurpose performing-arts hall.

FORT WORTH

Casa Manana puts on Broadway musicals, concerts, and plays in the country's first permanent musical arena theater (1958). At 3101 W. Lancaster in Amon Carter Square near Fort Worth's famous museums, this theater in the round offers a full summer season of road shows, featuring top names as well as local professionals. It is said a critic and former skeptic once said of Billy Rose's original, lavish outdoor playhouse: "Only two things live up to the claims of their press agents—the Grand Canyon and Fort Worth's Casa Manana." Call 332–6221 for information.

The highly acclaimed **Hip Pocket Theatre** takes its productions outdoors at Oak Acres Amphitheatre, 1620 Las Vegas Trail N. Customers are doubly satisfied: barbecue is served before each performance. Call 246–1269 for information and reservations.

Home of the **Fort Worth Theatre,** the $1.25 million **William Edrington Scott Theatre,** at 3505 W. Lancaster, is open for guided tours by appointment. Call 738–6509. Plays and film series are given year-round.

Fort Worth's summer **Shakespeare** series is given in Trinity Park.

SHOPPING. Dallas. There's no denying out-of-towners' fascination with *Neiman-Marcus,* especially at the original location, downtown at 1618 Main (at Ervay). The fourth-floor antiques are a special draw. Expect to compete storewide with hordes of locals during Last Call bargain days in late January and July.

The consensus on the town's best buy on Western boots is at down-to-earth *Mistletoe Boot Shop,* 942 E. Jefferson in Oak Cliff (I–35 south to the Jefferson exit, then one block).

The fashion-conscious woman can be seen maneuvering in "designer row" shops along Lovers La. between Inwood and Preston Roads in North Dallas. But the latest entries in the shopping sweepstakes are in the Galleria, Dallas Parkway north of LBJ Freeway in Far North Dallas, with such names as *Saks, Marshall Field, Gump's,* and *Tiffany's.*

If Galleria's ice rink is too crowded, try the one at Prestonwood Town Center, to the north at Dallas Parkway and Belt Line, with *Neiman-Marcus, Joske's* and *Lord & Taylor.* Between Galleria and Prestonwood are *Sakowitz Village* and a bevy of eating establishments. Valley View Mall, to the east of Galleria on LBJ Freeway between Montfort and Preston, offers *Sanger-Harris* and *Dillard's.*

Probably the most central shopping mall in Dallas, decorative NorthPark Center, at Northwest Highway (Loop 12) and North Central Expressway (U.S. 75), is home to *Neiman-Marcus, Joske's,* and *Lord & Taylor,* in addition to the Dallas Repertory Theatre. Kitty-corner to the mall at Central and Park Lane is Caruth Plaza, featuring sporty *Abercrombie & Fitch.*

A few blocks south of NorthPark and east of Central Expressway is Old Town mall at Lovers La. and Greenville Avenue in the heart of the North Dallas singles' stamping grounds. Old Town's specialty stores are bounded by a TGI Friday's and an all-night Tom Thumb supermarket.

The first mall of its kind in the country, Highland Park Shopping Center, Preston at Mockingbird in Highland Park, offers probably the swankiest *Sanger-Harris* department store in town. But parking at this Spanish-style center can be a problem, especially when the movie crowd moves in.

Arts and crafts aficionados can get their fix at, to name three centers, the *Craft Compound,* 6617 Snider Plaza near Lovers La. in Highland Park, with its crafts shops, galleries, antiques, and folk art; *Olla Podrida,* at 12215 Coit, west of Central Expressway between Forest La. and LBJ Freeway, an old barn converted into an artsy two-story "melting pot" of specialty shops; and the *Quadrangle,* 2800 Routh between Cedar Springs and McKinney near downtown in a historic section of Oak Lawn, with its Indian pueblo–style grouping of shops known for their pottery, jewelry, glassworks, baskets, and candles.

Traders Village, 2602 Mayfield Rd. in Grand Prairie, is a 106-acre Texas-size flea market where everything imaginable is bought and sold from 100 booths every Saturday and Sunday from 8:00 A.M. to dusk. Call (214) 647–2331 for information. In Dallas, try *Big D Bazaar,* 3636 Buckner; (214) 328–6117.

Other major shopping centers in Dallas include: Big Town Mall, U.S. 80 and 67 east in Mesquite; Town East Mall, LBJ Freeway at Town East Blvd. in Mesquite; Casa Linda Plaza, Garland Rd. and Buckner east of White Rock Lake in East Dallas; Red Bird Mall, east of Duncanville at 3662 W. Camp Wisdom and U.S. 67 South; Richardson Square Mall, 501 S. Plano Rd. in Richardson; European Crossroads, north of Bachman Lake and Love Field at 2829 W. Northwest Highway; and Irving Mall, west in Irving at Texas 183 and Belt Line.

Earmarked for a $2-million expansion, *Dallas Farmer's Market,* in the southeast corner of downtown, offers visitors a taste of the Texas truck-farming tradition. Depending on the season, trucks brim with tomatoes, corn, watermelons, potatoes, and grapefruit, among the countless offerings under three square blocks of huge sheds. Get there *early.* Call (214) 748–2082 for information.

Some 500,000 professional buyers from across the country and around the world converge on the Texas-size *Dallas Market Center* each year to spend $5 billion (wholesale) for residential and contract furnishings, gifts, decorative accessories, leisure goods, jewelry, toys, and apparel. At 2100 Stemmons Freeway, Market Center encompasses the Apparel Mart, the Decorative Center, the Home Furnishings Center, Market Hall, and the World Trade Center. Plantings and contemporary sculpture have been placed in and around the various buildings. Only the ground floor is open to the public.

Both Dallas and Fort Worth have plenty of exciting art galleries covering a range of specialties. Check the weekend-guide sections in the Friday editions of the *Dallas Morning News* and the *Dallas Times Herald* and the latest issue of *D* magazine for current offerings. Area universities and colleges have their own galleries too.

FORT WORTH

Fort Worth, where the West begins, can stagger the Western-wear shopper with sheer numbers. For example, the *Justin Boot Company Outlet,* three blocks south of downtown at 301 S. Jennings, houses thousands of wholesale overstock boots from its Fort Worth factory; *Luskey's,* downtown at 101 Houston, is a sure-find in western threads and several brands of boots, and *Shepler's,* south of I–30 in Arlington at 2500 E. Centennial Dr., offers more than an acre of floor space. The Fort Worth Stockyards area, Main and Exchange on the North Side, is home to specialty shops offering western apparel and merchandise of the historic cattle era.

A slice of downtown Fort Worth's present facelift, Sundance Square, with its turn-of-the-century architecture, features new restaurants, shops, and night-spots in low-rise buildings.

Cowtown does not lack for malls, either. At Hulen Mall, in southwest Fort Worth at 4800 S. Hulen St., *Sanger-Harris* and good snacks are the bywords. *Neiman-Marcus* is the calling card for Ridgmar Mall, 2060 Green Oaks at I–30 in west Fort Worth. Not to be confused with Ridgmar, the Ridglea shopping area, featuring the *Stripling and Cox* department store, lies to the southeast on Camp Bowie (U.S. 377/U.S. 80 Business) between I–30 and the Weatherford traffic circle.

Other major shopping centers in the Fort Worth area include:

Tandy Center, downtown at Throckmorton and Weatherford; Downtown Cowtown, 813 E. 9th St. (weekends only); Seminary South, I–35 at Seminary Dr.; Market Center, 4950 Highway 377 South (weekends only); North Hills Mall, 7624 Grapevine Hwy.; and Northeast Mall, northeast in Hurst at Texas 183/121 at I–820. In Arlington: Forum 303, 2900 Pioneer Parkway; Six Flags Mall, 411 Six Flags Dr.; and Carriage Plaza, 900 Copeland Road at Texas 157.

DINING OUT IN DALLAS. Partly because of antiquated liquor laws, which held sway until 1972, Dallas restaurants have been late in coming of age. (Even now, one must pay "membership fees" to drink in establishments outside the central "wet" area of town.) But since then, with a mushrooming, more sophisticated population, Dallas restaurants have increased in number and quality: the first, astronomically; the second, in a more measured fashion. Many of these new establishments are cynical products of marketing, and they tend to disappear as quickly as they materialize.

Finding a good restaurant in Dallas can be exponentially more difficult than that old needle-haystack search we've heard about all our lives. At least needles *look* bright and shiny, and haystraws don't have big-budget advertising campaigns designed to make them appear to be something they are not. Unfortunately, honesty is not the house policy in many local restaurants. If it were against the law to impersonate a restaurateur, most Dallas food handlers would be in jail. The odds are against you when you walk into any of the 4,000-odd restaurants in the Dallas area expecting to sit down to a rewarding dining experience. But a few restaurants are the product of commitment to good eating.

The search for a good restaurant is made even more difficult because most restaurateurs are attuned to Dallas diners' tendency to equate price—and sometimes pomposity—with culinary excellence. It is one of the central components of the Dallas psyche that you get what you pay for; therefore, a meal that costs more than your wristwatch *has* to be good. This notion has spawned a legion of restaurants that might best called pseudo-Continental, usually run by counterfeit Gallics whose cooking skills have yet to equal their self-esteem.

Of Dallas's high-ticket choices, Routh Street Cafe and Enjolie provide the most reliably extraordinary dining experience. Restaurants of this type have ever-escalating tabs that are correspondingly extraordinary. Dallas's big-deal restaurant tabs rival New York's, which is to be considered if one isn't on an expense account, as many of the patrons are. Be wary, especially, of off-the-menu options.

To eat with a view, consider the Hilton's Harper's Corner; stick with drinks at the Hyatt Regency's Antares, Reunion Tower.

As for native fare, don't expect trail-wagon specialties on every corner in Dallas. Certainly, Texana is available, at old favorites like Tolbert's Chili Parlor and newer ones like Hoffbrau Steaks. But Dallas's true indigenous cuisine subdivides into barbecue, southern, and Tex-Mex (which is particularly cheap, satisfying, and addictive).

Dallasites tend to take these areas for granted; they pride themselves on two other counts: the nouvelle and haute cuisine of the city's most pricey restaurants and the range of sometimes obscure ethnic food in the most inexpensive holes in the wall. Among the best funky, ethnic-food finds are Gonzalez (Mexican), Siam Orchid (Thai), Chito's (Mexican), and Kebab-n-Kurry (Indian).

Good restaurants are spread throughout the city (with the partial exception of Oak Cliff, which suffers from a no-alcohol, low-income history). North Dallas, the area between the LBJ Freeway and Belt Line Rd. near the Dallas Parkway in the township of Addison, is the site of the biggest boom. There are a few jewels in the midst of the paste flash and glitter, but too many North Dallas restaurants ride on their plush ambience.

Other restaurant-dense areas are Greenville Ave., which spans the city from north to south parallel to North Central Expy.; Lower Greenville (below Mockingbird) tends to funk; Upper Greenville (considered to be part of North Dallas) caters to more upscale, though not necessarily more discerning, tastes. McKinney Ave., near downtown, offers a small group of diverse options. And downtown Dallas has seen a restaurant boom of sorts with the active revitalization of the West End Historical District. For a taste of ethnic Dallas, the intersection of Maple and Wycliff is the center of Mexican restaurants and shops. Tex-Mex is ubiquitous, with its combination plates of tacos, enchiladas, tamales, and chalupas.

Both the *Dallas Times Herald* and *The Dallas Morning News* publish restaurant listings each Friday; the *Morning News's* are more extensive.

One holdover from Dallas's provincial heritage is restaurant hours. Many close by 10:00 P.M. As a side effect of Texas's blue law, many restaurants are closed on Sunday as well. Meals are taxed at 5%, the same rate for nearly everything.

The price classifications of the following restaurants, from inexpensive to deluxe, are based on the cost of an average three-course dinner for one person for food alone; beverages, tax, and tip would be extra. *Inexpensive,* less than $8; *Moderate,* $8 to $15; *Expensive,* $15 to $30; and *Deluxe,* more than $30.

Abbreviations for credit cards are: AE, American Express; CB, Carte Blanche; DC, Diners Club; MC, MasterCard; V, Visa. Most restaurants that do not accept credit cards will cash traveler's checks; few, however, will honor personal checks. Abbreviations for meal codes are: B, breakfast; L, lunch; D, dinner. Since restaurant hours and days of closing often change, you should call first to confirm.

All telephone numbers are area code 214.

BARBECUE AND CHILI

Inexpensive

Chickeria. 601 N. Haskall at Worth; 821–9072, situated in east Dallas. You've heard of the New American Cuisine. Chickeria has the New American Barbecue: grilled chicken and shrimp as well as ribs. L, D, Monday through Saturday. No credit cards.

Dan's. 3002 Canton; 741–0650. This downtown spot calls itself "home of the healthy plate." They're referring to the size of the typical serving, not the surgeon general's opinion. The offerings are, however, commendably grease free. The sausage in particular is terrific. No liquor. L, Monday through Friday. No credit cards.

Ribshack. 4615 W. Lovers Ln., North Dallas; 351–3400. The smoky, meaty, sugar-cured ribs are among the best in town; the setting is spotless and pleasant. Beer, wine. L, D, daily. No credit cards.

Salih's. 4801 Belt Line, Addison (north); 387–2900. One of the most clean-cut, pleasant barbecue experiences for the uninitiated. Faultless beef, sausage, ribs, and ham are served in a squeaky-clean setting that is a cross between a fern bar and a cafeteria. Beer. L, D, Monday through Saturday. Major credit cards.

Sonny Bryan's. 2202 Inwood Road, west of Dallas North Tollway near Harry Hines Blvd.; 357–7120. The sauce, which is legendary in Dallas, is the thing here. A cross section of Dallasites always crowds the tiny, dingy interior, where school-desk tops substitute for tables. Go early; the place closes up when the meat's all gone. Beer. L, daily. No credit cards.

Tolbert's Original Texas Chili Parlor. 4544 McKinney, north of downtown; 522–4340. Frank Tolbert is a tireless promoter who makes fine "red" Texas chili and homemade fries. Also memorable: donkey tails (hot dogs wrapped in flour tortillas, deep fried, and served with hot mustard). Alas, the original downtown Tolbert's is but a memory; the new McKinney location is airy and pleasant but lacking in soul. L, D, Monday through Saturday. AE, MC, V.

CAFETERIAS

Inexpensive

Highland Park Cafeteria. 4611 Cole Ave. in North Dallas; 526–3801. A local institution. HPC is probably the best place to sample reasonably priced southern-style home cooking. The array of dishes must be seen to be believed. Lines are always long, but they move quickly. (Also new branches at Las Colinas Tower, 225 E. John Carpenter Freeway, Irving, 556–0480; and 5100 Belt Line, 934–8025.) L, D, Monday through Saturday. No credit cards.

Luby's Cafeterias. Many locations; see the Yellow Pages. Above-average cafeteria food. L, D, daily. No credit cards.

DELICATESSENS

Whatever you say about Dallas, you can't say that it's a great city for deli food.

Inexpensive

Bagelstein's. 8104 Spring Valley (north, above LBJ Fwy. 635); 234–3787. Bagelstein's is notable for its seven kinds of bagels baked daily. No liquor. L, Tuesday through Sunday; D, Tuesday through Saturday. No credit cards.

Kuby's. 6601 Snider Plaza, Hillcrest Ave. at Lovers Ln.; 363–2231. This German-style sandwich and sausage purveyor is a Dallas institution. (Translation: it's nearly always crowded.) No liquor, L, Monday through Saturday. MC, V.

FAST FOOD

In addition to the standard national franchises, two local institutions are noteworthy:

Schlotzky's is renowned for its multi-ingredient (including ham, lunch meat, cheese, black olives, lettuce, tomato, and onion) sandwich served on home-baked bread. 5601 W. Lovers La.; 351–6587. 3529 McKinney Ave.; 528–3480. (Beer at preceding two.) 1503 Commerce; 744–3176. 13531 Montfort; 233–7554. 3203 W. Camp Wisdom; 339–9784. 13551 N. Central Expressway; 234–4249. 1734 S. Buckner; 391–3443.

Gonzalez (see *Mexican*) serves creditable, drive-through Tex-Mex breakfasts, lunches, and dinners.

HAMBURGERS

Inexpensive

Chip's. 4501 N. Central Expressway; 526–1092. Basic burgers done right and served in nifty surroundings. Check out the jukebox. Beer, wine; no cocktails. L, D, Monday through Saturday. No credit cards.

The Points are essentially bars, but they serve a huge, locally renowned burger. *The Point After,* 5724 E. Lovers; 691–3525. L, D, daily. *The Elm Street*

Point, 1324 Elm; 724–6552. L, D, Monday through Saturday. *The Locker Room,* 5021 W. Lovers; 352–6421. L, D, Monday through Saturday. *The Wycliff Point,* 2525 Wycliff; 528–2030. L, D, daily. *The Maple Point,* 5415 Maple; 630–7640. L, D, daily. AE, MC, V.

Snuffer's. 3526 Greenville, northeast Dallas; 826–6850. This pub-restaurant has a limited menu offering one of the best—and largest—burgers in town. An order of the homemade fries will easily do for two; the size is ridiculously huge. Serves late. L, D, daily. AE, MC, V.

PIZZA

Generally speaking, Dallas isn't a city for pizza lovers. Only two earn the respect of cognoscenti: Expect to wait at *Ciao,* Cedar Springs at Throckmorton; 521–0110. *Adriano's* (the Quadrangle, 2800 Routh; 871–2262) serves great, Spago-style pizzas with imaginative toppings (see "Italian").

HEALTH FOOD

Moderate

Francis Simun's. 6922 Snider Plaza, Hillcrest Ave. at Lovers Ln.; 824–4910. Very upscale for a health-food restaurant: pretty pastel decor and classical background music. Great house salad, superb whole-grain-crust quiche, creamy apricot mousse. No liquor. L, D, Monday through Saturday. Sunday brunch. No credit cards.

Inexpensive

Bluebonnet Natural Foods Grocery. 2106 Greenville, northeast Dallas; 824–1740. Austin-style (laid-back) health food establishment and juice bar with limited, flavorful fare. Try a fresh papaya smoothie and black-bean nachos. No liquor. L, daily. MC, V.

Harthomp & Moran Natural Foods Grocery. 9191 Forest Ln., far north Dallas; 231–6083. Outstanding fare, especially fruit salad. Awkward seating. Same owners as H&M Natural Foods Grocery. No liquor. L, Monday through Saturday, MC, V.

Kalachandji's. 5430 Gurley Ave., east Dallas; 821–1048. It's Hare Krishna–run, but don't let that scare you away. For a $5.50 prix fixe, a different, extensive Indian dinner is served each night. Eat in the courtyard, surrounded by stained glass. No liquor. D, Tuesday through Saturday. MC, V.

SEAFOOD

Surprisingly for a landlocked city, Dallas has a growing flotilla of seafood restaurants, most of them vying for preeminence in serving faultlessly fresh fish.

Expensive

Atlantic Cafe. 4546 McKinney at Knox; 559–4441. This chic, sophisticated restaurant may well serve the best seafood in town. The servings are Texas-size, the service is attentive, and the wine list is well-selected. L, D, daily. Sunday brunch. Major credit cards.

Café Pacific. 24 Highland Park Village, Preston Rd. at Mockingbird Ln.; 526–1170. Classy brass-and-glass decor. The food is good and so are the drinks, including a great Ramos gin fizz and piña colada. Very popular with the nearby Highland Park crowd, so expect a wait. L, D, daily. AE, MC, V.

Jozef's. 2719 McKinney Ave., north of downtown; 826–5560. Start with the smoked trout, which is an enjoyably out-of-the-ordinary appetizer. After that, stick with simpler choices, since Jozef's is not known for its sauces. The decor is neither here nor there: nice enough but forgettable. L, Monday through Friday; D, daily. Major credit cards.

Moderate

Oysters. 4580 Belt Line Rd. in Addison, north of far north Dallas; 386–0122. Nicely prepared oysters, shrimp, and fresh fish in a cozy, casual dining room. L, Monday through Saturday; D, daily. Major credit cards.

Rocco. 2520 Cedar Springs Rd., north of downtown; 747–6226. Exquisite seafood in a delicately nautical new-wave setting. Do have the terrific cornbread on the side, and ice cream with framboise (raspberry liqueur) for dessert. Informal and very chic. L, D, daily. AE, V.

Rusty Scupper. 4951 Belt Line Rd., Addison, far north; 960–0884. Surprisingly good seafood (for national chain) is served amid airy, fern-bar surroundings. Great sourdough bread, vegetables, and shrimp Mexical; terrible desserts. L, Monday through Friday; D, daily. AE, V.

S & D Oyster Co. 2701 McKinney Ave., north of downtown; 823–6350. A crowd of dedicated regulars is always lined up outside the door, drinking beer while they await admittance to the simple, renovated warehouse. Oysters on the half shell, red snapper, boiled shrimp, and other Gulf-coast seafood are what they're here for. As at Rusty Scupper, forget about dessert. Beer, wine, no mixed drinks. L, D, Monday through Saturday. MC.

Turtle Cove. 2731 W. Northwest Highway, northwest Dallas; 350–9034. Relaxed, pretty surroundings and SRO crowds for the seafood, which is excellent, fresh, and mesquite broiled. Mesquite-broiled vegetables sound unlikely but are terrific, a better option than salad. L, D, daily. AE, MC, V.

Inexpensive

Aw Shucks. 3601 Greenville Ave. (at Longview), in East Dallas; 821–9449. This tiny, informal establishment has some of the freshest, simplest seafood in the area. Beer served; no liquor. L, D, Monday-Saturday. Closed Sunday. No credit cards.

Hebert's Seafood Bar. 1900 Pacific; 760–8456. Commendable New Orleans–style seafood bar in a tiny downtown location. Beer, wine; no cocktails. L, Monday through Friday. AE, MC, V.

Mother Shucker's. 3957 Belt Line Rd. between Midway and Marsh; 788–2772. Simple seafood—raw, boiled or fried—is the attraction here. Soft-shell crabs and crawfish are two of the more unusual options. L, D, Monday through Saturday. AE, MC, V.

SOUTHERN

Moderate

Dovie's. 14671 Midway Rd., in Addison, north of Dallas; 233–9846. Definitely the nicest setting in which to try southern fare. The food has ups and downs, but the restored home makes for an enjoyable setting. B, Monday through Friday; L, D, daily. Major credit cards.

Inexpensive

Black-eyed Pea. 3857 Cedar Springs; 521–4580. 4814 Greenville; 361–5979. 5290 Belt Line, Addison; 233–8227. 1915 N. Central Expressway (at Park Blvd.), Plano; 423–5565. This local chain serves passable chicken-fried steak, stuffed peppers, etc. The noise level is a problem at the Belt Line and Greenville locations. L, D, daily. AE, MC. V.

Bubba's. 6617 Hillcrest Ave., south of Lovers Ln.; 373–6527. The bright, new slate-gray-and-lipstick-red decor is like a Salvador Dali vision. But the cooking couldn't be more old-fashioned: fried chicken, yeast rolls, down-home vegetables, and fruit cobbler. Skip Bubba's breakfast, though. No liquor. B, L, D, daily. No credit cards.

Dixie House. 2822 McKinney Ave., north of downtown; 824–0891. 3647 W. Northwest Hwy.; 353–0769. 14925 Midway, Addison; 239–5144. 6400 Gaston (at Abrams); 826–2412. These formula restaurants turn out dependable if uninspired southern classics. The result is informal and popular. L, D, daily. AE, MC. V.

Gennie's Bishop Grill. 308 N. Bishop; 946–1752. Tucked away in the decidedly un-chic Oak Cliff section of town, Gennie's turns out memorable yeast rolls, chicken-fried steak, and banana pudding. The food is authentic, and the service is cafeteria-style. No liquor. L, Monday through Friday. No credit cards.

Rosemarie's. 1411 N. Zang; 946–4142. Chow down on simple, basic southern food and good rolls in truck-stop diner decor in Oak Cliff. No liquor. B, L, Monday through Friday. No credit cards.

Upper Crust. Olla Podrida Shopping Center, 12215 Coit Rd., south of LBJ Fwy.; 661–5738. The small menu changes daily and features excellent homemade offerings. Situated in an offbeat, crafts-oriented shopping center. Liquor with membership. L, Monday through Saturday; D, Thursday. AE, MC, V.

STEAK

Steak chains abound in Dallas, but truly outstanding steak restaurants are surprisingly few.

Ruth's Chris Steak House. 6940 Greenville, northeast Dallas; 691–6940. Top-grade meat for those willing to pay top-grade prices. Minimal atmosphere, considering the tab. L, Monday through Friday; D, daily. Major credit cards.

Hoffbrau. 3205 Knox, North Dallas; 559–2680. Cold beer, chunky fried potatoes, and steaks pan sauteed with lemon butter are the essence of this reasonably priced menu. The decor and the jukebox are rowdy and western; the clientele always seems to be having a good time. L, Monday through Saturday; D, daily. Major credit cards.

AMERICAN-INTERNATIONAL

Deluxe

Enjolie. Mandalay Four Seasons Hotel, 221 S. Las Colinas Blvd., Irving; 556–0800. The Mandalay's top-of-the-line restaurant offers discreetly classy surroundings. Don't miss the knockout pheasant mousse and the decadent desserts. The complementary cheese tray and selection of petit fours add to the experience without adding to the tab. L, D, Monday through Saturday. AE, MC, V. (Also under *French.*)

The Mansion. 2821 Turtle Creek Blvd., North Dallas; 526–2121. The Mansion's elegant setting and late-night supper make it a favorite stopping point for visiting celebrities. The new, Wolfgang Puck-consulted menu is perhaps the best in town. Tie and jacket required for men. B, L, D, daily. No CB.

The Riviera. 7709 Inwood near Lovers; 351–0094. Classic Continental cuisine in upbeat setting reminiscent of southern Europe. D, Monday through Sunday. Major credit cards.

Routh Street Cafe. 3005 Routh St. (at Cedar Springs); 871–7161. A creative, changing menu served in an austere, lovely setting adds up to Dallas' most exciting dining experience. D, Monday through Saturday. AE, MC, V.

Expensive

Ewald's. 5415 W. Lovers Ln. near Dallas North Tollway; 357–1622. This chef-owned restaurant is a longtime favorite of Dallas natives, who come for the high-quality veal and beef dishes. There isn't a breath of pretentiousness in the place. The decor is nice enough, though a bit dated. D, Monday through Saturday. AE, MC, V.

Francisco's. 2917 Fairmount St., north of downtown; 749–0906. No nouvelle cuisine here; instead, there are variations on classic themes. Helpful service, and a terrific clear soup of sliced mushrooms floating in delicate consomme and topped with pastry, are pluses. L, Monday through Friday; D, Monday through Saturday. AE, MC, V.

Old Warsaw. 2610 Maple Ave., north of downtown; 528–0032. In its heyday, the peak dining experience available in Dallas. Still worth it for the extraordinary, classy-bordello plushness of the setting. Stick to simple choices, though; the elaborate offerings on the menu are disappointing. D, daily. Major credit cards.

Moderate

Bradford. Bradford Hotel, 302 S. Houston; 761–9090. One of the few options in downtown's west end, the Bradford is a pleasant choice. Stick with homemade soups and simpler entrées. B, L, D, daily. Major credit cards.

Café d'Or. Mandalay Four Seasons Hotel, 221 S. Las Colinas Blvd., Irving (west of Dallas, off Rte, 114); 556–0800. Appetizers and salads are the standouts at this ambitious, reasonably priced coffee shop of the Mandalay. B, daily; L, Monday through Saturday; D, daily. AE, MC, V.

The Grille. Adolphus Hotel, 1321 Commerce; 742–8200. This English club look-alike is across the lobby from the far more famous French Room. The food rarely comes close to the French Room's heights, but neither do the prices. It's still terrific for hotel food. Breakfast, though, is distinctly overpriced. B, Monday through Saturday; brunch, Sunday; L, D, Monday through Saturday. Major credit cards.

Jennivine. 3605 McKinney Ave., north of downtown; 528–6010. The service and food are uneven, but the imaginative, seafood-oriented English and French menu, which changes daily, keeps patrons coming back to this relaxed spot. Good selection of wines by the glass. Small patio for outdoor dining. L, Tuesday through Saturday; D, Monday through Saturday. Major credit cards.

Le Rendez-Vous. 3237 McKinney (at Hall), north of downtown; 745–1985. The closest thing to a bistro in Dallas. Late hours (till 2:00 A.M.) and a light menu make it a good standby. L, D, daily except Monday. Major credit cards.

Inexpensive

Bennigan's. 2410 Walnut Hill (at I-35); 350–3127. 5260 Belt Line (across from Prestonwood Mall); 233–2107. 8139 Park Lane; 696–2080. 721 N. Watson, Arlington; 261–2548. This bar/restaurant chain features munchy fare and an intensive singles scene. L, D, daily. Major credit cards.

Bronx. 3835 Cedar Springs Rd., north of Oak Lawn Ave. 521–5821. Not a bargain but a blessing for late-night sustenance, especially as a source of good coffee and dessert. Daily specials are good bets. Sophisticated, comfortable neighborhood bar. Substantially gay patronage. L, D, Monday through Friday; Sunday brunch. Major credit cards.

Dalt's. 5100 Belt Line, east of Dallas North Parkway in Addison. Suite 410; 386–9078. A marble-and-brass re-creation of drugstore soda-fountain decor. The food is munchie material, not the stuff of serious dining. L, D, daily. Major credit cards.

AUSTRIAN

Expensive

Belvedere. 4242 Lomo Alto Dr., north of downtown; 528–6510. A sibling of the Chimney (see below) that almost, but not quite, lives up to the Chimney's standards. The atmosphere is less intimate than the Chimney's but still warm. At both restaurants, appetizers and desserts are eminently skippable. L, D, Monday through Saturday. Major credit cards.

The Chimney. Willow Creek Shopping Center, 9739 N. Central Expressway at Walnut Hill exit, North Dallas; 369–6466. The Rehsteak Chimney—astonishingly tender, subtly sauced venison tournedos, served at dinner only—is a local legend. The candlelight-and-soft-piano-music setting is quietly classy. L, D, Monday through Saturday. Major credit cards.

CHINESE

Although there are Chinese restaurants around every corner in Dallas, most are mediocre, relying on canned vegetables and MSG. Four stand out as exceptions: *Uncle Tai's, Forbidden City, Yunnan Dynasty,* and *Bamboo Pavilion.*

Expensive

Uncle Tai's. Level 3, Galleria, Dallas Parkway at LBJ, far north Dallas; 934–9998. High-priced, high-quality fare in an austerely chic setting. Don't miss the sauteed sliced pheasant (or the crispy walnuts for dessert). L, D, Monday–Saturday. Major credit cards.

Moderate

Bamboo Pavilion. 1790 Promenade Center, on Coit between Belt Line Road and Arapaho, in Richardson, north of Far North Dallas; 680–0599. This sibling of Szechwan Pavilion offers the same high-quality, moderately priced fare in a nicer setting. Must-try: walnut shrimp. L, D, daily. Alcohol served to members only. AE, MC, V.

Forbidden City. 5290 Belt Line, in Addison, far north; 960–2999. Unusually classy decor is the backdrop for carefully prepared dishes. L, D, daily. Major credit cards.

Szechwan Pavilion. 8409 Preston Rd. at Northwest Highway, North Dallas. 368–4303. Szechwan Pavilion couldn't look more average and unassuming; the food, however, is far above average. Alcohol served to members only. L, D, daily. AE, MC, V.

Yunnan Dynasty. Caruth Plaza, 9100 N. Central Expressway (at Park La.); 739–1110. The setting is tasteful and contemporary, and the food is consistently among the best Chinese in the city. Special honors go to the steamed fish with garlic and black-bean sauce. L, D, daily. AE, MC, V.

Inexpensive

Fang-ti China. Twin Bridge Shopping Center, 6752 Shady Brook Ln. near Northwest Hwy., North Dallas; 987–3877. Open until six in the morning on weekends (and merely till 4:00 A.M. on weekdays), Fangti's above-average food starts to look great in the wee hours, considering the alternatives, which are nearly nonexistent in Dallas. Chances are good of meeting Fang-ti herself, who is proud of her status as the only female Chinese chef in the city. L, D, daily. Serves late. No CB.

Texaco Lunch Box. 3801 Ross Ave. (at Washington Ave.), downtown; 821–5036. The food is ordinary fast-food caliber but worth a visit so you can say you've been there. Where else can you fill up with unleaded and eggrolls to go? (Texaco Lunch Box sells gasoline and lunches.) Beer, wine. L, Monday through Saturday. No credit cards.

CZECHOSLOVAKIAN

Moderate

Bohemia. 2810 N. Henderson, east of North Central Expy., North of downtown; 826–6209. Hearty, well-prepared eastern-European food is served in delicately charming surroundings. Don't miss the homemade apple strudel. Beer, wine; no cocktails. D, Tuesday through Sunday. AE, MC, V.

ETHIOPIAN

Inexpensive

Queen of Sheba. 3527 McKinney (at Lemmon); 521–0491. The unknown terrain of Ethiopian food, which is unusual and *very* spicy, is not for the faint of heart. Expect to spend some time here; the philosophy behind the service is very unhurried. Beer, wine; no cocktails. L, Saturday and Sunday. D, daily. No credit cards.

Red Sea. 2926 Oak Lawn Ave., north of downtown; 528–8476. The food and service are much like Blue Nile's, but the coffeeshop–like setting is less appealing. Beer, wine; no cocktails. L, D, daily.

FRENCH

Deluxe

Café Royal. 650 N. Pearl (Plaza of the Americas); 747–7222. The warm, rich decor sets the stage for nouvelle cuisine at its best (when the kitchen is on). Veal steak with lime butter is always a sure bet, though. Discreet piano music adds to the feeling of leisurely luxury (sometimes too leisurely on the part of the service). L, Monday through Friday; D, Monday through Saturday. Major credit cards.

French Room. Adolphus Hotel, 1321 Commerce St.; 742–8200. The most luxurious restaurant in town: stunning baroque decor and good-to-great nouvelle cuisine. Langoustine bisque for an appetizer and the feuilletee of seasonal fruit for dessert are musts. D, Monday through Saturday. Major credit cards.

Expensive

L'Ambiance. 2408 Cedar Springs Rd., north of downtown; 748–1291. This former filling station is now an accepted bastion of nouvelle cuisine. Salads and soups are standouts. L, Monday through Friday; D, Monday through Saturday. Major credit cards.

Café de Paris. the Quadrangle Shopping Center, 2800 Routh, north of downtown; 653–1027. Lace curtains and tiny floral prints characterize this charming restaurant. Appetizers and entrées are dependably good, but desserts, including a warm fruit tart with whipped cream, are even better. L, D, Monday through Saturday. Major credit cards.

Calluaud. 2619 McKinney Ave., north of downtown; 823–5380. A Dallas classic, with elegant, masculine decor. Don't miss the veal with hazelnut sauce. L, Monday–Friday, D, Monday–Saturday. AE, MC, V.

Jean Claude. 2404 Cedar Springs Rd., north of downtown; 871–0818. Owner-chef Jean Claude Prevot's commitment to his restaurant can be seen every night as he prepares dinner with his assistants. The fixed-price menu (currently $37.50 per person), which changes daily, is a bargain. (Appetizer, salad, main course, and dessert are included.) The chocolate soufflé is the stuff of dreams. D, Tuesday through Saturday. AE, MC, V.

Pyramid Room. Fairmont Hotel, Akard at Rose Ave., downtown; 748–5454. Dallas's first sophisticated Continental restaurant has spawned many successors but is still worth a visit. The atmosphere of opulence is highlighted by maximum pampering, with such touches as matchbooks embossed with diners' names. L, Monday through Friday; D, daily except Monday. Major credit cards.

Les Saisons. 165 Turtle Creek Village Shopping Center, Oak Lawn Ave. at Blackburn St., north of downtown; 528–1102. Traditional French food and atmosphere at their best. Although unelevated, the ground-floor view of downtown Dallas is still a pleasant accompaniment to dinner. L, D, daily. Major credit cards.

INDIAN

Expensive

Sahib. Caruth Plaza (NE corner Park & 9100 N. Central Expressway); 987–2301. The setting is subtly beautiful; the northern-Indian food is often its match. L, D, daily. No DC.

Inexpensive

Kebab-n-Kurry. 401 N. Central Expressway (between Belt Line and Arapaho), Richardson, north of Dallas; 231–5556. This tiny, charming restaurant is one of the best finds in the area. Beautifully authentic Indian food is served in an unlikely strip shopping-center location. No liquor. L, D, daily. AE, MC, V.

Tanjore. 5409 Belt Line, at Forest Bluff (in North Dallas); 960–0070. Lunch buffet is the drawing card; those new to Indian food will appreciate the seasoning, which is easy on the American palate. L, D, Monday through Saturday. Major credit cards.

ITALIAN

Expensive

Mario's. 135 Turtle Creek Village Shopping Center, Oak Lawn Ave. at Blackburn St., north of downtown; 521–1135. If one of your party wants Italian and another wants Continental fare, Mario's is the compromise of choice. Far more formal—and expensive—than any other Italian restaurant in town. L, D, daily. Major credit cards.

La Tosca. 7713 Inwood Rd., south of Lovers Ln., North Dallas; 352–8373. The black-and-white decor is almost new wave in its minimalist chic. Homemade pasta and offbeat specialties such as octopus salad are featured. D, Tuesday through Sunday. Major credit cards.

Sergio & Luciano. 4900 Belt Line in Addison, north of far north Dallas; 387–4441. Pleasant if unspectacular surroundings serve as a backdrop for stellar food. Homemade pasta, unusual lunchtime salads, and fresh, simply prepared fish are the best choices from a consistently fine menu. L, Monday through Saturday; D, daily. AE, MC, V.

Moderate

Bugatti. 2574 Walnut Hill Ln., northwest Dallas; 350–2470. A terrific value: Outstanding pasta and good veal dishes are served in pretty and relaxing surroundings at reasonable prices. Tortellini alla crema, fettucine della casa, and the mushroom soup are must-order items. Skip the forgettable desserts, though. L, Monday through Friday; D, Monday through Saturday. Major credit cards.

Cremona. 3136 Routh St. in Chelsea Square Shopping Center, north of downtown; 742–4330. Fine, no-frills Italian fare in pleasantly spare surroundings: ladder-back chairs, white tablecloths, and hardwood floors—and that's about it. The pasta consistently outshines the veal. L, D, Monday through Saturday. No credit cards.

Da Piccolo. 4537 Cole Ave. (at Knox St.), North Dallas; 521–1191. This tiny, informal spot offers homemade pasta and superior veal. L, Wednesday through Friday; D, Wednesday through Monday. No CB.

DiPalma. 1520 Greenville Ave., East Dallas; 824–4500. Primarily a chic, take-out place with a menu leaning toward chicken and pasta dishes. The entrées are uneven, but desserts like fresh pear cake are noteworthy. L, D, Monday through Saturday. MC, V.

Sergio's. The Quadrangle Shopping Center, 2800 Routh St., north of downtown; 742–3872. Sergio's has its ups and downs, but the homemade pasta and sauces generally excel. Eating in the courtyard is pleasant on Dallas's rare perfect spring and fall days. L, D, Monday through Saturday. Major credit cards.

Inexpensive

Adriano's. The Quadrangle, 2800 Routh St.; 871–2262. The atomsphere is high-tech; the pizza is in the tradition of L.A.'s Spago—with unusual toppings. L, Monday through Saturday. D, daily. AE, MC, V.

Ciao. Cedar Springs at Throckmorton; 521–0110. An open kitchen and an engaging, art-deco decor add to the appeal of the pizza-intensive menu here. L, D, daily. AE, MC, V.

JAPANESE

Expensive

Kobe Steaks. Quorum Plaza Shopping Center, Belt Line Rd. at Dallas Parkway, north Dallas; 934–8150. Plush, contemporary Japanese-style steakhouse; chef prepares meals at hibachi tables. D, daily. Major credit cards.

Moderate

Mr. Sushi, 4860 Belt Line Rd. (at Inwood Rd.), Addison; 385–0168. Sushi and cooked Japanese dishes are featured at this lively, upscale restaurant. L, Monday through Saturday. D, daily. AE, MC, V.

Sakura. 7402 Greenville Ave. (in Old Vickery Park), North Dallas; 361–9282. Newly reopened and remodeled, with tatami and American-style seating. Aficionados say the sushi bar is the best in town. L, Monday through Friday; D, daily. Major credit cards.

Inexpensive

Fuji-Ya. 13050 Coit (at LBJ Fwy. 635, North Dallas); 690–8396. Go for the authentic food; the setting is very casual. Liquor with membership. L, D, daily except Monday.

MEXICAN

Moderate

Café Cancún. 4131 Lomo Alto Dr., North Dallas; 559–4011. Caruth Plaza Shopping Center, 9100 N. Central Expressway (at Park), North Dallas; 369–3712. Pretty, peach-colored, tropical setting. Imaginative dishes far removed from city's standard Tex-Mex: enchiladas verdes (chicken enchiladas with green tomatillo sauce), corn-cheese soup, black beans. L, D, daily. Major credit cards.

Café Rincon. 2818 Harry Hines, downtown; 742–4906. The setting is refreshingly spare, and the fare includes Tex-Mex as well as specialty Mexican dishes. Sopa de albondige—meat broth with meatballs with mint leaves and cilantro—is a standout. L. Monday through Friday, D Monday through Saturday. AE, MC, V.

Casa Rosa. 165 Inwood Village Shopping Center, Lovers Ln. at Inwood Road; 350–5227. Out-of-the-ordinary Tex-Mex in an attractive setting, much like Café Cancún. L, Monday through Friday; D, daily. Major credit cards.

Chiquita. 3810 Congress Street (at Oak Lawn Ave.), north of downtown; 521–0721. Ordinary Tex-Mex and more interesting, more expensive Mexico City–style specialties such as a rich, cheesy tortilla soup and filete a la Chiquita (filet mignon Mexican-style). Bright, pastel decor. L, D, Monday through Saturday. AE, MC, V.

La Calle Doce. 415 W. 12th Street; 941–4304. A rare find in the Oak Cliff section. In a pretty restored home. The Mexican specialties are better than the Tex-Mex combination plates. Liquor with membership. L, Monday through Friday; D, Monday through Saturday. No CB.

Joe T. Garcia's. 4440 Belt Line Rd., in Addison (north of Dallas); 458–7373. Family-style dinner (one price, one dinner) served in festive surroundings; a clone of the famous Fort Worth original. L, D, Monday through Saturday. MC, V.

Mario & Alberto's. 425 Preston Valley Center (LBJ Freeway 635 at Preston, North Dallas); 980–7296. Same owners and menu as Chiquita. As at its sibling restaurant, the smart money is on the Mexico City–style dishes rather than the very ordinary Tex-Mex. Liquor with membership. L, D, Monday through Saturday. AE, MC, V.

Moctezuma's. 3202 McKinney Ave., north of downtown; 559–3010. The consistently acceptable menu (offering standard Tex-Mex as well as more off-the-beaten-path choices), pretty setting (including an outdoor patio), and close-to-downtown location attract a steady crowd. L, D, daily. Major credit cards.

Ninfa's. This Houston-based chain, with extensive menu, has two immense outposts in the Dallas area. Service can be inconsistent; be prepared to wait in line at peak times. 1515 Inwood; 638–6865. 2250 Belt Line Rd.; 661–2671. 2011 Copeland, Arlington; 261–0267. All locations L, D, daily. No CB.

Raphael's. 3701 McKinney Ave., north of downtown; 521–9640. 6782 Greenville Ave., North Dallas; 369–5232. Marathon waits at the original McKinney location. Food fine, especially bean soup, chicken enchiladas, strawberry or peach sopaipillas—but you can do as well or better elsewhere. L, D, Monday through Saturday. Major credit cards.

Inexpensive

La Botica. 1900 N. Haskell; 824–2005. Home-cooked Tex-Mex in humble surroundings. Live entertainment weekends. L, Tuesday through Friday; D, Tuesday through Saturday. AE, V, MC.

Chito's. 4447 Maple Ave., north of downtown; 526–9027. This small, little-known place serves really tasty, authentically home-style Tex-Mex. Nothing fancy but well worth a visit. Beer, wine. L, D, daily except Wednesday. MC, V.

Escondido. 4024 Maple; 526–1721. The almost absurdly shabby premises give "hole in the wall" a whole new meaning. Check the spray-can graffiti on the ceiling. A funky and fun place to eat basic Tex-Mex. L, Monday through Friday; D, Monday through Saturday. No credit cards.

Gonzales. 4333 Maple; 528–2960. Excellent, inexpensive home-style cooking. The only authentic drive-through Tex-Mex in town! Try a potato-egg burrito for breakfast. Quick service. Clean, cheerful interior, or get it to go. Beer only. B, L, D, daily. AE, MC, V.

Herrera. 3902 Maple; 526–9427. The original Maple location is possibly the best-known Tex-Mex dive in the city. Jimmy's special and Pepe's special both offer an overwhelming sampling of Tex-Mex. There is always a line going out the door. No liquor; brown-bagging allowed. L, D, daily except Tuesday. New location at 5427 Denton Dr., north of downtown; 630–2599. Same down-home Tex-Mex but roomier, less funky surroundings; liquor, too. Monday through Sunday, 11:00 A.M. to 10:00 P.M. Major credit cards.

Mexico. 2911 Routh St.; 760–8639. Offbeat interpretations of Mexican cuisine are served in an attractive, spacious setting. L, D, Tuesday through Sunday. MC, V, AE.

Pepe's. 3011 Routh St., north of downtown; 698–9445. Call it preppy-Mex: Tex-Mex served to a predominantly preppy crowd. Surprisingly good and authentic fare in clean surroundings. L, D, Monday through Saturday. No credit cards.

SWEDISH

Moderate to Expensive

Three Vikings. 2831 Greenville Ave., East Dallas; 827–6770. Happily, the city's only Swedish restaurant is also a fine, family-owned one. Veal Oscar and the salmon steak with dill sauce are proven favorites. Relaxed woods-and-plants decor. D, Monday through Saturday. Major credit cards.

THAI

Inexpensive

Siam Orchid. 1730 W. Mockingbird Ln., near Harry Hines Blvd.; 631–5482. *Moo sartey*—grilled pork on a skewer, served with peanut sauce—may change your life. Other standouts are *pud thai* (rice noodles, shrimp, pork, bean sprouts, chili peppers, and peanuts) and *gang ped* (chicken curry with a rosy, coconut-based sauce). L, D, Monday through Saturday. Major credit cards.

VIETNAMESE

Inexpensive

Mai's. 4812 Bryan St. (east of Fitzhugh Ave.), downtown; 826–9887. A small, authentic menu. No liquor. L, D, Wednesday through Sunday. No credit cards.

DINING OUT IN FORT WORTH. Until a few years ago the restaurant fare in Fort Worth was largely limited to standard southwestern mainstays: Tex-Mex and barbecue. To find anything more sophisticated than that, one would need to drive 45 mi. east to Dallas. But a revitalization of the downtown area and the construction of several world-class downtown hotels has changed all that. Now it is possible to find anything from frijoles to pâté de foie gras in Fort Worth. The price classifications below follow the same dollar ranges as those for Dallas, above.

All telephone numbers are area code 817.

AMERICAN-INTERNATIONAL

Expensive

The Balcony. 6100 Camp Bowie; 731–3719. The Balcony is anything but innovative, but it is a place for reliable, old-style Continental cuisine: fried shrimp, beef variations, and veal cordon bleu. L, Monday through Friday; D, Saturday; closed Sunday. All major credit cards.

Brasserie la Salle. Americana Hotel, Tandy Center, 2nd St.; 870–1000. The Brasserie's offerings may seem overpriced until you consider what else is available in Fort Worth at 4:00 A.M.: Its eclectic classics (eggs Benedict, burgers, pasta) are available around the clock. No DC.

The Carriage House. 5136 Camp Bowie Blvd.; 732–2873. Stick to the steak in this Fort Worth standard, and you'll be pleased you came. Venture elsewhere into the uneven menu, and you'll wonder why this is an establishment favorite. L, Monday through Friday; D, Monday through Saturday; Sunday brunch. All major credit cards.

Crystal Cactus. Hyatt Regency Hotel, 815 Main; 870–1234. The Hyatt Regency has brought a new level of ambition to downtown dining in Fort Worth and has largely succeeded, with imaginative offerings along the lines of rock-lobster salad with tarragon dressing. D, daily; Sunday brunch. All major credit cards.

Old Swiss House. 5412 Camp Bowie; 738–8091. This old-timer among local Continental restaurants is either constant or boring, depending on your feelings about innovation or the lack thereof. No one could complain about the reliable perfection of the service, though. D, Monday through Saturday; closed Sunday. All major credit cards.

Moderate

Melting Pot. Ridgmar Mall, 2166 Green Oaks Road; 731–1502. Predictably enough, eclecticism is the name of the game at the Melting Pot. The menu leans to reasonably priced croissant, pasta, and omelet variations. L, D, Monday through Saturday; closed Sunday. No CB, DC.

Inexpensive

Massey's. 1805 Eighth Ave.; 924–8242. Chicken-fried steak is Massey's *raison d'être,* though you'd never catch the homespun patrons or staff using such a term. Seafood and Mexican fare are also served, but only the rankest tenderfoot would choose them. Concentrate instead on the definitive CFS and accompaniments of cream gravy and biscuits; the salad and vegetables are best forgotten. L, D, daily. MC, V.

BARBECUE

Inexpensive

Angelo's. 2533 White Settlement Rd.; 332–0357. Only Dallas's Sonny Bryan's rivals Angelo's for the ability to attract hordes of local barbecue devotees. Happily, Angelo's setting is large and relatively clean. The ribs are the thing here, so take care to arrive after 5:00 P.M., when they're served. L, D, Monday through Saturday; closed Sunday. No credit cards.

Dick's Kountry Barbecue. 316 S. Saginaw Blvd., north Fort Worth; 232–2532. Offers basic barbecued ribs, ham, beef, and staggeringly good side-orders (cole slaw, potato salad, red beans) in a log-cabin setting. L, D daily. No credit cards.

BURGERS

Inexpensive

Billy Miner's. 150 W. 3rd St. (at Houston St.) 877–3301. This newcomer serves what may well be the best burger in town. L, D, daily. MC, V, AE.

Kincaid's. 4901 Camp Bowie; 732–2881. Unprepossessing is an understatement for the "ambience" at Kinkaid's—which is understandable enough, considering that Kincaid's is a grocery store. The specialty du jour is always the classic burger, and the seating is in your car. L, D, Monday through Saturday; closed Sunday. No credit cards.

CHILI

Inexpensive

Lone Star Chili Parlor. 113 E. Exchange; 624–0111. As much bar as eatery, LSCP wisely confines its menu to what it does well: chili and a few related options. The building's libationary history dates back to 1905. L, D, Monday through Saturday; closed Sunday. No CB, DC.

STEAKHOUSES

Expensive

Cattlemen's. 2458 N. Main; 624–3945. Cattlemen's takes a textbook-Texan approach to dining out. The setting (including wall-to-wall cattle portraits) could hardly be more rustic, and the location is inevitable: the stockyards. Carnivores only need apply, since steak, naturally enough, is the attraction here. L, Monday through Friday; D, Monday through Saturday; closed Sunday. All major credit cards.

SEAFOOD

Moderate

Bill Martin's Second Edition. 4404 White Settlement Road; 737–4004. Nothing fancy here, just a wide variety of fried and broiled fish served up in a family atmosphere. This place has long been popular for its homemade hush puppies, along with fish selections ranging from fried whitefish fillets to fresh lobster. L, D, daily. No DC.

Inexpensive

J.J.'s Oyster Bar. 929 University; 335–2756. Oysters—fried or on the half shell—are the obvious attraction here. L, D, daily. No credit cards.

Texas Oyster Bar. 2520 Commerce; 429–5979. Tucked away inside Billy-Bob's Texas; serves oysters, shrimp, crablegs, and lobster flown in daily. Beer, wine, cocktails. L, D, daily; all major credit cards.

HEALTH FOOD

Inexpensive

The Back Porch. 2500 W. Berry; 923–0841. With its stockyard heritage, Fort Worth isn't exactly renowned as a center for the natural-foods crowd. But the Back Porch offers tasty and healthy fare to appease those who prefer to pursue health rather than cholesterol. The whole-wheat pizza, the pay-by-the-ounce salad bar, and the homemade soups are don't-miss propositions. L, D, Monday through Saturday; closed Sunday. No credit cards.

CHINESE

Moderate

Szechuan. 5712 Locke (near Camp Bowie); 738–7300. The decor is one cut above the standard off-the-shelf Chinese found in the rest of the city, and the spicy, if not incendiary, fare is a standout by several cuts. L, D, daily. No CB, DC.

FRENCH

Expensive

Café Bowie. 4930 Camp Bowie; 735–1521. Situated in a graceful old frame house. Café Bowie consistently serves up impeccable French fare, earning it best-of-the-city consideration. Though the uncrowded seating arrangement indicates intimate conversation, the perhaps overzealous service simultaneously contraindicates it. L, D, Monday through Saturday; Sunday, brunch only. No CB, DC.

Michel. 3851 Camp Bowie; 732–1231. Michel Baudouis, brother of famed Dallas restaurateur Jean Claude Prevot, has made his mark in Fort Worth with this eponymous establishment. The subtle gray-and-white setting provides a suitable backdrop for the imaginative menu, which changes daily. L, Tuesday through Friday; D, Tuesday through Saturday; closed Sunday and Monday. All major credit cards.

L'Oustau. 300 Main Street; 332–8900. This relative newcomer to the Fort Worth culinary scene is also one of the best choices in the city for high-priced, high-quality dining. Nouvelle cuisine, which is still big news in Cowtown, reigns on the menu. Saturday, dinner only; L, Monday through Friday; D, Monday through Saturday; closed Sunday. MC, V only; personal checks accepted.

GERMAN

Moderate

Edelweiss. 3801-A Southwest Blvd.; 738–5934. Cheese soup, sausages, and potato pancakes are served up in this beer hall, but the real attraction is—what else?—the beer (and the oompah music). D, Monday through Saturday; closed Sunday. All major credit cards.

ITALIAN

Moderate

Sardine's. 3410 Camp Bowie; 332–9937. At Sardine's, dramatically original (for Fort Worth) Italian food is enriched by live jazz. D, Tuesday through Sunday; closed Monday. All major credit cards.

MEXICAN

Moderate

Joe T. Garcia's. 2201 N. Commerce; 626–4356. Fort Worth's most famous purveyor of Tex-Mex is an institution, not a mere restaurant. Joe T's, as familiars like to call it, is a great place for the indecisive, since there are no choices: Everybody gets "the dinner," which includes nachos, enchiladas, guacamole, rice, beans, and tortillas. The killer margarita is a must for neophytes. L, daily; D, Monday through Saturday. No credit cards.

MIDDLE EASTERN

Moderate

Hedary's. 3308 Fairfield (Ridglea Center off Camp Bowie Blvd.); 626–4356. Middle Eastern food in Cowtown seems unlikely enough, but Hedary's Middle Eastern food is authentic and laudable in philosophy (the menu boasts "no hot table, freezer, chemicals, or can opener"). The hummus bit-tahini (a dip of ground chickpeas, sesame seeds, lemon juice, and garlic) is a must. The setting is pleasantly relaxed. D, Tuesday through Sunday; closed Monday. All major credit cards.

NIGHT LIFE IN DALLAS. Bar hopping is most plausible in two areas of town. The first, and far and away the more extensive, is Greenville Avenue. Mockingbird Lane bisects Greenville into lower Greenville (south of Mockingbird), which is considered to be part of East Dallas, and upper Greenville (north of Mockingbird), which is considered to be part of North Dallas. Upper Greenville attracts a more flashy crowd; lower Greenville, those more interested in funkiness.

The second is Knox Street in Highland Park, just west of North Central Expressway. Although Highland Park is an affluent preppy enclave, the night life is fairly relaxed.

All area codes are 214.

Acapulco Bar. 5111 Greenville; 692–9856. Popular disco with young professional crowd. Gaming tables, blackjack lessons.

Andrew's. 3301 McKinney Ave. (at Hall), north of downtown; 521–6535. 14930 Midway (at Belt Line); 385–1613. Archetypal exposed-brick-and-wrought-iron decor. Specialty drinks, house salad, black-bean soup, and boiled shrimp. Forgettable solo entertainment.

At the Top of the Dome. Hyatt Regency's Reunion Tower (downtown), Reunion Blvd; 651–1234. Revolves atop Reunion Tower. Casual dress. A much better idea than dinner at the overpriced Antares.

Café Dallas. 5500 Greenville Ave. (Old Town Shopping Center, northeast of downtown); 987–0066. A disco that has outlived the trend and continues to be a hot singles bar. Strict dress code.

Cardinal Puff's. 4615 Greenville Ave., northeast of downtown; 369–1969. Live music. Fireplace for winter months; outdoor garden for warm weather. College-age crowd.

Club Mercedes. 7035 Greenville; 696–8686. Live music featured in this hot new club. Dance floor; late-night menu.

Comedy Corner. 8202 Park Ln. (at Greenville Ave.), North Dallas; 361–7461. All-comedy: mostly national names; amateur night too.

Confetti. 5208 Greenville Ave. (at Lovers Ln.); 369–6977. Once the hottest bar in town. Party theme includes confetti and costumed patrons. Something for everyone: recorded music featuring '50s–'80s hits; dance floor, 10-ft. TV, billiards.

Exposure. 4516 McKinney Ave; 528–0210. Excellent, imaginative food and a chic clientele.

The Grape. 2808 Greenville Ave., East Dallas; 823–0133.Cozy and inviting, romantic in a funky way. Try the famed mushroom soup. Extensive wine list, as the name indicates.

Greenville Avenue Country Club. 3619 Greenville Ave., East Dallas; 826–5650. The garden with a swimming pool and a bar in back is the warm-weather attraction.

Greenville Bar & Grill. 2821 Greenville Ave., East Dallas; 823–6691. A historic bar with live Dixieland jazz and a loud neighborhood crowd.

In Cahoots. NorthPark East Shopping Center, Park at Central; 692–5412. Popular singles club with DJ. Gaming tables.

Joe Miller's. 3531 McKinney Ave., north of downtown; 521–2261. This is the place if you like media hangouts or strong drinks. Three drinks and you qualify as legally dead.

Knox Street Pub. 3230 Knox St., North Dallas; 526–9476. A classy pub with neighborhood clientele; jukebox.

La Cave. 2926 N. Henderson St., North Dallas; 826–2190. More than 300 wines by the bottle and six for tasting by the glass. The food is secondary. Not as comfortable as the Grape.

Longhorn Ballroom. 216 Corinth St., downtown; 428–3128. This is the real thing—a country dance hall. Live music and free dance lessons.

Mistral. Loews Anatole Hotel, 2201 Stemmons Freeway; 748–1200. A futuristic snow-white disco with good, expensive food.

NFL. 3520 Oak Lawn Ave., North Dallas; 559–4890. Friendly, rowdy. Live Irish music, darts, pool.

Nick's Uptown. 3606 Greenville Ave., East Dallas; 827–4802. This renovated drugstore is the site of national and regional big-name music. The noise level gives a whole new meaning to *deafening*. Dance floor.

Palm Bar. Adolphus Hotel, 1321 Commerce (at Akard); 742–8100. Elegant pub atmosphere downtown. Terrific place for lunch, too.

Piaf's. 4527 Travis St., North Dallas; 526–3730. A comfortable fern bar with above-average food.

Prohibition Room. 703 McKinney Ave; 954–4407. Located in downtown's West End Historical District. There is live jazz.

Quiet Man. 3120 Knox St., North Dallas; 526–6180. Neighborhood bar for '60s survivors (and burnouts). Darts, chess, backgammon, and other games. Very casual.

St. Martin's. 3020 Greenville Ave., East Dallas; 826–0940. A soothing, blue-toned wine bar. Baroque music and one of the city's best Sunday brunches. Dinners are overpriced, though.

Stoneleigh P. 2926 Maple Ave. (at Wolf), north of downtown; 741–0824. A rebuilt version of an incinerated Dallas legend. Headquarters for the self-proclaimed hip and artsy. Exceptionally good food. Notoriously eclectic jukebox.

Strictly Tabu. 4111 Lomo Alto Dr. (at Lemmon Ave.), North Dallas; 522–8101. The oldest jazz club in town—and looks it. Fusion-oriented jazz. A more or less Italian menu, but eat elsewhere.

TGI Friday's. Old Town Shopping Center, 5500 Greenville Ave., North Dallas; 363–5353. Also at 5150 Belt Line, Addison, north of Dallas; 386–5824. The archetypal singles bar but suitable for family meals too.

Venetian Room. Fairmont Hotel, Ross and Akard; 748–5454. The city's plushest showroom tends to middle-of-the-road names. There is also dancing to a live orchestra before and between shows. Semiformal dress.

NIGHT LIFE IN FORT WORTH. Fort Worth offers a wide diversity of nightspots and watering holes, ranging from the ubiquitous American fern bar to the quintessential Texas beer joint, an institution basic to the city's sociological heritage. Visitors seeking a slice of true Texana should opt for the latter category, the best examples of which can be found in the historic stockyards area on the city's North Side. All telephones are area code 817.

Billy Bob's Texas. 2520 N. Commerce; 625–6491. Within a stone's throw of the stockyards, this multi-acre indoor playpen bills itself as the world's largest honkytonk. It belongs in the Las Vegas class for entertainment bookings, which have ranged from Rosanne Cash to Bob Hope. In addition to a dance floor large enough to reenact the battle of the Alamo (the club has a seating capacity of 6,000), Billy Bob's features three restaurants, a gift shop, an indoor bull-riding arena, and multiple bars. Visitors eager to rub shoulders with those who daily dip their feet in cattle manure should consider this place a must-see.

The Blue Bird Night Club. 3515 Horne; 737–0453. This small, predominantly black tavern has been one of the mainstay stops on the city's nightclub circuit for quite a few years, largely because of the live jazz and rhythm and blues bands featured there.

Duffy's. One Tandy Center; 332–9501. This urbane downtown bar provides a good example of how diversified the city's bar scene has become in the past few years. Situated in one of the city's new architectural landmarks, this establishment could easily pass for part of midtown Manhattan or the Chicago Loop.

The Hop. 2905 W. Berry; 923–9949. A college clientele dominates this jazz-rock club, near Texas Christian University. The atmosphere is low key and less frenetic than one might expect for a college hangout. The fare includes spaghetti and pizza.

J. R.'s Place. 3400 Bernie Anderson Road (at Camp Bowie Blvd.); 735–8851. This place may sound country and western, but it's actually a first-rate jazz club, with a house trio, a vocalist, and on Monday nights, an audience-participation jam session.

Pickin' Parlour. 103 W. Exchange; 624–2592. Country-and-Western music, featuring the Hill City Cowboy Band. Tues.-Sat. No credit cards.

Rangoon Racquet Club. 4936 Camp Bowie; 737–5551. This subdued little pub caters to the over-30 affluent crowd and features preppy-looking waitresses in tennis skirts, as well as some of the heartiest homemade hamburgers to be found in the area.

Ricochet. Americana Hotel, 200 Main; 870–9885. This plush downtown nightspot is just what you might expect to find in the architectural showplace that houses it. The club caters to the expense-account set and features floor shows that have included '50s and '60s rock acts like the Shirelles and the Belmonts.

Waterworks. Hilton Inn, Interstate 20 and Commerce St.; 335–7000. More than a fern bar, this is a horticulturist's dream, where massive greenery meets chrome and glass to provide the city with one of its most urbane bars. The live music ranges from country to rock.

White Elephant Saloon. 106 E. Exchange Ave.; 624–1887. This stockyards bar, more than 100 years old, offers patrons a chance to drink and dance in an atmosphere that looks like something from the Gunsmoke set. The bar frequently has live country bands.

AUSTIN

Political and Intellectual Capital

by
OMEGA CLAY

Omega Clay is on the staff of the University of Texas Press in Austin. She is also restaurant reviewer and contributor to Third Coast *magazine of Austin. Before coming to Austin she was a reporter for the* Durham Morning Herald.

Texas has a strong image to many people outside the state, an image made up of stereotypes tied into bits of the romantic Old West: cowboys driving Cadillacs; tumbleweeds rolling across parched land; oil money. But visitors who come to Austin expecting a population outfitted in Tony Lamas and string ties may be in for a surprise. Austin is home to widely disparate groups of people, and here, more than in any other city in Texas, there is a strong liberal tradition and a tolerance for differences.

Austin is so pleasant a place to live in that salaries in the area are noticeably lower than in the rest of Texas, let alone the rest of the U.S.

One of Austin's unique features is its reputation as a music center. After being identified with traditional country music for years, it became the birthplace of "progressive" country in the early 1970s, music popularized by Jerry Jeff Walker, Gary P. Nunn, and Ray Wylie Hubbard and showcased on the famous PBS television program *Austin City Limits. Austin City Limits* is still filmed here each fall in the studios of KLRU-TV at the University of Texas; and Austin is now a proving ground for music of all types, from the country ballads of its most famous citizen, Willie Nelson, to rock 'n' roll by Joe Ely and blues by Albert Collins.

Austin grew from the frontier villages of Waterloo and Montopolis, settled in 1839 on the banks of the Colorado River, and was named for Stephen F. Austin, the first U.S. colonizer of the land that is now Texas. Austin was made the state capital by the third Congress of the Republic of Texas, on the basis of its central location, its mild climate, the beauty of its terrain, and the availability of water, stone, and timber.

More than a hundred years later Austin retains its mild climate, its clean water, and much of the beauty of its terrain—in spite of a rapidly increasing population (345,053 in a recent census). The rolling Hill Country to the west of town, largely undeveloped, and is considered by Texans to be some of the most beautiful land in the state. From the west, the Colorado River (*not* the same one that flows through Grand Canyon) winds through the city; it is still used for fishing and boating. The river has different names as it winds through Austin: "Lake Austin" on the west, for example, and "Town Lake" in south-central Austin. Austin's extensive park system contributes to the city's livability; no matter where you are, you're not far from a city park of some kind. The parks form a greenbelt providing relief from traffic and asphalt, with public tennis courts, pools, playgrounds, and softball fields.

The heart of the downtown business district in central Austin is dominated by the state capitol building, on Congress Avenue between 11th and 14th streets. The capitol grounds are a favorite stop for visitors; the grassy slopes, shaded by large oak trees, are perfect for a stroll or a picnic. State government office buildings, most built out of native pink granite, surround the capitol. Situated on a slight rise, the capitol faces south, overlooking the entire length of Congress Avenue to the Colorado River (which is called Town Lake where it intersects the city). Running north and south, Congress Avenue is one of the

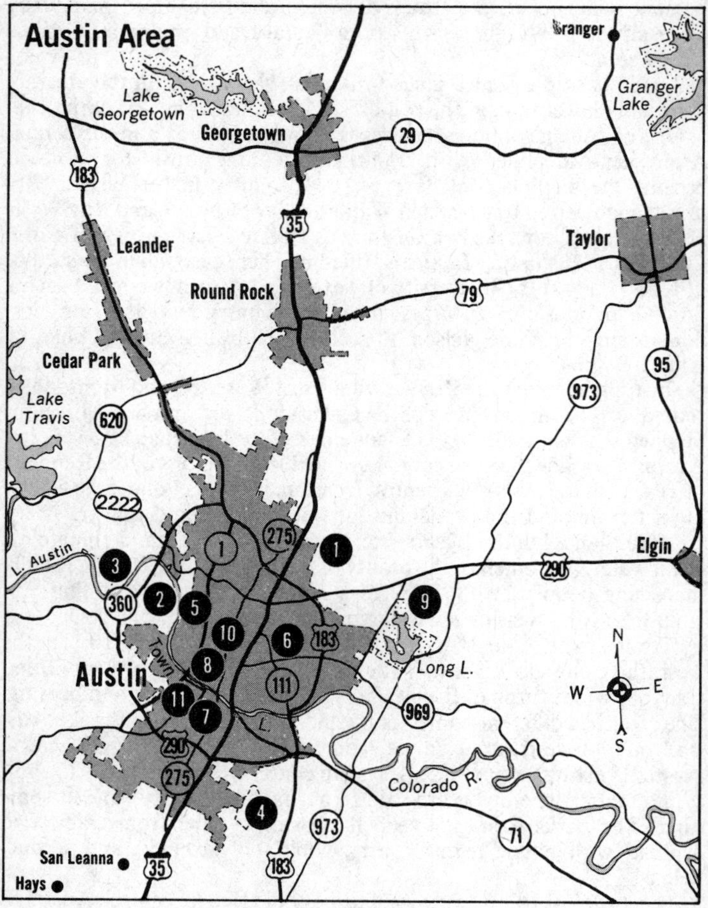

Points of Interest

1) Jourdan-Bachman Pioneer Settlers Memorial Park
2) Laguna-Gloria Art Museum
3) Lake Austin Metropolitan Park
4) McKinney Falls State Park
5) Mt. Bonnell Park
6) Mueller Municipal Airport
7) Palmer Auditorium, City Coliseum and Auditorium Shores
8) State Capitol
9) Walter E. Long Lake and Park
10) University of Texas
11) Zilker Park

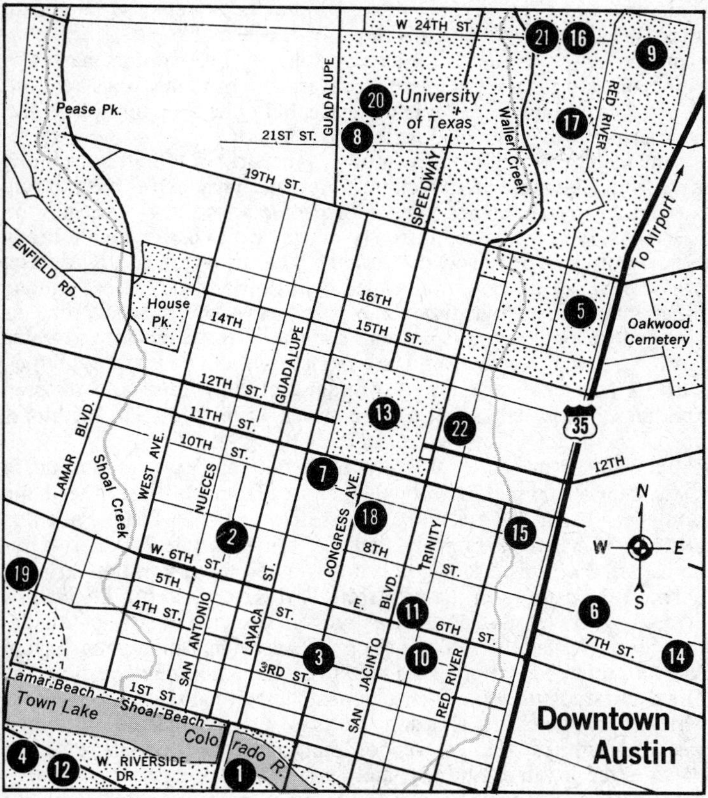

Points of Interest

1) Auditorium Shores
2) Bremond Block
3) Greyhound Station
4) City Coliseum
5) Frank C. Erwin Special Events Center
6) French Legation
7) Governor's Mansion
8) Harry Ransom Center
9) LBJ Library and Museum
10) O. Henry Home
11) Old Pecan Street
12) Palmer Auditorium and Convention Center
13) State Capitol
14) State Cemetery
15) Symphony Square
16) Texas Memorial Museum
17) Texas Memorial Stadium
18) Trailways Station
19) Train Station
20) University Main Building and Tower
21) University Performing Arts Center
22) Waterloo Park

main arteries of the city; between 11th and 1st streets it is the "main street" of downtown. Austin's downtown is a madhouse of new construction but offers the visitor an array of shops, restaurants, bars, and points of historic interest. There are several tall bank buildings here and large office buildings are going up apace, but older structures have also been attractively renovated for adaptive reuse.

One major attraction of downtown is the strip of 6th Street running west from Interstate 35 to Congress Avenue. This area is busy during the day but really comes alive with people after dark, especially on weekends. A renaissance of growth on this street has created a heavy concentration of bars and restaurants. The unrestrained nightlife on 6th Street has caused it to be called "a little Bourbon Street," among other things; at certain times, the police have experienced problems with crowd control, seedy panhandlers, public drunkenness, and traffic jams. No stay in Austin would be complete without a visit to 6th Street, with its fern bars, restaurants, vintage-clothing shops, and restored buildings. The Pecan Street Café, between Trinity and San Jacinto, is one of the better places for a snack.

Central Austin also includes the University of Texas campus, north of the capitol complex. The residential area from Martin Luther King Boulevard (19th St.) and Guadalupe Street, west to Pease Park and north to 30th Street, is largely student oriented. Hyde Park and Hemphill Park, both historic neighborhoods noted for restoration, are just north of the campus in the area from Red River Street to Guadalupe Street east to west, and north to about 45th Street. The strip of Guadalupe Street that abuts the campus on the west side, running north from Martin Luther King Boulevard to 29th Street, is commonly called "the Drag" by students. Like most campus commercial districts, this area is full of small clothing shops, bookstores, and movie theaters, and on weekends groups of street vendors may often be found here selling handcrafted jewelry, clothing, and leather goods.

Interstate 35 is the dividing line in most residents' minds between east and central Austin. East Austin is mainly a concentration of Mexican-American and black neighborhoods. This area is generally benign, but visitors should exercise some caution after dark. The nature of 6th Street, for example, changes considerably east of Interstate 35; here there are no expensive renovations or chi-chi shops, but small neighborhood bars, grocery stores, and older homes. Historic sites worth visiting in East Austin include the French legation, with its beautiful collection of period furnishings, and the state cemetery, where Stephen F. Austin is buried.

North Austin begins around 51st Street and encompasses recent urban sprawl. This is probably the fastest-growing area of Austin and is completely residential-commercial, indistinguishable from the kind of urban areas that surround cities everywhere. U.S. 183, or Research Boulevard, is the major east-west connection in north Austin, running from Interstate 35 to Loop 1, and is characterized by mile after mile of shopping centers.

West Austin is generally considered to be the area from Town Lake west of Pease Park, including the large upper-middle-class suburb of West Lake Hills. This area is largely residential, with limited or controlled commercial growth; there are many lovely neighborhoods and restored homes in this district, the headquarters of Austin's old and/or big money. Mount Bonnell, the highest point in Austin, is situated along affluent Mount Bonnell Road on the edge of Lake Austin; it offers a panoramic view of the city and the winding river. Toward the northwest, Mount Bonnell Road intersects FM 2222, one of the most scenic drives through the celebrated Hill Country west of the city.

The entire area south of Town Lake, from Zilker Park on the west to McKinney Falls Park on the east, is usually referred to as South Austin. From Riverside Drive on the shore of Town Lake to the major east-west thoroughfare, U.S. 290 or Ben White Blvd., South Austin is a mixture of established residential areas and commercial zones. There are very pleasant residential areas in Barton Hills, south of Zilker Park, and in Travis Heights, situated around Stacy Park. Travis Heights in particular has become a popular neighborhood for restoration, and what was once a student enclave has become rather pricey. South of Travis Heights on South Congress Avenue is Saint Edwards University, a 180-acre campus with approximately twenty-four hundred students. South Austin's urban sprawl begins at U.S. 290 and continues south and west to the small rural communities of Manchaca and Oak Hill.

Austin's two roles as the seat of state government and the home of the University of Texas have probably done the most to shape its development. Even though the pink granite dome of the capitol dominates the landscape, the university has a wider, more liberalizing influence. And tied to Austin's tradition as a politically and culturally liberal spot in the great expanse of Texas, is its image as fertile ground for the arts. There may be more potters, painters, writers, sculptors, dancers, actors, singers, and musicians per square inch here than anywhere in the state. There is a feminist bookstore. There is even a fairly large number of hippies left over from the 1960s. And whereas other Texas cities may raze old downtown structures to make room for reflecting-glass bank buildings, Austin's cityscape integrates the old with the new, making it a comfortable place to live and a unique place to visit.

PRACTICAL INFORMATION FOR AUSTIN

HOW TO GET THERE. By air. Austin has one airport, Robert C. Mueller Municipal, which recently underwent an $8-million improvement-and-expansion program. The airport is framed by I–35 and U.S. 290 and surrounded by residential neighborhoods, which may make the aerial descent into Austin a little hair-raising; on the plus side, it makes for a conveniently short ride from the airport to downtown.

Most visitors from out of state will have to change planes in Dallas or Houston to reach Austin. Airlines serving Austin are American, Continental, Delta, Eastern, USAir, Southwest, America West, Pan Am, TWA, Muse, and United. Commuter lines include American Eagle, which runs between Austin and San Antonio or Abilene; Air Spirit; Fort Worth Air; Texas Air; and Wise, which flies between Austin and San Angelo.

By car. I–35 leads right into Austin from the north, coming from Waco and, farther north, the Dallas–Fort Worth Metroplex. U.S. 290 comes into Austin from the east, from Houston.

The driving times to Austin from other cities, in hours, are: Dallas–Fort Worth Metroplex, 3½; Houston, 3½; San Antonio, 1¼.

By bus. Trailways and Greyhound connect Austin to most Texas cities and points beyond, but routes from out of state are often long and circuitous. Both bus terminals are downtown on Congress Ave., necessitating a taxi ride to the concentration of midrange hotels and motels along I–35.

By train. The Amtrak passenger station is near downtown at 250 N. Lamar Blvd. Passenger service to and from Austin is limited; the city is served by Amtrak's Eagle line, which passes through every day but Thursday. From Austin the Eagle leaves northbound for Chicago via Dallas and Texarkana on Sunday, Tuesday, and Friday at 10:57 A.M. On Monday, Wednesday, and Saturday it comes through out of Chicago headed for San Antonio and Los Angeles, leaving at 7:08 P.M. Overnight sleeper cars are available on the Eagle for an extra charge, and it is permissible to bring ice chests for use in your private room with your own beer, wine, or cocktails. For schedules and fares, check your local phone directory for Amtrak's toll-free information-and-reservations number. In Austin, the number to call is 476–5684 or toll-free (800) 872–7245.

TELEPHONES. The area code for Austin, parts of central Texas, and all of south Texas is 512. You do not need to dial the area code if it is the same as the one from which you are calling. There are five other area codes within Texas. For directory assistance in Austin, dial 1411; for directory assistance for numbers within the 512 area, dial 1–555–1212. For numbers outside the 512 area, dial 1–(area code)–555–1212, and to find toll-free business numbers, dial 1–800–555–1212. In case of emergency dial 911.

HOTELS AND MOTELS. Accommodations in Austin range from functional motels on the interstate highway to gracefully renovated downtown hotels. The mid-price motels and chains are concentrated along I–35, which runs through the city north to south. These motels are mostly comparable in price, so it pays the visitor to take one with a central location. Mueller Airport is small, with few accommodations nearby, so many hotels and motels offer free transportation to and from the airport. Several of the more expensive hotels offer lovely river views for a slightly higher price. Most motels offer "packages," special rates based on double occupancy, weekend occupancy, or family size; these are mentioned only briefly here but are worth inquiring about. In general, Austin's hotel-motel rates are lower than those in many parts of the country. Categories, determined by price, are: *Expensive,* $60 and up; *Moderate,* $40 to $59; and *Inexpensive,* less than $40.

Expensive

Austin Hilton. 6000 Middle Fiskville Rd. (one block west of I–35 at U.S. 290); 451–5757. Bentley's Restaurant, Peachtree Pantry coffee shop, and Goldy's lounge. Advance reservations required; small pets allowed. The Rainbow Weekend package includes deluxe room, cheese and wine, and continental breakfast both mornings. The Honeymoon package includes deluxe room, chilled champagne, full breakfast.

The Brookhollow Hotel. 935 La Posada Dr. (at I–35 and U.S. 290); 459–3335. All suites have full kitchens and fireplaces. Jacuzzi spa, sports court, clubhouse, pool, jogging track. Reduced rates for longer stays. The Escape Weekend package includes complimentary wine and breakfast.

The Driskill Hotel. 604 Brazos; 474–5911, (800) 228–0808. The Driskill's Romanesque architecture and old-fashioned elegance make it one of the nicest places in town to stay. The hotel is in the heart of downtown, near the historic 6th St. area with its active night life and restaurants. Features the Driskill Dining Room, the Driskill Bar & Grill, the Lobby piano bar. Suites available; children under 12 free. Offers a Luxurious Honeymoon package and a Romantic Weekend package. For big spenders, the penthouse runs $475 a night. Most rooms, however, are in the new "tower."

Hyatt Regency. 208 Barton Springs Rd., at S. Congress; 477–1234 or (800) 228–9000. Situated on the south shore of Town Lake, convenient to downtown, the Hyatt features a 17-story open-atrium lobby with restaurant and lounge, heated pool, spa, jogging and cycling trails, and courtesy airport transportation. The VIP floor is complete with concierge, complementary wine, free breakfast, and an assortment of other amenities. Reservations and deposit required. The Weekend at Hyatt package provides deluxe accommodations and entertainment.

Marriott Hotel. 6121 N. I–35 (at U.S. 290); 458–6161 or (800) 228–9290. North of town, convenient to the airport. Amenities, in newly remodeled facilities, include sauna, pool, and free airport limousine services. Dining at Diamond Lil's Emporium and Saloon, and sipping at Cafe de Vin, a new French-style wine bar serving lunch and early evening drinks. Offers a Weekend Special plan (limited availability, reservations required). The Escape Plan includes deluxe accommodations, dinner, and breakfast for two. Small pets allowed.

The Stephen F. Austin Hotel. 701 Congress Ave.; 476–4361. Situated in the business district three blocks from the capitol, the Stephen F. Austin calls itself "Austin's world-class hotel." Nicely renovated, it has a restaurant, a formal dining room, and a bar. Weekend Special package includes luxury room accommodations, fresh flowers, and chilled champagne on arrival.

Moderate

Best Western Chariot Inn. 7300 N. I–35; 452–9371. North of downtown. Chariot Club bar, restaurant, coffee shop.

Best Western Colonial Inn. 3909 S. I–35; 444–0531. Children under 12 free. Coffee shop, restaurant, laundry facilities.

Best Western Villa Capri. 2400 N. I–35; 476–6171. Adjacent to the LBJ Library and the University of Texas, convenient to downtown. Recommended for its central location and reliable service. Free airport transportation, two Olympic-size swimming pools, full-service restaurant, convention center, lounge. Suites for families or groups. Getaway Weekend package for two.

Granada Motor Inn. 5656 N. I-35; 452–2581; or (800) 2-RAMADA. Convenient to three shopping centers, 1 mi. from the university. Next Door Kitchen restaurant, free airport limousine.

Holiday Inn Town Lake. South I–35 at Town Lake; 472–8211. Features Pecan Tree Restaurant, and Pistachio's Lounge with live entertainment on the top floor. Lakefront swimming pool, airport transportation. Reservations with deposit or credit card required. **Holiday Inn North:** 6911 N. I–35; 459–4251.

Howard Johnson's. 7800 N. I–35 (at U.S. 183); 836–8520 or (800) 654–2000. Situated north of the center of town, Howard Johnson's has airport courtesy cars, laundry service, and 24-hour satellite TV viewing. Children under 18 free. There is an On the Move package, double occupancy for seven nights; the Weekend Wonder package includes cocktails and Continental breakfast.

North Ramada Inn. 9220 N. I–35; 837–2920; the national Ramada Inn toll-free number is (800) 2–RAMADA. Pancake Haus restaurant, Mortimers Lounge. Children under 18 free, airport transportation, small pets allowed.

Quality Inn South. 2200 S. I–35 (at the Oltorf exit); 444–0561. South of the center of town. Restaurant, live entertainment, and happy hour at the Attic Club. Free shuttle to the airport. Children under 18 free.

Highland Mall La Quinta. 5812 N. I–35 (at U.S. 290E); 459–4381; **North La Quinta.** 7100 N. I–35 (at St. John's exit); 452–9401; **Oltorf La Quinta.** 1603 E. Oltorf (off I–35 South); 447–6661. In all these La Quintas, children under 18 free, 24-hour restaurant; **La Quinta Motor Inns'** toll-free number (800) 531–5900.

Ramada Inn Capitol. 300 E. 11th; 476–7151. One block from the state capitol building, five blocks from the university campus. All rooms refurbished; free airport limousine.

Sheraton Crest Inn. 111 E. 1st St.; 478–9611 or (800) 325–3535. Situated at 1st and Congress near the Town Lake hike-and-bike trail, with a view of the state capitol building. Restaurant, live music nightly at the 111 Club, free airport transportation. Weekend Special package. Reservations required.

Town Lake Ramada Inn. 1001 S. I–35; 444–3611; or (800) 2–RAMADA. Rooms with river views available. Greens 'n Glass restaurant and lounge.

TraveLodge, Austin Midtown. 4001 N. I–35; 454–6721 or (800) 255–3050. Centrally situated, offers a courtesy-car pickup from the airport. Restaurant, meeting rooms, beauty salon. Weekender Special: $34 singles per night, Friday through Sunday, reservations one week in advance. Family rates. **Travelodge Motor Hotel:** 4323 S. I–35; 447–5511.

Inexpensive

Austin Rio Motel. 4800 N. I–35 (at 51st St. exit); 452–9493.

Best Western Cross Country Inn. 6201 U.S. 290 East; 452–8861. One block east of the interstate, just north of the airport. Children under 17 free.

Capitol Rodeway Inn. 1201 N. I–35; 472–8331 or (800) 228–2000. Near 12th St. close to downtown. Children under 16 free. Getaway Weekend package.

Drury Inn. 919 E. Koenig Lane (at I–35 and U.S. 290); Special weekend rates. 454–1144 or (800) 325–8300.

EZ Travel Motor Hotel. 9106 N. I–35 (at Rundberg La. exit); 837–7900. North of the center of town. Laundry, kitchenettes, 24-hour restaurant next door.

Imperial 400 Motel. 901 S. Congress; 444–3651 or (800) 252–9649.

Stars Passport Inn. 3105 N. I–35; 478–1631 or (800) 238–6161. Conveniently situated on the interstate near the LBJ Library, the university campus, and the capitol. Features 24-hour full-service restaurant.

University Rodeway Inn: 2900 N. I-35; 477–6395.

RESORTS. Lakeway Resorts. Situated on Lake Travis, 30 minutes from downtown, off FM 620; 261–6600, (800) 252–9222 (in Texas only), or (800) 531–5001. A resort community comprising the *Lakeway Inn,* with 140 rooms, and the *World of Tennis Resort,* with two-, three-, and four-bedroom condominiums. Features two 18-hole golf courses, an equestrian center, tennis courts, waterskiing, pool, marina, yacht club, restaurant, shops. The Hill Country Honeymoon package for two nights includes breakfast and dinner and wine or champagne; Golf Unlimited, for two nights, features no greens fees, guaranteed tee times, unlimited golf on Yaupon and Live Oak courses; Tennis Mini-Clinic package is for two nights, Friday or Tuesday arrival, with six hours of instruction, unlimited court time, unlimited sauna, steam room, and Jacuzzi. All packages include reduced rates on recreational facilities.

Woodcreek Resort. Situated on RR 12, 2 mi. north of Wimberley and 55 minutes from downtown Austin; 847–2221 or (800) 252–9303 (in Texas only). Recreational facilities include 12 tennis courts, two swimming pools, an 18-hole golf course, horseback riding, boating, volleyball, basketball, shuffleboard, and a full spa with racquetball courts, saunas, a hot tub, and an exercise room. Restaurant. The Unlimited Golf package features three days and two nights, includes unlimited tennis, one free day in the spa, two breakfasts, and free cocktails. The Woodcreek Resort Pass provides unlimited use of all recreational facilities, Sunday through Thursday, excluding horseback rides and golf carts.

HOW TO GET AROUND. By car. Austin is easy to explore by car. Metered parking spaces downtown can be scarce because of construction, but there are plenty of parking garages. No cars are allowed to park on, or even drive through, the university campus without a university-issued parking permit, and there are campus police stationed at every entrance to enforce this rule. Visitors should park on the periphery of the campus, or in the public parking lot near the LBJ Library. It might be wise to stay off the bridges during weekday rush hours; otherwise, driving in Austin presents no special problems, and it is the most convenient and efficient way to get around.

From the airport. A taxi from the airport to downtown is about $5.00 plus tip. A city bus leaves for downtown every 35 to 40 minutes on weekdays; the fare is 50 cents. There are courtesy limousines to the major downtown hotels, but no limousine service for hire.

Rental cars. If you are not traveling by car, it is highly recommended that you rent one during your stay. The national chain rental agencies are all situated at or near the airport. There are considerable differences in rates and conditions among the companies, so it pays to shop around. Most rental agencies charge a daily rate plus a mileage rate, but some companies offer unlimited free mileage, whereas others allow from 100 to 300 free miles and charge for mileage after that point.

Of the nine or so companies at or near the airport, these have the most reasonable rates: *Budget Rent a Car,* at the airport and at 3330 Manor Rd.; 478–6437. Weekend rates are effective Thursday noon to Monday. Credit card required. Rates for an economy car are $33.50 daily, with unlimited free mileage. *Airways Rent a Car,* 3515 Manor Rd.; 476–3519 or (800) 521–4000. Credit card required. *Dollar Rent a Car,* at the airport and at 3112 Manor Rd.; 474–1497 or (800) 421–6868. Rates for an economy car include unlimited free mileage. Major credit card, or fill out a credit application with the company.

If you aren't planning on driving out of town and don't require a stylish vehicle, there are local companies that rent for half of what some national companies charge. *Rent-a-Wreck* has two locations: 6829 Guadalupe (454–8621), and 1030 S. Lamar (441–9609). *Action Rent a Car, Inc.,* 5300 Burnet Rd. (454–0976), has a wide selection of cars. Their rates are based on the age of the car, not its size, and they have 1970–78 models. There is a two-day minimum. Credit card or $100 cash deposit.

Rental recreational vehicles and campers. *Sunset R V Center,* 15232 N. IH-35 (251–2491), rents motor homes and tent trailers. Rates for a 22-ft. Eldorado are $79 a day; custom vans go for $49 a day plus 10¢ a mile. *Texas Camper Corral,* 2010 S. Lamar (835–0174) rents tent trailers for $150 a week, $100 deposit, or 18-ft. travel trailers for $150 a week.

By city bus. It is possible to get from one point to another using Austin Transit System buses, but chances are, it won't be the most convenient or the quickest way. There are 30 routes serving the city and surrounding areas, and the transit system publishes 15 separate route maps with schedules. A newcomer to Austin will need to have almost all these route maps in hand, and try to coordinate them with a good city map in order to plot a course. Because the route maps are separate, it may be difficult to work out transfer points; and if you miss a bus, be prepared to wait anywhere from 30 minutes to an hour for the next one. Fares are 50¢ for adults and 25¢ for the elderly, the handicapped, and children ages 6 to 12. Exact change is required. Transfers are 5¢ and valid for two hours. An Anytime Ticket, valid all hours, costs $5, and you can also buy a monthly pass, a commuter pass, or a shopper pass. For route and transfer information, contact the Austin Transit System, 505 N. Pleasant Valley Rd., P.O. Box 1943, Austin, TX 78767. The customer-service and information number is 474–1200.

By taxi. You won't see a cab on every corner in Austin. The only place where it's possible to hail a cab is at the airport; otherwise, a phone call is required to one of the three companies in town. Service is comparable among the companies, and they are all open 24 hours a day, but there is some difference in rates. *Yellow-Checker Cab Co.,* 509 E. 5th St.; 472–1111. The meter starts at $1, plus $1 a mile afterward. *Harlem Cab Co.,* 1129 E. 11th St.; 472–2404. $1 for the first 1/5 mi., 20¢ for every following 1/5 mi. *Roy's Taxi,* 90 East Ave.; 476–6911. Charges $1 for call, plus $1 for the first 1/5 mi., plus 20¢ for every following 1/5 mi.

TOURIST INFORMATION. The Convention and Visitors Council of the Austin Chamber of Commerce is at 901 W. Riverside Dr., Austin, TX 78767; 478–0098. The department has a great many free brochures on things to see and do in the Austin area, and a friendly staff. One publication, "A Driving Tour of Austin," maps out a driving and walking route to 30 historical, cultural, and recreational points of interest. *Texas Monthly* magazine has a helpful listings section; the restaurant listings focus on the better eateries, and the nightlife section is a good newcomer's guide to the 6th St. area. Locally published *Third Coast* magazine also has a large listings section, and the giveaway *Austin Chronicle* covers the pop music scene very thoroughly. The number for the Tourist Information Bureau is 475–2878.

SEASONAL EVENTS. January. The *Austin Boat, Sport, and Motorcycle Show* comes to Palmer Auditorium the third weekend of the month. **February.** *Carnaval Brasileiro* in City Coliseum: a Rio-style celebration of samba rhythms, nonstop dancing, tropical refreshments, face and body painting, and a costume contest. Be prepared for the bizarre. **March.** Spring winds bring the *Kite Flying Contest* in Zilker Park the second Saturday of the month. The third Sunday is the Capitol 10,000, 6.2-mi. (10,000m.) foot race starting at the capitol building and winding through the city to the finish line on Auditorium Shores. The second-largest 10,000m. race in the country, it had 23,251 finishers in 1984. The third week of March, the *Austin-Travis County Livestock Show and Rodeo* comes to the Texas Heritage Center on Decker Lane, east of town, with a rodeo, livestock show and auction, carnival midway, barbecue cookoff, quarter-horse show, and country-and-western music and dancing. **April.** The first weekend of the month ushers in the *Texas Relays* on campus. The *Highland Lakes Bluebonnet Trail* is held the second and third weekends; maps put out by the chambers of commerce in Austin, Marble Falls, Buchanan Dam, Burnet, Llano, and Kingsland point out historic sites and list special activities along the 150-mi. wildflower trail. The *Legends of Golf Tournament* is held the last week of April at Onion Creek, with some of the most famous names in golf. **May.** *Cinco de Mayo* is held on May 5 at Fiesta Gardens. This celebration commemorates Mexico's military victory over the French in the 1800s. The first weekend of the month brings *Flora Rama,* the annual garden show at the Garden Center in Zilker Park. *Fiesta Laguna Gloria* is held the third weekend of May at the Laguna Gloria Art Museum, with artists selling their work, demonstrations of various techniques, and an art auction of donated works. **June.** June 19 is the *Juneteenth Celebration,* commemorating emancipation for black Texans. The last week in June brings the *Williamson County Sheriff's Posse Rodeo and Western Week* in Georgetown. **July.** *Independence Day* on the 4th is always celebrated with a fireworks display over the lake at Auditorium Shores and a performance by the Austin Symphony. The *Governor's Cup Sailing Regatta* is held on Lake Travis the first weekend in July, and a *summer musical* is usually put on the third week of the month at the outdoor theater in Zilker Park. **August.** *Aqua Festival* is probably the biggest event of the year, an annual celebration focusing on water, sun, and sports. There are more than 75 events every year; they include: a rowing regatta, family concerts, a lighted water parade at night, stock-car races, autocross and motocross, a rodeo, a skeet shoot, ethnic nights, volleyball games, and raft races. **September.** The *Ethnic Folk Festival* is held in the early fall in Fiesta Gardens. Devoted chili lovers can't miss the *Republic of Texas Chilympiad,* held the third weekend of the month in nearby San Marcos. **October.** Local artists display and sell their work at the *Highland Lakes Arts and Crafts Trail,* held the last weekend of the month in Burnet, Llano, Marble Falls, Kingsland, and Buchanan Dam. **November.** The first week of the month brings *Wurstfest,* a celebration of German culture and cuisine in New Braunfels, a short drive southwest of Austin. A variety of artwork is for sale and display at the *Austin Artists' Harvest,* held the first weekend of the month at Palmer Auditorium. **December.** Zilker Park's *Parade of Lights* is in full swing the week before Christmas.

TOURS. *Gray Lines of Austin,* 7115 Burnet Rd. #118 (459–1300, evenings 345–6810 or 836–2255). Three-hour tours twice daily at 9:30 A.M. and 1:30 P.M. for $12.50 that includes trips to Sixth Street, Barton Springs, the LBJ Library, Town Lake, the governor's mansion, the capitol, and historic homes. Also available are trips to the LBJ Ranch and Fredericksburg and out-of-town tours to San Antonio and the Mexican Border. Call for details.

Town Lake Riverboat excursions begin every Saturday and Sunday at 4:00 P.M. The old-fashioned red-and-white riverboat leaves the dock at the Hyatt Regency Hotel on Barton Springs Road (at S. Congress) and cruises Town Lake for an hour and a half. Admission is $6 for adults, $4 for children under 12. The riverboat does not run during December, January, and February. For more details, call 327–1388.

SPECIAL-INTEREST SIGHTSEEING. Texas State Capitol Building. In any photograph of the Austin skyline, one of the most familiar landmarks is the dome of the capitol building. Situated on 25 acres in the center of downtown, the capitol is a favorite stop for tourists. The building was constructed in 1888 of native pink granite, and its architectural style bears more than a passing resemblance to the nation's capitol building. The height of the dome is 309 ft., 8 in.—seven feet higher than that of the U.S. Capitol.

In the center of the building, the rotunda opens onto four floors, where portraits of the five presidents of the Republic of Texas and the past governors of the state of Texas are displayed. During sessions of the legislature, visitors may view House and Senate proceedings from chamber balconies on the third floor. The capitol building is open from 6:00 A.M. to 11:00 P.M., seven days a week. Free guided tours are conducted every 15 minutes, from 8:15 A.M. to 4:30 P.M., Monday through Friday, and every half hour on weekends. For details, call Capitol Guided Tours at 475–3070. A tourist-information center in the south foyer is open daily from 8:00 A.M. to 5:00 P.M. Operated by the highway department, the center provides free information and maps, including a helpful guide to all the buildings and points of interest in the capitol complex. Free visitor parking is provided in designated lots on the southeast corner of 11th St. and Congress Ave. and in the mid-1500 block of Congress Ave.

The University of Texas Campus. The University of Texas opened in 1883 with 218 students; in fall 1981, there were 48,145 students enrolled on a campus consisting of more than 300 acres and 110 buildings. Much of the university's physical growth can be attributed to the discovery of oil on university-owned land in 1924. UT's doctoral programs in linguistics, Spanish, German, and botany rank among the top five in the country; its undergraduate business program has been ranked fifth in the U.S.

Visitors are welcome on campus, but parking can be a problem. Metered spaces are available at the north end of Memorial Stadium off 23rd St., and more parking is usually available at the *UT Visitor Center* (471–1420 or 471–1421), in the Nowotny Building in the restored Little Campus area at the southwest corner of Martin L. King and IH-35. The visitor center is open daily from 9:00 A.M. to 5:00 P.M. and provides maps, exhibits, and information on university programs. On the west side of campus, a good stopping place is the *General Information and Referral Service* (471–1506), on the ground floor of the Main Building. A student-guided walking tour of campus leaves at 11:00 A.M. and 2:00 P.M. Open from 8:30 A.M. to 5:00 P.M. while classes are in session, the information center also has maps, brochures, and information on upcoming events. The Main Building, or *UT Tower,* is the central administration building and a landmark on the Austin skyline. The tower rises 27 stories and has a 17-bell carillon, which chimes the quarter hours, at the top.

UT has the eighth largest academic library in the country. At the main library, *Perry-Castaneda* (471–5553), on-site use is available without charge; to check out books, there is a $15 deposit and a $2 fee. The *Texas Union,* at Guadalupe and 24th St. (471–5651), is the community center of the university; the information desk on the ground-floor lobby provides maps, shuttle-bus schedules, and brochures. Personnel can answer questions about Union activities and campus events through the use of a campus-wide calendar computer terminal. Or call the 24-hour information number, 471–4747, for a recorded rundown of campus events. *Astronomy Department Observatory,* at the top of Painter Hall at 24th St. and Inner Campus Dr., houses a telescope with a 9-in. lens. The observatory is open to the public every Saturday night from 9:00–11:00 P.M. Admission is free; call 471–4461 for further details. The observatory's Skywatcher Report, 471–5007, gives a two-minute recorded message on the current positions of the planets and stars. (For information on campus museums and art galleries, see *Museums;* for information on research-library collections and the LBJ Library, see *Libraries.*)

CITY PARKS. Zilker Park is Austin's largest and most used city recreation area, only five minutes from downtown on 391 acres fronting the south shore of Town Lake. Probably the most popular feature of the park is Barton Springs Pool, fed by natural springs that originate in the surrounding Hill Country. The unusually cold, clear water attracts swimmers all year long. The pool is open from 10:00 A.M. to dusk on weekends and from noon to dusk on weekdays. There is no admission fee to enter Zilker, but there is a parking fee on weekends, and a small fee for the pool.

The Zilker Park Garden Center features a wide range of flowering Texas plants, as well as azalea and rose gardens. One of its most beautiful sections is the Oriental Garden, designed and built single-handedly by Japanese-born Isamu Taniguchi; here, wooden bridges span small ponds full of water lilies, and narrow footpaths lead to a thatched bamboo teahouse. The garden center also has an authentic Swedish pioneer cabin, a blacksmith shop, a mineral trail, and a fragrance garden with herbs and plants for the blind.

At the northwest end of Zilker, the Austin Nature Center (327–8180) offers a hands-on approach to experiencing nature and the environment. There are exhibits at the main building, a walking trail, a picnic area, and access to Town Lake. The center has nature programs for children, and bird and wildflower walks for families.

A favorite feature of the park for children is the Zilker Park Eagle (478–8167), a miniature train offering 15-minute rides for 80¢ and 95¢. There are seven Zilker playing fields, used for city soccer games on weekends and for general kite flying and frisbee throwing. Zilker Park Boat Rentals (478–3852) operates from the south end of Barton Springs pool, and canoeists can paddle down Barton Creek into Town Lake. Canoe-rental hours are 9:00 A.M. to 7:00 P.M. during the summer; hours vary during the winter.

Auditorium Shores. This grassy area on the south bank of Town Lake, a bit west of S. Congress Ave., is the setting for the City Coliseum and the Palmer Auditorium and Convention Center.

Mount Bonnell Park. At 785 ft., Mount Bonnell is the highest point in Austin, and offers beautiful views of city, lake, and surrounding hills. Visitors have to park halfway up and climb to the top; the ascent is easy, consisting of wide, gradual stone steps bordered by trees. A maze of footpaths leads from the summit to the lake below. Mount Bonnell is a favorite spot for picnickers during the day and for stargazers at night. To the north, Mount Bonnell Road leads to FM 2222, one of the most scenic routes through the Hill Country.

Waterloo Park. Red River St., between 11th and 15th Sts.; 477–6511. Named for one of the first settlements in Austin's history, Waterloo is an open, well-tended park between the campus and downtown. Ideal for brown-bag lunching beside Waller Creek. Open seven days a week, 6:00 A.M. to 10:00 P.M.

Mayfield Park. 3800 W. 35th St.; 477–6511. Peacocks strut the grounds and roost in the trees in this dense park, adjacent to Laguna Gloria Art Museum and Lake Austin. There are two marked trails. A good place for birdwatching and picnicking (on the ground; there are no tables). Open Monday through Friday, 8:00 A.M. to 5:00 P.M.; Saturday, 9:00 A.M. to 5:00 P.M.; Sunday, 1:00 P.M. to 5:00 P.M.

Lake Austin Metropolitan Park, with 1,152 acres fronting Lake Austin, is a 15-mi. drive from town on scenic FM 2222. There are overnight camping facilities, free public boat ramps, picnic grounds, and a swimming beach. There is a small admission charge, and swimming areas are often crowded. For further details, call 327–1418.

Walter E. Long Lake and Park is a newly developed area 6 mi. east of Austin off Webberville Road. Boat ramps are available, fishing is permitted, and a lifeguard is on duty for swimmers.

Jourdan-Bachman Pioneer Settler's Memorial Park. 11418 Sprinkle Cut-off Rd.; 837–1215. Situated on a 70-acre tract in northeast Austin, the Pioneer Settler's Park gives pre-arranged groups of visitors a glimpse of what daily farm life was like in the mid-1800s in central Texas. Activities include quilting bees, furniture making, and hoedowns. Hours are Monday through Friday, 9:00 A.M. to 1:00 P.M.; call for tour arrangements and information on children's programs.

CAMPING. Public campgrounds are available in five of the six state parks surrounding Austin and at sites run by Lower Colorado River Authority (LCRA) in the lake district northwest of the city. The only in-town, centrally situated campground is *Pecan Grove RV Park,* 1518 Barton Springs Rd.; 472–1067. Pecan Grove is just south of the river, several blocks outside Zilker Park; there are hookups, showers, a laundry, and tree-shaded lots, with daily, weekly, or monthly rates. May be displaced by development.

The *Austin Capitol KOA* campground, 7009 S. I–35 (444–6322), is located south of the city. It accepts tents, trailers, or motor homes and offers showers, a laundry, a game room, a swimming pool, and a television room.

A complete listing of all campgrounds in the state, "Texas Public Campgrounds," may be obtained by writing Travel and Information Division, State Department of Highways and Public Transportation, P.O. Box 5064, Austin, TX 78763. A free map of privately owned campgrounds is also available from the Texas Association of Campground Operators, 1301 N. Watson Rd., Arlington, TX 76011.

LAKE PARKS. The LCRA administers a number of parks on the lakes along the Colorado River west of Austin: Lake Buchanan, Lake LBJ, and Lake Travis, as well as two parks on Lake Bastrop, north of Bastrop State Park. Swimming and fishing are permissible at all the following parks, and restroom facilities and drinking water are available at all except Pace Bend. Each campsite is equipped with a picnic table and a cooking grill. There is a 14-day limit.

Black Rock. 473–3217. Ten acres on Lake Buchanan; 20 campsites, boat ramp, playground, RV dumping station, restroom for the handicapped. No fee.

Shaw Island. 473–3217. Four acres on Lake Buchanan; 15 campsites. No fee.

Arkansas Bend. 451–7548. 195 acres on Lake Travis; boat ramp, 12 picnicking sites, but no camping. No fee.

Cypress Creek. 451–7548. 15 acres on Lake Travis; boat ramp, 10 picnicking sites, but no camping. No fee.

Mansfield Dam. 478–9606. 42 acres on Lake Travis; 36 campsites, boat ramp, six additional picnicking sites. No fee.

Pace Bend. 478–9606. 1,520 acres on Lake Travis; 150 campsites, two boat ramps. No fee.

Sandy Creek. 473–3217. 25 acres on Lake Travis; 31 campsites, RV dumping station, restroom for the handicapped. No fee.

North Shore. 321–3307. 23 acres on Lake Bastrop; 74 campsites, boat ramp, showers, dump stations, electrical hookups, rental cabins, restrooms for the handicapped. Entrance and use fees.

South Shore. 321–3307. 14 acres on Lake Bastrop; 81 campsites, boat ramp. Has all the camping facilities North Shore has. Entrance and use fees.

STATE PARKS. The Texas Parks and Wildlife Department publishes a free, comprehensive pamphlet with a guide to the state's recreation areas, parks, and historic sites and structures. Included in the pamphlet are camping regulations, entrance fees, reservation information, and a complete listing of the phone numbers of all state parks. Call or write: Texas Parks and Wildlife Department, 4200 Smith School Rd., Austin, TX 78744; (800) 792–1112, or 479–4800 in Austin. Fees for all the following parks except Longhorn Cavern ($3.50 tour fee) and LBJ (free) are $2 per day, per vehicle. Reservations for cabins, campsites, and screened shelters are accepted daily at each park from 8:00 A.M. to 5:00 P.M.; the spring and early-summer months are peak camping times in Texas, so campers should be sure to call ahead.

Bastrop State Park. 32 mi. southeast of Austin on TX 21, 1 mi. east of Bastrop; 321–2101. Bastrop is situated in the Lost Pines area, a disjunct loblolly-pine woodland 100 miles from the main body of East Texas pine woods. The 3,503-acre park is covered with 70 sq. mi. of pine-and-oak woodland. There are 13 rustic cabins with cooking facilities, overlooking a small lake. Camping amenities include picnic tables, grills, water, restrooms, showers, and trailer hookups for electricity, water, and sewage. The park also has a swimming pool with two children's wading pools, and a 9-hole golf course open year-round.

Buescher State Park. About 40 mi. southeast of Austin off TX 71 on FR 153; 237–2241. Buescher is only a few miles east of Bastrop State Park, and the terrain is identical. The park has 40 campsites with water and electricity, 65 picnic sites, and three restrooms, two with showers. Four screened shelters with electricity, picnic table, water, and grill are available. A 25-acre lake provides good fishing, but swim at your own risk. There are no hiking trails, but there is a 14-mi. scenic drive on Park Rd. 1, between Buescher and Bastrop.

Inks Lake State Park. About 60 mi. from Austin in the Highland Lakes area on Park Road 4; 793–2223. This 1,200-acre park features cedar and oak woodlands, a diversity of wildflowers and pink gneiss, and granite outcroppings. There is archaeological evidence that the area was used as an Indian hunting ground, and wildlife is still abundant. Recreational facilities include swimming, boating, canoeing, waterskiing, scuba diving, and fishing. Campsites are available with tables, grills, electrical hookups, restrooms, and showers. There are screened shelters as well as primitive camping for backpackers. The park has a 9-hole golf course, a grocery store, and a public boat ramp. Canoes, fishing boats, and paddle boats may be rented.

LBJ State Historical Park. A little more than 50 mi. west of Austin, off US 290; 644–2252. This park is adjacent to the LBJ Ranch, a popular tourist stop. On 718 acres, the park has a visitors' center with a museum and theater, picnic sites, a nature trail, a swimming pool, and wildlife enclosures. This is a day-use area only, without camping facilities. Free bus tours, run by the LBJ National Historic Park, depart from the visitors' center daily and include: a drive past Lyndon Johnson's first schoolhouse; a tour of his birthplace and family cemetery; and a drive through the LBJ Ranch, a working ranch where the "Texas

White House" sits facing the Pedernales River. (The LBJ State Historic Park and the LBJ National Historic Park are really one package.)

Longhorn Cavern State Park. 62 mi. from Austin in the Highland Lakes area on Park Rd. 4, 6 mi. from U.S. 281; 756–4680. At least a million years old, this large cavern descends to 130 feet below ground level in its most remote chamber; calcite crystals and clusters of stalactites and stalagmites line the walls. The cavern's temperature remains constant at 64 degrees. There are a snack bar, a gift shop, and a picnic area; camping is available at Inks Lake State Park, a five-minute drive away. Tours are conducted every hour from 10:00 A.M. to 5:00 P.M., seven days a week, from June 1 to August 31. From September 1 through May 31, tours are held Monday through Friday at 10:00 A.M., 1:00 P.M., and 3:00 P.M. and every hour on weekends. The cavern is closed Mondays and Tuesdays, October through February.

McKinney Falls State Park. 13 mi. southeast of downtown Austin, off Nuckols Crossing Rd.; 243–1643. Onion Creek winds through the park for 1.7 mi., with large pools, occasional rapids, and two beautiful waterfalls. There are bald cypress, Texas oak, and pecan trees and a variety of wildlife, including deer, quail, and armadillos. The park has 84 campsites with water, electricity, picnic tables, and grills; restrooms and showers are available, and there is a separate picnic area with a playground. Preserved along the hiking trail are the ruins of the Thomas F. McKinney homestead, dating from the mid-1800s.

Pedernales Falls State Park. About 46 mi. west of Austin on RR 3232, off U.S. 290 West; (512) 868–7304. This 4,800-acre park stretches for 6 mi. along the Pedernales River and for 3 mi. along the south side of the beautiful Pedernales Falls Gorge. Formerly the Circle Bar Ranch, the land is dotted with springs, streams, and canyons. Deer, turkeys, raccoons, and many birds are abundant. The park has 69 multi-use campsites, each with electrical and water hookups, a picnic table, a grill, and a tent pad. A sewage-disposal station for RVs and restrooms with showers are also in the camping area. There are 50 additional picnic sites. The 8.2-mi. Wolfe Mountain trail is popular for hiking and backpacking, and primitive camping is permitted in this area.

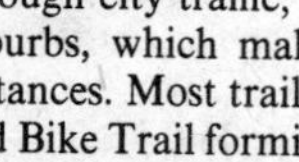

PARTICIPANT SPORTS. With its mild, sunbelt climate, surrounded by water and blessed with a number of parks, Austin is a perfect place for almost any recreational sport. **Running** is probably the single most popular sport among residents, and no wonder: There are miles of off-road trails, many designed specifically for runners. No one need risk life and limb jogging through city traffic; and unlike many cities, Austin is not yet tightly ringed by suburbs, which makes it easy to run in the country without traveling long distances. Most trails are in the central area of town, with the Town Lake Hike and Bike Trail forming the backbone of the system. The Town Lake Trail winds around the lake for 8.4 mi. and feeds into several shorter trails. Most of it is surfaced with crushed granite gravel, which is easy on feet and legs. Parking is available on either side of Lamar Blvd. south of the lake, at Festival Beach just east of I–35, in lots west of S. 1st St., or at Municipal Auditorium. For maps of trails and further information, contact the Austin Parks and Recreation Department, 1500 Riverside Dr.; 477–6511.

Fishing is available in any of the lakes around Austin. There are many public parks as well as private lodges and marinas that offer fishing facilities (see *Lake Parks*). Fish caught in the Highland Lakes area just west of Austin include white bass, crappie, large-mouth bass, catfish, and perch. All fishermen must have a Texas license; the cost is $8 for a 14-day nonresident license, $15 annually for nonresidents, and $8 annually for residents.

The open expanse of Lake Travis west of the city is excellent for **sailing** and **scuba diving. Swimming** is permitted in all lakes except Town Lake, and there are good swimming beaches at Lake Austin Metropolitan Park. **Waterskiing** and **pleasure boating** are allowed on all the lakes except Town Lake, where gasoline engine motorboats are prohibited (electric motors allowed). Boat-launching ramps are found in most public parks and campgrounds. There are five public boat launches in Austin: Walsh Boat Landing is in a residential area of west Austin, off Enfield Road, and there are launches at the hike-and-bike trail on West 1st St., at the Congress Avenue Bridge and East 1st St., at Waller Beach, and at Longhorn Shores.

All **hunting** in Texas is done on private property leased from the owner. Deer hunting is very popular in areas west of Austin. Contact the chambers of commerce in those communities for information on ranchers who have hunting leases. A Texas license is also required; resident fee is $8; nonresident fee, $100.75.

There are five public **golf** courses in Austin, but a couple were shaky in mid-1984. *Jimmy Clay Golf Course,* 5200 Nuckols Crossing Rd.; 447–1938. The newest and largest municipal Course, in South Austin next to McKinney Falls State Park, was closed because of problems with overflow from an adjoining sewage treatment plant. *Riverside Golf Course,* 5712 E. Riverside; 477–6511. Formerly the Austin Country Club course, this course was leased from another owner, and there was hope that it would be bought. *Lions Municipal Golf Course,* 2901 Enfield Rd. and Lake Austin Blvd.; 477–6963. An 18-hole course with practice area in west Austin, accessible to Loop 1. *Morris Williams Golf Course,* 4305 Manor Rd.; 926–1298. *Hancock Golf Course* at E. 41st St. and Red River; 453–0276. This is the oldest course, with 9 holes. Centrally situated, but maintenance is often poor. Greens fees are $5.50 weekdays, $7 weekends, for nine holes, with special rates for players under 18 and over 62. Golfing is a year-round activity here, so tee times may be required.

There are 153 public **tennis** courts in Austin. For players who don't want to take a chance on being unable to find an empty court in one of the parks, there are four tennis centers, with a total of 35 well-maintained courts. The tennis centers offer low-cost reservations, made by phone or in person, up to two days in advance. *Caswell Tennis Center,* 24th St. and Lamar Blvd.; 478–6268, 9 courts. *Austin High Tennis Center,* 1715 W. 1st St.; 476–5662, 8 courts. *Pharr Tennis Center,* 4201 Brookview Rd.; 478–8799, 8 courts. *South Austin Tennis Center,* 1000 Cumberland Rd.; 442–1466, 10 courts. *The Austin Recreation Center,* 1213 Shoal Creek Blvd. (476–5662), operates on a first come–first served basis for its four courts; fees are $4 per person, or annual membership cards are available for 90 minutes of singles or two hours of doubles.

Racquetball is available at *Royal Court Club,* 2415 Twin Oaks Dr.; 459–7638; *Supreme Court Racquet Club, North:* 9638 N. Lamar; 835–4113; *Plaza 183:* 13450 Hwy. 183N, 250–1683; *Downtown:* 115B Pecan St.; and *South:* 1020 Walsh Tarlton La.; 327–4580; *Total Fitness and Racquetball,* 9518 Anderson Mill Rd., 250–1666 and 111 E. Logan, 255–8535.

In spite of Austin's hot summers, you can **ice skate** all year round at the indoor *Northcross Ice Rink,* 2525 W. Anderson Lane; 451–5102. The rink is in Northcross Mall and can get very crowded on weekends. Monday is $2 night.

For **horseback riding** in the rolling Hill County west of town, contact *Lakeway Equestrian Center,* 2401 FM 620; 263–5012. Other stables that rent horses are *Sidewinder Stables,* 4821 Johnson Rd, E. of Hwy 183S; 247–4298. 500 acres on the southeast city limits. *Nameless Valley Ranch,* 23421 Nameless Rd.; 267–1168, in Leander, northwest of Austin.

SPECTATOR SPORTS. The *University of Texas Longhorns* compete in football, baseball, basketball, cross country, golf, indoor and outdoor track and field, tennis, swimming, and diving. Information about the university sports program and when and where events will be held is available through Sports News; 471–7437. Although football games are not usually sold out, it would be wise to call early for tickets. Tickets for all sports may be obtained at the ticket office in Bellmont Hall # 102 (Bellmont is in the football stadium on campus); 471–3333, Monday through Friday, 9:00 A.M. to noon and 1:00 to 4:00 P.M. The office is also open on days of home football games from 9:00 A.M. to noon.

Austin has no professional teams of its own. Occasionally the San Antonio Spurs or the Houston Rockets basketball teams play exhibition games in the Frank Erwin Special Events Center on campus; 447–6060 (ticket office). A *horseracing track, stables, and rodeo area* may be found at Manor Downs, off U.S. 290 East near Manor, just east of Austin. Quarter-horse races are held on scheduled days, and post time is 12:00 noon. Call 272–4042 for schedule and ticket information.

HISTORIC SITES. The French Legation. 802 San Marcos St.; 472–8180. Built in 1840 by Comte Alphonse Duboise de Saligny, French ambassador to the Republic of Texas, the legation contains a beautiful collection of imported period French furniture. Outbuildings include an authentic French country kitchen. This is the only foreign legation ever built outside Washington, D.C. Admission $2 for adults, 50¢ for children under 12. Open from 1:00 to 5:00 P.M., Tuesday through Sunday.

The Bremond Block. Between 7th and 9th Sts. and San Antonio and Guadalupe Sts. The houses here are representative of the architecture of the late nineteenth century. John and Elizabeth Bremond moved from Philadelphia to

Austin in 1846 and built the first home on the block in 1863. When their children married, they also built homes on the block. The architectural variations among the houses make a walk through the area interesting. Parking on 7th St.

The Millet Opera House. 110 E. 9th St. Built in 1878 by Capt. C. F. Millet, contractor and lumberyard owner, the building is now the home of the Austin Club. Many of the great and near great, including Edwin Booth, Otis Skinner, and Lily Langtry, performed here.

The Old Locomotive. Trinity and 4th St. This old locomotive, circa 1924, stands as the last of the steam engines to operate out of Austin on the Southern Pacific Railroad. Children love it.

The Old Bakery and Emporium. 1006 Congress Ave.; 477–5961. Built in 1876 by Charles Lundberg, a Swedish immigrant, and restored in 1963 by the Heritage Society and Junior League. Hand-crafted items made by senior citizens are for sale, as are coffee and baked goods. Admission free. Open Monday through Friday, 9:00 A.M. to 4:00 P.M. Also open Saturdays in the summer.

Saint David's Episcopal Church. 7th and San Jacinto Sts. Completed in 1854, this is the oldest Protestant church west of the Mississippi. Some of the stained glass is by Tiffany, and the bell, cast in Philadelphia and originally designed for the state capitol, is still in use.

Saint Mary's Cathedral. 10th and Brazos Sts. Built of native limestone in 1884, this church has beautiful German and French stained glass.

The State Cemetery. E. 7th and Comal Sts. This cemetery contains the graves of Stephen F. Austin and seven governors of Texas, as well as 234 graves of lesser officials and their wives and 2,047 graves of Confederate army veterans and their wives. One interesting feature of the cemetery is Elisabet Ney's recumbent statue of Gen. Albert Sidney Johnson, secretary of war of the Republic of Texas, killed at the Battle of Shiloh in 1862.

Santa Rita No. 1. The first drilling rig to strike oil on University of Texas land, Santa Rita has been preserved and is now at Martin Luther King Blvd. and San Jacinto St., on the southern edge of the university campus.

The Governor's Mansion. 11th and Colorado Sts.; 475–2121. Built in 1855, this 20-room mansion is the oldest building in the capitol complex. Its Corinthian columns and wide verandas typify the antebellum style of the Republic of Texas. The first floor contains furnishings of Texas' past governors and a collection of antique furniture and art. Admission free. Tours are conducted Monday through Friday, every 20 minutes from 10:00 A.M. to noon.

LBJ State Historical Park. See *State Parks,* above.

Treaty Oak. 503 Baylor St. This tree is estimated to be from 500 to 600 years old, and its picture hangs in the Hall of Fame of Forestry in Washington, D.C. Its giant branches shade more than ¼ acre of ground and spread 127 ft. Stephen F. Austin is reputed to have signed the first boundary agreement between Indians and settlers under its branches.

Symphony Square. 11th and Red River streets; 476–5098. These quaint limestone-and-mortar buildings house the Austin Symphony Orchestra Society. The complex includes a 500-seat amphitheater and stage of Greek design, Doyle House (a youth-education center), and the triangular Jeremiah Hamilton Building. Musical performances for children are scheduled often, along with weekend performances showcasing new musical talent from the area. Free tours by appointment. Open 9:00 A.M. to 5:00 P.M., Monday through Friday.

Old Pecan Street. This street is now named 6th St. The area between I–35 and Congress Ave. was originally the primary east-west business district, and many of the old buildings have been restored. The street has retail stores, restaurants, theaters, art galleries, bars, and specialty shops. The charm of the area has always been its diversity: thrift shops next to expensive restaurants.

Paramount Theater for the Performing Arts. 713 Congress Ave.; 472–5411. This is one of the few remaining grand vaudeville houses in Texas and has been beautifully restored. Call the box office for information on shows.

LIBRARIES. Lyndon Baines Johnson Library and Museum. 2313 Red River St.; 397–5136 (information) or 397–5279 (tours). One of seven presidential libraries administered by the National Archives, the LBJ Library consists of two parts: the library itself, which houses 31 million historical documents used primarily by scholars; and the museum, with historical and cultural exhibits, open to the public. Each year an estimated 450,000 people visit the library and museum, situated on 14 acres on the university campus. The library is second only to the Alamo in terms of popularity with Texas tourists. Exhibits in the museum include glimpses of Johnson, his family, and his political programs; displays of gifts given to him by foreign leaders and the American public; and "Life in the White House" as explained by Lady Bird Johnson. The museum also contains a replica room of the White House Oval Office as it looked during Johnson's presidency. A recent $2.3-million renovation added an orientation theater showing films, a First Lady Theater, a Great Society Hall, and an expanded Vietnam-war exhibit. Admission free. Open seven days a week, 9:00 A.M. to 5:00 P.M. Closed only on Christmas Day.

Harry Ransom Center. 21st and Guadalupe Sts.; 471–7324. Situated on the university campus, the center houses the Huntington Art Gallery (see *Museums*) and the special collections of the Humanities Research Center, an internationally recognized library of rare books and manuscripts. The center has notable collections in English, American, and French literature, with an associated iconography collection. Its special-collection rooms may be seen by appointment only. The photography collection on the sixth floor contains 200,000 photographs, 15,000 books and periodicals, and 2,000 pieces of photographic equipment. Also exhibited at the Ransom Center is a Gutenberg Bible, printed in 1455 and one of only five copies in the U.S. Admission free. Open 9:00 A.M. to 5:00 P.M., Monday through Saturday; 1:00 P.M. to 5:00 P.M., Sunday.

Nettie Lee Benson Latin American Collection. Sid Richardson Hall # 1.109, university campus; 471–3818. The Benson Latin American Collection has approximately 338,000 volumes and 2 million pages of manuscripts, as well as thousands of photographs and maps. The private library of Genaro García, noted Mexican historian, forms the nucleus of its research collection, augmented by acquisitions from Paraguay, Chile, Argentina, and Guatemala. Visitors may apply at the front desk for special stack permits, but because of the relative scarcity of Latin American materials, many are designated for library use only. Open Monday through Thursday, 9:00 A.M. to 10:00 P.M.; Friday, 9:00 A.M. to 6:00 P.M.; Saturday, noon to 5:00 P.M.; and Sunday, 2:00 to 6:00 P.M.

Eugene C. Barker Texas History Center. Sid Richardson Hall #2.109, university campus; 471–5961. The Barker History Center has the single most extensive collection of Texana and Texas-history material to be found anywhere. The collection dates back to 1883 and includes a library of 120,000 volumes, a newspaper-and-map unit, a special collection of publications by and about the university, and an archives-and-manuscript unit based on the Bexar Archives, a record of the Spanish and Mexican colonies in Texas. The collection also has a wealth of information related to ethnic history, particularly German, Mexican, and Jewish immigration and settlement. Open 8:00 A.M. to 5:00 P.M., Monday through Saturday.

MUSEUMS. O. Henry Home and Museum. 409 E. 5th St.; 472–1903. Short-story writer William Sydney Porter, known by his pen name of O. Henry, lived in this small Victorian house in 1893, when it was on 4th St. It is furnished with period pieces, and O. Henry's personal effects are displayed. Rooms are not roped off, so visitors may walk freely through the house and browse. Admission free. Open Tuesday through Saturday, 11:00 A.M. to 4:30 P.M., and Sunday, 2:00 to 4:30 P.M.

Texas Confederate Museum. 11th and Brazos Sts.; 472–2596. Presently the home of the Daughters of the Confederacy Museum and the Daughters of the Republic of Texas Museum. Built in 1857, it once housed patent, deed, and land documents of the Republic of Texas. Relics of the Confederacy, items used by early Texas settlers, and records and exhibits of the Texas Republic are displayed. Admission free. Open 9:00 A.M. to noon and 1:00 to 5:00 P.M., weekdays.

Neill-Cochran Museum House. 2310 San Gabriel St.; 478–2335. Built in 1855, this house is an example of southern Greek-revival architecture, using native Texas limestone and pine. It served as a family home for more than half its existence and is now owned by the Colonial Dames of America, who have restored the house and maintain its antique furnishings. Admission $1 for adults, 50¢ for students and children. Open for tours Wednesday through Sunday at 2:00, 3:00, and 4:30 P.M.

Texas Memorial Museum. 2400 Trinity St.; 471–1604. Situated on the University of Texas campus, this museum features exhibits on geology and paleontology, including Texas minerals and dinosaur fossils; the animals and plants of Texas and their habitats; prehistoric peoples from around the world, including rock art, pre-Colombian pottery, and basketry; and Texas history, from sixteenth-century Spanish exploration to the post–Civil War era. Admission free. Open Monday through Friday, 8:00 A.M. to 5:00 P.M.; Saturday and Sunday, 1:00 to 5:00 P.M.

Laguna Gloria Art Museum. 3809 W. 35th St.; 458–8191. Laguna Gloria is housed in a 1916 Mediterranean-style villa on 29 acres on the shore of Lake

Austin. Its focus is American art since 1900, including painting, sculpture, photography, and architecture. Exhibits change continually, and there is also an ongoing exhibit series on regional art. The museum sponsors films, lectures, tours, and performances and runs an art school. Admission free. Tuesday, Wednesday, Friday, and Saturday, 10:00 A.M. to 5:00 P.M. Thursday, 10:00 A.M. to 9:00 P.M.; Sunday, 1:00 to 5:00 P.M.

Elisabet Ney Museum. 44th St. and Ave., H; 458–2255. Ney, a prominent German sculptor before coming to Texas, built this fortresslike studio-home in 1892, after receiving a commission for statues of Stephen F. Austin and Sam Houston. The museum houses many of her works in plaster, marble, and bronze, and some historic memorabilia. Admission free. Tuesday through Friday, 11:00 A.M. to 4:30 P.M.; Saturday and Sunday, 2:00 to 4:30 P.M.

George Washington Carver Museum. 1165 Angelina St.; 472–4809. This museum has changing exhibits of Texas folk art and Afro-American folk crafts. Admission free. Tuesday and Wednesday, 10:00 A.M. to 6:00 P.M.; Thursday, noon to 8:00 P.M.; Friday and Saturday, noon to 5:00 P.M.

Huntington Art Gallery. This collection is on the university campus at two locations. The gallery in the UT art building, 23rd and San Jacinto (471–1833), has changing exhibits. The Harry Ransom Center, at 21st and Guadalupe (471–7324), houses the Michener Collection of 20th-Century American Painting, Greek and Roman statuary reproductions, contemporary Latin American art, paintings and bronzes of the American West, and ancient Greek and Italian pottery. Admission free. Call 471–7324 for a recorded listing of current and future exhibits. Open Monday through Saturday, 9:00 A.M. to 5:00 P.M.; Sunday, 1:00 to 5:00 P.M.

Texas Archives and Library Buildings. 1201 Brazos St.; 475–2996. Just east of the capitol grounds, the archives building has historic relics and items used by early Texas settlers on display. There is also an excellent genealogical section. Admission free. Open Monday through Friday, 8:00 A.M. to 5:00 P.M.

Dougherty Arts Center. 1110 Barton Springs Rd.; 477–5824. Features changing exhibits of contemporary art, crafts, and photography by local and Texas artists. Admission free. Tuesday through Friday, 9:00 A.M. to 5:00 P.M.; Saturday and Sunday, 1:00 to 4:00 P.M.

STAGE. Austin has a small but lively theatrical community. *B. Iden Payne Theater,* 23rd and San Jacinto Sts., on campus; 471–1444: The University of Texas drama department stages many different productions here throughout the year, often with guest directors and performers; call for schedule and ticket information. *Esther's at the Ritz,* Ritz Theater, 320 E. 6th; 479–0054. This is the showcase for Esther's Follies, Austin's own versatile comedy troupe, performing original vaudeville, satire, and parody. This is one of the best shows in town, though some of the local references may stymie nonresidents. *Zachary Scott Theater Center* (Austin civic theater), 1421 W. Riverside; 476–0541: Eleven productions per year, using local talent under professional direction. *Mary Moody Northen Theater,* on the campus of Saint

Edward's University, 3001 S. Congress Ave.; 444–8398: Theater in the round; the productions usually feature a well-known visiting actor or actress. *Paramount Theater for the Performing Arts,* 713 Congress Ave.; 472–5411: Built in 1915, the building has been restored and offers Broadway entertainment as well as musical events. *Capitol City Playhouse,* 214 W. 4th; 472–2966. Produces a lot of original local material.

SHOPPING. You have to go to Dallas or Houston if you want Saks, Bloomingdale's, or Neiman-Marcus. What Austin does have for the shopper is a variety of arts-and-crafts and specialty shops that carry unique, handmade items. *El Taller,* 723 E. 6th; 473–8693: An art gallery on the IH-35 end of Sixth Street specializing in work with a strong Southwestern flavor, featuring many posters and prints.

Charles Lewis Co., 2301 Hancock Dr.; 452–5406: Direct importers of Mexican antique furniture, embroidered clothing, and some preconquest art objects. Usually carries a fine collection of Mexican-village folk art, including wood carvings, festival-dance masks, weavings, and clay figures; and has good imports from Peru, Guatemala, and South America. *Earthsea,* 3700 Kerbey Lane; 451–7042: Carries an extensive collection of shells, coral, and feathers, many made into unusual items and jewelry. *Clarksville Pottery,* 1013 W. Lynn; 478–9079: This little shop in a west-Austin neighborhood carries porcelain and stoneware items handmade by local artists. *Clayworks Studio and Gallery,* 1211 E. 6th St.; 474–9551: A working studio for potters, Clayworks also has a nicely arranged gallery of decorative and functional pottery for sale.

If you're looking for cowboy boots or other kinds of western apparel, there are several good stores to choose from. Most western-wear stores carry an assortment of cowboy boots and hats, several brands of blue-jeans, western belts and buckles, western-style shirts, work clothes, and often tack and saddle equipment. *Allen's Boot Center,* 1522 S. Congress Ave.; 447–1413. *Callahan's General Store,* 501 Bastrop Hwy. (U.S. 183 South); 385–3452. *The Lariat Ranch Wear and Saddle Shop,* 1610 S. Congress Ave.; 444–2111. *Tiny's Western Shop,* 2213 Airport Rd.; 476–1277. *Shepler's,* 6001 Middle Fiskville Rd.; 454–3000.

Austin has a number of stores that specialize in vintage or antique clothing or high-quality used clothing on consignment. The following list is only a sample of some of the more interesting shops. **Vintage Clothing.** *Old Time Teenie's,* 1126 W. 6th St.; 477–2022: This wonderfully eccentric little shop carries truly antique clothes, most in very good condition, not always cheap. *The Bazaar,* 2404 Guadalupe St.; 478–3536: Vintage clothes and the feather boas, seamed hose, and theatrical makeup to go with them. *Henry's Memrys Vintage Clothing,* 423 E. 6th; 474–6428: A really nice selection of vintage clothing in the heart of the Old Pecan Street district. **Resale Shops.** *Rethreads Consignment Boutique,* 1806 W. 35th St.; 459–3325. *Act II Resale Shop,* 3339 Hancock St.; 451–0076. *Second Time Around,* 3704 Crawford; 451–6845. **For Children.** *Monkey Business,* 5504 Burnet Rd.; 458–4364: Resale and consignment clothes, toys, furniture, baby accessories. *The Jelly Bean Tree,* 7437 Burnet Rd.; 452–1694.

Although *Highland Mall,* on the northeast side of town remains popular, the malling hotspot is now *Barton Creek Square,* a monster center at Loop 360 and the MoPac Freeway.

DINING OUT. There are a wide variety of restaurants to choose from in Austin, from Tex-Mex to Szechuan; and dining out here is less expensive than in many other parts of the country. The following restaurants represent a sample of the better-known, tried-and-true places. Price classifications are based on the cost of a typical meal for one person, exclusive of drinks, tax, or tip, and they are meant only as a general guide. *Inexpensive:* less than $6; *Moderate:* $6 to $15; *Expensive:* $15 to $25. Credit-card abbreviations: AE, American Express; MC, Mastercard; V, Visa; DC, Diners Club.

Expensive

Austin's Courtyard. 1205 N. Lamar Blvd.; 476–7095. A good place for an elegant, romantic dinner. The menu changes daily, but can include wild game, abalone, duck, quail, rainbow trout with king crab and oysters, and a wide variety of veal dishes. Bar. D, Monday through Saturday. AE, MC, V, DC.

Basil's. 900 W. 10th St.; 477–5576. Considered by many to be the best Italian restaurant in town. Be prepared for generous portions of pasta and superb seafood entrées (shrimp and oysters especially recommended). Also be prepared to empty your wallet and to wait for a table. No reservations taken. Beer and wine. D, daily. MC, V, AE.

Green Pastures. 811 W. Live Oak; 444–4747. Austin's *grande dame* restaurant, housed in an old mansion on the south side of town, with peacocks strutting the grounds. Excellent service, good food, big checks. The Sunday brunch is much favored in certain circles, Monday–Saturday; D, Monday–Saturday; Sunday brunch buffet 11:00–2:00. AE, MC, V.

Inn at Brushy Creek. In Round Rock, north of Austin, on the west side of I-35 at the Taylor exit; 255–2555. This quaint stone inn offers some of the best food in central Texas: game hen Normandie with herbed stuffing, Portuguese soup, a perfectly executed bearnaise sauce. Dry county; free corkage (means bring your own wine). Reservations required. D, Thursday through Saturday. AE, DC, MC, V.

Jeffrey's. 1204 W. Lynn; 477–5584. Creative Continental cooking in a small, elegant setting. Try the delicate trout in dill sauce, calves' liver moutarde, or exceptional venison. Wine and beer. No reservations taken; and waits can get long, but you can go next door to the Clarksville Cafe and they'll come and get you when your turn comes. D, daily. MC, V, AE, DC.

Moderate

Chez Nous, 510 Neches; 473–2413. A few steps off Sixth Street, Chez Nous features very well executed French country cooking, nothing super-fancy, but well done. The veal and the fish are highly recommended. All in all, an unpretentious atmosphere that welcomes black tie and blue jeans with equal enthusiasm from 11:30 A.M. to 11:00 P.M. L, D, Tuesday through Saturday. AE, MC, V.

County Line. 6500 W. Bee Cave Rd., 327–1742; and 5204 Farm-to-Market Road 2222, 346–3664. That Texas staple, barbecue, served up with an inspiring view of the rolling Hill Country. A paradise of ribs, brisket, and sausage for the carnivore. Home-baked bread. Bar. D, daily. MC, V.

San Miguel. 2330 W. North Loop; 459–4121. The elegant, authentic Mexican fare served here is a far cry from the Tex-Mex served in most places: enchiladas filled with crabmeat and topped with sour-cream sauce; chicken-vegetable soup; shrimp cocktail. Pleasing stucco-and-tile decor. Bar. D, daily; Sunday brunch. DC, MC, V.

Sweetish Hill. 1202–B W. 6th St.; 472–7319. Pleasant patio dining and an innovative Continental menu—stuffed shoulder of lamb, fish soup, etc. Cakes, tortes, croissants and other confections from the bakery, an Austin institution that is open only from 8:00 A.M. to 3:30 P.M. daily. Wine list. B, L, Tuesday through Friday; D, Tuesday through Saturday; Saturday and Sunday brunch. MC, V.

Tortuga's. 3010 W. Anderson Lane in Creekside Square; 458–2243. Texas-Caribbean food served in colorful surroundings. Try pork ribs in a pineapple-rum glaze, green enchiladas, zucchini with parmesan. Bar. Buffet lunch, Monday through Friday; D, daily; Sunday brunch. AE, MC, V, DC.

Yunnan Dynasty. 2900 W. Anderson Lane; 454–6677. Journey beyond chow mein; here you can find stir-fried eggplant in garlic sauce, and scallops with water chestnuts and mushrooms. Bar. L, D, daily. All major credit cards.

Inexpensive

Another Raw Deal. 1110 W. 6th St.; 473–0015. Plain Texas cooking—steaks, chops, chicken, beans, home fries. The atmosphere is often smoky and noisy, since this is a popular place to drink as well as to eat. Bar. L, D, daily. MC, V, AE, DC.

El Azteca. 2600 E. 7th St.; 477–4701. A little bit of everything on the menu: flautas, chicken mole, pork chops, beef rib, and no fewer than 10 vegetarian plates. The Guerra family has operated this popular restaurant for almost 20 years. L, D, daily except Sunday. AE, MC, V.

China Palace. 6605 Airport Rd.; 451–7104. An extensive menu that includes the familiar (kung pao chicken) and the not-so-familiar (shrimp in black-bean sauce, hot-and-spicy bean curd). Also classic Chinese-American fare, from egg-drop soup to egg roll. Bar. L, D, daily. MC, V.

Jaime's Spanish Village. 802 Red River St.; 476–5149. A homey, comfortable place to eat; friendly service. Tex-Mex food at its best: good fajitas, guacamole, chile con queso. Bar. L, D, daily. Major credit cards.

The Nighthawk. 336 S. Congress Ave.; 474–7701. A meat-and-potatoes tradition, the Nighthawk has been around since 1932. Old West decor, friendly waitresses in a family atmosphere. You can't go wrong with any of the steaks. Bar. B, L, D, daily. MC, V, AE, DC.

The Omelettry. 4811 Burnet Rd.; 453–5062. Also, *Omelettry West,* 2304 Lake Austin Blvd.; 478–8645. Serve every variation on the omelet, from guacamole to black olive to spinach and bacon. Excellent salads and hamburgers, tasty homemade desserts. No smoking. No bar. B, L, D, daily. No credit cards or checks.

La Tapatia. 1501 E. 6th St.; 477–2355. This large, friendly restaurant serves good, basic Tex-Mex food to the accompaniment of wonderful mariachi music. Enjoy green enchiladas with chicken to the strains of "La Paloma" on the accordian. L, D, daily. AE, MC, V.

Luby's Cafeterias. Many locations; see the Yellow Pages. Excellent cafeteria food. No credit cards. **Furr's** and **Marimont** are two other good cafeterias.

COUNTRY-AND-WESTERN MUSIC. One of Austin's unique assets is its music scene. Known for more than ten years as a "second Nashville" for country music, Austin also attracts top-quality performers from other musical spheres—rock 'n' roll, blues, jazz, and folk-ethnic. So many musicians live and work here that it's possible to find good live music in bars and clubs any night of the week. (See a selection in *Night Life,* below). Country music, of course, is at the heart of it all. In the early 1970s, Willie Nelson and his band moved back to Austin from Nashville; this marked the beginning of the migration to Austin of a host of superb country musicians and resulted in the birth of "progressive" country music. That music phenomenon has left its mark; you can still catch such well-known names as Jerry Jeff Walker, Michael Murphey, Gary P. Nunn, B. W. Stephenson, Ray Wylie Hubbard, and Kinky Friedman playing in bars around town. But the nationally known acts and the well-known names who choose to live and record here aren't what gives Austin its musical vitality and makes it such a wonderful place for music lovers—it's the corps of high-quality local performers who come from all parts of the country to live in Austin and play the bars and clubs.

NIGHT LIFE. Going out after dark in Austin usually means going to a bar to listen to live music. The only real "strip" of bars is on the length of East 6th St. from I–35 to Congress Ave. Also known as historic Old Pecan Street, this area has experienced a renaissance of growth in the past few years. Many new businesses have moved in and renovated the old buildings, and most of these businesses have been bars. One result is frequent traffic jams and unruly crowds on the street at night, especially on weekends. For mob-scene barhopping, this is still the place to go; but there are good alternatives. Austin has a selection of both traditional- and progressive-country-music clubs, some good rock 'n' roll and blues spots, and the occasional quiet, relaxing tavern. There is a smaller concentration of bar/restaurants on West 6th St. much farther west of Congress, around Lamar St.

Antone's. 2915 Guadalupe St.; 474–5314. This is the third location for Antone's, traditionally the best purveyor of class-act rhythm and blues—including Muddy Waters, B. B. King, and Bobby "Blue" Bland. Full bar, food.

The Broken Spoke. 3101 S. Lamar Blvd.; 442–6189. The granddaddy of old-fashioned country honkytonks, the Spoke has excellent regional dance bands on the weekends. Also serves food, with a great chicken-fried steak. Beer, wine, and setups. Checks accepted.

Cactus Cafe. In the University of Texas Student Union Building, west side of campus; 471–5651. Not a place you'd think to go honkytonking, but the Cactus Cafe and the Texas Tavern, also in the Union building, book good local and regional acts with a reasonable cover.

Continental Club. 1315 S. Congress Ave.; 443–7141. Leave your tie and heels at home; the CC is base for a crowd of old-time Austin music hippies and hangers-on. It's usually packed, the toilets leak, and the dance floor is way too small, but that's called "character." Good rock 'n' roll and blues. Full bar.

Double Eagle. 5337 Hwy 290W; 892–2151 for recording; 892–3452 for other information. A far south club that serves up large portions of solid country and country-rock. On a big night the parking lot is pick-um-up trucks as far as the eye can see. All major credit cards.

Flying Circus. 1025 Barton Springs Rd.; 478–4585. A beer garden smack up against the side of a hill that's starting to book some very good local talent. Lots of nice-looking people in here looking each over.

Hut's Drive-In. 807 W. 6th St.; 472–0693. Some of Austin's top bands play here, mostly rock and blues, and only on Thursday and Sunday nights. A smooth stucco interior, expansive bar, and small dance floor that's always being used. Full bar. AE, MC, V.

Liberty Lunch. 405 W. 2nd St.; 477–0461. A large, paved dance floor under the stars is the perfect showcase for bands from the '60s and local dance bands (the Mexican jazz of Beto y los Fairlanes, reggae by the Lotions). A colorful mural, full bar, and tables and chairs—all outdoors. MC, V.

Maggie Mae's. 323 E. 6th St.; 478–8541. Dart games upstairs and traditional folk music below; a hangout for soccer players, rugby players, and British Isles types far from home. You can get Guinness here for a hefty price, and there's an endless selection of imported brew. Seating is at a premium. Beer and wine. AE, MC, V.

Scholz Garten. 1607 San Jacinto; 477–4171. Scholz's has been going for so long that it's an Austin institution. Inside, it's a chicken-fried-steak diner; outside in the beer garden, tables are lined up under the trees and usually crowded with government workers and lawyers. Full bar; live music Thursday nights. MC, V.

The Shorthorn Lounge. 5500 N. Lamar Blvd; 451–5822. A relatively small place with an army of devoted regulars. Two-step to traditional country music. No urban cowboys here; this is the real thing. It's worth your trouble to watch for an appearance of the delightful Tommy Hancock and the Supernatural Family Band doing old country numbers, Spanish, Lubbock rockabilly, and purely idiosyncratic stuff. No credit cards.

Soap Creek Saloon. 1201 S. Congress; 443–1966. The third location for a beloved old hippy institution that has managed to survive by changing very gently with the times. Features folkies, country, ethnic, and old-time rockers. Live music nightly; no credit cards.

SAN ANTONIO

Spanish Missions, Mexican Marketplace, River Walk—and the Alamo

by
NANCY HASTON FOSTER

Nancy Haston Foster, a resident of San Antonio, writes a monthly column for San Antonio *magazine, is co-author of a guidebook on San Antonio, and author of another one on Texas missions.*

San Antonio is the city where other Texans go for a laid-back vacation without defecting from the Lone Star State.

That says something about this history-laden place. Ask most native Texans which is the most colorful, endearing town in the state, and they'll probably mention San Antonio, after a few obligatory remarks about their own hometown. For sightseeing and relaxed fun, San Antonio simply has more.

With its Mexican ambience, historic weathered Spanish missions, River Walk, and yes, that old firehorse of Texas independence, the Alamo, it is a natural haven for visitors and tourists. In fact, tourism is one of its major industries.

We can be grateful, however, that San Antonio has not yet been over-"tourized." Despite its share of "Nowhere else but San Antonio" T-shirts and Alamo souvenirs, the town itself doesn't suffer from a bad case of it.

It still retains a small-town flavor (though it isn't small, with its population of around 850,000 and a metro area of 1.3 million) with natural charm. It's less slick and commercialized than Dallas and Houston. It has won many a clean-city award, but it still has some respectable dirt and smells that waft from tiny shops hawking tacos and herbs.

But although many foreigners and Yankees come to San Antonio expecting to find a rip-snortin' dusty town with inebriated cowboys wandering about, this is far from the case.

San Antonio is your usual American metropolis with a few moderately tall buildings downtown ringed by freeways and sprawling suburbs, all ensconced on a fairly flat and rolling hill terrain with plenty of trees.

In short, viewed from the air or freeway, San Antonio looks much like other U.S. cities. But there the similarity ends. Once you visit downtown's River Walk, the centuries-old San José Mission, the festive Mexican Market, or the Retama Polo Center, you find that San Antonio most definitely is *not* an urban Xerox copy.

And delightfully so.

Will Rogers called San Antonio one of the four most unusual cities in America. No doubt some other cities might rise up on their hind legs to contest this, but old Will probably had something. San Antonio *is* a one of a kind.

What to See Downtown

To understand and savor San Antonio, start in the heart of downtown, on the River Walk. San Antonio is a river city, but not in the way you might expect.

The San Antonio River is no behemoth Missouri or even Allegheny. In fact, it's so narrow that it's barely navigable by small barges. That's the beauty of it. A little old lady could throw a Frisbee over it, and you can easily walk across the many rock bridges. The river meanders about downtown in such loops that you can't help encountering it. For about two miles on the river there are shops, restaurants, and landscaped parkland, close to river level, a full story lower than street level. This is labeled the River Walk, and many modern hotels overlook it or are nearby. It's a real treat to sit on your room balcony and watch the lively festivities on the river (though it's also a little more expensive than staying on the downtown fringe or farther out).

Walk up and down the River Walk. (The 400 block of East Commerce is a good starting point.) It has a cosmopolitan, European feel. Eat at one of the sidewalk cafés with umbrella-shaded tables and do what everybody else does on the river—people watch. The River Walk is a little like New Orleans, full of weirdly dressed characters and laced with conventional tourists and natives. Also sounds of music—Mexican mariachis playing their trumpets, jazz, or country-and-western. Aromas of spicy Mexican food or sizzling steaks add to the ambience.

Most nights you will hear amplified bongo drums and whistling in the vicinity of S. Alamo St. and Market St. off River Walk. This is Bongo Joe, a local character, who has been doing this for many years, He runs a good line of patter with the audience, too.

The Alamo

San Antonio is a very walkable town, at least downtown.

Once you've soaked up a little of the slower-paced lifestyle on the river, saunter on over to the Alamo. You can't come to San Antonio without seeing the biggest tourist attraction in the state.

The Alamo is just a couple of blocks east of the river. This is as pleasant a place as any to soak up some Texas tales and history. Even on a hot day, the shade trees and colorfully flowered grounds are an oasis. (See *Historic Sites* below.)

Prior to 1718 (considered to be San Antonio's founding date) Spaniards explored the area as early as 1691 and named the native river San Antonio de Padua, after St. Anthony of Padua. So San Antonio is old. And it has taken advantage of this, restoring many of its historic buildings.

From the Alamo, you have a multiple choice for sight-seeing.

You can continue walking about three blocks south on Alamo Street to HemisFair Plaza and other points in the downtown area (the farthest being about ten blocks) or take several modes of transportation. You can ride the city via motorized streetcars (only ten cents) or try the various tour buses that originate from the Alamo. Some of them, such as the streetcar tours, stop at places for you to shop and look.

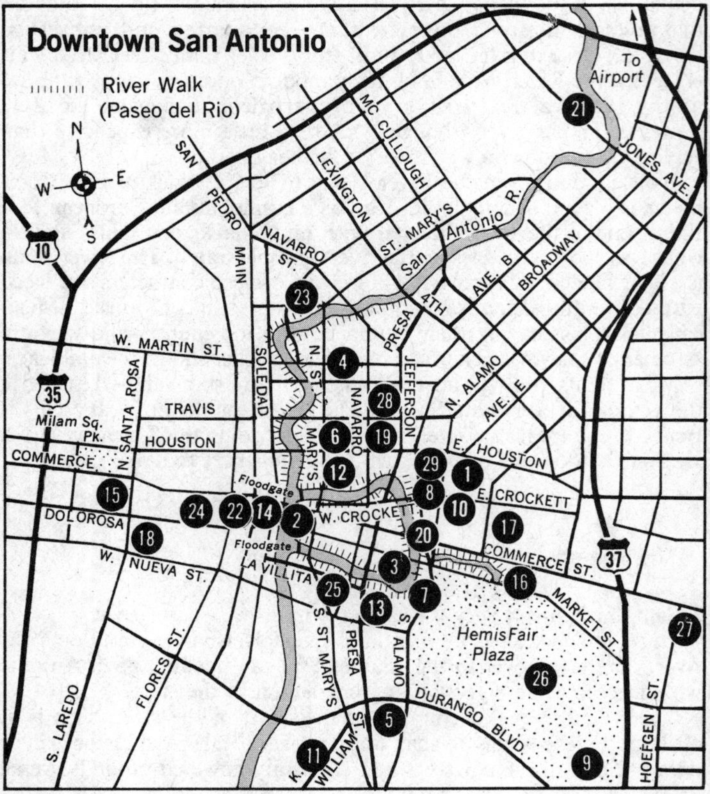

Points of Interest:

1) Alamo
2) MBank-Alamo Building
3) Arneson River Theater
4) Bus Station
5) Four Seasons Plaza Nacional
6) Gunter Hotel
7) Hilton Palacio Hotel
8) Hyatt Regency Hotel
9) Institute of Texan Cultures
10) Joske's
11) King William Historic Area
12) La Mansion Del Rio Hotel
13) La Villita
14) Main Plaza
15) Market Square
16) Marriott Hotel
17) Menger Hotel
18) Navarro State Historic Site
19) St. Anthony Inter-Continental Hotel
20) San Antonio Convention Center and Visitors Bureau
21) San Antonio Museum of Art
22) San Fernando Cathedral
23) Southwest Craft Center
24) Spanish Governor's Palace
25) Tower Life Building
26) Tower of the Americas
27) Train Station
28) Travis Park
29) Visitor Information Center

HemisFair Plaza

HemisFair Plaza, at Alamo and Market Streets, is a landscaped ninety-two-acre complex of convention buildings, Victorian houses, restaurants, shops, theaters, and museums. It was the site of the city's World's Fair celebration in 1968, celebrating San Antonio's 250th anniversary.

The most obvious landmark here is the Tower of the Americas, which juts 750 feet into the skyline and has a revolving restaurant at the top. You can get a spectacular panoramic view of the city while dining here—though, considering the food, just drinks might be sufficient—or go onto the observation deck for a cheaper one.

Don't miss the Institute of Texan Cultures or the San Antonio Museum of Transportation, both on the grounds of the plaza and good for children. The institute is a remarkably unboring museum, with colorful exhibits of the ethnic groups that settled Texas and of old country stores, dental offices, and so on. (This is also the site of the Texas Folklife Festival, a huge ethnic block party held for four days in early August that attracts thousands every year.)

The Museum of Transportation has many vintage autos, trolleys, horse-drawn carriages, and trains on display. Also in the area is the beautiful Lila Cockrell Theatre which has an extended arm of the San Antonio River at its doorstep. You can catch a performance of the San Antonio Symphony here, and there are many other major cultural attractions.

To revert back to some more history, just walk across South Alamo Street to La Villita.

La Villita

La Villita is a quaint restored village that dates back probably to the mid-1700's, though no one knows for sure. This little town grew up to house settlers other than the Franciscan fathers and soldiers who founded San Antonio. Some of the present restored adobe cottages date back at least to the 1830s and 1850s.

Walk through the stone streets with old-fashioned lamp posts and see artisans and artists plying their crafts and selling their wares. Antique shops, Mexican boutiques, and restaurants are harbored in the old buildings. La Villita is also the host site of the largest event of Fiesta, (SA's biggest annual celebration): "A Night in Old San Antonio," a giant block party with ethnic food, music, and dance around April 21st.

From La Villita, you might walk four blocks west to Main Plaza to view the beautiful Gothic San Fernando Cathedral, one of Texas' oldest

Catholic parish churches. Part of it dates back to the mid-1700s, though the outside structure was finished in 1873.

Then, just a block west on Commerce Street, you can glance in passing at the Spanish Governor's Palace, which dates back to 1749. Spanish governors ruling the Texas province sometimes lived here.

Market Square

Had enough history for a while? For the perfect antidote, head two more blocks west on Commerce Street and relax at Market Square. It's time for a little fiesta and some cool spirits anyway, particulary if it's a warm Texas day.

Market Square is a mini Mexican market, slightly "Anglo-ized," in downtown San Antonio. We doubt, for example, that you'd find air conditioning at real Mexican markets, but there are still enough of the aromas and festive atmosphere of Mexico to satisfy most gringos.

Market Square is a whole block of shops, restaurants, bars, art galleries, and of course El Mercado, a large building housing vendors hawking Mexican imports at reasonable prices. Stroll up and down the stone promenade, with its old-fashioned streetlights, and buy an obligatory sombrero or watch the colorful Mexican singers and dancers who frequently perform outside. Sit at one of the sidewalk cafés and drink a cool *cerveza* (beer) and down some native Tex-Mex food.

Exploring the Rest of Town

This is about as far as you would want to take a walking tour downtown, though conceivably you might hike over to the Southwest Craft Center, at Augusta Street and the San Antonio River, possibly using the River Walk. This peaceful respite from urbania is a complex of old French-architecture buildings built around 1851 as a Catholic girls' school, the Ursuline Academy. Now it houses artists and artisans giving lessons and selling their wares. Eat in their informal lunchroom or take a sandwich outside beneath the trees by the river.

It's best to rent a car or join one of the many tour buses to see the rest of San Antonio. The traffic isn't as bad or as furious as in some cities, so it's relatively easy to drive yourself. But do take a good map. Being such an old city, San Antonio is laid out haphazardly, and streets frequently make crazy abrupt turns. Don't be alarmed if you get lost; just ask for directions. Even the natives still get lost sometimes.

On the northern fringe of downtown is one of San Antonio's jewels. The San Antonio Museum of Art, a splendid combination of art exhibits in a renovated old Lone Star Brewery building. It has received national acclaim for its innovative use of old architecture; and it gets some of the really big touring exhibits that don't stop at other regional museums. Regular galleries include modern—and contemporary—art, earlier American art, early Texas furniture, and more.

This is just another example of how San Antonio has made use of its historic buildings instead of bulldozing them over, thanks in great part to the San Antonio Conservation Society, one of the oldest and most tenacious such groups in the country. In fact, folks come here from all over to see how conservation is done; witness the River Walk and the King William residential area.

The King William area of elegant old Victorian homes, also on the edge of downtown, but to the south, was the very first in the state to be zoned as a historic district. Amble along this yesterday neighborhood or take a horse-and-carriage ride (see *Tours* below) to soak up a little nostalgia. The houses here were built in the late 1800s by prominent German merchants, who made this San Antonio's first "wealthy neighborhood." One house, the Steves Homestead, is open to the public.

Missions

On the same side of town, the south, are the charming Spanish missions. These old stone structures give a striking feeling of another era. San Antonio is the only city in the country where you can see five eighteenth-century missions (the Alamo, downtown, was the original one, established in 1718) and bring alive most vividly Spain's attempt to colonize the New World at that time.

These four other missions, established from 1720 to 1731, comprise the San Antonio Missions National Historical Park and can be seen by driving and following the Mission Trail signs. All are within the city limits. The most notable one is Mission San José. The largest and probably most beautiful, San José has a care-forgotten pastoral setting to it. Besides browsing on the large grounds and in the various buildings and lovely chapel on a relaxing day, try to catch a colorful mariachi mass on Sunday at noon. If you've got the time, all the missions are worth seeing, with their exquisite bell towers and rustic Spanish-colonial architecture (see *Historic Sites,* below).

Other Attractions

What does San Antonio have to offer besides an overabundance of history? Plenty.

Polo, for instance. San Antonio has one of the world's best facilities for watching top-notch games, at the Retama Polo Center just outside northeast San Antonio.

Or parks and gardens. Drive out north of downtown on Broadway and enjoy 343-acre Brackenridge Park, where the renowned San Antonio Zoo is situated, along with riding stables (you can rent a horse), the Witte Museum (natural history and Texana), and Sunken Gardens. The 33-acre San Antonio Botanical Center, with its rustic setting of native Texas plants and old cabins that bely the usual dull hothouse gardens, isn't far away.

Just a little farther out in this same part of town is a don't-miss for art lovers, the McNay Art Museum, a private museum with a lot of treasures, such as paintings by Cezanne, Gauguin, and Picasso, along with western American art. A former estate, the Spanish buildings and grounds are worth seeing on their own account.

While out in this general area you might take a look at the neighborhoods: Alamo Heights, Terrell Hills, and Olmos Park are three older suburbs where "old family" San Antonio lives.

Like most cities, San Antonio has a mixed economic structure, with poorer Mexican barrios to the west, black sections in the east, and Anglos in the south. But the tables have been turned somewhat in recent years, with the so-called minority (Mexican-American) becoming in reality the majority and holding many of the elected governmental positions. But ethnicity is one of the things that makes this city unique. The Spanish, French, Germans, and Mexicans all had a hand in forging it, and remnants of their cultures have been retained in both architecture and festivals.

Fiesta

Fiesta, *the* big ten-day bash of the year held annually the week containing April 21, has a lot of Mexican influence, with mariachi music, *charreadas* (Mexican rodeos), and colorful costumes. Don't miss this Texas version of Mardi Gras if you go in for festivals, ethnic foods, dance, and parades. There are events going on all day for ten days all over the city.

Other big influences on San Antonio have been the military and the cattle business. There are five air-force and army bases that call it home and make the feds one of the biggest industries in town. Defending the territory and later the state and nation with forts, has been one of San Antonio's preoccupations ever since Spain first tried to protect its new real estate.

And yes, San Antonio once did look like the saloon town you see in movies, because it *was* a saloon town, where cattle drives converged. The Union Stock Yards are the oldest south of Kansas City. (Agribusiness is still a big industry here.) San Antonio was a bawdy and lively city in those days and to some extent still has a lot of that quality left.

San Antonio likes to have fun and enjoy life. And that's what most visitors find appealing about it. The slower-paced lifestyle inherited from the original Mexican inhabitants is comfortable.

So enjoy the city's vittles in its offbeat restaurants, its music and night life, its concerts in the downtown parks—whatever suits your fancy. But make it casual. The winters are mild, but the summers can be *muy caliente* (very hot), frequently in the 90s. Which more or less dictates cool, casual dress to go along with that casual lifestyle.

PRACTICAL INFORMATION FOR SAN ANTONIO

HOW TO GET THERE. San Antonio is in the south-central part of the state and easy to get to. Since Texas has such a good highway system and well-kept roadside parks, many people drive. But there are plenty of direct and connecting air flights from all over the country, as well as good bus linkage. There is limited train service.

By car. Excellent interstate freeways, including I–10 from Houston and I–35 from Dallas–Fort Worth and Austin.

The driving times to San Antonio from other cities, in hours, are: Austin, 1½; Dallas–Fort Worth, 5; El Paso, 12; Laredo, 3, Corpus Christi, 3; Houston, 3½.

By air. Mexicana, American, American Eagle, Continental, Delta, Eastern, Fort Worth Air, Ozark, Southwest, TWA, United, and U.S. Air. Regular daily limousine service between airport and downtown hotels.

By bus. Both Greyhound and Trailways have heavy schedules into San Antonio. The Greyhound terminal is at 500 N. St. Mary's; call 227–8351 for information. The Trailways terminal is at 301 Broadway; for information on Austin and Dallas–Fort Worth, call 226–6821; for Corpus Christi and the Rio Grande Valley, 226–7059; for Houston, 226–6970.

By train. Amtrak service from New Orleans, Los Angeles, and Chicago (all three times weekly) on superliner equipment. The Amtrak passenger station is at 1174 E. Commerce. For toll-free information call (800) 872–7245.

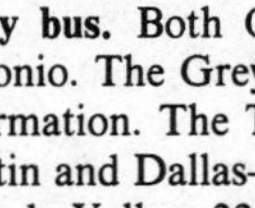

TELEPHONES. The area code for San Antonio and Bexar County is 512. If calling from outside San Antonio for directory assistance, call (512) 555–1212. If in San Antonio, just dial 1411. To see whether a business in San Antonio has a toll-free 800 number, dial 1–800–555–1212.

Points of Interest:

1) Alamo KOA Campground
2) Botanical Center
3) Brackenridge Park, including the San Antonio Zoo, Witte Museum, and Sunken Gardens.
4) Buckhorn Hall of Horns (Lone Star Brewery)
5) Concepcion Mission
6) Espada Mission
7) McNay Art Museum
8) North Star Mall
9) Pearl Brewery
10) San Jose Mission
11) San Juan Capistrano Mission
12) San Pedro Park
13) USAA Building
14) University of Texas Health Science Center at San Antonio

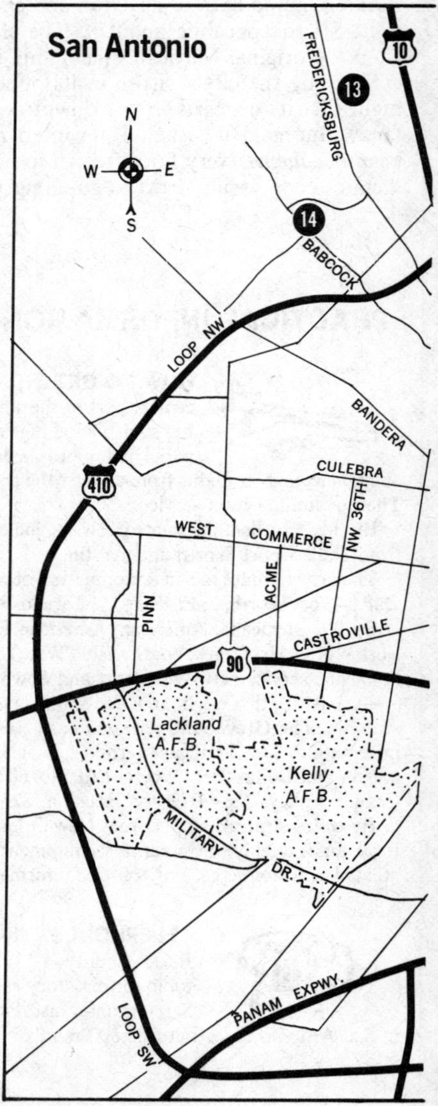

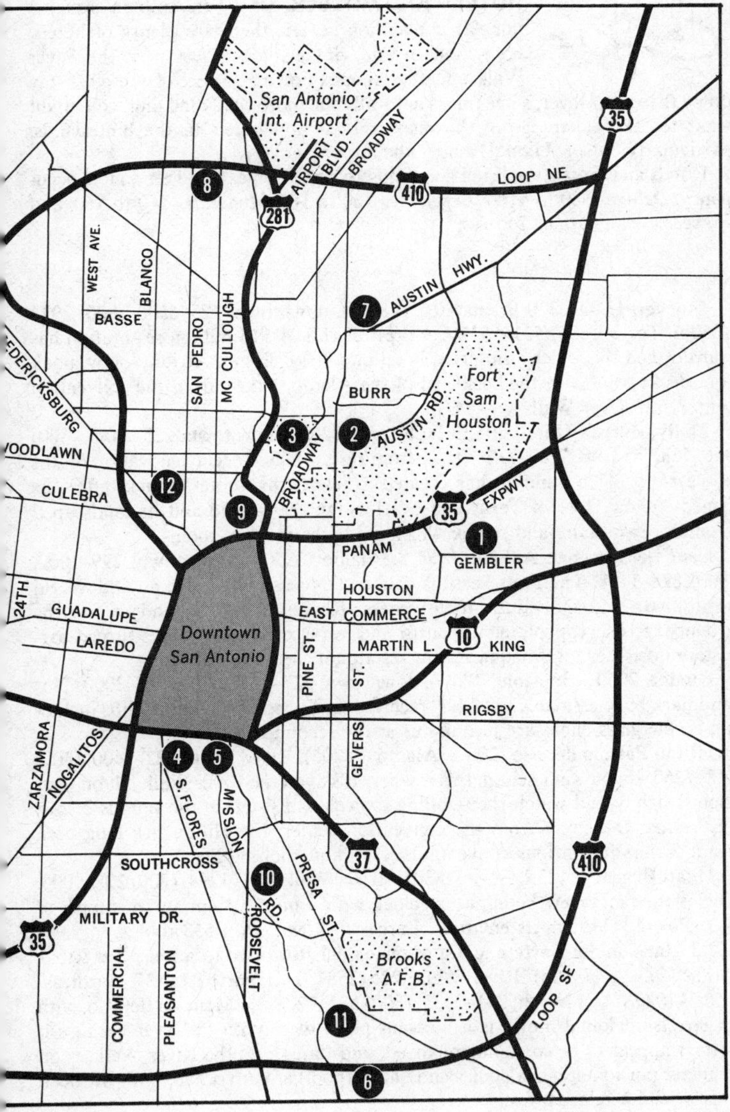
San Antonio
Int. Airport
AIRPORT BLVD.
BROADWAY
35
LOOP NE
410
281
8
WEST AVE.
BLANCO
AUSTIN HWY.
7
BASSE
SAN PEDRO
MC CULLOUGH
FREDERICKSBURG
Fort
Sam
Houston
BURR
AUSTIN RD
3
2
AUSTIN RD.
WOODLAWN
BROADWAY
12
CULEBRA
9
35
EXPWY.
1
PANAM
GEMBLER
HOUSTON
24TH
GUADALUPE
EAST COMMERCE
Downtown
San Antonio
10
LAREDO
MARTIN L.
KING
PINE ST.
ST.
RIGSBY
ZARZAMORA
NOGALITOS
4
5
GEVERS
S. FLORES
MISSION
37
410
SOUTHCROSS
10
PRESA
RD.
ST.
MILITARY DR.
35
ROOSEVELT
Brooks
A.F.B.
COMMERCIAL
PLEASANTON
LOOP SE
11
6

HOTELS AND MOTELS. Since San Antonio is such a popular convention center, there are plenty of hotels, both modern and vintage, downtown near the River Walk and the Alamo. For a real feel of the city, stay down there. However, since this is naturally the more costly lodging, you might want to take advantage of the many motels and hotels in the hinterlands, particularly out on Loop 410 near the airport.

Hotels and motels are listed according to price range, based on double occupancy: *Deluxe,* $80 to $130; *Expensive,* $60 to $80; *Moderate,* $40 to $60; and *Inexpensive,* less than $40.

Deluxe

Crockett Hotel. 320 Bonham St. (78205), downtown; 225–6500, (800) 292–1050 in Texas; (800) 531–5537 from rest of U.S. A $15 million restoration has transformed this older, utilitarian hotel into a stylish inn. Atrium lobby, pool, roof deck. Almost in the backyard of the Alamo, blocks from the convention center and River Walk.

Emily Morgan Hotel, 705 E. Houston (78205), downtown; 225–8486, (800) 356–5683 in Texas, (800) 824–6674 from rest of U.S. Recent renovation of this 60-year-old office building has created a new luxury hotel, named after the famed Yellow Rose of Texas and overlooking the Alamo and its landscaped grounds. Swimming and sauna; whirlpool baths in most rooms.

Four Seasons San Antonio. 555 S. Alamo (78205), downtown; 229–1000, (800) 828–1188. The Four Seasons deliberately sets out to give an Old World atmosphere and individual attentiveness. Rooms are large, and so are the grounds: greenery, pool, tennis courts, and restored historic-houses-turned-bar-restaurants. Elegant Anaqua Room restaurant, health club, sauna.

Gunter. 205 E. Houston (78205), downtown; 227–3241, (800) 531–3000. This landmark businessman's hotel has received an European flavor facelift, including a new glass enclosure jutting out at the second level.

Hilton Palacio del Rio. 200 S. Alamo (78205), River Walk; 222–1400, (800) 442–7260. If you want action, this is where it's at on the River Walk. Sit on your room balcony and watch the strolling crowds and listen to the sounds below. Just across the street from the convention center, the Hilton has long been headquarters for various conventions. Pool and roof garden.

Hyatt Regency. 123 Losoya (78205), River Walk; 222–1234, (800) 228–9000. This is the fancy new hotel on the block with a huge atrium and a snippet of river flowing through its environs. Largest in town, with 633 rooms.

La Mansion del Norte and **La Mansion del Rio.** Two locations. Del Rio is at 112 College (78205), River Walk; 225–2581. Del Norte is at 37 Northeast Loop 410 (78216), North; 341–3535, (800) 531–7208. La Mansion del Rio, with its Spanish-colonial motif, is a pleasant place to stay on the river because it doesn't appear to be so commercialized, and though on the River Walk, is on a quieter portion of it. Balconies and patios (pool) at both hotels, with Mexican music, lend a relaxed, festive air.

Marriott Hotel. 711 E. River Walk, on Market St. (78205); 224–4555, (800) 228–9290. Another modernistic, high-rise convention hotel, just across the street from the convention center. Atrium pool, sauna.

St. Anthony Inter-Continental San Antonio. 300 E. Travis (78205), downtown; 227–4392, (800) 327–0200. This is an old-line hostelry to which people have returned for its low-profile elegance. New owners have restored the 1909 hotel, retaining its antiques and live background music in the lobby around happy hour. New pool deck. Overlooks Travis Park.

Expensive

El Tropicano. 110 Lexington (78205), downtown; 223–9461. A frequent convention meeting ground. Pool.

Holiday Inn Airport. 77 Northeast Loop 410 (78216), north; 349–9900. (Toll free, call 800–HOLIDAY.) The Holiday Inn Airport is a new modern high-rise.

Marriott Inn. 611 Northwest Loop 410 (78216), north; 340–6060, (800) 228–9290. High-rise modern, not far from the airport.

Menger Hotel. 204 Alamo Plaza (78205), downtown; 223–4361, (800) 241–3848. You can't get any closer to the Alamo than this, right across the street. And you can't get any closer to Texas inn history than the Menger, which dates back to 1859. All sorts of folks, such as Teddy Roosevelt (who supposedly recruited his Rough Riders here in the bar), Robert E. Lee, Oscar Wilde, and Sarah Bernhardt stopped by here, *the* hotel in its heyday. Now it's not quite as posh, and unfortunately the owners haven't restored the original part of the old hotel to its former splendor. But it's still fun to stay here in the heart of things. Pool and patio.

Moderate

Best Western Northport Inn. 2635 Northeast Loop 410 (78217), northeast; 653–9110, (800) 528–1234. Pool and 24-hour restaurant.

Broadway Plaza. 1111 Northeast Loop 410 (78209), north; 828–9031. A modern high-rise motor hotel close to the airport. Entertainment in the bar.

Holiday Inns. *Holiday Inn Alamo,* 318 W. Durango (78207), downtown; 225–3211. *Holiday Inn Northeast,* 3855 N. Pan Am Expressway (78219), east; 226–4361. *Holiday Inn Northwest,* 6023 Northwest Expressway (78201), northwest; 732–5141; *Holiday Inn North-Airport,* 77 N.E. Loop 410 (78216), north; 349–9900.

Howard Johnson. 9603 I–35 North, (78233), northeast; 655–2120, (800) 654–2000. Motel with pool; 24-hour café.

Lexington. 4934 Northwest Loop 410 (78216), northwest; 680–3351, (800) 527–1877. Pool and kitchenettes. Not far from the medical center.

Oak Hills Motor Inn. 7401 Wurzbach (78229), northwest; 696–9900. Next to the South Texas Medical Center, therefore convenient for medical meetings and patients' relatives.

La Quinta Motor Inns. *La Quinta Airport East,* 333 Northeast Loop 410 (78216), north; 828–0781. *La Quinta Airport West,* 219 Northeast Loop 410 (78216), north; 342–4291. *La Quinta Downtown,* 1001 E. Commerce (78205), downtown; 222–9181. *La Quinta Market Square,* 900 Dolorosa (78207); 222–

9181. *La Quinta Lackland,* 6511 Military Dr. W. (78242), west; 674–3200. *La Quinta South,* 7202 S. Pan Am Expressway, south; 922–2111. *La Quinta Turtle Creek,* 9542 I–10 West (78230), northwest; 690–8810. *La Quinta Vance Jackson,* 5922 Northwest Expressway (78201), northwest; 734–7931. *La Quinta Windsor Park,* 6410 I–35 North (78218), northeast; 653–6619.

Ramada Inns. *Ramada Inn Airport,* 333 Northwest Loop 410 (78216), north; 344–4581. *Ramada Inn North,* 1131 Austin Hwy. (78209), northeast; 824–1441, (800) 228–2828. The Ramada Inn Airport is near shopping malls and close to the airport.

Sheraton San Antonio. 1400 Austin Hwy. (78209), northeast; 824–5371, (800) 325–3535. Includes a 21-acre conference center with pools, tennis courts, 9-hole golf course.

Texian Inns. *Texian Inn Downtown,* IH-10 at Houston St. (78207), downtown; 225–1111. *Texian Inn Northwest,* IH 10 at Wurzbach (78240), northwest; 690–8000, (800) 531–1000.

TraveLodges. *TraveLodge on the River,* 100 Villita (78205), downtown; 226–2271. *TraveLodge Northwest,* 9806 I–10 West (78230), northwest; 696–0810, (800) 255–3050.

Inexpensive

Best Western Inns. *Best Western Continental,* 9735 I-35 North (78233), northeast; 655–3510. *Best Western Town House,* 942 Northeast Loop 410 (78209), north; 826–6311, (800) 528–1234.

Motel 6. 9503 IH-35N, northeast; 653–7320.

Rodeway Inns. *Rodeway Inn Downtown,* 900 N. Main (78212), downtown; 223–2951. *Rodeway Inn Wonderland,* 6804 Northwest Expressway (78201), northwest; 734–7111, (800) 228–2000.

Town & Country. 6901 San Pedro (78216), north; 344–4511. Pools, restaurant.

Warren Inn. 5050 Fredericksburg Rd., northwest; 342–1179. Kitchenettes in all rooms.

HOW TO GET AROUND. Most of Texas is a car society, and San Antonio is no exception. Most folks like to see the city by car, particularly if they want to see sites outside of downtown. But on the other hand, San Antonio has so much to do and see downtown that you can do very well by staying there and walking or taking the VIA motorized streetcar (fare 10¢), which stops at downtown tourist sites every few minutes. Most sites (but not the missions) are within a very reasonable walking distance.

However, if you want to drive yourself or let someone else do it, there are many national auto-rental companies at the airport, and the public bus system VIA (227–2020) is a very good one that goes to all areas of the city. VIA costs only 40¢ within Loop 410 or 75¢ for express buses. Taxi fare rates are $2.45 for the first mile, $1.00 for each additional mile.

From the airport. A taxicab to the downtown hotels, down McAllister Fwy, will cost about $11.00 plus tip, a 15-minute ride. A VIA limousine service does the same for $5.00. Or the VIA express bus leaves for the downtown hotel area every 45 minutes from 6:00 A.M. to 8:00 P.M. for 75¢.

TOURIST INFORMATION. Get free brochures and information from the Visitor Information Center at 317 Alamo Plaza (downtown, right across from the Alamo), open daily; 299–8155. Or write ahead to the San Antonio Convention & Visitors Bureau, P.O. Box 2277, San Antonio, TX 78298; 299–8123. Toll-free in Texas, 800–292–1010; from the rest of the U.S. toll-free, 800–531–5700.

SEASONAL EVENTS. Check the exact dates of all of these events with the Convention and Visitors Bureau (see above).

January. Look for the *Sport and Boat Show* at the Convention Center. Things start going western with the *Great Country River Festival,* a freebie country-and-western-music event held at Arneson River Theater on the River Walk downtown. Nonstop music outdoors with big-name artists. **February.** The ten-day San Antonio *Livestock Show and Rodeo* at Freeman Coliseum. **March** is the time for all good Irishmen to celebrate Saint Patrick's Day with the river dyed green for the occasion.

April. *Fiesta* is the biggest festival held in San Antonio, rather akin to Mardi Gras, but a Mexican version. It lasts ten days, always around April 21 (San Jacinto Day). The town comes alive with parades, live entertainment, ethnic festivals, sports events, Mexican rodeos, etc. The Battle of Flowers is the big parade, but the River Parade is one of the more unusual. Don't miss "A Night in Old San Antonio," a giant block party held in quaint La Villita, with good ethnic foods cooked right there—and foot-stomping live music. But beware; it's spelled "crowded." Go early.

May ushers in *Cinco de Mayo* (May 5), a Mexican holiday celebrated big in San Antonio, particularly at Market Square, with music and food. *Armed Forces Week* also falls in May. What with five bases, the military is *in* in San Antonio. Tours of the bases and their military museums, and an air show at Randolph AFB. **June.** The highly acclaimed *San Antonio Festival,* three weeks of performing and creative arts events throughout the city (overlaps from May to June). In June, July, and August, the *Fiesta Noche del Rio* has three shows of Latin music and dance weekly at the Arneson River Theater (Tues., Fri., Sat.). And the river is also the June site of the two-day *Stroh-ling Down the River Celebration,* with beaucoup free band entertainment.

July. Naturally July 4th isn't ignored. Market Square is jumping, and the military bases have fireworks displays. **August** brings in another big urban block party, the *Texas Folklife Festival,* held for four days at the Institute of Texan Cultures at HemisFair Plaza. Ethnic food, dance, and crafts. Then there's *Semana de las Misiones,* a week-long commemoration of the historic missions, with tours and a fair, and the *Carver Jazz Festival,* a rare delight of big-name jazz entertainers held at Carver Community Center.

September. *Diez y Seis de Septiembre* (September 16) is celebrated in style for a week (this is Mexico's version of July 4th) with many events, including La Feria del Rio. **October** seems to be ethnic month with the *Greek Funstival* and *Oktoberfest* going on. Also the *Texas Open PGA Golf Tournament* and the *River Art Show.* **November.** A fairly slow month for festivals, but look for Spurs' basketball games (NBA) and San Antonio Symphony performances.

December is a delightful time to be in San Antonio; it's full of colorful Mexican traditions. Try the *Fiesta Navidena* in El Mercado at Market Square, with Mexican music, foods, and *Piñata* parties. Then don't miss *Fiesta de las Luminarias* on the River Walk. That's when it's all lit up with candles in paper sacks at night. Or *Las Posadas* (with candle-bearing singers), also on the River Walk. And then top it all off by watching the outdoor production of *Los Pastores,* a Christmas pageant at Mission San José. *¡IFeliz Navidad!*

TOURS. There are numerous sightseeing tours available in San Antonio. The mode depends upon your whims and your time. Besides bus, there are carriage, river barge, and streetcar.

City tours. Naturally *VIA Gray Line* (227–5251) offers several bus tours, ranging from 2¼ hours to an all-day one (7¼ hours). One tour covers the Alamo and the missions; another Brackenridge Park, Fort Sam Houston, Sunken Gardens, McNay Art Institute; and another La Villita, El Mercado, San Fernando Cathedral, the King William district, and the Lone Star Brewery Museum. Others are combinations of these, with the all-day tour taking in the whole works. Prices run from $7.75 to $21.50. (*VIA* also has Express streetcars that leave on the hour on Saturdays and Sundays and shuttle to downtown and Brackenridge Park sites for one price. $4, adults.)

Get a breath of fresh air by taking the 1907 trolley (San Antonio Trolley System; 533–3992) for a 50-minute tour of downtown and King William ($3.50). All the above tours leave from in front of the Alamo, and information can be found there. The trolleys usually leave on the half-hour daily roughly between midmorning and late afternoon.

Off-beat tours. How about horse-and-carriage rides? Several leave from in front of the Alamo daily, mornings and evenings. Most charge around $15–20 per couple for ½ hour, more for the tour of King William district. One of the services, Yellow Rose, can be reached at 225–6490. And then there's the San Antonio River Tour on barges along the scenic River Walk. Tours leave every fifteen minutes daily, roughly between 10:00 A.M. and 8:00 P.M. (9:00 A.M.–10:30 P.M. in the summer) at the Paseo del Rio boat dock across from the Hilton Hotel at Commerce Street. $1.25.

SPECIAL-INTEREST SIGHTSEEING. This section includes those sightseeing spots not covered in other sections such as *Historic Sites* or *Museums.*

Heart of Texas Show. This color multimedia show, at 307 Alamo Plaza, may help give you a handle on what Texas is all about, down to the sound of rattlesnakes. Open daily 10:00 A.M. to 6:00 P.M.; shows 11:00 A.M. to 5:00 P.M., on the hour. Adults, $3.25; children, $1.50; 222–2400.

Lone Star Brewery and Buckhorn Hall of Horns. Yes, this is the home of the Lone Star Beer trucks that help keep Texas happy. It also houses exhibits of stuffed wildlife, fish, and birds; plus the old Buckhorn Saloon and O. Henry's house, both relocated at 600 Lone Star Blvd. Open daily, 9:30 A.M. to 5:00 P.M. Adults, $2.00; children $1.00; 226–8301. Beer samples, of course. Plant tours on a limited basis.

Military Base Tours. Most of the air force and army bases are open to the public, except *Kelly Air Force Base,* which does, however, schedule tours; 925–7951. *Fort Sam Houston* is an old historic base with several military museums; 221–1211. And *Brooks Air Force Base* has its Hanger 9 Museum plus the Aerospace Medical Division; for tours call 536–2203. *Lackland Air Force Base* (671–2907), with its older World War II planes on display, and *Randolph Air Force Base* (652–1110) are also worth a drive through.

Pearl Brewery. 312 Pearl Parkway; 226–0231. No plant tours, but you can get a free beer at their Jersey Lilly (sic) hospitality center and see the replica of Judge Roy Bean's old saloon and courthouse. Monday through Friday 10:00 A.M. to 4:00 P.M. Free.

USAA Building. Does *big* impress you? Try the nation's second-largest office building; the 3.1-million-sq.-ft. headquarters of United Services Automobile Association. Call first to join weekly public tours; 690–2335. 9800 Fredericksburg Road.

UT Health Science Center at San Antonio. There is always lots going on at this University of Texas medical school and research center. Take a self-guided tour or arrange for group ones at 691–6327. 7703 Floyd Curl Drive.

RIVER WALK (PASEO DEL RIO). This is what makes San Antonio San Antonio, what makes natives and tourists alike keep coming back downtown: the River Walk, a two-mile landscaped, parklike area following the San Antonio River's course with shops, sidewalk restaurants, art galleries, and bars alongside. La Villita borders the Walk at the Arneson River Theater.

All this is below street level amid tall trees and blooming greenery, giving a relaxed but cosmopolitan atmosphere. Drink a cool longneck beer at one of the sidewalk cafés and join the other people oglers watching the parade of humanity saunter by. River Walk is not quite as weird as some promenades in New Orleans or San Francisco but nevertheless has a polyglot flavor of politicians rubbing elbows with artists and "river people" alike.

The River Walk is awake 24 hours, turning from daytime languid to nighttime lively, with Irish ditties or jazz and—naturally—country-and-western music wafting about. The river is romantic all lit up at night, particularly at Christmastime, when it is lined with candle-lit paper sacks (this is the Fiesta de las Luminarias). Look for seasonal events such as the River Art Show and the Great Country River Festival on the river. And during the summer, there is live Mexican entertainment at the outdoor Arneson River Theater on Tuesday, Friday, Saturday, and Sunday nights.

How to get to the River Walk? You can't miss it; the little San Antonio River twists and turns all around downtown. There are numerous steps down at various bridges. Perhaps the most obvious ones are at Commerce and Losoya and next to the Hilton Palacio del Rio Hotel.

Don't miss the boat tour rides (see the *Tours* section), and for information about the River Walk call the San Antonio River Association (227–4262) or read their monthly newspaper *Showboat,* distributed in hotels and shops.

HEMISFAIR PLAZA. This is a 92-acre complex downtown at 200 South Alamo that comprises all sorts of facilities, including the convention center, restaurants, shops, and museums. Its most visible landmark is the 750-foot *Tower of the Americas,* where, if acrophobia and glass elevators don't bother you, you can see the circumference of the city from the observation deck. Open 10:00 A.M. to 11:00 P.M., daily. Adults, $1; children, 50¢. (There is also a revolving restaurant in the top of the tower.)

Stroll around the plaza; it's landscaped and has some renovated old homes retained when the city redid this area for its 1968 World's Fair, celebrating San Antonio's 250th birthday. The interesting *Institute of Texan Cultures* is housed here, as well as the *San Antonio Museum of Transportation* and the *Mexican Cultural Institute* (see *Museums*). Also the *sports arena* and the elegant *Lila Cockrell Theatre,* where the San Antonio Symphony plays and other cultural events are held. And that old standby the *Melodrama Playhouse & Saloon.* (Throw in some college branches and federal buildings, and you've got the HemisFair Plaza.) Call 299–8570 for information. The area is open at all times.

PARKS. San Antonio has dozens of parks and plazas to relax in, the most notable and popular being *Brackenridge Park,* at 3800 Broadway, northeast of downtown. This comfortably aged park has a skyride, a golf course, riding stables, a daily miniature-railroad ride for the kiddies, a zoo, and hiking paths. Sunken Gardens and the Witte Museum are also there. Brackenridge is the site of the underground springs that are the source of the San Antonio River.

Adjoining Brackenridge Park is Koehler Park (pronounced "K-ler"). Koehler, the founder of the Pearl Brewery, was outraged that old Brackenridge donated his park with the stipulation that no alcoholic beverages be served in it, so Koehler gave more parkland to the city with the stipulation that drinking such must never be prohibited in *his* park.

Another park of interest is *San Pedro* (1500 San Pedro), an oldie, possibly the second oldest municipal playground in the U.S. Both of these parks are open seven days, and entry is free. Or for unspoiled wilderness, try the newer *Friedrich Park,* 230 acres devoted to a sanctuary for wildlife and plant life; it has seven nature trails. A few miles north of town just off I–10 on Milsa Road; 299–3211. Open Wednesday through Sunday, 9:00 A.M. to 5:00 P.M.

NATIONAL PARKS. The *San Antonio Missions National Historical Park* includes the separate sites of four 18th-century missions built by the colonizing Spanish and the Catholic church. (The Alamo is the fifth, but it is operated as a state historic site.) They're all within the city limits and can be toured by following the signs marked "Mission Trail." (See the *Historic Sites* section for more details.) No camping or lodging facilities.

ZOO. Big kids and little ones alike will find the *San Antonio Zoo* much fun. It's one of the top ten in the nation, with around 3,000 specimens, and its homey, natural terrain with rock walls and streams makes it a good place to spend the day. Take an elephant ride and visit the animal nursery. In Brackenridge Park at 3903 N. Saint Mary's; 734–7183. Open daily, 9:30 A.M. to 5:00 P.M., but till 6:30 P.M. in the summer. Adults, $3.00; children, $1.00.

GARDENS. To see what the flora of Texas are all about, take in the *San Antonio Botanical Center.* This 33-acre center probably has the best collection of native plants in the state. This is no hothouse garden; it shows the realistic landscape of various sections of Texas, even down to a log cabin and "lake" for East Texas. Trails for hiking and viewing, plus formal gardens. Open Wednesday through Sunday, 9:00 A.M. to 6:00 P.M. Adults, $1.25; children, 50¢. 555 Funston Place; 821–5115.

The *Sunken Gardens* in Brackenridge Park at 3800 N. Saint Mary's are more traditional, in the Oriental vein. Lush greenery and blooms, with stone bridges and pools. Open daily during daylight hours. Free.

CAMPING. For outdoorsy types, there's an Alamo KOA Kampground with a good midtown location at 602 Gembler Road; 224–9296. Tent sites ($11.75 for two people) and trailer/RV hookups ($14.25 for two people). Swimming pool, laundry, playgrounds, showers and restrooms, fishing. City golf course next door.

HUNTING. Obviously you can't go loaded for bear right in San Antonio; it's no longer the wild, wild west. But many ranching facilities in surrounding counties are open to the public for hunting. Besides the usual deer in season, many ranches stock exotic game for year-round hunting. Call the Kerrville County Chamber of Commerce at (512) 896–1155 and the Bandera Chamber of Commerce at (512) 796–4312 for information (both areas are part of the Hill Country to the northwest of San Antonio).

PARTICIPANT SPORTS. With all the wide-open space, Texans take their outdoor sports seriously. That's why you'll find a lot of good golf courses and tennis courts. **Golf:** Four city-owned championship courses and one private course are open to the public. Look in the Yellow Pages under Golf Courses–Public (Municipal) for phones. **Tennis:** Many courts across town in the parks, but the McFarlin Tennis Center at 1503 San Pedro (732–1223) is the largest. Fee. **Swimming:** 21 pools in various city parks, with the indoor San Antonio Natatorium being a nice facility at 1430 W. Durango; 226–8541.

Try Brackenridge and McAllister Parks for **jogging** and the stables at Brackenridge for **horseback riding** ($8 an hour). Or if you're a **skeet and trap** enthusiast, call up the National Gun Club; 688–3291.

SPECTATOR SPORTS. The biggie professional sport in San Antonio is basketball, and the Spurs. Led by the "Iceman" George Gervin, the NBA Spurs play in the Convention Center Arena from October through April. For baseball, try the San Antonio Dodgers, a class-AA Texas League team that plays at V. J. Keefe Field. A pro football team, the San Antonio Gunslingers, competes in the USFL. Then there are also auto racing (Alamo Dragway), the PGA Texas Open in October, the annual San Antonio Livestock Show Rodeo in February, and world-class competition at the Pentathlon Center at Fort Sam Houston. And for horsin' around, look to the plush Retama Polo Center for international matches, and the fascinating *charreadas,* or Mexican rodeos, held at the San Antonio Charro Association Ranch. See newspapers for details of these activities during your visit.

CHILDREN'S ACTIVITIES. *Brackenridge Park,* at 3800 Broadway, is a good place to start with the kids. It has the excellent San Antonio Zoo (see above), a riding stable (732–8881), a skyride (732–8481), and a miniature railroad (735–8641). Then there's the *San Antonio Museum of Transportation* (226–5544), with classic cars, and the *Hertzberg Circus Collection* (299–7810), both downtown. Or try San Antonio College's *Planetarium* (733–2910) and its Sunday-evening shows. The *Buckhorn Hall of Horns* and the *military museums* at Lackland Air Force Base, Brooks Air Force Base, and Fort Sam Houston are also good possibilities (see *Special-Interest Sightseeing,* above). Two caves are only about 15 mi. from San Antonio: Natural Bridge Caverns near I–35 (512–651–6101) and Cascade Caverns near I–10 (512–755–9285). The *Institute of Texan Cultures* will interest even non-Texan youngsters, with its live demonstrations. HemisFair Plaza; 226–7651.

HISTORIC SITES. *Downtown Area:* **The Alamo.** Texas' biggest historic tourist attraction is situated conveniently downtown on Alamo Plaza and Alamo St. (what else?). You'll recognize the weathered old stone structure easily. It's been called variously the shrine or cradle of Texas liberty, and it did stir up things in Texas' fight for independence from Mexico in 1836. On March 6, 1836, some 188 defenders (including Jim Bowie and Davy Crockett) died here, under the onslaught of General Santa Anna's army of several thousand men. This led to Texans later yelling at the Battle of San Jacinto, near Houston, "Remember the Alamo!"—and winning the war.

The Alamo was first established in 1718 as Mission San Antonio de Valero at another location in San Antonio, eventually moving to its present location in the 1720s. The chapel building and barracks are all that is left of the original mission and fort. The grounds are peaceful, and colorful plants bloom year-round. Attractions include a museum, slide shows, and a souvenir shop. Free admission and guided tours. Open Monday through Saturday, 9:00 A.M. to 5:30 P.M.; Sunday, 10:00 A.M. to 5:30 P.M.; 225–1391.

La Villita. Just a few blocks south of the Alamo on Alamo St. is this old restored village dating back several hundred years. After the missions were founded in San Antonio settlers began to build adobe homes nearby in this "little village," and a few still remain. Now it's full of art galleries, shops, and artisans and is a frequent site for fiestas, or festivals. Quaint place for strolling; may be reached from the River Walk up a long flight of steps. Area open at all times. Free.

Bexar County Courthouse. on Main Plaza cast an eye toward this 1890s courthouse, a marvelous example of Romanesque architecture built in pink (red) granite and sandstone.

San Fernando Cathedral. This centuries-old church is where Santa Anna raised the flag of no quarter during the Alamo siege. Founded by the original Canary Island colonists, the lovely old cathedral at 114 Military Plaza is open daily, still in use.

Spanish Governor's Palace. Nearby the cathedral is this 1749 remnant of Spanish architecture, called the governor's palace. Though perhaps not the actual home of Spanish governors, it did house local officials. It is well restored, with period furnishings and an inviting courtyard and fountain. At 105 Plaza de Armas; 224–0601. Adults, 50¢; children, 25¢. Open 9:00 A.M. to 5:00 P.M., Monday through Saturday; 10:00 A.M. to 5:00 P.M., Sunday.

Navarro State Historic Site. A restored home of an early Texas patriot. At 228 S. Laredo; 226–4801. Circa 1850; includes the home, kitchen, and office. Open 10:00 A.M. to 4:00 P.M., Tuesday through Saturday. Adults, $1.00; children, 25¢.

Old Ursuline Academy (Southwest Craft Center). Don't miss these picturesque old French buildings built by the Ursuline Sisters in 1851 as the city's first school on the San Antonio River. Restored, it's now the Southwest Craft Center at 300 Augusta, where creative artisans work, sell, and teach classes in pottery, weaving, etc. See the beautiful Gothic chapel and brownbag it in the pleasant courtyard. (Or eat at their informal Copper Kitchen, weekdays for lunch.) Open roughly 10:00 A.M. to 4:00 P.M. Monday through Friday, til 3:00 P.M. on Saturday. 224–1848.

MISSIONS AND OTHER CITY AREAS

San Antonio Missions National Historical Park. This is one of the unique features of San Antonio. The city is almost embarrassingly endowed with Spanish Catholic missions, five of them. The Alamo, or Mission San Antonio de Valero, was the first to be founded, in 1718. Four more followed, and they're the ones included in this national park, on the "Mission Trail." The missions were built by the Spanish to colonize the New World in the early 18th century, and each compound included a church, residences, trade schools, and granary in a fortified square. They were made mainly of adobe and native stone, and even today they operate as parish churches. With their peaceful grounds, they survive in the south part of town as remnants of a long-ago past of Spanish life and architecture. To follow the Mission Trail signs, go south on S. Alamo (beginning at Market Street). If your time is limited, see at least Mission San José. Missions' hours are 9:00 A.M. to 6:00 P.M., daily; no admission. 229–6000.

Mission Concepción. Established here in 1731 and the oldest unrestored Texas mission. Has twin towers and some original frescoes. At 807 Mission Road.

Mission San José. This is the flagship of the missions, the largest and most beautiful. Here you can best picture what life was like then. The beautifully carved church (with "Rosa's Window") is surrounded by the Indian quarters, with the *acequia* (aqueduct) to bring water from the San Antonio River to irrigate the fields. The harvest was stored in the granary. If possible, attend the beautiful mariachi mass at noon on Sundays. At 3200 block of Roosevelt Ave. and Mission Road; 922–2731.

Mission San Juan Capistrano. At 9101 Graf, this is very peaceful and quaint, with the church's open bell tower a good photo subject. Established here in 1731; much of the original square is preserved.

Mission San Francisco de la Espada. Referred to as Mission Espada, it's on the edge of town at 10040 Espada, giving it a feel for the remoteness of mission life. Be sure to see the Espada Aqueduct, about 1½ mi. north of the mission, between it and Mission San Juan. This unusual irrigation system, dating back to 1731–40, may be the oldest in the U.S. still in use.

King William Historic Area. This elegant late-1800s Victorian residential neighborhood to the south of downtown has been restored. One house, the Steves Homestead, at 509 King William, is open to the public for a fee, but only during certain hours; call 225–5924.

Yturri-Edmunds Home and Mill. At 257 Yellowstone; 534–8237 or 224–6163. A circa 1840–60 adobe-block structure and restored grist mill. Guided tours and demonstrations. Small fee.

Fort Sam Houston and Quadrangle. This historic fort, still in use, is worth driving around in. Mamie and Ike Eisenhower met and lived here. And Geronimo was once confined here in the quadrangle—now a good place for a picnic, what with the tame deer, peacocks, and ducks wandering around. Main gate at New Braunfels and Grayson; 221–1211. Open daily.

MUSEUMS. San Antonio Museum of Art. The museum's unusual abode is one of San Antonio's pride and joys and has received national recognition for historic preservation. This complex of buildings at 200 W. Jones Avenue, built at the turn of the century, used to be the Lone Star Brewery. Booze was transformed well into art; this museum is now one of the top ones in the country, receiving the larger traveling exhibits such as the renowned "Pre-Colombian Art of Costa Rica." Check ahead to see what national touring exhibit may be there during your visit. Regular galleries include contemporary and Modern Art (with the likes of Hans Hofmann and Frank Stella), and 18th- and 19th-century art with American works by Benjamin West, John Singleton Copley, Gilbert Stuart, and Edward Hicks. Other standing exhibits are early Texas furniture and decorative arts, pre-Colombian art, photography, and Spanish colonial art. Gift and snack shops. Open 10:00 A.M. to 5:00 P.M., Tuesday, Wednesday, Friday, and Saturday; Thursday till 9:00 P.M.; Sunday, 12 noon to 5:00 P.M. (In summer, open till 6:00 P.M.) through Sunday. Adults, $3; children, $1. 226–5544. (Note: A ticket into any of San Antonio's three city museums, the Museum of Art, Witte, or the Museum of Transportation, gets you into the other two free that day).

From 1913 to 1933 a streetcar ran past the building that now houses the museum. An old streetcar, called the **"Old 300,"** has been lovingly restored and now makes a run from the museum to the Pearl Brewery and back. This very slow ride, which operates twice a day weekdays and six times a day weekends, is free for museum ticket holders. This ride does not operate Monday.

McNay Art Museum. This is another fine art museum in an unusual setting, the old Spanish-style estate of Marian Koogler McNay, which includes spacious grounds. This private museum at 6000 N. New Braunfels, has a lot of biggies on display: Cezanne, Gauguin, Picasso, van Gogh, and El Greco, for example. There is also an extensive print collection. Charming patio and gardens. Open 9:00 A.M. to 5:00 P.M., Tuesday through Saturday; 2:00 to 5:00 P.M., Sunday. Free. 824–5368.

Institute of Texan Cultures. This is one museum that is fun to go to; even the kids won't be bored. Located in HemisFair Plaza at the corner of Bowie and Durango streets, it's chockful of colorful exhibits of the ethnic groups that settled Texas, plus such restorations as an old dental office, a post office, and a general store. There are also live demonstrations at the teepee, the loom, and the sharecropper's cabin. Media show. Open 9:00 A.M. to 5:00 P.M., Tuesday through Sunday. Free. 226–7651.

Museum of Transportation. Spiffed-up old classic cars, plus carriages, stagecoaches, and a trolley at this museum at HemisFair Plaza. Open 10:00 A.M. to 5:00 P.M., Tuesday, Wednesday, Friday, and Saturday; Thursday till 9:00 P.M.; Sunday, 12 noon to 5:00 P.M. (In summer open till 6:00 P.M.) Adults, $3; children, $1. 226–5544.

Witte Museum. Pronounced "Witty." In Brackenridge Park at 3801 Broadway. Features Indian, dinosaur, natural-history, and Texas exhibits, with log cabins on the grounds. Open 10:00 A.M. to 5:00 P.M., Tuesday, Wednesday, Friday, and Saturday; Thursday till 9:00 P.M.; Sunday, 12 noon to 5:00 P.M. (In summer open till 6:00 P.M.) Adults, $3; children, $1.

Hertzberg Circus Collection. On the corner of S. Presa and W. Market Sts., downtown; 299–7810. Lots of circus memorabilia for big-top fans. Posters, photos, costumes. Open 9:00 A.M. to 5:30 P.M., Monday through Saturday (and on Sundays 1:00 to 5:00 P.M., May through October). Free 299–7810.

Military Museums. Several of the local bases have small, interesting museums. *Fort Sam Houston:* both a military museum (221–6117) and an army medical museum (221–2358). *Brooks Air Force Base:* Hangar 9 Museum (536–2203). *Lackland Air Force Base:* history and traditions museum and *real* older jets and World War II planes at the parade ground for close-up viewing (671–2907).

Mexican Cultural Institute. Exhibits contemporary Mexican and South American artists. HemisFair Plaza, 9:00 A.M. to 6:00 P.M., Monday through Friday; till 5:00 P.M. Saturday and Sunday. 227–0123.

MUSIC AND DANCE. If you go for lively music and dance, you're in the right place. Naturally, the emphasis in festivals and casual entertainment is on Mexican or country-and-western music. But there's plenty of classical music. The *San Antonio Symphony,* based at the Lila Cockrell Theatre in HemisFair Plaza, performs regularly between September and May, including pops and park concerts; 223–5591. The *San Antonio Performing Arts Association* brings in top names such as Nureyev, Perlman, and the Joffrey Ballet. There are also the *San Antonio Choral Society,* the *Texas Bach Choir,* and several chamber-music groups; check the newspaper for times and places. And look for the free Brown Bag Days concerts in downtown parks, at noon weekly from April through September.

Three weeks of performing and creative arts events throughout the city mark the renowned *San Antonio Festival* in late May and early June.

For colorful Mexican folk dances and songs, go to the *Arneson River Theater* on the River Walk on Tuesday, Friday, Saturday, or Sunday evenings during the summer. Either Fiesta Noche del Rio (226–4651) or Ballet Folklorico de San Antonio (733–3708) will be performing outdoors. Admission. (For other musical performances see *Calendar of Events* above.)

STAGE. San Antonio has several local theater companies. The oldest, a community theater, is *San Antonio Little Theatre,* which gives year-round productions running the gamut of drama, comedy, and musicals; 735–6922. Or you can sneer at the villains at the *Melodrama Playhouse and Saloon* down at HemisFair Plaza; 271–0300. Shows in this renovated 1890s general store are held Thursday through Sunday evenings. For touring Broadway shows and big-name entertainers, check out the *Majestic Performing Arts Center* and the *San Antonio Performing Arts Association.*

SHOPPING. Your best bet here is to take advantage of San Antonio's proximity to Mexico and pick up some reasonably priced Mexican imports. Besides, the shopping in San Antonio is colorful, particularly at **Market Square,** patterned after a Mexican market and conveniently situated downtown, at 514 W. Commerce near Milam Park. The square encompasses shops, art galleries, restaurants, and bars, with live entertainment frequently in the open plaza area. Market Square is worth a whole day's visit. Then there's the Mexican market building itself, called *El Mercado,* which includes stalls and cubbyholes of 30-odd small businesses, with merchandise such as piñatas, pottery, jewelry, clothes, chili powder, and toys. Some of the offerings are cheap trinkets, but some are exquisite, expensive creations. All the merchandise is interesting—and usually at good prices—but look around, since prices vary for the same items. The Market Square area is open at all times, but the El Mercado shops are open from 10:00 A.M. to 6:00 P.M. daily (sometimes later in the summer) 299–8600. (Don't forget that *La Villita* has shops too.)

Colorful Mexican dresses, men's *guayabera* shirts, and custom boots are good things to shop for downtown and throughout San Antonio. Although there are department stores and specialty shops downtown, much of the retail action may now be found in the seven major malls in the suburban areas. Perhaps *North Star Mall,* at Loop 410 and San Pedro on the north side of town and near the airport, the oldest, has the best variety of local and regional stores.

For an unusual shopping adventure, try *Los Patios,* a blend of stores and restaurants in a peaceful, rustic setting on 32 acres on Salado Creek in northeast San Antonio on Loop 410 NE.

DINING OUT. You'll find food in San Antonio reasonably priced—and sometimes the best of it in the unlikeliest no-frills places. That's part of the city's unpretentious charm. And you can't go away without at least trying some Mexican food. Price categories are for dinner for one person, not including alcohol, tips, or tax. *Expensive,* \$15 to \$35; *Moderate,* \$5 to \$15; *Inexpensive,* less than \$5. Credit-card abbreviations: AE, American Express; CB, Carte Blanche; DC, Diners Club; MC, MasterCard; V, Visa.

Expensive

Anaqua Room. Four Seasons San Antonio Hotel, 555 S. Alamo, downtown; 229–1000. An elegant dining room currently serving American fare, such as chicken, roast lamb, salmon, or duckling. Overlooks landscaped courtyard. B, L, D, daily. Major credit cards.

Arthur's. 4001 Broadway, northeast; 826–3200. Formal, vaguely Oriental decor, with continental fare, fresh seafood, and dessert soufflés. Entertainment in bar. L, D, daily. Major credit cards.

Las Canarias. La Mansion del Rio Hotel, 112 College, River Walk; 225–4000. Continental food in a Spanish-colonial decor overlooking the river. Flamenco guitarist and dancers gratis at D. L, D, daily. Major credit cards.

Chez Ardid. 1919 San Pedro, north; 732–3203. French cuisine under aegis of owner-chef Guillermo Ardid. Crepes, lamb, seafood, mocha cake served in a restored mansion setting. D, Tuesday through Saturday. Reservations required. AE, MC, V.

Crescendo. Hyatt Regency Hotel, 123 Losoya, River Walk; 222–1234. Another lavish hotel dining room. Mexican and Italian comestibles, plus steak. View of river, with piano music wafting in from the atrium. D, daily; Sunday brunch. Major credit cards.

Fig Tree. 515 Villita, River Walk; 224–1976. One of the most expensive in town, dinner entrees alone are around $35—which buys you lots of ambience (overlooks the river and La Villita) in a historic building, with intimate dining rooms and fancy china and crystal. Continental food. Suggest reservations. D, daily. Major credit cards. Bar outside overlooking the river.

Little Rhein Steakhouse. 231 S. Alamo, River Walk; 225–2111. In this cozy restored 1847 rock house can be found some tasty steaks and lamb chops, but they're not inexpensive. On the edge of La Villita. Some tables outdoors overlooking the river. Casual. D, daily. Major credit cards.

La Louisiane. 2632 Broadway, northeast; 225–7984. Creole and French dishes in an ornate, intimate setting. Good prime rib. Used to be the grande dame of San Antonio restaurants before all those upstart competitors moved in. Good service. L, D, Tuesday through Saturday. Major credit cards.

La Provence. 206 E. Locust, north; 225–0722. Dine in French opulence in this restored old mansion. Naturally the cuisine is French and the service attentive. Lobster a specialty. D, Tuesday through Saturday. Major credit cards.

McTad's. 205 North Presa, downtown; 227–4700. Housed in a restored 1880s building complete with courtyard, this continental-fare restaurant/bar is also popular for cocktail time. Live background music. B,L,D, Monday through Friday; L,D, Saturday. AE, MC,V.

PJ's. One Riverwalk Place (700 N. St. Mary's), downtown; 225–8400. Continental, with Italian specialties. L, D, Monday through Friday; D, Saturday. Major credit cards. (The bar is also excellent.)

Moderate

Bayous. 517 N. Presa, River Walk; 223–6403; and 2617 Wagonwheel, northeast; 828–5726. Louisiana-style seafood, with fresh oysters and boiled shrimp at Happy Hour bargain prices at the bar. L, D, daily. Major credit cards.

Cappy's. 5011 Broadway, Alamo Heights; 828–9669. An old lumberyard building turned into an intimate restaurant of hanging baskets and wooden beams. Gourmet offerings of American-International dishes. L, D, daily. AE, MC, V.

Casa Rio. 430 E. Commerce, River Walk; 225–6718. Does a booming outdoor Mexican-food business because of its prime location right on River Walk. Not San Antonio's top Mexican fare but good. Can be quite inexpensive. Mariachis nightly. L, D, daily. Major credit cards.

Checkers. 4901 Broadway, Alamo Heights; 822–6129. Casual chic surroundings for light lunches to steak. L,D, Monday through Friday; D only Saturday. AE, MC, V.

Crumpets. 5800 Broadway, Alamo Heights; 821–5454. Highly thought-of European cuisine in a casual but chic atmosphere. Pig out on their freshly baked croissants. Also bakery and outdoor tables. L, D, Monday through Saturday; Brunch, Sunday. AE, MC, V.

Earl Abel's. 4200 Broadway, northeast; 822–3358. A popular old 24-hour restaurant serving reasonable, solid American food in a motel-atmosphere setting. Open 24 hours daily. No credit cards.

La Fonda. 2415 N. Main, north; 733–0621. Old line San Antonio has been going here for years for bland Mexican-food luncheons and to see each other. L, D, Monday through Saturday. No credit cards.

Grey Moss Inn. 19010 Scenic Loop Rd., northwest, approximately 12 mi. from Loop 410. Take Bandera Rd. (Hwy. 16), turn right on Scenic Loop Rd.; 695–8301. Romantic spot for dinner in country-inn and woodsy setting. Charcoal-broiled steaks and chicken. D, Tuesday through Sunday. AE, MC, V.

Hunan Garden. 506 River Walk; 222–0808; and 8069 Callaghan, northwest; 349–5427. Hunan and Szechuan Chinese food, on the spicy side. L, D, daily. AE, MC, V.

Josephine Street. 400 E. Josephine, near downtown; 224–6169. A comfortable old neighborhood café with an old-fashioned wooden bar and loud conversation. Steaks (also chicken fried) a specialty. L, D, Monday through Friday; D, Saturday. AE, MC, V.

Kangaroo Court. 512 River Walk; 224–6821. A popular spot for natives and tourists alike, for people watching from outdoor umbrella tables. English-pub decor; sandwiches and seafood. L, D, daily. Major credit cards.

Little Mike's Ice House. 1722 S. Zarzamora, south; 223–7856. Some of the best Italian food in town is found in this small former icehouse. Also the most reasonably priced. Get "the works" for $4.75 at lunch. Must call beforehand for dinner. L, D, every day except Wednesday and Sunday. No credit cards.

Mama's. 9907 San Pedro, north; 349–2314. Casual: hanging baskets and wood. Burgers, steaks. L, D, daily. AE, MC, V.

Mama's Café. 9903 San Pedro, north; 342–3219; 2442 Nacogdoches, northeast; 826–8303. Both have steaks, liver, etc. in Texas highway-café chic. B, L, D, daily.

La Margarita. 120 Produce Row, Market Square; 227–7140. Either sit outdoors and watch the parade of humanity in lively Market Square or dine in the New Orleans–style building. Mexican food and oysters. Try the *fajitas.* L, D, daily. AE, MC, V.

Mario's. 325 S. Pecos, downtown; 223–9602. A popular 24-hour Mexican restaurant with good food—and mariachis in late evening. Open 24 hours daily. No credit cards.

Mi Tierra Café and Bakery. 218 Produce Row, Market Square; 225–1262. Another popular Mexican restaurant because of its being open 24 hours and being part of the Market Square action. At times so many tourist-minded gimmick entertainers stop at your table that it's difficult to eat in peace, but an interesting Mexican bakery and mariachis in the evening are the pluses. Open 24 hours daily. AE, MC, V.

Niki's Tokyo Inn. 819 W. Hildebrand, north; 736–5471. Japanese cuisine, such as shrimp tempura. D, Tuesday through Sunday; L, Saturday and Sunday.

Paesano's. 1715 McCullough, north; 226–9541. As you might suspect, Italian food, with shrimp paesano and veal francesca among the specialties. Decor nothing to shout about, but many movers and shakers consider this their favorite San Antonio Italian restaurant. L, D, Tuesday through Friday; D, Saturday and Sunday. MC, V.

Los Patios. 2015 Northeast Loop 410, northeast; 655–6190. A welcome retreat for lunch and shopping in this rustic acreage. Includes three restaurants: *Gazebo* (crepes, salads); *La Hacienda* (Mexican); and *Brazier* (steaks, chicken, seafood). All attractive, relaxing decor. L, daily. AE, MC, V.

Pearl's Oyster Company. 3011 N. St. Mary's, north; 734–0058. Seafood in a cozy, renovated gas station. L, D, daily. AE, MC,V.

Red Carpet. 107 E. Martin, downtown; 222–8581. Quality Continental fare. L, Monday through Friday; D, Monday through Saturday.

Settlement Inn. On I–10 at Boerne Stage Rd. Exit, about 12 mi. north of Loop 410; 698–2580. Now, for that real western setting, pardner, the inn in its old stagecoach building certainly qualifies. Tasty, all-you-can-eat barbecue platters. D, daily; L, Sunday. Major credit cards.

Tower of the Americas Restaurant. 222 HemisFair Plaza; 223–3101. The bonus here is the panoramic view of San Antonio from this revolving (one revolution per hour) restaurant in the Tower. Steaks, seafood, etc. The nighttime view is romantic. L, D, daily. Major credit cards.

Viet Nam. 3244 Broadway, northeast; 822–7461. Some of the best Vietnamese food in San Antonio in this small, no-frills place. The spring rolls are especially good. L, Monday through Saturday; D, daily. MC, V.

Inexpensive

Calico Cat Tea Room. 304 N. Presa, near River Walk; 226–4925. Locals patronize this informal, high-ceilinged room for the excellent homemade soups, quiches, and sandwiches and for the warm atmosphere of recorded classical music and bustling talk. L, Monday through Saturday. No credit cards.

La Casita. 1701 Babcock, northwest; 349–5208. Good, reasonably priced Mexican food. B,L,D Monday through Saturday. AE.

Copper Kitchen. 300 Augusta, in the Southwest Craft Center, downtown; 224–0123. Good soups and sandwiches in this self-serve eatery in a quaint restored Catholic school. L, Monday through Friday. No credit cards.

Four Ten Diner. 8315 Broadway, north; 822–6246. Thick pork chops and big hunks of cornbread in 1940s setting. L, D, daily. AE, MC, V.

La Fogata. 2427 Vance Jackson, northwest; 341–9930. To some aficionados, this small no-frills place has the best authentic Mexican food in town. Some outdoor seating; expect crowds. B, L, D Tuesday through Sunday. All major credit cards.

Hickory Hut Bar-B-Q. 3731 Colony Dr., northwest; 696–9134. Tasty barbecue in a rustic decor; self-serve set-up. L, D, daily. Checks.

Jim's Coffee Shops. Thirteen locations about town. Burgers, sandwiches, etc. Open 24 hours daily. Major credit cards.

Luby's Cafeterias. Many locations; see the Yellow Pages. Has some of the best food in town. L, D daily. No credit cards.

Schilo's Delicatessan. 424 E. Commerce, near River Walk; 223–6692. A genuine old-time deli (since 1917). L, Monday through Saturday. No credit cards.

NIGHT LIFE. Space limits prevent us from listing all San Antonio night life. So we've opted for a sampling of local bars and music across the available spectrum, seeking to provide both upscale and colorful regional haunts. Check ahead for live music hours.

The Beauregard. 320 Beauregard, King William; 223–1388. Casual. There is also a restaurant, patronized by both blue-collars and affluent King William residents. Jazz, blues, and folk music.

Bonham Exchange. 411 Bonham, downtown; 271–3811. A tastefully decorated bar for gay or straight, in a renovated downtown building.

Durty Nellie's Pub. Hilton Palacio del Rio, 200 S. Alamo, downtown; 222–1400. An Irish pub on River Walk. Piano player and sing-along.

Esquire Bar. 155 E. Commerce, downtown; 222–2521. Bankers and laborers alike go here. Esquire has a great long bar to belly up to. Mexican mariachis play nightly.

Farmer's Daughter. 542 N. W. W. White, east; 333–7391. A country-and-western dance hall for all generations.

Floore Country Store. About 12 mi. northwest of San Antonio in Helotes, just off Hwy. 16; 695–8827. Country-and-western; large outdoor dance floor. Parking can be a problem.

Karam's Kantina. At Market Square, 102 Produce Row, downtown; 225–0445. Local courthouse types and tourists frequent this tasteful bar. Mexican mariachi music in evenings.

The Landing. Hyatt Regency Hotel at 123 Losoya, downtown; 222–1234. The Happy Jazz Band plays . . . what else? At the hotel's River Walk level.

Lerma's. 1602 N. Zarzamora, west; 732–0477. Funky neighborhood night club where you can absorb some regional "conjunto" (a blend of Mexican and German).

Pioneer House. 8085 Callaghan, northwest; 341–9159. Bluegrass music.

Raffles. 1896 Nacogdoches, northeast; 826–7118. Uptown intimate bar where three-piece-suit professionals mingle.

St. Mary's Bar & Grill. 3000 N. St. Mary's, north; 736–2776. Some R&B, jazz, and rock in this restored 1920s building. Caters to young professional and college crowd.

Summertime only: On every third Friday of the month, from June through September, there are oom-pah-pah bands, dancing, costumes, beer, and food at the **Beethoven Maennerchor Home,** 422 Pereida, near the King William district south of downtown; 222–1521.

LAREDO

by
PAT HATHCOCK

Pat Hathcock, a journalist based in Austin, has written for various regional publications, including Texas Monthly. *A twenty-year aficionado of border towns, he has visited most of them, especially Matamoros and Nuevo Laredo, on a very regular basis.*

There are occasionally irredentist rumblings among Mexicans and Chicano groups about a restoration of South Texas to Mexico. It's all just vague talk, an extremist fringe nursing an old grievance.

The first-time visitor to Laredo might think that the talkers had managed to bring off their dream, so pervasive is the Mexican influence in that city. The music heard from stores, the language spoken in the streets, even the smell of the cooking oil from the cafés—all feel Mexican.

Above 90 percent of the population is of Mexican descent, and the remaining 10 or so percent, if they wish to live comfortably in the area, are to some degree bicultural. Laredo is a town where you get refried beans instead of hash browns with your breakfast.

Laredo was founded in 1775 by don Tomás Sánchez, a tough Mexican frontiersman (the frontier was as great an influence in northern Mexico as it was in the southwestern United States, and *norteños* have a reputation in Mexico much like that of Texans in the United States—bluff, hardy, a bit crude). The town was sited near the present-day San Agustin Plaza, in what is now downtown Laredo, and named for a Spanish city in the province of Santander, that part of Mexico then being called Nuevo (New) Santander. Descendants of Sánchez have remained prominent in Laredo politics unto the seventh generation.

The little settlement hung in there, fighting Indians and drought, until the Texans under Stephen F. Austin revolted in the north. Santa Anna's troops marched through Laredo on their way to their defeat at San Jacinto. For the next ten years, Mexicans contended that the border stood at the Nueces River, between Laredo and San Antonio, while Texans held it to be at the Rio Grande. In practice, the Texan government exercised no control over the area south of San Antonio.

In 1840 Laredo was the capital of the Republic of the Rio Grande, a separatist group of three Mexican states that had rebelled against the Mexican central government. The rebellion was soon controlled and the area restored to effective Mexican hegemony.

The Mexican War of 1846 established the border firmly at the Rio Grande. In 1848 the army built Fort Crawford, two years later renamed Fort McIntosh, to discourage Indian raiding and border banditry. The border had long been known for violence, and some of the men labeled by the government as bandits were considered by inhabitants of Mexican descent as more like freedom fighters.

In 1847 Mexicans from this side who preferred to remain Mexican citizens established Nuevo Laredo on the opposite bank of the river. (How fortunate that Sánchez didn't name his original settlement Nuevo Laredo; then the new town would have been Nuevo Nuevo Laredo.)

During the Civil War a regiment of Confederate troops was raised in Laredo. Colonel Santos Benavides was commander. Southern cotton was transshipped through Mexico to the mills of England, providing money to help the South hang on.

After the northern victory more Anglo Americans, many of them former Confederate soldiers, moved into the border country. (Anglo, by the way, is the common designation in the Southwest for non-Latin whites, so you will hear people with obviously Jewish or Polish names described as Anglos.)

The influx of outsiders accelerated the growth of the livestock industry in the area, already longtime cattle- and sheep-raising country.

The Streets of Laredo

Something about the very sound of the word *Laredo* is conducive to romantic speculations. It conjures up visions of narrow, dusty streets, shady saloons, blazing sun, dusky señoritas. Small wonder it became the setting for one of the favorite ballads of the cowboys.

Many of those dusty streets continue in existence today, but paving of outlying streets, once a political issue, now is under way. The downtown streets, laid out long ago for a small village and horse-drawn traffic, require some close-tolerance driving since there are now ninety thousand people—most with cars—in Laredo.

The downtown area between Iturbide and Water Streets is designated as the Villa de San Agustin Historical Zone. (The local historical society has worked up a series of walking tours for downtown; maps are available from the Chamber of Commerce.) Like most Spanish towns, Laredo was laid out around a plaza, rather than the courthouse square common in other parts of Texas. San Agustin Plaza, at San Agustin and Zaragoza, is a good place to begin your look around. The Museum of the Republic of the Rio Grande is on Zaragoza next to La Posada Hotel. On the east side facing the plaza is the handsome Saint Augustine church. Take a peek inside for the fine stained-glass windows. You can also just sit on a bench on the edge of the plaza and watch the world go by; everybody else is. There are two other plazas in the downtown area. One, Bruni, at Washington and San Bernardo, has the new city library; the other, Jarvis, at Matamoros and Salinas, has the federal building.

An aimless amble through downtown can be fun. Downtowns aren't dying in the Texas border towns as they are so many other places; their customers are mostly Mexican nationals, many of whom walk across from the other side. The stores stock lots of appliances, cameras, stereos, clothing, things prohibitively expensive or of poor quality on the Mexican side. Many other stores handle imported goods—Laredo is one of the busiest ports of entry in the United States—and not just Mexican stuff, either. There's a fascinating row of import stores in the 1400 block of Zaragoza.

Aimless ambling is fun in April or October; in August it can be deadly. Laredo is HOT, and those accustomed to more temperate climes should exercise caution. In the summer, the overhead sun can make it hot enough to fry an egg on your brainpan. Wear a hat; don't

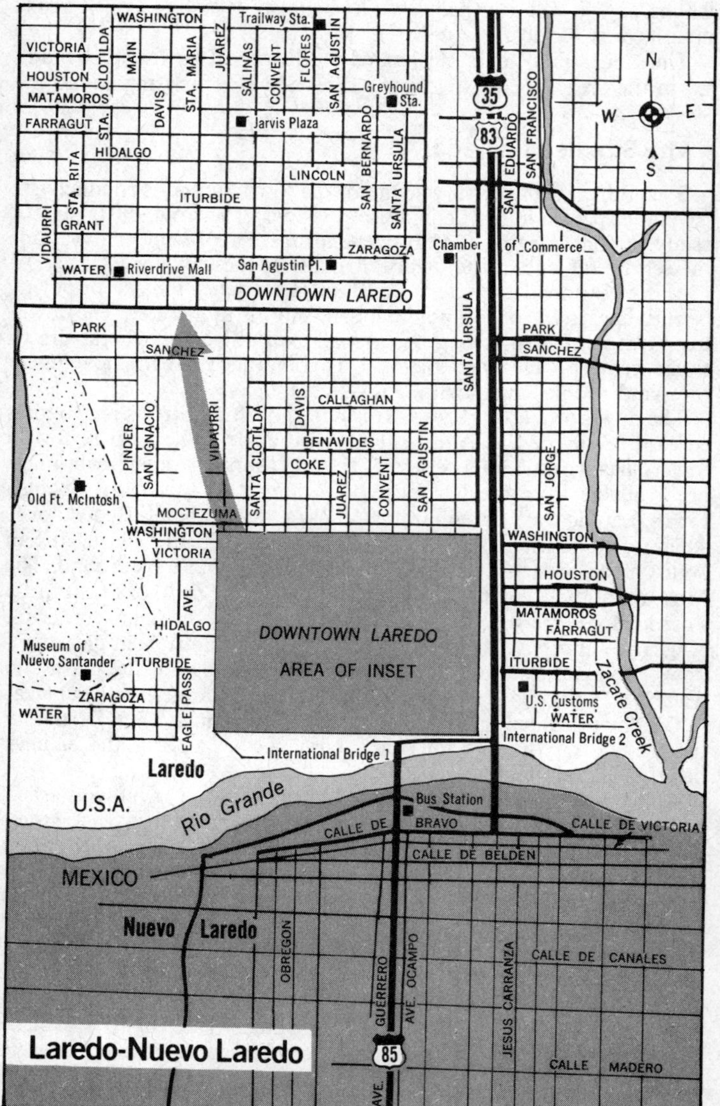
WASHINGTON
Trailway Sta.
VICTORIA
HOUSTON
MATAMOROS
FARRAGUT
HIDALGO
CLOTILDA
MAIN
DAVIS
STA. MARIA
JUAREZ
SALINAS
CONVENT
FLORES
SAN AGUSTIN
STA. RITA
Greyhound Sta.
Jarvis Plaza
LINCOLN
SAN BERNARDO
SANTA URSULA
ITURBIDE
GRANT
VIDAURRI
ZARAGOZA
WATER
Riverdrive Mall
San Agustin Pl.
Chamber of Commerce
DOWNTOWN LAREDO
35
83
SAN EDUARDO
SAN FRANCISCO
N
W
E
S
PARK
SANCHEZ
CALLAGHAN
BENAVIDES
COKE
PINDER
SAN IGNACIO
VIDAURRI
SANTA CLOTILDA
DAVIS
JUAREZ
CONVENT
SAN AGUSTIN
SANTA URSULA
SAN JORGE
Old Ft. McIntosh
MOCTEZUMA
WASHINGTON
VICTORIA
HOUSTON
MATAMOROS
FARRAGUT
ITURBIDE
HIDALGO
Museum of Nuevo Santander
ZARAGOZA
WATER
EAGLE PASS AVE.
DOWNTOWN LAREDO
AREA OF INSET
U.S. Customs
WATER
International Bridge 2
Zacate Creek
International Bridge 1
Laredo
U.S.A.
Rio Grande
Bus Station
CALLE DE BRAVO
CALLE DE VICTORIA
CALLE DE BELDEN
MEXICO
Nuevo Laredo
OBREGON
GUERRERO
AVE. OCAMPO
JESUS CARRANZA
CALLE DE CANALES
85
AVE.
CALLE MADERO
Laredo-Nuevo Laredo

overexert; step into a variety store and try to make the counter help understand that you want iced tea.

When you've seen all of downtown that you want, drive north to Washington, hang a left, and follow the street to the end. You will be on the grounds of old Fort McIntosh, now the home of two colleges—Laredo Junior College and Laredo State University—as well as various government agencies. The big old two-story houses on the north side of the street were formerly officers' quarters, built to the same plans as those you see all over the Southwest. They are now used for faculty housing. Go left at the end of the street and stop at the Museum of Nuevo Santander, the old military chapel. A staffer will walk you through the other three buildings of the museum.

PRACTICAL INFORMATION FOR LAREDO

HOW TO GET THERE. There was a happy day when you could ride the train to Laredo, kill a day there, and get on the Aztec Eagle in Nuevo Laredo for the trip on into the interior of Mexico. It was great—so of course Amtrak killed the route. You can still get to Laredo by train, but now only from Corpus Christi. Tex-Mex Railroad plans to begin five-days-a-week passenger service from Corpus Christi early in 1986. It'll be a four-hour trip, with bar car available.

You can also get to Laredo by car, plane, or bus. Laredo is the end of the line for I–35, a good highway most of the way. From Houston you can come in on U.S. 59. From the lower Rio Grande Valley, take U.S. 83.

The driving time to Laredo from other cities, in hours, are: San Antonio, 3; Corpus Christi, 3; Brownsville, 4.

American Eagle, a commuter airline, serves Laredo from San Antonio. So does Texas National, which also flies into here from the Rio Grande Valley. Royale flies in from Houston. An alternative might be to fly direct to San Antonio and take one of the many buses from there for about $12. Continental Trailways and Greyhound both serve Laredo. The bus stations are right downtown, and Laredo International Airport is close in, off Saunders Road (U.S. 59).

TELEPHONES. The area code for all of South Texas is 512. You do not need to dial the area code if it is the same as the one from which you are calling. Information is 1411 for local numbers, 1–555–1212 for other 512 calls, and 1 (area code) 555–1212 for other area codes.

HOTELS AND MOTELS. Laredo has more than 2,600 hotel and motel rooms, which is a lot for a city of 90,-000+. Still, there are times when rooms can get tight. The first weekend of whitewing-dove season, in early September, holiday weekends, when people pour in from all over Texas to shop and party—at these times a call ahead might be in order.

Much of the prosperity of Laredo's lodging business has depended on Mexican tourists who come from all over the country to shop. The devaluation of the peso has resulted in actual decline; room rates at many Laredo lodging places have dropped in the last two years. There might be some good deals on packages as owners try to make up for lost trade. But with the opening of a racetrack in neighboring Nuevo Laredo in 1983, many hotels and motels began counting on the many visitors from Texas and other states who now visit Laredo to take advantage of the year-round dog and horse racing across the border.

With a couple of exceptions, lodging in Laredo is pretty much good, solid chain fare, interchangeable with that anywhere but with prices much lower than in larger cities. The larger places have acceptable restaurants and lounges with live music, which abounds all around Laredo.

Categories, determined by price, are: *Expensive,* \$50 to \$75; *Moderate,* \$25 to \$50; *Inexpensive,* under \$25. Prices quoted are for doubles, and a 12% tax will be added to the bill in Laredo. Lodging places tend to be strung out along San Bernardo, which runs parallel to I-35 on the West Side, or clustered downtown. All have pools unless otherwise indicated. All are within easy walking or driving distance of Mexico.

Expensive

Hilton Inn, 1 S. Main; 722–2411, Texas toll-free 1–800–2–LAREDO. A very comfortable hotel, run by a European-trained manager, and convenient to downtown and the #1 bridge. A good restaurant and a sophisticated sound system in the Castillian Tower. (After dinner take your drink over by the window and watch the river. Sooner or later you will see someone swimming from the other side. That is either the Nuevo Laredo swim team working out, or the evidence of the total failure of United States immigration policy.) Hilton amenities include courtesy cars, transportation to the bridge (it's really an easy walk), and a sauna.

La Posada. 1000 Zaragoza; 722–1701. A beautiful job of adaptive renovation. La Posada was once a school; now it's tile, lots of greenery, gracious help, and a very charming place. Full service, courtesy car, and a block from the bridge. La Posada sits right on San Agustin Plaza. There are two excellent restaurants, plus a club-restaurant upstairs.

Moderate

Casa de Palmas. 5900 San Bernardo; 722–8133. Courtesy car, restaurant, and club, the Roundup, that's a favorite with locals.

El Centro Motel. 920 Matamoros; 723–4319. A small motel fairly close to the International Bridge. No pool or restaurant.

Evelyn Motor Inn. 2720 San Bernardo. Small—but clean and comfy and with a restaurant.

La Hacienda. 4914 San Bernardo; 722–2441. Pool, restaurant, lounge, courtesy car.

Holiday Inn-Civic Center. 800 Garden St.; 723–8704. A 208-room hotel, built especially for convention trade. All the amenities.

Holiday Inn. 5420 San Bernardo; 723–3603. Restaurant, courtesy car, and a lounge, the Torch Club, with live entertainment. Dependable chain.

Mayan Motor Inn. 3219 San Bernardo; 722–8181.

Monterrey Inn. 4820 San Bernardo; 722–7631. Close to the freeway for an easy run to the bridge and downtown. 72 rooms.

New Hamilton Hotel. 815 Salinas; 723–7421. The New Hamilton is not so new; it's the town's old commercial hotel, built in the 1920s, aging but entirely decent. The original Hamilton was the pride of Laredo late in the last century. Facing Jarvis Plaza, the Hamilton, with 250 rooms, is the biggest house in town, the kind of place where the local civic clubs meet. Full service, a restaurant, and a nice little lounge, the Club Capuchine. Good downtown location. No pool.

La Quinta Motor Inn. 3600 Santa Ursula; 722–0511. San Bernardo fronts on the freeway down to Calton Road; after that it's Santa Ursula, which lies between San Bernardo and the freeway. 24-hour restaurant on premises.

Rodeway Inn. 2620 Santa Ursula; 722–6321. A 76-room house, one of a good chain. Restaurant.

Sheraton Motor Inn. 7060 San Bernardo; 724–8221. A nice motel, restaurant, and another lounge, Bernardo's, with live music. Courtesy car. San Bernardo is the frontage road this far up, and although it's a way to downtown, it's a quick trip.

Siesta Motel. 4109 San Bernardo; 723–3661. Restaurant.

TraveLodge Motor Inn. 4910 San Bernardo; 722–5271. A big motel from a big chain. 147 rooms, restaurant, lounge.

Inexpensive

Rock bottom's not really that rocky in Laredo; these places all have pools. They'll all do fine if you're po'-boying the trip or you'd rather spend your money on board then bed. All are less than $25 double. **Alamo Courts,** 3302 San Bernardo, 722–9153; **Frontier Motel,** 4201 San Bernardo, 722–1756; **Loma Alta Motel,** 3915 San Bernardo, 722–9198; **Motel 6,** 5310 San Bernardo, 722–4666.

HOW TO GET AROUND. To get the most out of your Laredo trip, you will probably need a car. Taxi stands abound, and there is a public bus system (call 722–0951 for routes and schedules), but driving will give you a lot more flexibility. Budget, National, Avis, and Hertz all have offices at the airport. All but Avis will write you an insurance policy for Mexico so you can drive your rental car in Nuevo Laredo, Mexico.

GOING TO MEXICO

It's the easiest way to go abroad: just pay 10¢ and walk over or pay 50¢ and drive across. Mexican customs will peer into your car and nod you through. If you are staying in the border zone that's all there is to it. You are allowed to return to the U.S. with $400 worth of goods, technically, but in fact there are a great many exceptions from the limit on goods from a developing country. Ask at U.S. Customs about the exceptions; they'll provide literature on exceptions for personal and household use. You are allowed one liter of liquor per 21-year-old-or-over per month, but the state of Texas will extort a 50¢ tax on it even if you're not from Texas and don't intend to drink it in Texas. Some agricultural products may not be brought back, nor may parrots or any other animal.

Coming back to the U.S. you will be required to state your citizenship (don't clown—these guys are serious) and declare what you brought back. Occasionally they'll pull someone out of the line of cars and look through things, so if you're tempted to pick up a bit of contraband, do it only if you can maintain a look of innocence and have lots of luck.

If you drive your own car across the bridge, be sure that your insurance policy has an endorsement for the Mexican border zone, or buy insurance for the Mexican side from a Laredo agency (Sanborn's, 3920 Santa Ursula Ave., 512–722–0931, is a good one). Traffic accidents are criminal rather than civil matters in Mexico and can be very unpleasant. In Mexico you are guilty until proven innocent. The small expense of insurance is more than justified by the peace of mind it buys.

TOURIST INFORMATION. There is a Texas Tourist Bureau on I-35 on the far-north edge of town, but the best local source is the Laredo Chamber of Commerce, P.O. Box 790, 78040; street address: 2310 San Bernardo; (512) 722–9895. Write before you get there, and they'll send you a packet of literature or answer any questions you might have. They promote tourism intensively and have current information about activities on both sides of the border. It's really a good place to stop and find out what's going on.

SEASONAL EVENTS. The big celebration of the year is a week of activities around *George Washington's Birthday,* a very old tradition on the border for some reason. Stores all along the border have Washington's Birthday sales slanted to Mexican trade. Washington's Birthday features dances, parades, a carnival, a queen, a Jalapeñofest that's lots of grins, ethnic food—about what you'd expect, but fun because of the border flavor.

The Border Olympics, held the first week in March, is the first outdoor track meet of the season in this country. It draws student athletes—high school and college—from all over the Southwest and Mexico.

Expomex, the big fair in Nuevo Laredo, takes place around the 16th of September. It draws some big-name Mexican talent.

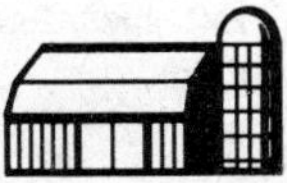

SPECIAL-INTEREST SIGHTSEEING. If you come in on I-35, you know what the South Texas brush country looks like. If you didn't, you might enjoy a run down the river on U.S. 83 to San Ygnacio. It's a chance to look at an oil patch if you've never seen one, some typical ranch country, and a bit of farming. If the weather's clear you can see mountains down to the south. San Ygnacio is a small old town that has discovered it's historic, so there's some nice restoration work going on, and a small museum. Birders dote on the many varieties available along this stretch of the river. If you still haven't seen enough brush you can go on down to Zapata, then catch Texas 16 to Texas 649 and see some really big country, bleak to most but enchanting to some. 649 meets Texas 359 at Mirando City. 359 going west will take you back to Laredo.

FISHING. It might seem unlikely in this desiccated country, but there is some pretty good fishing around Laredo. Lake Casa Blanca on the eastern edge of town has black bass, cats, panfish, and striper-white hybrids. Laredo is the closest sizable town to the headwaters of Falcon Reservoir, a 70-mi.-long monster on the Rio Grande. You can get to the lake at San Ygnacio, about 30 mi. from Laredo, but Zapata has boat rentals and camping facilities, and it's a few miles farther on. Falcon has the reputation of being the best lake in Texas for white bass; the whites run heaviest in the winter and early spring.

HUNTING. Webb County consistently produces some of the largest whitetail bucks in Texas. The whitewing-dove season in early September is practically a national holiday along the border, with people coming from all over the state to shoot birds and to party on the other side. Deer season begins around the middle of November and runs through the end of the year. Hunting is on leases, there being no public land. The Laredo Chamber of Commerce (512–722–9895) can give you information on leases or put you in touch with local outfitters. There is also spectacular hunting on the Mexican side, and Rio Bravo Outdoor Adventures, Inc., 815 Lafayette, 78040, (512) 722–1573, can help with the arrangements. A Texas hunting license is $8.00 for residents, $100.75 for nonresidents, and you must also have a $3.00 stamp if you're going to hunt whitewings. Licenses and stamps are obtainable at most sporting-goods stores.

SPECTATOR SPORTS. *Nuevo Laredo Downs,* a track that opened in early 1983, features thoroughbred and quarterhorse racing and greyhounds. The ponies run Saturday afternoons, and the pups run Wednesday through Sunday evenings, year round. You can drive to the track, about seven miles south of the bridge, or catch a bus from Mall del Norte, Riverdrive Mall, or the principal hotels and motels. Roundtrip $5. Track admission 50¢, finish-line box seats $1. Full-service restaurants, snacks, bars. For further info, call the Texas office, 726–0540 or write Nuevo Laredo Downs, 1000 Zaragoza, Laredo 78040.

There are also frequent *boxing* matches in Nuevo Laredo, and the city has a Mexican major league *baseball* team that had a good season last year.

People obsessed with the Anglo-Saxon concept of fairness find it hard to call bullfighting a sport, but some people find they really like the drama of it all. It's gauche to cheer for the bull and dumb to bet on him. The fights are not scheduled regularly but take place most often on the Sunday of a holiday weekend. There are two rings in Nuevo Laredo, a small one, *La Herradura,* by the Expomex grounds at 125 Washington, and a larger one, *La Fiesta,* about 6 mi. south of the bridge out on the Monterrey highway. Admission to La Herradura was U.S. $3, $5 reserved in September 1982, but prices will depend on the condition of the peso. Call the Laredo Chamber of Commerce for schedules and prices.

There is *horse racing* at LIFE Downs, out U.S. 59 in Laredo, but there is no pair-mutuel betting in Texas. If you're one of those who claim they like to go to the track just to see 'em run, this is where you can do it. Call 722–5662 for info.

HISTORIC SITES. For a city as old as Laredo, there seems a paucity of interesting old places. The entire downtown of Laredo is designated a historical zone, with the *Museum of the Republic of the Rio Grande* at San Agustin Plaza the single most interesting old building. Nearly a century and a half old, it has a hodgepodge of relics dating back to the last century, including three rooms furnished in the style of those days. It's open Monday through Saturday 9:00 A.M. to 4:00 P.M. and is free; contributions accepted.

On the grounds of old Fort McIntosh in the *Nuevo Santander Museum,* housed in buildings that once served military functions. The headquarters is in the old chapel. An attendant will go around with you and let you into the other three buildings. One of them, the commissary, is probably pre-1850. One of the exhibits is of various types of construction used for *jacales.* The *jacal* was a type of hut that once furnished shelter for most of the poorer folks in the border country and has since furnished the name for half the beer joints in South Texas.

SHOPPING. There is an old border stereotype of the tourist coming back across the bridge with a bottle of booze, a plaster bull, and a silly-looking hat. Ten or fifteen years ago, Mexican curio-stand owners used to importune passing tourists with, "Come see my jonk." Their marketing techniques have improved since then, but they are still importunate, and a great deal of what they sell is still junk. But there is much of merit among the junk, and even junk can be fun. That plaster bull might be good for a grin back home, and the hat might look great as a wall decoration. The bottle of booze was surely a great bargain. In the following, the discussion is entirely about shopping across the border in Nuevo Laredo. Prices in U.S. dollars are as of summer 1984, and can be expected to vary considerably over time because of exchange fluctuations.

Kahlua goes for around U.S. $5 a bottle, excellent tequila for a dollar or so less. As a change from the Cuervo or Sauza rut that so many tequila drinkers seem to be in, try Herradura, smooth stuff much favored in Mexico—look for the blue horseshoe on the bottle—or Viuda de Romero, which means Romero's widow. Non-tequila drinkers might propound some theories about what happened to Romero.

Another good buy in Mexican liquor is Castillo rum, with an interesting smoky taste, good with soda. Or try Presidente brandy. Somehow they manage to make a pretty good brandy out of wine that is definitely wanting. (In Mexico beer is the wine of the country; it's conceded to be among the best in the world.)

The big attraction in Mexico shopping is handicrafts. The border towns are usually the second-best place to buy them—the best being the city where they are made—but on the border you get the products of all regions, and prices are low because competition is stiff.

The big market in Nuevo Laredo rebuilt after a fire, should be finished by the time this comes out. It's three blocks down Guerrero on the right. Walk through slowly; if you see something you like, don't buy immediately. Prices vary from stand to stand; check around. If you still like it, come back and haggle. Look closely at goods you're serious about buying; check the stitching in that embroidered dress—cheaper ones are sometimes already starting to come apart and have less-intricate needlework. Dresses start at about U.S. $8.00—an outstanding buy. If you're thinking of buying something made of leather, sniff it. A funky smell may indicate a bad job of tanning.

DINING OUT. South Texas-Northern Mexico is a region with a singular style of cooking, utilizing what's cheap and common. Do you remember that great scene in *Giant* when they brought out the barbecued cow's head and Liz Taylor swooned? That was *barbacoa de cabeza,* a weekend standard in Laredo. Go native: Stop anyplace that advertises "*Barbocoa hoy,*" ice down some beer, get a stack of tortillas and some hot sauce, and drive out to Casa Blanca Park for a picnic. Or try *mariachis.* All those little restaurants that advertise *mariachis* don't have live music; it's a local name for a soft taco made with a flour tortilla. When there's *barbacoa de cabeza* you will be able to find mariachis made from brains *(sesos)* or tongue *(lengua,* like language). Give it a chance.

The brush country is big for sheep and goat raising and though, strangely, lamb does not appear much on local menus, goat kid, *cabrito,* is a standby. Walking down Guerrero, you'll see the little lovelies cooking *al pastor,* shepherd-style, all spread-eagled over pits of mesquite coals in the windows of restaurants that specialize in *cabrito.* Goat has had some bad ink in the squemish press, and some people think of it as being like eating horsemeat, but it's really wonderful. Order *pierna de cabrito,* leg. Or if you're feeling adventurous, try *machitos,* the heart, liver, and lights all bound about with tripes and barbecued on a skewer. Or *cabecita,* which is just *cabeza* (head) in its diminutive-goat form.

Not everything's funky ethnic by any means; there are many fine restaurants where you can get a filet mignon and fries, but most everything has a funny little border twist on it. If you have lunch on the Mexican side, pass on the dessert, walk over to La Flor de Michoacán, on the east side of Guerrero in the first block beyond the bridge, and try a *paleta.* Visitors from the U.K. call them ice lollies, you'd call them Popsicles made from fresh fruit juice; you'll also call them good. Those made from fruit and water are 60 pesos, and those with milk are 80 pesos. Try *nuez,* pecan made with milk. You may find some little bits of nutshell in it, but that just reminds you that these weren't turned out by a machine. La Flor also has *licuados,* Mexican fruit smoothies, in an assortment of flavors for 130 pesos.

Inexpensive is less than $8 for a meal for one, not counting drinks, taxes, and tips; *moderate* is from $8 to $15; and *expensive* $15 and up. It's possible that your American plastic won't go everywhere on the other side.

Expensive

El Tesoro Club. Upstairs in La Posada, 1000 Zaragoza; 722–1701. A private club with coat and tie after seven, very much white linen and crystal. The menu features such things as veal Oscar; a dinner for two with duck à la orange, crabmeat, and more; a nice homemade black-bean soup; and mangoes flambé and strawberries Romanoff in season. Nice wine list. Live music and dancing from 8:00 to 11:00 P.M. Tuesday through Saturday. Open 5:00 P.M. to midnight, weekdays, 6:00 P.M. to 1:00 A.M. Saturday, closed Sunday. Major credit cards.

Moderate to Expensive

Goldings Hatari. 1702 Santa Maria; 723–9733. Where Laredans (and Mexicans with dollars) go for steak. The local joke is that the wealthy Mexican family that owns this restaurant keeps it so they'll be sure of getting a good steak when they're in town. A good steak menu and a 23-entry wine list. The Hatari Special has *carne asada* (steak), quail, broiled or fried shrimp, and finger ribs. The little bar adjoining has more Africana. Restaurant 11:30 A.M. to 11:00 P.M.; bar 5:00 P.M. to 2:00 A.M. Major credit cards.

The Tack Room. 1000 Zaragoza, 727–1701. Another pearl from La Posada. The Tack Room's strong on steaks, but is also good for seafood and Canadian baby-back ribs. Major credit cards. Sunday–Thursday 4:00 P.M.–Midnight, Friday and Saturday 4:00 P.M.–1.00 A.M.

Moderate

El Azador Suiso. 4120 San Bernardo; 724–9646. Family dining, informal atmosphere. Mexican cuisine, steak, chicken. The rich authentic flavor of old Mexico. Major credit cards. Noon to 3:00 P.M. and 6:00 to 11:00 P.M. Monday–Saturday. Closed Sunday.

Favarato's. 1916 San Bernardo; 722–1802. Specializes in Italian food and Continental cuisine, plus steaks and seafoods. Relaxed atmosphere. Most major credit cards. Noon to 10:00 P.M. Sundays; 11 A.M. to 11:30 P.M. Tuesday through Saturday. Closed Mondays.

La Palapa. 5300 San Dario; 727–7115. Homecooking served buffet style in a relaxed atmosphere. Family dining. Mexican cuisine offers authentic south-of-the-border flavor in Texas. Major credit cards. Open Sunday–Saturday 10:30 A.M.–11:00 P.M.

The Unicorn. 3810 San Bernardo; 727–9166. Mexican cuisine, plus steaks, seafood, chicken, hamburgers. Homestyle cooking. Major credit cards. 11:00 A.M.–midnight Monday–Saturday. Closed Sundays.

Inexpensive

Cotulla-Style Pit B-B-Q. 4502 McPherson; 724–5747. South Texas TexMex, *barbacoa de cabeza,* various flavors of *mariachis.* Go have them for breakfast on Sunday. Tuesday through Saturday, 8:00 A.M. to 5:45 P.M.; Sunday, 8:00 A.M. to 2:45 P.M. AE, V.

La Hacienda, 4801 Gallagher (two long blocks east on Calton Rd. from the freeway frontage, then a short halfblock to the right); 722–2441. Wonderful Mexican food—*fajitas* (skirt steak marinated and grilled), *cabrito,* combination plates—and it's all good. 7:00 A.M. to 10:00 P.M., Monday–Saturday. Closed Sundays. Major credit cards.

Luby's. 600 W. Calton; 722–3397. A block down from the Mall del Norte, this is the place to come when you gotta have good old American bland. This cafeteria has had the largest average bill and the largest number of customers in the Luby's chain because the shoppers from Mexico are so enthralled by this particular kind of American fast food. Daily, 10:45 A.M. to 8:00 P.M. No credit cards.

Hungry Farmer. 620 W. Calton Rd.; 727–7202. Family dining, informal atmosphere. Steaks are the specialty, with seafood and chicken also on the menu. Major credit cards. 11:00 A.M.–10:00 P.M. Sunday–Thursday; 11:00 A.M. –11:00 P.M. Friday and Saturday.

Rosita's Restaurant. 1005 San Bernardo; 723–1900. Homecooking, families especially welcome. Mexican cuisine. No credit cards. 9:00 A.M.–10:00 P.M. Monday–Thursday; 9:00 A.M.–11:00 P.M. Fridays and Saturdays. Closed Sundays.

NIGHT LIFE AND BARS. There is a lot going on on both sides of the border. Mexico has a reputation for vice on the border—and for good reason. You must understand that when a cabbie offers to take you to see a show it's not going to be anything like what you'd see at the art theater up by the university. And when they offer to take you to Boys' Town, it's not an institution for orphaned lads, it's the *zona de tolerancia,* the area where prostitution is tolerated. Proceed with caution unless you're an old border hand. Otherwise, enjoy the music and the other people having a good time.

If you elect to stay on the Texas side during the evening, a dozen or so of the larger hotels and motels offer lounges where you can relax amid comfortable surroundings. Many offer live music, especially on the weekends, and happy hours are standard attractions. Many lounges even offer complimentary hors d'oeuvres.

Crazy Horse. Cotulla, Texas; 879–2046. In South Texas, it's nothing to drive 65 miles to go partying, and the Crazy Horse throws some of the best parties around. Bands booked include foot-tapping norteño music and national caliber C&W stars. Two dance floors and a bunch of bars under one roof. Wednesday through Saturday, 8:00 P.M. until 2 A.M., Sunday 7:00–midnight. Cover.

El Tesoro. 1000 Zaragoza. 722–1701. An elegant private club at La Posada (complimentary cards for hotel guests). Live music and dancing from 8:00 to 11:00 P.M. Tuesday through Saturday. Coat and tie required.

The Import Lot. 1000 Zaragoza; 722–1701. A downstairs nitery that's definitely not a beer joint. Look down upon the river and hobnob with slick locals and other travelers. Monday through Thursday, 5:00 P.M. until 1:00 A.M. Friday and Saturday 5:00 P.M. until 2:00 A.M.

The Round-up. 5900 San Bernardo in the Ramada Inn, Laredo; 722–8133. If you like country music but don't like funky honkytonks, this place is for you. The best local talent and some pretty fair out-of-towners play the Round-up. No live music Sundays. Monday through Saturday noon to 2:00 A.M.; Sunday, noon to midnight. No cover. Major credit cards.

EL PASO

by
EDNA GUNDERSEN

Edna Gundersen has been a feature writer for the El Paso Times *since 1977. Currently restaurant critic, she also writes travel and entertainment articles for the paper and for the Gannett News Service, serving more than 100 dailies. She has lived in El Paso for more than twenty years; her journalistic work in the area has won numerous awards, including two from the Texas Associated Press Managing Editors Association.*

El Paso, with its modern downtown skyline, young, mushrooming industry, and vast stretches of new suburbia, is often mistaken for a budding city with a brief past. Yet many of its most provocative memoirs predate the American Revolution.

In 1521, twenty-nine years after the first voyage of Christopher Columbus, Hernando Cortez of Spain conquered the Aztecs and claimed Mexico for his country. Shortly thereafter, Álvar Núñez Cabeza de Vaca, one of many subsequent Spanish explorers, landed in Florida and later arrived in Mexico City, proclaiming tales of the Seven Cities of Gold that supposedly lay north of Mexico. A centuries-long quest for riches was launched.

El Paso's history germinates in those fables of wealth and the massive gold hunt that followed. Local historians mark El Paso's beginnings on a dusty August day in 1581, when Chumascado, a seventy-year-old Spanish officer, and his band of soldiers and Indian servants traveled northward from Mexico and happened upon the valley where the Rio Grande slices through a string of mountain ranges. As with the annals of many southwestern towns, some pages are spattered with blood. When Chumascado's party entered New Mexico, one of three padres decided to return home. He was killed by Indians a few miles away. The two remaining priests resolved to stay and Christianize the heathen. They, too, were murdered after the Spanish soldiers reluctantly allowed them to remain in El Paso.

But Indians could not stymie the indomitable explorers, and a steady stream of Spanish soldiers passed through this area in search of the legendary gold deposits in New Mexico. Almost seventeen years after Chumascado stumbled onto the luscious valley nestled between desert mountains, Juan de Oñate, Spanish colonist and conquistador and the first real founder of El Paso, led an expedition of four hundred men, ten priests, and nearly two hundred families into New Mexico. First he reached the Rio Grande at what is today San Elizario Presidio. A few days later, Oñate crossed the river where El Paso now lies. He named the area El Paso del Rio del Norte, or the Pass to the River to the North. That was 1598, twenty-two years before the Pilgrims would land at Plymouth Rock.

The first of this area's historic missions was not built until more than fifty years after Oñate's momentous river crossing. Under the direction of a Spanish missionary, Indians constructed Misión Nuestra Señora de Guadalupe—Our Lady of Guadalupe Mission—between 1658 and 1659 in Juárez. After the bloody Pueblo (Indian) Revolt of 1680, Spanish refugees fled Santa Fe and retreated south to El Paso, where two villages were established for the bands of Indians who remained loyal to Spain, whether by choice or by intimidation. Residents at Ysleta, named after the Isleta Pueblo just south of Albuquerque, and Socorro, which means "help" in Spanish, built missions where they began to worship a new god.

An Island of Progress

The Spanish influence remains strong today. About 65 percent of El Paso's population is Hispanic, and locals often jokingly plot to secede from Texas, a land that seems foreign to the inhabitants of the state's most distant western point. El Paso is 791 miles from Galveston, 830 miles from Beaumont, and 806 miles from Brownsville. In fact, it is closer to San Diego than to Houston, a metropolis that lies 743 miles east, a distance greater than the drive between Buffalo, N.Y., and Atlanta.

Though isolated, El Paso is no bump in the road, nor is it a sleepy hamlet unconnected to the progress and pitfalls of the twentieth century. El Paso's population exceeds 430,000, and Juárez claims 900,000 inhabitants. The two cities share both culture and economy, as is evidenced by the average of three million El Paso–Juárez border crossings per month. About fifteen thousand Juarenses work daily in El Paso. Additionally, American businesses maintain several twin-plant operations, where factories in El Paso prepare raw materials for assembly by sister plants across the border. The finished goods are then returned to the States to be packaged and sold by such makers as Atari, RCA, and Samsonite.

Though less frantic than its bigger cousins of the East Coast, El Paso is a busy hub of manufacturing, transportation, and military defense. The army payroll at Fort Bliss alone exceeds $303 million annually. The city's growth over the past decade has been the third highest of all U.S. urban areas. Among the primary income sources is western wear, of which El Paso is the undisputed southwest capital. Makers of handcrafted boots, including Larry Mahan, Tony Lama, and Justin, produce one million pairs each year—and still can't meet the demand. Clothing is another leading industry. Farah Manufacturing, only one of a hundred El Paso apparel firms, sells pants throughout the world. The factory and headquarters, a building one-half-mile long, employs three thousand workers; supervisors make the rounds on roller skates.

The Special Spirit of El Paso

With all the hustle and bustle, El Paso doesn't allow itself to be swept into the impersonal fog that characterizes so many big cities these days. The prevailing attitude is still one of *mañana,* or tomorrow, a philosophy of living borrowed from south of the border. Anything that can wait until later should and often does in El Paso. It is the kind of firmly entrenched leisurely pace that, if resisted by the uninitiated visitor, results only in the visitor's needless anxiety. This notion of dawdling through the day by no means halts the wheels of progress. It only briefly applies the brake for vitally important breathers: tickling babies, watching a sunset, taking short siestas, sipping *cerveza* (beer).

Part of the population's laid-back demeanor may be attributed to El Paso's climate. With weather so beautiful, keeping one's nose to the grindstone is an unrealistic expectation. Situated at the northern edge of Mexico's Chihuahuan Desert, El Paso enjoys warm days from March through October. The sun has failed to shine only 39 days since 1966. Winters are mild, though an occasional light snowfall—which abruptly halts business and closes schools—is not impossible. During the summer temperatures climb past 100 degrees, but the absence of humidity makes life bearable. The annual precipitation rate hovers at about 7.7 inches.

The City's Spokes

The major segments of El Paso seem to fan out from a point near the center of town, under a conglomerate of freeway ramps known as the Spaghetti Bowl. The bowl is the junction between Interstate 10 and the North-South freeway, a loop of which takes drivers to the Cordova port of entry to Juárez. Beneath the new-fashioned cement tangles of the Spaghetti Bowl lies El Paso's own "Boot Hill" and perhaps a fitting starting point for a city tour: the Concordia Cemetery. Many of the town's founding families are buried here, and there is even a special section for the Chinese inhabitants of yesteryear, including coolie laborers who died while constructing the railway.

The most famous tombstone is that of gunfighter, or "shooter," John Wesley Hardin, who met his end playing cards in the Acme Saloon downtown. The bar was a favorite meeting place for the likes of Wyatt Earp and Bat Masterson. Hardin, however, surpassed their reputations, holding the title of fastest gun in town. He claimed to have killed forty men. In August of 1895, Hardin was shot in the head by Constable John Selman. The local newspaper reported his death noting, "Except for being dead, Hardin looked remarkably well."

Just east of Concordia Cemetery are the busiest sections of the city, Downtown and Central El Paso. The skyline boasts several new buildings, including the gray, towering county jail, another reminder of Old West gunfights. During the late 1800s Downtown El Paso was one of the region's most notorious shoot-out arenas. At one spot on Santa Fe Street, Marshal Dallas Stoudenmire killed three men within five seconds. Johnny Hale, a rancher, had been accused by a posse of rustling Mexican cattle. Hale drew his gun and killed a constable in the group of lawmen. In reaction, Stoudenmire charged forward with guns blazing, killing a bystander accidently and fatally wounding Hale and one of Hale's supporters who foolishly pulled a gun.

One of Downtown's impressive landmarks is the Hotel Paso del Norte, constructed in 1912 (and currently closed for extensive renovation). The lobby, dominated by a huge Tiffany stained-glass dome overhead, is filled with mahogany and marble. Who slept here? Pancho Villa and Zsa Zsa Gabor—in separate instances, of course. San Jacinto Plaza is the nucleus of Downtown. The original city square and park once embraced pools with live alligators. Today it is the main congregation point of El Paso and the site of much sidewalk evangelism.

West and uphill from Downtown is the edge of West Side El Paso, which begins with the lovely hodgepodge of architecture in the old Sunset Heights and Kern Place neighborhoods. The University of Texas at El Paso (UTEP), one-and-a-half miles west of Downtown just off I–10, bears an architectural style that is simultaneously harmonious and incongruous with its environment. The buildings are patterned after motifs in Bhutan, a country on the northeastern border of India. Designers decided early this century that the desert hills of El Paso bore an uncanny resemblance to the terrain of Bhutan and the Himalayas.

Farther west on Interstate 10, but still in El Paso, the Rio Grande switches from an international border to the dividing line between Texas and New Mexico. A few feet from this confluence of boundaries is the peak of a modest mountain, where a statue of Christ stands. Called either Christ of the Rockies or Sierra de Cristo Rey, the Catholic shrine was sculpted by El Pasoan Urbici Soler in 1938. The summit can be reached by a foot trail of slightly more than one mile.

Neighborhoods thick with cottonwoods line the Rio Grande in an area known as the Upper Valley. The Upper Valley follows the Rio Grande from northwest of the University of Texas at El Paso to the city limits and somewhat beyond. Here is the true oasis in El Paso's stark landscape. Trees, shrubs, and wild grasses have sprung from a rich soil that bears chilies, alfalfa, cotton, and onions. The fertile strip stretches from the western limits of El Paso to Las Cruces, New Mexico, forty miles to the northwest.

North of Concordia Cemetery, along the new North-South freeway to Alamogordo, New Mexico, is Northeast El Paso, home of Fort Bliss, the largest air-defense center in the free world. The military population exceeds eighty thousand; in 1981, troops from twenty foreign countries worked at Fort Bliss, site of a German air-force training school.

The origin of Fort Bliss is confusing, because the fort shifted locations several times during its rocky history. The first military post was established in 1849 in what is now the western part of Downtown, including the El Paso Civic Center. It next moved to Magoffin Street in Central El Paso, then to Camp Concordia, near the Concordia

Cemetery, and then to Garrison Town, which now includes San Jacinto Plaza. Fort Bliss again relocated, pitching camp on the banks of the Rio Grande on Simeon Hart's property. Today that area harbors the University of Texas at El Paso and La Hacienda Restaurant.

Fort Bliss finally found a permanent niche. Construction at the current location, called Lanoria Mesa, began in 1892, and the first garrison of officers arrived in 1893. Over the years, Fort Bliss soldiers fought several formidable enemies, among them Geronimo and Pancho Villa. Today, there are fifteen thousand military retirees residing in El Paso, many of them in Northeast, where they lived while on active duty.

A drive east of Concordia Cemetery introduces the newcomer to the grass roots of El Paso. The East Side includes the city's newest and most immense suburban grounds. It is also the shopping axis of El Paso. The town's largest malls are situated along Interstate 10's eastern branch, which also links a number of refineries and manufacturing companies.

Farther east, along the Rio Grande, lies the Lower Valley, another rich farming area that brims with tales of Spanish conquests and Old West showdowns. The Lower Valley follows the Rio Grande southeast from just past East El Paso east of Delta Street and south of I–10, and is the site of the missions. The Lower Valley also embraces the Tigua Indians, who, like the Zuni, Taos, and other Rio Grande tribes, belong to the Pueblo group of native North Americans. The Tiguas are the oldest identifiable ethnic group in Texas. Their reservation, 122 S. Old Pueblo Road, features dances from 11:00 A.M. to 1:00 P.M. and 2:00 to 3:00 P.M. on Saturdays and Sundays. The museum houses arts and crafts, including jewelry and pottery, and the restaurant serves the hottest chili verde in town. Group tours are available. For more information, call 859–3916 or 859–3917.

Juárez

Of course, no description of El Paso would be complete without mention of Ciudad Juárez to the south. The city was named after Mexican president Benito Juárez, who in 1865 took refuge there during his struggle against the imperial rule of Maximilian of Austria. Most of Ciudad Juárez's claims to fame, in fact, seem to be rooted in war. Its most illustrious chapter has to be its 1911 takeover by General Francisco "Pancho" Villa and his revolutionary army.

Juárez offers a field day of extremes. Judging by a quick tour of its residential areas, inhabitants seem to live in either stunning mansions or cardboard shacks. Sadly, abject poverty is the more common situation, and even Juárez middle-class members have harder lives than poverty-level Americans.

Just as El Paso reflects a good deal of cultural assimilation, Juárez has borrowed from the American way. As if to symbolize its cohesive relationship with the its brothers to the north, Juárez holds a treasured American icon—the only standing Lincoln-memorial statue outside the United States. It is on Avenida Lincoln near the ProNaF (government-run craft store).

The Mountains

El Paso mapmakers generally divide the city according to populated sections. Yet the most prominent part of the city has the fewest inhabitants and remains untitled. It is simply "the Mountains." The Franklin Mountains are undeniably El Paso's prettiest feature. Loaded with tales of ghosts and motherlodes, the rugged range annually attracts thousands of hikers, climbers, and just plain lookers. People are drawn to the beauty and danger of the peaks and arroyos, which brim with deer, hawks, semiprecious gemstones, lead, tin, and desert plants—from cholla and prickly pear to ocotillo and yucca. The highest point along the jagged ridge is North Franklin Peak, at 7,192 feet above sea level.

To experience the mountains, a logical starting point is Scenic Drive, which extends from Richmond Avenue by way of Alabama on the Northeast Side to Rim Road by way of Mesa on the Westside. Scenic Point, a small parking lot with a few telescopes, offers a panoramic view of El Paso from 4,221 feet above sea level. Fossils of prehistoric fish are embedded in the limestone 200 feet above this lookout, where mastadons once roamed.

A second stop should be the Ranger Peak Aerial Tramway, reached by taking McKinley up the mountain from Alabama on the Northeast Side. A cable car rides 2,300 feet to an observation deck and a television transmitting tower on Ranger Peak, 5,653 feet above sea level. The seven thousand-square-mile view engulfs portions of three states—Chihuahua in Mexico, New Mexico, and Texas—and a host of other ranges, including the Hueco, Juárez, and Mimbres Mountains in three different directions. Cable-car rides cost two dollars for adults and one dollar for children under twelve. For information call 566–6622.

The next mountain visit should be paid to McKelligon Canyon, a popular picnic spot that harbors an amphitheater where jazz and rock concerts are staged, as well as the annual Southwest pageant *Viva! El Paso!* Once a game-and-bird refuge, McKelligon is a park founded during the Depression to provide construction work for jobless El Pasoans. The canyon is open daily to hikers, campers, picnickers, and sightseers.

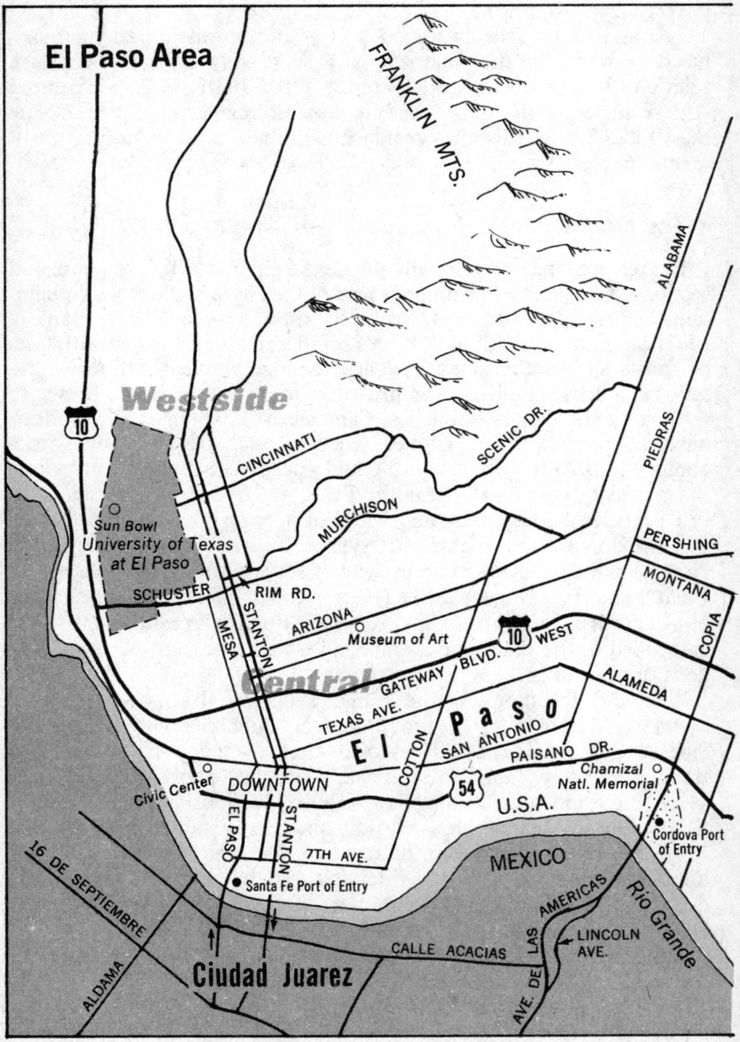
El Paso Area
FRANKLIN MTS.
Westside
10
CINCINNATI
SCENIC DR.
ALABAMA
PIEDRAS
Sun Bowl
University of Texas
at El Paso
MURCHISON
PERSHING
MONTANA
SCHUSTER
RIM RD.
STANTON
MESA
ARIZONA
Museum of Art
10 WEST
COPIA
GATEWAY BLVD.
Central
ALAMEDA
TEXAS AVE.
El Paso
SAN ANTONIO
COTTON
PAISANO DR.
Chamizal
Natl. Memorial
Civic Center
DOWNTOWN
54
U.S.A.
EL PASO
STANTON
7TH AVE.
Cordova Port
of Entry
MEXICO
Santa Fe Port of Entry
16 DE SEPTIEMBRE
AMERICAS
Rio Grande
LINCOLN
AVE.
CALLE ACACIAS
AVE. DE LAS
ALDAMA
Ciudad Juarez

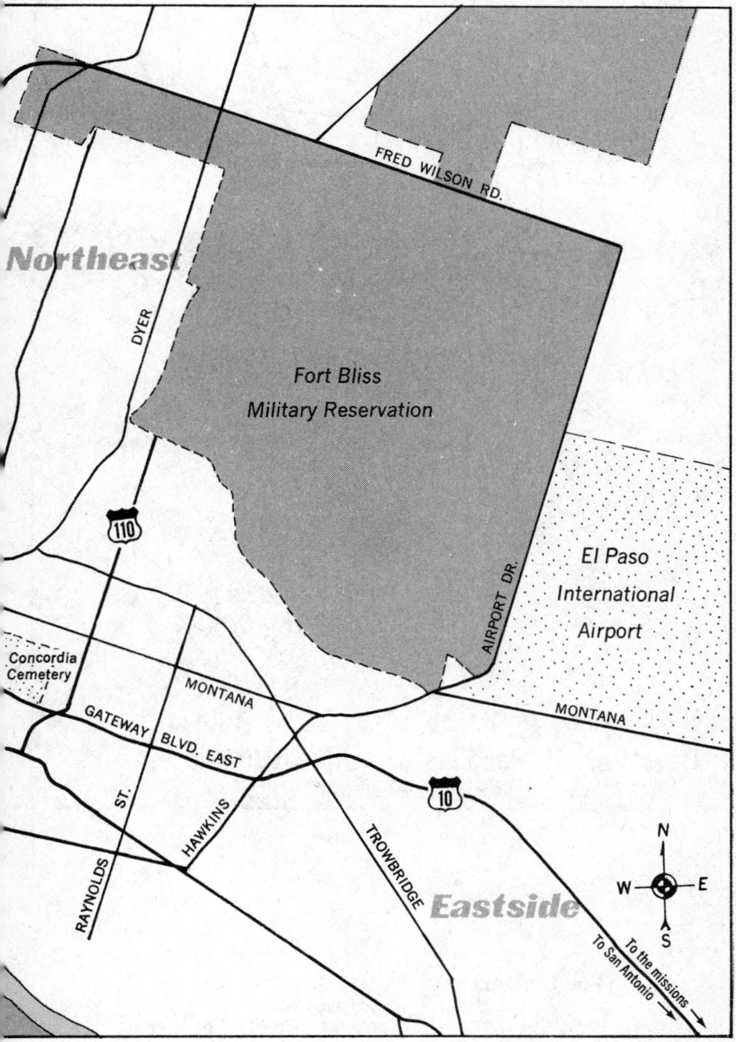
FRED WILSON RD.
Northeast
DYER
Fort Bliss
Military Reservation
110
El Paso
International
Airport
AIRPORT DR.
Concordia
Cemetery
MONTANA
MONTANA
GATEWAY BLVD. EAST
10
ST.
RAYNOLDS
HAWKINS
TROWBRIDGE
Eastside
N
W
E
S
To the missions
To San Antonio

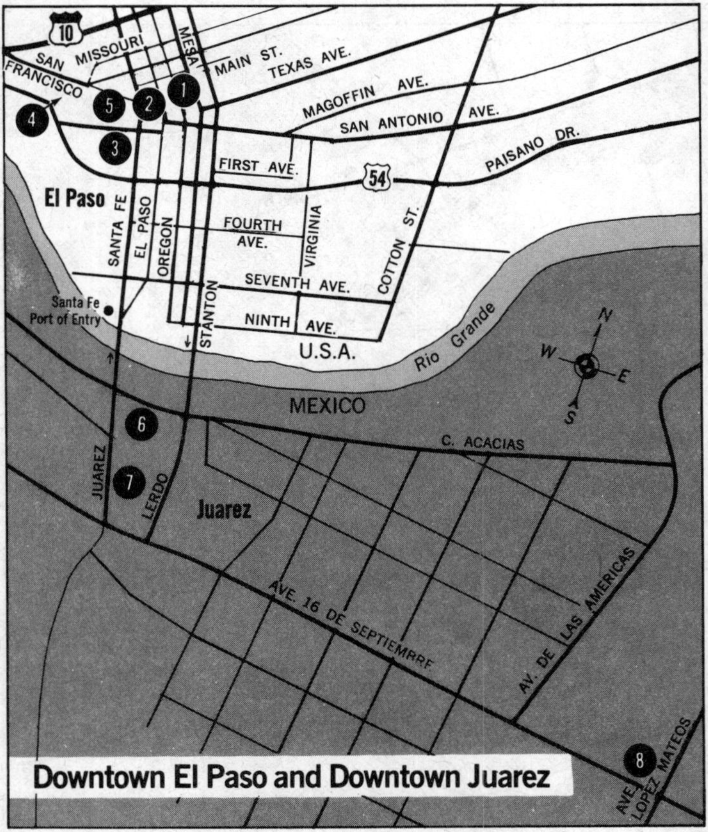

Downtown El Paso and Downtown Juarez

Points of Interest:

1) San Jacinto Plaza
2) Greyhound Station
3) Trailways Station
4) Union Depot
5) El Paso Civic Center Plaza
6) Mexican Tourist Information
7) Plaza Monumental Bullring
8) ProNaF

Finally, tourists who want to see the Franklin Mountains from the inside out should take the seven-mile drive across Trans Mountain Road, one of the highest roads in Texas. It slices through the range from Northeast El Paso to the West Side, passing petroglyph sites and Fusselman Canyon, the largest canyon in the Franklins.

PRACTICAL INFORMATION FOR EL PASO

HOW TO GET THERE. By bus. *Greyhound,* 544–7200, is Downtown at 111 San Francisco. *Trailways,* 533–5921, is nearby at 200 W. San Antonio. *Texas, New Mexico and Oklahoma Coaches Inc.,* which offers tours to Carlsbad in addition to its regular routes, is at 111 San Francisco; 532–3404. *Transportes Chihuahuenses,* 544–7200, offers numerous routes throughout Mexico. In El Paso, their buses leave from the Greyhound station.

By air. The major airlines that serve El Paso at El Paso International Airport are *America West,* (800) 247–5692; *American Airlines,* 533–9909; *Delta,* 779–2288; *Eastern,* 532–6854; and *Frontier,* 779–6266; *United,* 779–1036; and *Western,* (800) 227–6105. *Southwest Airlines,* 859–1221, also serves El Paso, flying among most big Texas cities, including Corpus Christi, Dallas, and Houston, and to points as far as San Diego, New Orleans, and Los Angeles. The Juárez International Airport is served by *Aeroméxico,* 544–9290, which has offices in El Paso at 303 N. Oregon, Downtown. For information on *Mexicana,* which flies throughout Mexico, phone (800) 292–7871.

By train. *Amtrak,* situated in the historic and recently renovated Union Depot at 700 San Francisco, takes an eastern route to Houston and New Orleans and travels west to Tucson. Call 545–2247 or (800) 421–8320.

By car. The main arteries leading into El Paso are: I–10, which runs east and west and serves as the primary freeway through the city; U.S. 54, known as Dyer Street in town, which travels northeast to Alamogordo and entwines with I–10 and the Cordova port of entry to Juárez just east of Downtown; and U.S. 62/180, called Montana in town, which travels east to Carlsbad. At Las Cruces, 45 mi. north of town, I–10 connects with I–25, which runs north to Albuquerque and Denver. I–10 links El Paso with Tucson to the west and with Abilene and San Antonio to the east.

The driving times to El Paso from other cities or areas, in hours, are: Big Bend National Park, 6½; Abilene, 9; San Antonio, 11; Dallas–Fort Worth Metroplex, 11 to 12; Santa Fe, 6; Phoenix, 5.

TELEPHONES. The area code for El Paso and much of West Texas is 915. For Las Cruces and all New Mexico locations it is 505. In El Paso dial 1–411 for information. Outside El Paso dial (915) 555–1212. For Fort Bliss directory assistance, phone 568–2121. For directory assistance in Juárez, dial 1–32–40131 from El Paso; from outside El Paso, dial 010 and ask the operator for Juárez directory assistance. To dial direct to Juárez from El Paso, dial 1–32 and then the five-digit number. At a pay phone, local calls cost 25¢ and calls to Juárez cost $1.

El Paso, unlike most of the rest of Texas, which is on Central Time, is on Mountain Time. This means that it is *two* hours earlier on the clock than the East Coast, and *one* hour later than the West Coast.

HOTELS AND MOTELS. Prices quoted are for a double room for two. Categories are defined as follows: *Expensive,* $50 to $100; *Moderate,* $25 to $49; and *Inexpensive,* less than $25.

Expensive

Embassy Suites. 6100 Gateway East, East Side; 779–6222. Convenient to the airport. Gorgeous layout with rooms facing interior atrium gardens and indoor-outdoor pool. The view from the upstairs Isabella's restaurant is fabulous. King-sized and double-double beds. All rooms are suites with kitchenettes. Free cocktails 5:30 to 7:30 P.M. Free full breakfast. Pets permitted. Airport pickup. 185 rooms.

Hilton Inn. 2027 Airway, El Paso International Airport; 778–4241. Beautiful large pool but otherwise slightly rundown quarters. King- and queen-sized beds available. Pets permitted. Airport pickup. Playground, restaurant, lounge. 145 rooms.

Marriott. 1600 Airway at El Paso International Airport; 779–3300. Luxury through and through. Indoor-outdoor swimming pool, hydrotherapy pool. Terrific views of both Downtown El Paso and Juárez. Plush suites. La Cascada Mexican Restaurant, McGinty's Grill Specialty Restaurant, and McGinty's Lounge. 300 rooms.

Moderate

Caballero Motor Hotel. 6400 Montana, East Side; 772–4231. Convenient to the airport and Bassett Center. Heated pool, king- and queen-sized beds available. Pets permitted. Airport pickup. Restaurant and the popular Caballero Lounge. 101 rooms.

Execulodge. 4501 N. Mesa, West Side; 533–6801. Pool, king- and queen-sized beds available. Pets permitted. Airport pickup. Restaurant, lounge. 100 rooms.

Executive Inn. 500 Executive Center, West Side; 532–8981. Pool. King- and queen-sized beds available. Pets permitted. Airport pickup. Restaurant, lounge. 99 rooms.

Holiday Inn Airport. 6655 Gateway West, East Side; 778–6411. Pool, king-sized beds available. Airport pickup. Restaurant, lounge. 196 rooms.

Holiday Inn Downtown. 113 W. Missouri; 544–3300. A high rise with stunning views of the city. Pool. King-sized beds available. Pets permitted. Restaurant, lounge. 209 rooms.

Holiday Inn Mid-City. I–10 at Raynolds, East Side–central; 533–7521. Heated pool, king-sized beds available. Pets permitted. Airport pickup. Restaurant, lounge. 197 rooms.

Holiday Inn Sunland Park. I–10 at Sunland Park, West Side; 833–2900. Gorgeous new complex, convenient to the freeway, Downtown, and West Side, but quiet. Excellent restaurant.

Howard Johnson's Motor Lodge. 8887 Gateway West, East Side; 591–9471. Pool. King-sized beds available. Pets permitted. Airport pickup. Restaurant, lounge. 140 rooms.

Imperial 400 Motel. 6363 Montana, East Side; 778–3311. Heated pool, queen-sized beds available. Airport pickup. Kitchenettes. 59 rooms.

La Quinta Motor Inn. 6140 Gateway East, East Side; 778–9321. Pool. Pets permitted. Airport pickup. Restaurant. 121 rooms.

La Quinta Motor Inn. 11033 Gateway West, East Side; 591–2244. Pool. King-sized beds available. Pets permitted. 138 rooms.

Rodeway Inn. 6201 Gateway West, East Side; 778–6611. Convenient to the airport and Bassett Center. Sprawling complex. Pool. King-sized beds available. Airport pickup. Restaurant, lounge. 310 rooms.

Tom Penny Inn. 7144 Gateway East, East Side; 779–7700. Heated pool. King- and queen-sized beds available. Pets permitted. Airport pickup. Restaurant. 179 rooms.

TraveLodge East. 6308 Montana, East Side; 778–6661. Heated pool. King- and queen-sized beds available. 70 rooms.

TraveLodge El Paso Central. 409 E. Missouri, Downtown; 544–3333. Pool. King- and queen-sized beds available. Airport pick-up. Restaurant, lounge. 109 rooms.

Inexpensive

Budget Inn Motel. 5634 E. Paisano, East Side; 772–8875. Clean. Heated pool. King-sized beds available. Pets permitted. Lounge. 48 rooms.

Budget Lodge Motel. 1301 N. Mesa, West Side; 533–6821. Clean, quiet, convenient to Downtown but a comfortable distance from traffic congestion.

Colonia Motor Hotel. 8601 Dyer, Northeast; 755–7621. Pool. King- and queen-sized beds available. Pets allowed. Kitchenettes. Good Oriental-food restaurant. Lounge. 55 rooms.

Gardner Hotel. 311 E. Franklin, Downtown; 532–3661. The city's only youth hostel. Old but clean. Members, $7.50; nonmembers, $9.50.

Hawaiian Royale Motel. 8735 Dyer, Northeast; 755–2341. Pool. Pets allowed. Kitchenettes, playground. Restaurant. 60 rooms.

La Posta Motor Lodge. 4111 N. Mesa, West Side; 533–3986. Tiny, somewhat worn out. Pool. King-sized beds available. 37 rooms.

Sunset Inn Motel. 4532 N. Mesa, West Side; 533–8201. Pool. King-sized beds available. Pets permitted. Houses a passable Arabic-food restaurant and popular rock club. 120 rooms.

Warren Inn. 4748 N. Mesa, West Side; 544–4494. Spiffy and new. Free Continental breakfast. Pool, heated jacuzzi, color cable television, kitchens. Daily or weekly rates.

HOW TO GET AROUND. Buses. Sun City Area Transit, or SCAT, 533–3333, operates fairly modern buses with reliable air conditioning, even during June's 110-degree days. Schedules are light. You may wait an hour for a bus to outlying areas. And because the city is so spread out, a trip from one end of the city to another may require one or more transfers. Fares are 50¢, and transfers cost 20¢.

Juárez border buses are red. To go to the ProNaF, catch the bus at the corner of Paisano and Stanton in Downtown El Paso. The window sign should say "El Paso/Juárez" and "PTE LIBRE." This bus takes the Cordova or "free bridge" port of entry. Buses crossing the Stanton and Santa Fe bridges downtown may be caught on South El Paso St. until San Antonio, where they turn and continue to Stanton, then turn right and head for Juárez. These are marked "El Paso/Juárez" and "STA FE." In Juárez, the bus travels down Lerdo and makes a right turn at Avenida 16 de Septiembre. To see the Guadalupe Mission, get off at the last stop on this street and walk west three blocks. To visit the Juárez city market, get off at the first stop on this street and walk two blocks east.

From the airport. A taxi to downtown will cost about $9.00 plus tip, and should take twenty to thirty minutes. There is no airport bus or limousine service.

Taxis. Unfortunately, some cabdrivers in El Paso have a reputation for taking advantage of naïve newcomers. Be wary, but more important, be informed. Try to learn the route and mileage to a particular destination before you hail a cab. By the way, hailing a cab in El Paso is a tricky business, since operators tend to park in taxi zones rather than driving around in search of passengers. Calling a cab is a safer proposition, but you might wait for 45 minutes, unless you're Downtown. In Juárez, cabs are the easiest, most efficient means of getting around if you're not limiting your visit to a walk down Avenida Juárez. *Always* ask the price of the ride before you hop in the back seat.

Walking. Walking is not a very practical way to see El Paso. The Lower Valley missions may be 30 or 40 mi. from interesting points in West Side El Paso. Downtown, however, offers a walking tour that winds around historic buildings and a number of landmarks. A map detailing the tour is available at the Greater El Paso Tourist and Convention Bureau at the El Paso Civic Center. (See the *Tours* section, below.)

By car. Driving is the ideal way to experience the sprawling city. Roads are clearly marked and adequately maintained, and street maps are available at the tourist bureau, the El Paso Chamber of Commerce, and most service stations.

Several car-rental agencies, some offering worthwhile seven-day or weekend plans, are based at the airport.

TOURIST INFORMATION. Both the El Paso Chamber of Commerce, 534–0500, and the Greater El Paso Civic, Convention and Tourist Center, 534–0600, are situated at the El Paso Civic Center Plaza Downtown. A list of hotels may be obtained by writing the El Paso Chamber of Commerce, Ten Civic Center Plaza, P.O. Box 9738, El Paso, Texas 79987. For sightseeing information, write the Greater El Paso Tourist and Convention Bureau, Five Civic Center Plaza, El Paso, Texas 79999.

The El Paso Tourist Information Center, 859–3300, on I–10 at the Ave. of the Americas, provides literature, and, on request, will show a film about El Paso. The Texas Tourist Information Center is on I–10 East at the Texas–New Mexico border; 886–2511. It offers comprehensive literature featuring sights and highlights of El Paso and Texas.

The Mexico Tourist Information Center is just opposite the Stanton St. Bridge at Malecón, Juarez; phone 40123. There you can pick up brochures, maps, and hotel information about Juárez and other cities.

SEASONAL EVENTS. January. While others celebrate New Year's Day with a bowl of black-eyed peas, El Pasoans feast on menudo, a spicy Mexican tripe stew fabled to cure hangovers. Recovered, locals romp and stomp in **February** during the *Southwest International Livestock Show and Rodeo,* which kicks off with a Downtown parade and features 10 days of livestock shows, rodeo competition, and top country-and-western entertainment.

The winds of **March** bring the enchanting *Siglo de Oro Drama Festival,* two weeks of Spanish classical-drama competition at the Chamizal National Memorial Theater in El Paso. The Juárez bullfight season begins in **April.** The highlight of **May** is also a Juárez event, the annual *Cinco de Mayo Parade,* May 5. **June** is lively with native dances and ceremonies during the *Tigua Saint Anthony's Day Ceremony* at the Tigua Indian Reservation.

The usual array of fireworks and festivities toast Independence Day in **July,** when the four-day *El Paso Street Festival,* with continuous live entertainment, art exhibits, ethnic-food booths, and gunfighter "shoot-outs," is staged at the El Paso Civic Center and surrounding streets. The annual historical pageant *Viva! El Paso!* begins at McKelligon Canyon Amphitheater in Northeast El Paso, and the colorful coming-of-age ceremonies, featuring dazzling Mountain Spirit night dances, take place on the Mescalero Apache Indian Reservation near Ruidoso, northeast of El Paso.

August hosts the down-home *Cotton Festival* in Fabens, just east of El Paso on I–10. **September** brings slightly cooler temperatures, in the 90s, the sizzling *Texas Red Chili Cook-off,* and the three-day *Fiesta de las Flores,* a weekend carnival celebrating Mexican-American culture. September 16 is *Mexican Inde-*

pendence Day, and there is generally a parade and lots of tequila-laced celebration in Juárez.

Finally, Indian summer arrives in **October,** along with the annual *Menudo Cook-off* (menudo is a spicy tripe stew) in the El Paso Civic Center and a slew of cultural happenings. *Kermezaar* fills the El Paso Civic Center with regional arts and crafts. The *Socorro Art Fiesta* salutes the townfolk of tiny Socorro, Texas, in the Lower Valley, with a mini-parade and oodles of booths filled with crafts, antiques, and homemade Mexican goodies. The *Border Folk Festival* at the Chamizal National Memorial features a weekend of folk singers, musicians, and dancers from around the country.

On the second day of **November,** Juárez citizens observe *Day of the Dead* or *All Saints Day* at the Juárez Cemetery on Zaragosa Road. Flowers literally flood the street as inhabitants pay tribute to their lost relatives. A day of incredible feasting and toasting.

December is a glittery month in El Paso. A week before Christmas, the El Paso Electric Company lights an enormous star on a slope in the southern end of the Franklin Mountains. On Christmas Eve, El Paso embraces a charming custom of decorating yards and sidewalks with *luminarios,* lighted candles placed in sand-filled paper bags. Scenic Drive is typically festooned with the glowing baubles, but the biggest Christmas razzle dazzle may be found in the Eastridge neighborhood off McRae on the East Side, where residents transform their streets into a shimmering neon maze. The last month of the year also heralds many *Sun Bowl* activities, including the coronation of the Sun Queen, a basketball tounament, and the annual Sun Bowl football game televised from the University of Texas at El Paso.

TOURS. City tours. *The Gray Line,* 598–8878, offers sightseeing tours by bus through El Paso and Juárez. A four-hour tour to Juárez leaves at 9:30 A.M. and takes visitors to the city market, the ProNaF center, a glass factory, the Plaza Monumental bullring and the country-club neighborhood. The cost is $9.50. A slightly curtailed three-hour Juárez tour in the afternoon costs $9. Gray Line's four-hour El Paso tour costs $9. A combination tour, taking passengers to sights in both El Paso and Juárez, starts at 9:30 A.M. and costs $17.00 for adults and $8.50 for children under 11. Tours to the Juárez race track and to bullfights (seasonal) are also available.

Golden Tours, 779-0555, offers Juárez tours that begin at 9:30 A.M. and 2:00 P.M. Cost is $9.00 for adults and $4.50 for children 5 to 12. The tour visits a glass factory, the Chamizal Federal Park, the Guadalupe Mission, the ProNaF, the bullring, and the city market. An El Paso tour, beginning at 2:00 P.M., visits the Downtown area, the University of Texas at El Paso, Scenic Drive, Fort Bliss, the Tigua Indian Reservation, and neighborhoods along the Rio Grande. Nightly round-trip rides to the Juárez Race Track cost $6. Discounts and custom tours may be arranged for large groups.

The *Yellow Cab Company* at 900 S. Santa Fe., 532–9036, offers Juárez tours to the ProNaf, glass factories, Plaza Monumental or Balderas bullrings, Guadalupe Mission, the city market, and Mexican residential areas with more iron work than New Orleans' French Quarter.

Walking tour. The Greater El Paso Tourist and Convention Bureau has maps and keys to the walking tour, marked along downtown sidewalks by faded yellow footsteps. The tour begins in San Jacinto Plaza at the corner of Mills and Oregon, a point along the 1,600-mile Camino Real (King's Highway) that stretched from Mexico City to Santa Fe and was used by Spanish colonizers. Highlights of the tour include a mural by noted artist Tom Lea in the U.S. Courthouse, the Church of the Immaculate Conception, built in 1892 on a small rise to protect it from the annual spring flooding of the Rio Grande, and the rejuvenated Mills Building, designed by Henry C. Trost, a celebrated architect at the turn of the century.

PARKS, ZOOS, AND AMUSEMENT CENTERS. El Paso's newest recreational attraction is **Magic Landing,** a 23-acre theme park east of El Paso between the Avenue of the Americas and Zaragoza exits on I-10. The fun includes a steam-powered train, a carnival midway, game arcades, amusement rides, and a ferris wheel 15 stories tall. Phones 858–3000. **Ascarate,** a huge city park with a large lake, offers boating, baseball, tennis, handball, volleyball, a golf course, and picnic grounds. 772–3941. On the park grounds is **Western Playland Amusement Park,** with rides geared toward tots as well as brave-hearted adults; open weekends, March through Memorial Day, then Tuesday through Sunday evenings until Labor Day. Phone 772–3914 or 532–6969.

The **Chamizal National Memorial** is a park, museum, and theater dedicated to the settlement of a dispute between the United States and Mexico over a section of border territory. Established in 1973, the park commemorates the history of the border from 1848 to the final resolution of the boundary dispute in 1963. A film about the surveying of the border is shown on request in the 500-seat theater; 543–7880. The park's Mexico counterpart is the 760-acre **Chamizal Federal Park,** landscaped with more than 750,000 trees and a botanical garden.

The five-acre **El Paso Zoological Park,** 10 minutes from Downtown in Washington Park, Evergreen at Paisano, houses 250 mammals, birds, and reptiles. Phone 541–4600.

PARTICIPANT SPORTS. Ambitious **joggers** get a workout in the hilly parts of West El Paso and the especially challenging routes over Scenic Drive and Trans Mountain Road. Runners with less drive tackle the flat runs along the river levees in the Upper and Lower Valleys and throughout East El Paso.

El Paso's glorious sunshine is perfect **golf** weather: Ascarate Municipal Golf Course in Ascarate Park, 27 holes; 772–7381. Cielo Vista Municipal Golf Course at 1510 Hawkins near the Airport, 18 holes; 591–4927. Also, Dos Lagos in Anthony, northwest of El Paso, 18 holes; 882–2830.

Horseback riding is available by the hour at: Horse Country Stables, 11248 Montana; 593–0321. Indian Cliff Ranch, four miles north of the Fabens I–10 exit; 544–3200. Square Dance Stables, 13227 Montana; 592–1650.

Swimming is a popular sport almost year-round, but especially during the dog days of July and August. Almost all motels have pools. Ten public swimming pools also are available.

Tennis players swing in El Paso at 25 public courts, 18 of them lighted for night games. For locations and hours of pools and courts, call the El Paso Parks and Recreation Department; 594–8614.

Biking is popular in the Upper and Lower Valleys, less plagued by traffic congestion and better shaded. The city's only bona-fide bicycle route follows Yandell street between Paisano and the University of Texas at El Paso.

Roller-skating is available at: El Paso Skateland, 6550 N. Mesa, West Side; 581–4845. Rushfair Good-Time Center, 5250 Fairbanks, Northeast, 751–9092. Roller King, 10826 Pellicano, Eastside; 591–8822. Wheels Plus, 6369 Montana, Eastside; 779–3924.

Amateur **archery** buffs are admitted for open shooting Saturday and Sunday at the El Paso Archery Range on Fred Wilson Road, Northeast.

Water slides are the summer lures at Wetand Wild Water World, just northwest of El Paso at the KOA Campgrounds west of the I–10 Anthony exit; 886–3507.

Go-carts may be rented at Family Golf and Go-Carts, 10355 Dyer, Northeast, 821–8153.

SPECTATOR SPORTS. El Paso's Diablos team plays **baseball** during the spring and summer at Dudley Field, 3931 Findley; 544–1950. A variety of college sports are on tap year-round at the University of Texas at El Paso. The Miners play **football** in the Sun Bowl and **basketball** in the Special Events Center. A number of **track and field** events are open to the public as well. Phone 747–5234.

Professional **bullfights** are staged in the Plaza Monumental Bullring, 16 de Septiembre at Carril Panamericana in Juárez. The bullring, the fourth largest in the world, seats 17,000. Matches are set on certain Sundays from April through September. Amateur bullfights and Mexican rodeos are staged occasionally on Sundays.

Sunland Park Race Track features **horse racing** October to May at Sunland Park Drive and Doniphan, West Side. Dinner and drinks are available; 589–1131.

The most popular spectator sport for tourists undoubtedly is **greyhound racing.** The dogs run at 8:00 P.M. Wednesday through Sunday year-round at the Juárez Race Track, off Avenida 16 de Septiembre, east of the bullring. Follow the signs. Complete wagering facilities accept both U.S. and Mexican currency. The enclosed air-conditioned grandstand features the Jockey Club on the second level, where visitors get the best view and enjoy an indoor German beer garden. The El Paso office is at 5959 Gateway West; 778–6322.

The El Paso Speedway Park, 14900 Montana, East Side, is the site of **automobile racing** at 8:00 P.M. Fridays and Saturdays, April through October. Stock-car, formula-midget, and speedway bike races are featured. Drag races take place at the Sun City Dragway, on Montana 4 mi. east of the I–10-Ysleta cut-off, East Side.

Polo fans can watch the sport at 1:30 P.M. every Sunday from May to September at the Las Anitas Polo Field near the Zaragosa Bridge in the Lower Valley.

HISTORIC SITES. Lower Valley missions, within close proximity of one another, are vestiges of a history filled with violent religious clashes between the Indians who populated the rich farmland and the zealous Spaniard explorers and priests who sought to convert them. The **Ysleta Mission** was built in 1681 by Franciscan *padres* and the Tigua Indians. One of the oldest buildings in the United States, it predates the first missions of California by 90 years. In an outdoor niche is a statute of Saint Anthony, the Tiguas' patron saint. Take I–10 east to the Ysleta exit. Drive south 3 mi. to Ysleta, home of the Tigua Indians. The mission is between Zaragosa and Old Pueblo Rd. Phone 859–9848. Nearby is the Ysleta del Sur Pueblo Museum, 122 S. Old Pueblo Rd., off Alameda, which traces the history of the Pueblo Indians in the historic Candelaria house, built in the mid–1700s. Hours are daily, 9:00 A.M. to 5:00 P.M. Phone 859–7913.

The **Socorro Mission,** the oldest continuously active parish in the United States, was constructed in 1681. The handcarved roof beams were sculptured by the Piro Indians, who settled here after the Pueblo Revolt of 1680 but are no longer a distinct ethnic group. In the south sacristy is a hand-carved wooden statue of Saint Michael. According to legend, the statue was being transported from Mexico to a church in New Mexico, when the ox cart carrying it "miraculously" became mired in the Rio Grande mud near the church. It could not be budged, so locals assumed the statue was meant to remain in Socorro. Take I–10 east to the Ave. of the Americas. Go south, then left on Socorro Rd. Phone 859–7718.

San Elizario Presidio, on the famous Camino Real, was established in the 1780s as a fort to defend the Spanish against the Apaches. It was the county seat of El Paso until the railroad arrived in 1881. An adobe structure on the south side of the plaza is the old county jail, where many of the area's desperados were incarcerated. In 1877, San Elizario was chiseled into history when a company of Texas Rangers surrendered to a mob during the Salt War, a battle between locals over the ownership and prices of salt dug from flats near Guadalupe Peak. The resulting murders and executions made this one of the valley's bloodiest chapters. To reach San Elizario, take the route to Socorro Mission but continue on Socorro Road (FM 258) 5 mi.

The fourth mission of interest in the region is the **Guadalupe Mission** in Juárez, off the Avenida 16 de Septiembre, constructed of adobe between 1658 and 1668 by a Spanish missionary and local Indians. According to legend, shadows from the mission point to the Lost Padre Mine in the Franklin Mountains, where Spanish gold is said to be hidden.

The **Magoffin Home,** 1120 Magoffin Ave., near Downtown, is a furnished 20-room Territorial-style hacienda built in 1875 by pioneer El Pasoan Joseph Magoffin. The walls are 4-ft.-thick adobe. Inside are hand-hewn *vigas* (beams) and some furnishings that date to the time of the original owner. Open Wednesday through Sunday. Phone 533–5147.

SHOPPING. The two biggest conventional shopping complexes, both on the East Side, are *Cielo Vista Mall* at Hawkins and I–10, and *Bassett Center,* at I–10 and Geronimo. Either should meet any run-of-the mill shopping needs, as well as supply the usual assortment of specialty shops. Credit-card holders can take advantage of Cielo Vista's anchors: *Montgomery Ward, J. C. Penney, Sears, Joske's,* and *Dillard's.* Downtown, the leading department store serving shoppers on both sides of the border is the locally owned *Popular.*

COWBOY BOOTS

Several bootmakers, from the huge Tony Lama manufacturing company to the Downtown-basement Plainsman factory, maintain plants in El Paso, where the generous supply of both first-quality and irregular shoes keeps prices comparatively low. If you pay $500 for a top-of-the-line pair of ostrich boots in Houston, the El Paso price may be less than $300. Even so, boots are an expensive memento, and buyers should shop around for the lowest price tag and highest quality. The *BOOTrader,* 10787 Gateway West, East Side, carries 10,000 pairs with brands such as Justin, Nocona, Acme, Dingo, Dan Post, and Lucchese. It also offers Bailey and Resistol hats and personalized leather belts. *Cowtown Boot Company,* 11401 Gateway West, East Side, carries an extensive inventory of seconds. Among their biggest sellers are sharkskin boots. Prices are attractive. The small, family-operated *Desierto Leather Shop,* 1601 Montana near Downtown, features an elegant line of Plainsman boots in rare-reptile skins at below-average prices.

Tony Lama handcrafted boots are available at five factory outlets: 109 E. Overland, Downtown; 12151 Gateway West at Zaragosa, East Side; 7156 Gateway East, next to the main plant; 4900 Gateway West, West Side; and 9220 Dyer, in Northeast El Paso.

Champion rodeo cowboy Larry Mahan hung up his spurs and hopped on the bootmaking bandwagon a few years back. Rugged men's boots and delicate ladies' styles with blue butterflies and pale red flowers are among the pickings at *Larry Mahan's Factory Outlet Boot Stores,* 7661 N. Mesa, West Side; The *Champion Boot Company Factory Outlet,* 8070 Gateway East, East Side, sells boots at wholesale prices and has an interesting array of children's cowboy boots handmade in Juárez.

And the *Hondo Boot Company,* 5548 El Paso Drive, behind the Fox Plaza Shopping Center in Central El Paso, distributes Mexican-made Hondo boots with prices starting at $60.

DISCOUNT CLOTHING

Clothing is a big industry in El Paso, where several factory employees stitch on those trendy back-pocket labels that triple the value of denim jeans. *Farah Manufacturing* wears the pants in El Paso's trouser-making family, and it operates a factory outlet at 8889 Gateway West, next to its enormous manufacturing plant. *Trevino Outlet Mall,* I-10 at Lee Trevino, East Side, offers bargains in clothing, shoes, boots, fabric, sporting goods and even eyewear. Cut-rate designer wear is particularly reasonable at the center's *J. Brannam* store, 594–1111. *Jogamoe's,* headquarters for the Sasson label and a variety of El Paso-made Viola sportswear, has locations at 217 N. Stanton, Downtown; and 5140 Montana and 1840 Lee Trevino, both East Side. Great buys in the newest Ralph Lauren fashions may be found at the *Polo Factory Store* in Cielo Vista Mall. Four *AID Clothing* locations offer bargain-basement discounts on clothes for the whole family, as do both *ZIP Fashion Outlets,* 301 Cincinnati, West Side; and 8500 Dyer, Northeast.

SPECIAL PLACES

If you fly to El Paso, one of the first shopping stops to check out is *La Placita,* on the quaint hallway of gift shops at the El Paso International Airport, open daily, 9:00 A.M. to 7:00 P.M. *Dos Pajaros Gallery* showcases several prominent Southwest artists, including El Paso's Frederick Carter and Robert Carlson. *Indian Nation Trading Post* offers a wide selection of Southwest Indian jewelry, rugs, pottery, and sand paintings.

For kitchen-theme items, shop the *Coffee Emporium,* 5817 N. Mesa, West Side, or the *Dutch Oven,* Cielo Vista Mall, I-10 at Hawkins, East Side. Nice ceramics, desk accessories, and pretty things in general are offered at *The Looking Glass,* 3737 N. Mesa; *Charlotte's,* 5411 N. Mesa at Peppertree Square; and *Gifts with Grace,* 2801 N. Stanton, all on the West Side. Wine and wine knickknacks are sold in quantity at the *Vintage Year,* 6633 N. Mesa, and *Penrods Wine and Gourmet Delicatessen,* 4400 N. Mesa, both on the West Side.

Fine-art lovers interested in picking up examples of Southwestern works should visit *Casa Adobe Gallery,* 126 Shadow Mountain in Turtle Cove, West Side. The gallery represents master printmakers Amado Maurilio Pena, Jr., and Liese Jean Scott of Austin, as well as renowned local potters. The *Galeria Colonial,* 2717 N. Stanton, West Side, specializes in Mexican *bultos* and *retablos* —religious scenes painted on tin sheets—of the 18th and 19th centuries. *Ed Hill Gallery,* 2601-B N. Stanton, West Side, deals in fine contemporary prints and works by prominent Southwest artists, including Fritz Scholder. Intricate and ultra-geometric 14K gold originals are among the treasures at *Tiara Jewelry and Gallery,* 1500 Montana, near Downtown.

Two out-of-the-way points are worth shopping trips. In the tiny Lower Valley community of Socorro, in-the-know antique lovers buy fine country pine and Spanish Colonial furniture at *Caldarella's Socorro Trading Post,* at *The Bosque,* 10167 Socorro. *Socorro Gallery* features paintings by Las Viejas Artistas, "the old women artists." *La Mesilla,* off I-10 just south of Las Cruces, about 40 mi. northwest of El Paso, is a historic Spanish village with an enchanting old church. The plaza is surrounded by thick-walled adobe buildings that now serve as shops. The area is said to be among Billy the Kid's stomping grounds. The Kid was convicted of murder and jailed here, where the Butterfield Overland Stagecoach Line stopped from 1858 to 1861. Some La Mesilla musts: the *Double Eagle* restaurant, crammed with impressive antiques; *Galeria de las Artes,* carrying work by Marty Katon, Rosamond and Aldo Luongo; and the *William Bonney Gallery,* featuring fine Pueblo Indian pottery by Red Starr and Margaret and Luther.

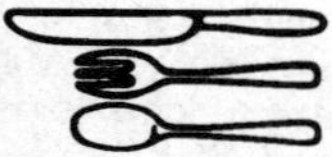

DINING OUT. Though many El Pasoans consider their town a steak-and-potatoes stronghold, visitors are immediately struck by the immense number of Mexican-food restaurants, the existence of which locals seem to take for granted—until they try ordering *tacos al carbón* in St. Louis. Not only does El Paso boast the finest and largest variety of authentic Mexican food in Texas, but it outdistances offerings in Juárez as well, a wry irony. Equally peculiar is the greater availability of fresh seafood in Juárez, despite Mexico's seemingly sluggish transportation system.

The price classifications for restaurants are based on the cost of an average dinner for one person for food only, excluding beverage, tax, and tip. *Inexpensive* means less than $6; *Moderate,* $7 to $14; and *Expensive,* more than $14. Abbreviations for credit cards: AE, American Express; CB, Carte Blanche; DC, Diners Club; MC, MasterCard; V, VISA. Most restaurants cash traveler's checks, and some will accept personal checks with a driver's license and a major credit card. Abbreviations for meal codes are: B for breakfast, L for lunch, and D for dinner.

AMERICAN-INTERNATIONAL

Expensive

Cafe Peppertree. 5411 N. Mesa in Peppertree Square, West Side; 581–8741. The decor is plush, the food extraordinary, from simple lamb and shrimp recipes to more unusual concoctions like deep-fried lobster, chicken and apple crepes, and calf fries (bull testicles). Extravagant Sunday brunch. L, D, Monday through Saturday. Major credit cards.

Cinders. 2280 Trawood, East Side; 598–0202. Steak, ribs, chicken, seafood—the works. Fresh fish is flown from California. The place is perpetually packed but comfortable. Waiters brag without shame over the restaurant's oysters, charbroiled turbot, and prime rib. Take their word for it. Pleasant piano bar. L, D, Monday through Friday; D, Saturday. Major credit cards.

Moderate

Harrigan's. 251 Shadow Mountain, West Side; 581–8771. Mainly crepes, sandwiches, and steak in a comely wood-and-stained-glass environment. The plate of nachos Acapulco would stuff even Orson Welles. L, D, daily; brunch, Sunday. AE, MC, V.

Isabella's. 6100 Gateway East atop Embassy Suites, East Side; 772–7798. Relaxing splendor and a sweeping view of El Paso and Juárez. Lobster Americana, steaks, tableside preparation of Caesar's salad, rainbow trout stuffed with shrimp, and a sampling of Mexican food. L, D, daily, Major credit cards.

Patrick's. 4501 N. Mesa at Executive Inn, West Side; 532–7945. At presstime, the only live lobster outlet in town. Excellent Caesar's salad, prime rib, seafood and chocolate raspberry cake. L, D, daily. Major credit cards.

Sioux Street. 1610 Sioux St., East Side; 772–1800. This gem of a restaurant harbors surprises such as pan-fried quail with rice pilaf and mushrooms, Puntas Sioux Street, loin-strip medallions topped with onions, chilies, and a spicy gravy. L, D, Monday through Saturday. Major credit cards.

STEAK HOUSES

Good beef, much of which comes from the huge cattle ranches of Chihuahua, Mexico, is readily available in El Paso.

Expensive

Billy Crews Dining Room. 1200 Country Club, Upper Valley; 589–2071. The attraction here is custom-cut steaks. Steaks 2-in. thick are not unusual. Thick salad dressings, hot rolls, and chocolate-cream pie are whipped up from scratch. Lots of southern plantation hospitality. D, daily. AE, DC, MC, V.

Cattleman's. 25 mi. east of El Paso on I-10, north at the Fabens exit on FM 793, 4.5 mi. to Indian Cliffs Ranch; 544–3200. A long drive but worthwhile. Even a Texas appetite is challenged by this rustic restaurant's 2-lb. "cowboy" T-bone. Steaks cut every which way but small are served with gravy, horseradish dressing, pineapple-tinged cole slaw, hearty ranch beans, baked potato, and hot bread. While you wait, saddle up one of the stable's fine fillies. Belgian horses pull hay wagons for free rides Sunday afternoons. L, D, Tuesday through Sunday. AE, MC, V.

Great American Land and Cattle Company. 7600 Alabama, Northeast; 751–5300. Perpetually packed, with only 25 tables, the Cattle Company has a waiting time that often exceeds two hours. Admission is precious on weekends. Call ahead to ask how long you'll have to wait. Despite the crush, service is hospitable and efficient. Luscious steaks of generous proportions, D, daily. DC, MC, V.

Moderate

Iron Tender. 1270 Giles, East Side; 592–4186. Also **Iron Tender West,** 533 Executive Center, West Side; 533–9579. The East Side location is festooned with branding irons and Old West knickknacks. The West Side spot is housed in a contemporary castle. Aromatic steak soup, laden with chunks of tenderloin, is the main attraction, with seconds and thirds on the house. Standard cuts as well as marinated steaks, chicken, and seafood draw a packed house every weekend. Vegetables lathered in *chile con queso* are a favorite side dish. L, D; Monday through Friday; D, Saturday and Sunday. AE, DC, MC, V.

Steak and Ale. 1000 Magruder, East Side; 779–6416. Tudor-style beef with some seafood accompaniment and an excellent salad bar. Crab-stuffed mushrooms and chocolate-mousse pie are royal choices, as is the Kensington Club, a marinated top sirloin. L, D, Monday through Saturday; D, Sunday. Major credit cards.

SEAFOOD

Live lobster in El Paso is scarce and expensive. Fresh fish? Try a pet store. El Paso is simply too landlocked to supply restaurants readily with hours-old shrimp, trout, or oysters. Even restaurants that boast seafood specialties usually rely on the frozen variety. If you get desperate, a few grocery stores, most notably Skaggs, sell fresh seafood at bearable prices.

Expensive

Pelican's. 130 Shadow Mountain, West Side; 581–1392. Also 9077 Gateway West, East Side; 591–8139. Fried cheese is a sumptuous appetizer, and the sautéed asparagus is brought sizzling to the table. Good main courses are broiled bacon-wrapped scallops or beer-battered shrimp. You'll walk the plank for Pelican's catch, the daily fresh special—and always a good deal. Prime rib and steaks are good buys here. D, Daily. Major credit cards.

Plantation St. Clair. 733 Camino Real, Upper Valley; 589–1122. Tucked under a cool umbrella of trees, this attractive eatery has earned distinction for its smoked meats and fish, especially mesquite-smoked and charbroiled shark or salmon. D, daily. MC, V, AE.

Moderate

The Crab Joint. 4000 N. Mesa, West Side; 532–6253. From catfish to orange ruffe and blue crab, almost everything served here is delightfully fresh. Among the offbeat items: an oyster club sandwich, or shrimp and orange sections tossed with romaine lettuce and red onions. L, D, daily.

Seafood Galley. Both on the East Side, 1711 Lee Trevino, 593–8388; and 1130 Geronimo, 778–8388. Oysters, lobster, fish and scallops, all reasonably price. Best bets: clam chowder and jumbo shrimp, butterflied and batter-fried. L, D, daily. MC, V AE.

POPULAR PIT STOPS

These restaurants defy categories—yet demand inclusion because they tend to ride the city's pulse. If you want to combine eating with conversation about local politics, local history, and locals in general, these are the hot spots.

Moderate

Beauregard's. 7351 Edison Way, East Side; 722–3235. Strictly Southern. Portions of such home-style standards as pot roast, meat loaf and peach cobbler are generous. Convenient to Cielo Vista Mall. L, D, Monday through Saturday. Major credit cards.

Bill Parks Bar-B-Q. 3130 Gateway East, central; 542–0960. The best—maybe the only—sweet-potato pie in town. The soul food here includes cornbread, greens and pork, and beef barbeque. Super casual—and always interesting chitchat. B, L, D Monday through Saturday. Cash only.

Chilo's. 310 E. Missouri, Downtown; 532–9745. Small and perky. Backgammon is the favorite barside pastime, while stuffed shrimp and Mexican appetizers occupy diners at the noisy tables. L, D, Monday through Friday. Major credit cards.

Cooper's. 508. N. Stanton, Downtown; 546–9378. Partially constructed with old railroad-car planks, Cooper's is one of *the* daytime watering holes and a crowded lunch niche. A Healthy Sandy, wholegrain bread with melted cheese, avocado, tomato, and alfalfa sprouts, pleases dieters, and capacious appetites go for the mushroom-cheeseburger splurge. L, D, Monday through Saturday. AE, MC, V.

Jaxon's. 4799 N. Mesa, West Side; 544–1188. This wildly successful hangout moved from cramped downtown headquarters to a roomier turf. The menu, described as "territorial" ranges from Mexican food a la Santa Fe to beef Wellington and chicken-pecan salad. L, D, daily. Major credit cards.

Mac's II Bistro. 5034 Doniphan, Upper Valley; 833–0939. Quaint and quirky, this quasi-French dining room holds only 26—shoulder to shoulder. From the smoked salmon Alfredo to the curried shrimp to the perfect bananas flambes, every course is a winner. D, Monday through Saturday. Major credit cards.

State Line. 1222 Sunland, West Side; 581–3371. Expect to cool your heels in the outdoor patio or bar unless you come early at this cavernous dining hall decked in 1940s can labels and jukeboxes. The menu includes steak and seafood, but most of us don't get past the barbecue, homemade bread, and gloriously fresh ice cream. Platters of gigantic ribs are served with cole slaw, beans, and potato salad. You always get more than you can put away. Football teams and other groups with boundless appetites should try the all-you-can-eat "country style" plan. D, Monday through Saturday. MC, V.

FAR EASTERN

Moderate

Kim Chee Jar. 9834 Dyer, Northeast; 757–1138. This modest Korean restaurant doubles as a grocery store. Try the *pi bim pop,* heaps of rice and vegetables topped with a fiery chile paste and fried egg. D, daily, except Tuesday. Cash only.

Mandarin Garden. 604 N. Mesa, West Side; 581–8199. Mandarin and Szechuan dishes served in a stark and quiet dining room. L, D, Tuesday through Saturday. MC, V. Checks accepted.

Peking Garden. 1810 Trawood, East Side; 593–5037 or 593–9813. The menu boasts an exceptional variety of authentic Szechuan, Hunan, and Mandarin food. The shredded beef Szechuan style is a heaping platter of beef slivers tossed with celery, carrots, bamboo shoots, and green onion in a light but throat-sizzling sauce. Top-notch appetizers include beef *cho cho,* marinated slabs on a stick. L, D, daily. MC, V.

Shogun Steak House. 1201 Airway, East Side; 775–1282. A lot of razzle dazzle, Benihana style, accompanies the preparation of excellent teppan dishes. The menu is brief: chicken, steak, lobster or shrimp. The results, outstanding. D, Tuesday through Sunday. Major credit cards.

Uncle Bao's. 9515 Gateway West, Suite A, East Side; 592–1101. For gourmands who delight in tongue-searing Szechuan dishes, this is the place to park your chopsticks. Delicious and daring recipes are sold under such irresistable names as The Dragon Teasing the Phoenix, Buddha Jumps the Wall, and Ants Climb a Tree. L, D, daily. Major credit cards.

Inexpensive

Chinese Palace. 8320 Dyer, Northeast; 757–1138. Chuck Norris ate here, the owners will proudly inform you, pointing to a faded snapshot of the martial arts movie star. The food is ordinary but good. Try the pineapple sticks: fried chicken in a sweet and sour syrup loaded with carrots, cucumber, and celery (no pineapple). L, D, daily. Major credit cards.

Japanese Kitchen. 4024 N. Mesa, West Side; 533–4267. Here you'll find El Paso's only sushi bar, but that's not the main attraction. A fabulous buffet, featuring everything from sushi and vegetables tempura to spare ribs and vanilla cake, is served every afternoon for under $5. No such bargains at dinner. L, D, daily. Major credit cards.

Pinetum. 4028 N. Mesa, West Side; 545–5375. Tiny alcoves, decorated with Oriental tapestries, are populated by shoppers, students, and escapees from the Downtown (all things being relative) rat race. Most dishes are quite mild, but the lunch tofu has some pizzazz. Complicated Chinese recipes may be had if ordered a day ahead. D, daily. MC, V.

Szechuan Restaurant. 1461 Lee Trevino, East Side; 594–8104. Cozy quarters and cheerful service go with the excellent Mongolian barbecue. L, D, daily. Major credit cards.

FRENCH

Expensive

Gigi de Paris. 3111 Yarbrough, East Side; 598–6033. The French tradition of coddling the appetite rules here, where chef Annette Gantenbein's delicate version of duck a l'Orange will have you examining Donald and Daffy with a newfound gastronomical lust. You cannot go wrong unless you abstain. L, D, Tuesday through Saturday. Major credit cards.

Stanton Room. 508 N. Stanton, Downtown; 533–1799. Brimming with charm, this modest café whips up tantalizing food and exquisite service. Steak Diane, *tournedos au poivre, veau dijonnaise,* smoked trout, Greek lemon soup, vichyssoise, and chocolate mousse are high on the request list. Crisp vegetables, buttery pasta, perfect soufflés—Paris by the book. Parties of six may reserve for the six-course, six-wine feast in a private dining room. D, Monday through Saturday. AE, MC, V. Reservations recommended.

GERMAN

Moderate

Gunther's Edelweiss. 11055 Gateway West at the Lomaland Exit, East Side; 592–1084. The cooking leans toward Bavaria with *Weisswurst,* pale-colored sausage from Munich; *Kartoffelpfannküchen,* potato pancakes; and *Schweinebraten,* pork loin roast. Holstein *Schnitzel* (cutlet) and Hungarian goulash, cubed beef in a thick gravy with sides of dumplings, are crowd-pleasers. L, D, Tuesday through Sunday. MC, V.

ITALIAN

Inexpensive to moderate

Bella Napoli. 6331 N. Mesa, West Side, 584–3321; Also 10600 Montana, East Side, 592–9500. *Osso buco,* a full-bodied veal stew, is a weekend specialty. Regulars crow about the chicken Jerusalem and the thin-crust pizza. L, D, Tuesday through Sunday. AE, MC, V.

Cappetto's Italian Restaurant. 2716 Montana, Central; 566–9357; and 5229 Sanders, Northeast; 755–1304. A very popular lunch spot. Nothing on the menu sparkles with ingenuity, but all dishes bear the restaurant's trademark wholesomeness. Veal is a specialty. Extremely casual. L, D, Monday through Friday; D, Saturday and Sunday. Checks accepted.

Como's Italian Restaurant. 4030 N. Mesa, West Side; 533–0287. Piping-hot pizza and stupendous manicotti bring gushes of praise. During holiday periods, the owners often dole out free glasses of wine and complementary homemade pastries. A friendly place with baskets and Chianti bottles dangling from the walls. L, D, Monday through Saturday. MC, V.

Italian Kitchen, 2923 Pershing, Central; 565–4041. Tiny and humble, the Italian Kitchen produces a rich lasagna that keeps the regulars a trifle on the pudgy side. Pizza munchers and spaghetti slurpers dominate. The veal with mushrooms and peppers is a rich stew. The Italian Plate offers rigatoni, spaghetti, lasagna, bread, soup, and antipasto salad. L, D, Monday-Saturday. AE, MC, V.

Sorrento Italian Restaurant. 5325 Dyer, Northeast; 565–3937. Cozy atmosphere, indulgent service. The spaghetti sauce is tangy—and no spumoni in town is better. L, D, Monday through Friday; D, Saturday and Sunday. DC, MC, V.

MEXICAN FOOD

The top Mexican-food eateries are in El Paso, *not* —as one might expect—in Juárez. Most native El Pasoans thrive on *jalapeños* and hot *salsas,* but not all Mexican dishes are tongue-searing volcanos. Waiters in the following restaurants are accustomed to tourists with blander palates and will gladly direct you to less fiery selections. If you are unfamiliar with Mexican menu lingo, don't hesitate to get a detailed description of the item. Otherwise, you may end up with a novice's nightmare, like *menudo,* tripe in a spicy soup, a border favorite and fabled hangover cure. Among the more exotic recipes worth a try are *mole,* a piquant sauce made with chocolate and draped over chicken; *chiles rellenos,* long green peppers stuffed with cheese and deep fried in an egg batter; and tamales, pork wrapped in an airy dough, sealed with a corn husk, and steamed.

Inexpensive to Moderate

Avila's. 7000 Gateway East, East Side; 772–5566. Here, find the town's best *fajitas*—strips of marinated skirt steak served with flour tortillas, guacamole and pico de gallo. One order fills two and leaves a corner for the steaming *sopaipillas* drizzled with honey. L, D, Monday through Saturday. Major credit cards.

El Bandido. Dillard's third floor, Cielo Vista Mall, 8401 Gateway West, East Side; 779–6969. The mild Mexican food here is not traumatizing to the uninitiated tongue. The beef *flautas* (tortilla "flutes" stuffed with meat and deep fried) are fat and fanciful. The tortilla soup and gazpacho, piquant and cold with chunks of crisp chilies, are ideal excuses for shopping breaks. A balcony overlooks the bustling mall. L, D, Monday through Saturday. AE, DC, MC, V.

Carlos and Mickey's. 1310 Magruder, East Side; 778–3323. California and Arizona influences flavor these Mexican dishes. Crab enchiladas are a specialty. The service is tops, and the Mexican decor is richly authentic. L, D, daily. AE, DC, MC, V.

Forti's Mexican Elder. 321 Chelsea, East Side; 772–0066. The Forti family dishes out the best, biggest *flautas* in town, hands down. These corn-tortilla tubes stuffed with shredded chicken or beef are flooded with *guacamole,* a creamy avocado dip, and sour cream. Impossible to finish, but you'll always try. The *tampiqueño* steak, served with *guacamole,* an enchilada, rice, and refried beans, is a specialty. Few can resist the sumptuous *flan,* a rich custard. L, D, daily. MC, V.

Griggs Restaurant, 9007 Montana, East Side; 598–3451. Also 5800 Doniphan, West Side; 584–0451. New Mexican cuisine, with more calories and less fire, is prepared carefully from scratch. The kitchen grinds *masa* for pork *tamales.* The tomato-heavy *salsa* is habit-forming, as are the bulging green-pepper-and-meat enchiladas and savory *chile con queso.* The *empañadas,* tender fruit turnovers served with ice cream, and the *sopaipillas,* light pastry pillows to be drenched with honey, are homemade. Chicken *sopa,* a thick stew, is one of several dishes that sets Griggs apart from its competitors. L, D, daily, except that the West Side location is closed Monday. DC, MC, V. Checks accepted.

Leo's. 6232 N. Mesa, West Side; 584–3621. Also 5315 Hondo Pass, Northeast; 757–0505. There are more Leo's locations across town, but these two are the best. The piping-hot nachos drip with a generous layer of Monterey Jack cheese. Chicken *tapatias* and enchiladas with green sauce are delightful tummy stuffers. L, D, Monday through Saturday. MC, V.

Inexpensive

Casa Jurado. 226 Cincinnati, near the University of Texas at El Paso; 532–6429. The Jurado family concocts creamy *chile con queso* and a refreshing summer meat salad, *salpicón,* cold shredded beef, spiced and served with corn tortillas. The chicken enchiladas and beef *flautas* are raved about. *Flan* is a fitting dessert that stomps out the fire. L, D, Monday through Saturday. MC, V.

El Cerezo. 610 N. Mesa, Downtown; 542–1745. At El Cerezo pork is prepared *al pastor,* or shepherd-style: slices are stacked on a vertical skewer and positioned before a fireplace. As the meat cooks, the done outer edges are shaved off and served in tacos and burritos. All meats are cooked slowly over mesquite wood, a costly pampering that results in an addictive smoky flavor. A must appetizer is the *queso fundido con chorizo,* a bowl of creamy melted cheese and Mexican sausage served with small corn tortillas. L, D, Monday through Saturday. Cash only.

Chope's. La Mesa, New Mexico; west of El Paso, off Doniphan; (505) 233–9976. The dining room is smaller than some coat closets, and consequently many patrons are asked to wait at the bar next door. An intercom system summons them when a table is free. The confusion is worthwhile. Food at Chope's is fresh, teasing, and hotter than July. Regionally picked chilies go into a steamy *salsa.* Open only three hours daily; lunch from noon to 1:00 P.M. and dinner from 6:00 to 8:00 P.M., Tuesday through Saturday. Cash only.

La Hacienda. 1720 W. Paisano, West Side; 532–5094. This spacious hacienda, once the home of Fort Bliss, now buzzes with business from noon till dusk. Favorites on the strictly Mexican-food menu are the steak *tampiqueño* and a filing Mexican plate. Service is sometimes slow but always courteous. L, D, Tuesday through Sunday.

El Rancho Escondido. 14549 Montana, East Side; 859–8065. Word of mouth vaulted this roadside café to prominence. Two kinds of *salsa*—one hot, the other explosive—demands lots of beer consumption. *Chile verde con carne* and red enchiladas topped with fried eggs are the oft-requested choices. D, Tuesday through Saturday.

NIGHT LIFE. This is the way diehard barflies approach partying in El Paso. Hit two or three (or four or five) local bars until the streets roll up and the taps run dry at 2:00 A.M. Then head for Juárez, where nightclubs never close and drinking ages are unheard of. El Paso night spots are generally spiffier, plusher, and more accommodating than their Juárez counterparts. But bars south of the border are livelier and much cheaper. This listing offers only a sampling of El Paso bars and does not focus on the hundreds of cozy neighborhood bars, most of which warmly welcome outsiders.

HANGOUTS

Bennigan's. 10497 Gateway West, East Side; 592–7200. This woods-and-brass bar boasts a packed house, especially during the two happy hours, one from 11:00 P.M. to 2:00 A.M. nightly, the other from 11:30 A.M. to 7:00 P.M. Monday through Saturday. Attracts a jubilant crowd of big spenders.

Dudley's. 1188 Yarbrough, East Side; 593–3820. A relaxing new bar with snappy decor, irresistible food, and giddy people.

Gasoline Alley. 2514 N. Mesa, near the University of Texas at El Paso; 532–5353. Monday night is sports night on a giant screen TV. Wednesday is dart-league night. Free popcorn nightly. Cheerful and charming, with mostly young folks. Nostalgic service-station decor. Live, mellow entertainment Thursday through Saturday nights.

Harrigan's. 251 Shadow Mountain, West Side; 581–8771. Politely termed a singles club and occasionally slurred as a pickup joint, Harrigan's has a nightly sardine scene that is a definitely *the* cruising ground for the youthful.

King's X. 4119 N. Mesa, West Side. One of the West Side's oldest and most consistently popular night spots. Serious drinkers. Features an island bar, shuffleboard, and electronic games.

Springfire's. 5024 Montana, East Side; 772–1182. Live entertainment with everything from folk to rock to jazz. Shoulder-to-shoulder crowds hop at this boisterous pizza-pasta joint, where the beer and the jokes flow nonstop.

TAKING IT EASY

Caballero Lounge. Caballero Motor Hotel, 6400 Montana, East Side; 772–4231. An international boiling pot: Fort Bliss army folks and tourists from Germany, Finland, Mexico, and Japan.

Jolly Ox Pub. In the Steak and Ale Restaurant, 1000 Magruder, East Side; 779–6416. A bustling club noted for its great easy-listening music. Attracts East Side business folk.

Kern Place Tavern. 214 Cincinnati, near the University of Texas at El Paso; 546–9013. In operation nearly 50 years, this classic neighborhood bar is the regular resting perch for many UTEP professors.

Knight's Club. Rodeway Inn, 6201 Gateway West, East Side; 778–6611. Live pop sounds for all ages. Dancing.

Pine Knot Jr. 2224 E. Yandell, Central; 532–5541. Popular among media folk and other nefarious types. Cheap drinks, boisterous atmosphere.

Teddy's. 17th floor, Holiday Inn Downtown, 113 W. Missouri; 544–3300. "Unwind time" begins at 5:00 P.M. Monday through Saturday with a complimentary supper buffet. The taped music format offers country-and-western, rock, and pop music, as well as some disco.

WESTERN

The Anthony Gap Saloon and Dance Hall. 113 N. Main, Anthony, Texas (Anthony straddles the New Mexico-Texas border just west of El Paso); 886–2171. The legendary hoedown fort that brought such diverse acts as John Lee Hooker, Greezy Wheels, and Ruby Star to the tiny burg of Anthony recently reopened with an expanded mahogany dance floor and more of the same good music that characterized its first life. Bucking-machine contest; frenetic dancing; excessive drinking.

Lariat Lounge. 8601 Dyer, Northeast; 755–1689. Lots of down-home dancing. Northeast El Paso grass-roots working-class heroes—military and civilian alike—flock here.

ROCK

Big Apple. Gateway East at Yarbrough, East Side; 593–1241. As much an amusement park as a nightclub, with outdoor seating, shrimp and oyster bars, waterfalls and entertainment ranging from Tex-Mex rock to Duke Jupiter. All genres, including progressive jazz, are showcased in this 1,000-seat house. Open only for special engagements.

Dallas. 1840 Lee Trevino, East Side; 598–1309. El Paso's most perpetually packed club. No-frills rock and stiff drinks.

Mr. K's. 4026–A N. Mesa, West Side; 545–5172. Home of popular rocker Mike Cancellare and his Buckwheat Blues Band. Classic rock and blues are featured more than top 40.

Phoenix. 1461 Lee Trevino, East Side; 598–6545. A huge nightclub with a sprawling dance floor. SRO on weekends.

Sound Seas Performance Warehouse. 1903 Texas, near Downtown; no phone at the club. Information: 833–1736. El Paso's only punk haven. Catch local bands like Moral Cripples and Rhythm Pigs.

Tree Top Lounge. 1160 Airway, East Side; 772–3166. *The* quintessential rock haven for listeners who demand state-of-the-art amplification. A professional lighting system and the hottest, cleanest PA in town. Local and visiting bands dish out mega-decibels of traditional rock 'n' roll.

DISCO

Graham's. 9505 Viscount, East Side; 595–0036. This gigantic rock disco offers more than a huge dance floor and canned sounds at a concert volume. There are a dozen TV sets, 19 pool tables, five bars, and frequent performances by magicians, clowns, and male strippers.

Old Plantation. 219 S. Ochoa, Downtown; 533–6055. A notorious gay bar, but in-the-know heteros flock here for consistently great disco sounds, the large dance floor, and an uninhibited atmosphere. One of the largest and best discos on either side of the border. Always packed.

TEXAS

INDEX

(The letters H and R indicate hotel and restaurant listings.)